D1623836

THE MANY NOT THE FEW

The Many not the Few

The Stolen History of the Battle of Britain

Richard North

BLOOMSBURY

NEW YORK • LONDON • NEW DELHI • SYDNEY

Published by Bloomsbury USA, New York

All papers used by Bloomsbury USA are natural, recyclable products made from wood grown in well-managed forests. The manufacturing processes conform to the environmental regulations of the country of origin.

LIBRARY OF CONGRESS CATALOGING-IN-PUBLICATION DATA HAS BEEN APPLIED FOR.

ISBN: 978-1-62040-100-2

First U.S. Edition 2013

1 3 5 7 9 10 8 6 4 2

Typeset by Fakenham Prepress Solutions, Fakenham, Norfolk NR21 8NN
Printed in the U.S.A.

Contents

Never in the field of human conflict was so much owed by so many to so few.

Winston Churchill, *Their Finest Hour.* 20 August 1940

The searchlights are in position, the guns are ready, the people's army of volunteers is ready – they are the ones who are really fighting this war …

Quentin Reynolds, *London can take it.* 16 October 1940

Acknowledgements

How this book came to be written is as much part of this story as the story itself. Born in North London just a few years after the end of the war, I was brought up with the Battle of Britain. As a boy, I built my quota of Airfix Spitfires and Hurricanes, Me 109 fighters, Stuka dive bombers and, when it finally came available, the fabulous model of the twin-engined Heinkel 111 bomber. With my school friends, no group of boys could have more avidly discussed the specifications and the merits of the different aircraft, or studied more carefully the tactics and the events of 1940.

London, even in my childhood, was still pockmarked with bomb sites, which we spent endless time exploring. Neighbours, the parents of our friends and our relatives all had their own stories, to which we boys listened, wide-eyed. When old enough, we joined the air cadets and my very first flying experience, in a dual control Chipmunk, virtually duplicated the path one of the combat flights of fighter ace Douglas Bader during the war.

With a flying scholarship under my belt and a private flying licence gained shortly after my eighteenth birthday, I found myself living and working on a former fighter station in Essex, a satellite airfield which had housed Hurricanes during the battle. In the bright summer mornings, standing amid the wartime hangers, it took little effort to imagine the sounds of Merlins and aircraft rising to meet the enemy. That and much, much more had made the Battle of Britain as much part of my life as it possibly could be, short of actually living through it.

Decades later, on the seventieth anniversary, when tributes were flowing for the diminishing band of men directly involved in the events, I decided to offer my own personal homage to "the few". I chose to do this by means of an internet diary, or blog. This had been done before, but I reasoned that if my own skills could make the battle a little more accessible to a wider audience, it would be worth doing again.

With that as my objective, 70 years to the very day after the battle had started,

I published the first entry. Then presenting a daily narrative on every single one of the 114 days of the battle, my sole intention was to record a summary of events. However, as I added more and more detail, I found increasing difficulty in keeping to the conventional narrative. Long before the end, I had concluded that it did not hang together.

Curiosity now aroused, I began to read more widely and then research more thoroughly. With a distance of more than 40 years between my first flight and now, what flying skills I had ever possessed had long since been replaced by an entirely new skill-set, including a PhD as a formal qualification in research, all supporting my day job as a political researcher. With a new eye, and access to material which had previously only been obtainable with difficulty, if at all, I set to work.

What made the book possible though was the way the research environment has changed. First, much of the basic labour has been done, so that one can rely on such authorities as Francis K. Mason for their detailed analyses of the air battle, and on and the likes of Rear Admiral Ansel for his evaluation of the prospects for the invasion of England – to name but two of over a hundred key writers. But what has really changed is the advent of the internet. Far more material is available, far quicker, and at considerably less cost than it ever has been. Furthermore, the net has been enriched by new material that would never otherwise have seen the light of day.

Add to this the ability now to obtain books from around the world, even rare, out-of-print copies, at astonishing speed and low cost, and it is possible to achieve far more in less time than traditional researchers, with large support teams, could ever do. Running my own online forum also allowed me to test theories, and air information, with members from all over the world adding comments and sending more material. This made for a more balanced and complete work than I imagined possible, and I thank them all for it.

That said, as with my previous book on the British occupation of Iraq, very many people helped with the making of this book. The technology may have vastly improved the process but it also makes writing a more lonely occupation. As before, therefore, I must single out my long-suffering and patient wife Mary who provided so much support during the long hours of parturition. Again, my colleague Christopher Booker helped with encouragement and advice, and especially with the fearsome issue of structure, and my publisher Robin

Baird-Smith kept me on the rails. I thank them both and also Jim Greenhalf, who has been a very special friend.

Special thanks also go to Peter Troy, for his interest and encouragement, and his comments on early drafts, which helped shape the narrative. To the editor of the website *Think Defence* who freely provided me with a huge amount of material, I also owe many thanks, as well as John-Paul Mc Kenna, who was extraordinarily helpful in getting research material to me. And even in this electronic age, real human beings have given me real and valuable assistance. I must thank Belinda Brown of the New Zealand High Commission, the hugely effective researchers at the Fleet Air Arm Museum at Yeovil, Nick Baldwin, Archivist at the Great Ormond Street Hospital for Sick Children and Christine Wagg of the Peabody Trust. I am also indebted to Andreas Winkel, editor of the website *storm boot kommando.de,* who supplied me with some original photographs of the German invasion fleet.

Reflecting how much the research environment has changed though, recognition must go to the hundreds or even thousands of anonymous – or, at least, unknown to me – people, from the researchers and administrators of the National Archives, to private website designers and owners who have put information and photographs in the public domain for all comers to use. That I should have made so much use of it is rather appropriate in a book that celebrates the achievements of the people.

Despite all that, this is not a revisionist history. I would assert that we are currently living through that – a history that was changed after the event, for reasons I explore. This is an attempt to revert to the original – a *reversionist* history, if you like. It returns to a more faithful narrative which better describes events which still shape our destinies.

As importantly, in seeking to discover how and why the distortions occurred, I come to the startling conclusion that they were largely deliberate, a so far successful attempt to steal our history. That is a story on its own, and one which has important implications for us all. He who steals our history, steals our identity. If we are to learn from history, it must be the right history, the true account, not a counterfeit put in place to conceal a theft.

Bradford
West Yorkshire
10 July 2011

Foreword

By Christopher Booker

Only rarely is it given to a book to show one of the most famous episodes in history in such a dramatically new light that we can never see it in the same way again. Such is the achievement of this remarkable new account of the Battle of Britain by Dr Richard North.

For 70 years we have lived with a picture of the historic events in 1940 which has become one of the most enduring and familiar myths of our time. If a single image could sum up that picture it is of the gallant pilots of those Spitfires and Hurricanes criss-crossing the skies above Kent and Sussex, so successfully defying the aerial armadas being hurled against them that this did more than anything else to avert a threatened invasion.

The myth tells us that, when Britain stood alone after the fall of France, Hitler's mind immediately turned to the military conquest of England, a precondition of which would be to win command of the air. Hence his launching in mid-August of a full-scale assault on the airfields of southern England. With the RAF's resources allegedly stretched almost to breaking point, and the invasion barges gathering in ports across the Channel, Hitler then made what is painted as a fundamental strategic blunder, when on 7 September he switched his bomber fleets from the airfields to launch a full-scale offensive on London.

Barely a week later came what has come to be regarded as the highpoint of the battle, on 15 September, "Battle of Britain Day". The newspapers bannered across their front pages that the RAF had shot down no fewer than "185 German aircraft". Although the assault on London continued, by October the outcome of the battle was assured. Invasion had been called off. Britain and civilization were saved. In Churchill's immortal words, more often quoted than any others of the time, "never in the field of human conflict was so much owed by so many to so few".

Such is the essence of the "myth", congealed over the decades in countless books, films, newspaper articles and television documentaries. But such is the picture which North's new version dismantles, reassembles and extends in so many respects that it turns much of that mythical version upside down.

Above all, by a *tour de force* of original research, North is able to set the events of those months in a vastly wider perspective. Instead of focusing just on the heroic role of Fighter Command, he steps back to show us very much more of what was going on at the time, including much that has previously been obscured, downplayed or completely overlooked. The Battle of Britain, it turns out, was an altogether larger and more complex web of events than it has too often been portrayed to be. And, as so often in history, the three-dimensional reality turns out to be much more interesting than the two-dimensional simplicities of the myth.

For a start, North confirms that there was never any practical possibility of an invasion of England, as Hitler soon knew. His real game, to an extent which has never been properly recognized, was not to conquer Britain but to neutralize her into withdrawing from the war, No fewer than five times between July and October 1940, he secretly put forward peace proposals which would allow Britain to remain an independent nation, with most of her worldwide empire intact – so long as she ceased to be at war with Germany.

To this end, Hitler rested his hopes on destroying Britain's will to continue fighting, by offering a resolution of the conflict which the battle-weary British people would find it hard to resist. If necessary, they should force Churchill to resign, in favour of a new government which would represent their wish to come to some peaceful accommodation with him, Hitler's purpose was to free himself from the distraction of Britain, so that he could concentrate on what was already his real aim, an invasion of the Bolshevik empire to the east.

Immediately after the fall of France, the German High Command had analysed the need to subdue Britain's resistance under three headings. The first was to be a major blockade by air and sea, designed to bring her economy to a halt by destroying her ability to feed her people and to keep her key industries functioning, thus depriving her of the means to defend herself. The second strategy would be an aerial assault on her cities intended to break the morale of the British people, to the point where they would be willing to accept Hitler's offer of peace. Only in third place, as an addendum to the others, was the possibility of mounting a physical invasion.

It was this grand plan which essentially shaped the drama which was to follow. The Battle of Britain proper began, not with the aerial offensive launched on 13 August, "Eagle Day", but a month earlier, with a concerted attempt in July to cut off her economic lifelines and her maritime supplies. This centred partly on a relentless campaign to sink the small ships which brought down the east coast so much of what London and southern England needed to survive, such as coal to keep power stations running and the lights on. But it also involved raids on many of Britain's key ports, such as Dover, Southampton, Bristol, Swansea, Liverpool, Hull, even Falmouth.

One reason why the scale of these July attacks has never been fully appreciated – as was to remain true of much else that followed – was the very strict censorship, which prevented much of the havoc they were wreaking from being reported. All newspaper readers or BBC listeners were allowed to know of a devastating attack on Bristol, for instance, was a brief report that that there had been "a raid on a town in the west of England". As North discovered, much of what was going on all over Britain in 1940 remained virtually unrecorded for decades. Only the internet and the painstaking efforts put into compiling local historical websites and archives has made it possible for much of this to be put together.

The second phase of the battle was the assault in August on Britain's air power. Again this was targeted not just at the airfields – the RAF survived these attacks much better than is often allowed – but at aircraft factories across the kingdom, from Southampton, Luton, Bristol, Birmingham and Coventry to northern cities such as Leeds and Manchester. Particularly when these raids took place at night, there was inevitably much collateral damage from bombs which missed their intended targets, and it was at this time that, for the inhabitants of many British cities, what would be remembered as "the Blitz" began.

Only in September, when the third phase of the battle began with the launching of the blitz on London, were the British people allowed to know something of the horror of the aerial offensive which had already caused havoc in other cities. Initially most of the destruction was centred around London's East End and what was then the largest port in the world. For the first time, the assault of the *Luftwaffe* was deliberately aimed at civilian targets and at destroying the British people's morale and social cohesion. This leads to one of the most fascinating episodes in North's narrative.

Never fully reconstructed before has been the chilling story of how hundreds of thousands of East Enders were desperate to find refuge from the mass-bombing, from which they were hopelessly ill-protected by the perfunctory surface shelters provided by government policy and local councils. Above all Londoners wanted to shelter safely underground in tube stations. But initially the authorities, led by Churchill's Cabinet, were adamant that armed guards must be placed on station entrances to keep the public out.

Only after 50 East Londoners, led by a Communist Phil Piratin, marched "up West", demanding to join the customers of one of London's most luxurious hotels in a shelter beneath the Savoy, did the debate over the inadequacies of London's shelter provision come to a head. So strong by now was the anger of East Enders, who felt abandoned by the authorities (only the tireless efforts of the Salvation Army and other voluntary organizations made it possible for many blitz victims to find food and shelter), that the government finally gave way. The policy reversal which opened up the underground to provide bomb shelters was to provide some of the most haunting images of the war.

The significance of this, however, was that it reflected Hitler's wish to divide British society in such a way that the poorer classes might rise up to demand peace at almost any price. In this respect he certainly blundered in eventually allowing his bombers also to strike at the richer West End of London, most notably in the bombing of Buckingham Palace, since this did much to show the British that all classes were now in this fight together,

But as North describes, the potential division Hitler hoped to promote was most vividly expressed in a running conflict between Churchill, who continued to portray "his" Battle of Britain as centred on the heroic exploits of Fighter Command, and J. B. Priestley who, in his hugely popular weekly radio broadcasts, was quick to recognize that the real front-line protagonists in the battle were now "the people". Like the US broadcaster Quentin Reynolds, he spoke for all those who nightly suffered the effects of the bombing, and all those who were fighting heroically alongside them to keep society functioning, from firemen, civil defence and ambulance workers to the crews of the ships which were keeping London and Britain supplied with the necessities of life.

So fixated was Churchill on the crucial part in saving Britain he saw having been played by "the few" that, when the invasion fear finally subsided in October, he was quite happy to proclaim the Battle of Britain as having ended in victory. In fact, the struggle had been much more level-pegging than the government propaganda machine and the media liked to pretend (the true German losses on 15 September, for instance, had been not 185 as claimed but only 56). By the end of October the *Luftwaffe's* total losses had been 1,680 aircraft, the RAF's 1,642 – so that, in that respect, the result had been not so much a victory as a score draw.

Nevertheless this was very far from being the end of the "Battle of Britain". The blitz continued uninterrupted, not just on London but on towns and cities across the country. In October 1940, when Hitler made his last serious effort to draw Britain to the peace table, the Germans dropped more bombs on Britain than in any other month of the war. London and many other cities, including Coventry, would still have to endure raids heavier than any they had seen to date for another eight months, lasting right through to 10 May 1941.

But suddenly after that night the raids stopped. This was the moment which marked the true end of the Battle of Britain. It came about, not because of any recognition that the British had won, but simply because Hitler was moving his bomber fleets across to the east, to prepare for what had been his real under-lying goal all along, his advance into Russia.

The real battle of Britain was one which had been going on for almost a year, directly involving millions of people who had bravely endured destruction and horror on a scale never faced by any previous generation. They and Britain had survived – and in that sense they all shared in an extraordinary victory. Certainly Churchill's favoured "Few" had played their part. But as others recognized at the time, such as Priestley, Reynolds and George Orwell – and as Richard North vividly shows in this enthralling and long overdue reappraisal of the "myth" – what ultimately made that survival possible were the efforts and the courage of the "Many".

Introduction

There's one going down in flames! Somebody's hit a German and he's coming down with a long streak – coming down completely out of control – a long streak of smoke.

Charles Gardner, BBC Journalist, 14 July 1940

On Sunday 14 July 1940, the BBC decided to cover the action. With aerial battles visible to cliff-top watchers along the south coast of England, its reporter Charles Gardner joined the crowds to witness German attempts to stop an eleven-ship convoy being run through the Straits of Dover.

At close to eleven in the morning, a Dornier twin-engined medium bomber escorted by ten Messerschmitt 109 fighters made the first attack. Then, in the early afternoon, a force of about 120 enemy aircraft collected behind Calais and approached the convoy. At around three in the afternoon, as the sky reverberated to the drone of aircraft, Gardner began to make his now famous recording:

> The Germans are dive-bombing a convoy out to sea! There are one, two, three, four, five, six, seven German dive-bombers! – Junkers Eighty-Sevens! There's one going down on its target now – Bomb! No! He missed the ships – it hasn't hit a single ship. There are about ten ships in the convoy, but he hasn't hit a single one and … There! You can hear our anti-aircraft going at them now. There are one, two, three, four, five, six … there are about ten German machines dive-bombing the British convoy, which is just out to sea in the Channel.[1]

Despite the large numbers of German aircraft, there were just three single-seater Hurricane fighters thrown into the fray. Heavily outnumbered and outclassed by the superior Me 109s, they belonged to Red Section of No. 615 Squadron (Sqn). As they went into action, the excited Gardner described the fighting:

> I can't see anything. No! – We thought he had got a German one at the top then, but now the British fighters are coming up! Here they come. The Germans are coming in an absolute steep dive, and you can see their bombs actually leave the machines and come into the water. You can hear our guns going like anything now. I am looking round now – I can hear machine gun fire, but I can't see our Spitfires, they must be somewhere there. Oh! Here's one coming down!

Like most journalists of his day, Gardner had not acquired any expertise in aircraft recognition. He had that in common with many Royal Air Force (RAF) fighter pilots, some of whom flying Spitfires in early September 1939 had shot down two Hurricanes. Others were later to claim Heinkel 113 fighters as trophies – a type that did not exist.[2] Gardner saw Spitfires when only Hurricanes were in action. As he watched the spectacle, he joyously exclaimed:

> There's one going down in flames! Somebody's hit a German and he's coming down with a long streak – coming down completely out of control – a long streak of smoke. And now a man's baled out by parachute! The pilot's baled out by parachute! He's a Junkers Eighty-Seven and he's going slap into the sea. And there he goes – SMASH! A terrific column of water and there was a Junkers Eight-Seven. Only one man got out by parachute, so presumably there was only a crew of one in it!

Fortunately for Gardner's immediate reputation, these comments were for radio. A Hurricane had now become a "Junkers Eighty-Seven" and it was this from which a mortally wounded Pilot Officer M. R. Mudie had just bailed out – the "crew of one". Mudie was eventually picked up by the Royal Navy and hastily transferred to Dover Hospital, where he died the following day.[3] By then, Gardner's commentary had been broadcast. The BBC's own listener research noted that it was "enormously appreciated". But some were troubled by the "football style". A policy of treating war as a sport "would be asking for trouble".[4]

What was not explored at the time was how much of the narrative was factually wrong. For instance, Gardner had been confident that the ships had escaped unscathed. They had not. The collier SS *Island Queen* had been badly damaged. Taken in tow by the trawler *Kingston Alalite*, she sank before reaching harbour, with three crewmen lost. Less than two miles south of Dover Pier, the SS *Mons* had been damaged. The Norwegian steamer *Balder* took a hit and caught fire. The flames were extinguished but she had to be towed into Dover Harbour. The escort destroyer HMS *Vanessa* had her main engines disabled and she too had to be towed into port.[5] Yet, to all of this drama, Gardner had been oblivious.

However, despite its manifest and egregious errors, the piece has been rebroadcast many times and it is still celebrated by the BBC on its website – with no reference to or acknowledgement of its errors. That, in many ways, typifies the Battle of Britain "experience". The account of the battle is flawed, yet it is repeated again and again, without any acknowledgement of its errors. It has become obscured by myths.

Part of this book is an exploration of these myths. Mainly, it is a fundamental re-evaluation of the Battle of Britain, addressing the simple question: who won? The traditional answer is "the few", that gallant band of Fighter Command pilots in their Spitfires and Hurricanes, led by Air Chief Marshal Sir Hugh Dowding, the man who should not have been there. By some strange stroke of fate, he had been due to retire on 14 July 1940, but had been asked to stay on by the then Chief of the Air Staff, Air Chief Marshal Sir Cyril Newall. The man with a nickname of "Stuffy", a man with many enemies who would have been pleased to see him go, was now assured a place in history.[6]

Desperately outnumbered, "the few" fought off the Nazi hordes in their Messerschmitt fighters, their Dorniers, Heinkels and Stukas. As to the essence of the myth, in the summer of 1940 Britain stood alone against the dark forces of Nazi Germany, prostrate after the fall of France and the "miracle" of Dunkirk. All that stood between it and invasion was Fighter Command. In a series of battles, the gallant "few" stopped the German air force establishing air superiority. The turning point came on 15 September 1940, when in an epic battle, the *Luftwaffe* was sent packing, a victory which caused the invasion to be postponed and then cancelled. The fighter pilots had saved the nation, Europe and the entire free world.

One myth was immortalized by the famous Low cartoon of 14 June, on the fall of France.[7] It depicted a defiant soldier on a rocky shore surrounded by tumultuous waves, shaking his fist at the encroaching Nazi bomber fleet, voicing Churchill's sentiment: "Very well, alone!" But we were not alone, the point made by a Fougasse cartoon in Punch magazine on 17 July. It showed two British soldiers sitting, overlooking the white cliffs of Dover. One is saying "So our poor old Empire is alone in the world". The other replies "Aye, so we are – the whole 500 million of us".

Nor were we reliant wholly on the Empire. While, Great Britain supplied 2,341 aircrew to Fighter Command, they came from all over the world. From Australia came 32, Barbados 1, Belgium 28, Canada 112, Czechoslovakia 88, France 13, Ireland 10, Jamaica 1, Newfoundland 1, New Zealand 127, Poland 145, Rhodesia 3, South Africa 25 and the USA 9. This does not count career officers from the Empire and Dominions who had joined the RAF prior to hostilities, including Air Vice-Marshal Park.[8]

Nor was Fighter Command just a fighter organization. It was also the umbrella body for Anti-Aircraft Command, alongside which there was the Balloon Command and the Observer Corps. At its height, the Anti-Aircraft Command alone mustered seven divisions, numbering over 350,000 personnel drawn from the Royal Artillery, the Royal Engineers, the Auxiliary Territorial Service (the women's branch of the Territorial Army), the Royal Marines and the Home Guard. They were led by Major General Sir Frederick Pile, working under the general direction of Hugh Dowding. The two men were friends.

At the beginning of 1940 there were only 695 heavy anti-aircraft guns (many of which were becoming old and on loan from the Navy) along with 253 light guns, against a projected requirement of 2,232 heavy and 1,200 light guns. Despite this, the Command claimed approximately 300 aircraft shot down during the battle of Britain – unfortunately, not all of them German.[9]

Nevertheless, in 1941, on the basis of the exploits of "the few" alone, historians were invited to make comparisons between the Battle of Britain and Marathon, Trafalgar and the Marne.[10] Many obliged and continue to do so, not least historian Richard Overy. He finds "more than a touch of irony" that the battle was won by a "tiny military élite". The few, he wrote, saved the many from a terrible ordeal.[11] But they did not. This was a war of the many.

Even in the RAF, there were the Bomber and Coastal Commands. They were part of the fight. Many aircrew paid the ultimate price, in particular those in the 200 Blenheim bombers of No. 2 Group, which carried out multiple attacks on invasion barges in the Channel ports. They also attacked enemy airfields and other targets, including shipping, displaying almost suicidal bravery at times.[12] These Commands also had a strong multi-national flavour and, in the case of Coastal Command, there was No. 10 Sqn Royal Australian Air Force, the Australian crew of which were in England at the time hostilities broke out. It had been intended that they would train in England before returning to Australia with their aircraft, but on the outbreak of war, the Australian Government agreed to keep them in Britain, where they had distinguished careers.[13]

Then there were the other uniformed military services – especially the Royal Navy, often alongside the Merchant Marine – which populated the battlefield.[14] But, above all, this was the people's war. Part of that amorphous group, and making up a crucial part of the Order of Battle, was a network of organizations, ranging from local authorities, air raid precautions (to become Civil Defence) services, the firemen of what was to become the National Fire Service (NFS), the police, fire watchers, nurses, doctors and the whole range of voluntary services from the Red Cross and St John's Ambulance Brigade, to the Women's Voluntary Service (WVS) and the Salvation Army, and many, many more.[15]

In the dark days of 1940, these and millions of ordinary British people were tested to the extreme of human endurance and sometimes beyond. Their skill, their courage and, above all else, their endurance made the difference. Under direct attack from their bombers, they held on and defied the Germans. Had they broken, the war would have come to an abrupt end. By their endeavours, but also with the considerable help of the British Commonwealth, the Empire and the fighting men and women of conquered and captive nations, Churchill's island people prevailed.

That so many took part, and contributed mightily to the fight – many more giving their lives than the few – is not an arcane academic issue. How we see ourselves is important. Overy, very expertly and succinctly, defines the orthodoxy, and wants us to see ourselves reliant on the élite. But this is a top-down myth that defines the ordinary people as supplicants. This is a false image of the British people, even if it is one that present-day politicians are only too keen to endorse. But the British people actually took the brunt of the enemy attack, and survived, largely through their own efforts. The true image is of a self-reliant nation, which saved itself, to an extent in spite of, rather than because of the politicians and Overy's élite. This makes us different from the people of the myth.

This thesis, however, has to be proven and, to do so, we have to look anew at the battle, the people who fought it, the challenges they faced and how they responded. And to understand this complex battle, we need to look at a much wider perspective than the air war, putting events in their political and social context, reintegrating the events, bringing together all the inter-related parts, to present – as far as is possible – a rounded whole.

However, this book goes further. How and why our history has become so distorted is an important part of our history, and we look at how that happened.

The results are startling, and lend strong support to an argument that our history was not simply changed, but stolen. We want it back.

That is the underlying message of this book.

1.

Battle lines

What General Weygand called the "Battle of France" is over. I expect that the battle of Britain is about to begin. Upon this battle depends the survival of Christian civilisation. Upon it depends our own British life and the long continuity of our institutions and our Empire. The whole fury and might of the enemy must very soon be turned on us. Hitler knows that he will have to break us in this island or lose the war.

Winston Churchill, 18 June 1940[1]

In setting the scene for the battle to come, two days after France had capitulated, Churchill had Hitler wanting to "break us in this island", predicting that he would do so by means of an invasion. Although that was to shape the now traditional version of the Battle of Britain, there were two other ways to achieve that end. On 25 May 1940 – in response to a request from Churchill to assess Britain's prospects for fighting on after the fall of France – the Joint Chiefs of Staff had identified them.[2] The first was an "unrestricted air attack", not as a prelude to invasion, but aimed specifically at breaking public morale. The other was a "blockade".

The idea of an "unrestricted air attack", later dubbed the "Blitz", was held in the same awe as was the post-war threat of nuclear annihilation. The period immediately after the fall of France, in terms of public nervousness, could almost be equated with the Cuba Crisis of 1962. The bomber was the original weapon of mass destruction, employed on what was called "terror bombing", a concept which stemmed from the 1920s and the theories of Italian General, Giulio Douhet. He held that destroying a country's "vital centres" – government, military headquarters and industry – could break a people's will to fight, the so-called "morale effect", and secure a rapid end to a war. The essence of his theories, though, was that airpower could mount an offensive that could win a war decisively in lieu of a ground offensive.[3]

This thesis was reflected in observations by the then former Conservative Prime Minister Stanley Baldwin, chairman for five years of the Committee of Imperial Defence, having sat continuously for ten years on that committee. Responding to a Commons debate on disarmament, on 10 November 1932, he declared: "the bomber will always get through". "Any town which is within reach of an aerodrome", he said, "can be bombed within the first five minutes of war from the air, to an extent which was inconceivable in the last war, and the question will be whose morale will be shattered quickest by that preliminary bombing?" He went on to say that: "The only defence is in offence, which means that you have to kill more women and children more quickly than the enemy if you want to save yourselves".[4]

The potential of the bomber was then brought to a wider audience by the 1936 film, *Things to Come*. With a script written by H. G. Wells, it had "Everytown" (based on London) being overwhelmed by a single, massive air attack.[5] Seemingly confirming the prophets of doom, there was the bombing of Guernica, in the Spanish Civil War, followed by the Nazi bombing of Warsaw and Rotterdam, depicted in newsreels shown in the nation's cinemas.

Thus, the British Chiefs of Staff, in common with virtually the entire nation – and especially the political élites – genuinely believed that this so-called "terror bombing" could bring defeat. The proletariat "were bound to crack, run, panic, even go mad, lacking the courage and self-discipline of their masters or those regimented in the forces". In the chaos that followed, the government (or its replacement) would be forced to capitulate.[6] Furthermore, this was a view shared by Hitler, the *Luftwaffe* High Command and its so-called England Committee, a unit established to provide specialized guidance on target selection. They all believed that the poorer working classes could "be incited against the rich ruling class to bring about a revolution".[7]

In sharp contrast, the blockade option was more of a slow strangulation of Britain's supplies, but it was also potentially a war winner. A blockade had been instrumental in causing the downfall of Germany in 1918, by bringing that unhappy nation to the brink of starvation. Hitler, a man of that war and of long, bitter memories, meant to turn the tables. On 29 November 1939, he had issued Führer Directive No. 9 to set up the German version of the blockade. The directive was amended on 24 May 1940 but the aim remained the same: to "cripple the English economy by attacking it at decisive points".[8]

To help him in this aim, Hitler had his Commander-in-Chief (C-in-C) naval forces, Grand Admiral Erich Räder. A career officer, formerly captain of Kaiser Wilhem II's private yacht in the run-up to the First World War, Räder had fought in the Battle of Jutland in 1916 and had remained a naval officer in the lean, inter-war years. He had risen to Rear Admiral in 1922 and become C-in-C of the Weimar Republic Navy in 1928, then building the *Kriegsmarine* for the new Chancellor. He had at his disposal cruisers and ultra modern battleships, including *Bismark*, *Scharnhorst* and *Gneisenau*, his U-boat fleet under the command of Admiral Karl Dönitz, and long-distance Focke Wulf 200 "Condor" bombers, plus surface torpedo boats, raiders and mine layers.

With the *Luftwaffe*, Hitler also planned attacks on all the principal ports in England, by bombing and mining. And, with the fall of France, the Germans had moved into Channel and Atlantic ports and airfields. Medium-range aircraft, fast motor torpedo boats, called E-boats by the British and S-boats by the Germans (S for *schnell* – as in fast), destroyers and even the long-range artillery in the Pas de Calais region could all take part.

Whatever the form of attack which comprised the Battle of Britain, for the British, it was a defensive battle that they could not afford to lose. Britain had to survive, in order then to rebuild her offensive strength and take the fight to the enemy. Whether she could avoid losing would depend, the British Service Chiefs thought, on three things. The first two were: "whether the morale of our people will withstand the strain of air bombardment"; and Britain's ability "to import the absolute essential minimum of commodities necessary to sustain life and to keep our war industries in action". Last, and by inference least, was the "capacity to resist invasion".[9]

Given that their report was written before the fall of France, it was remarkably prescient. Just over a month later, Colonel General Alfred Jodl, Chief of Operation Staff of the German Armed Forces Supreme Command (OKW), came to the same conclusions in his own report labelled: "The continuation of the war against England". This document had him declaring: "If political measures do not succeed, England's will to resist will have to be broken by force", whence he then listed the three forceful options: "siege – this includes war on the high sea and from the air against all shipments to and from England, the first against the English Airforce and all economic resources important to her war effort; terror attacks against English centres of population; and a landing of troops with the objective of occupying England".

"Germany's final victory over England is only a question of time", Jodl then wrote. "Hostile operational attacks of great strength are no longer possible. Germany, therefore, can choose a form of warfare which husbands her own strength and avoids risks". "Together with propaganda and temporary terror attacks – said to be reprisal actions – this increasing weakening of English food supply will paralyse the will of her people to resist and finally break it, and thus force the government to capitulate", Jodl added, then going on to consider a landing in England. This could only be contemplated, he wrote, after Germany has gained control of the air:

> A landing in England, therefore, should not have as its objective the military conquest of the island an objective which can be obtained by the Luftwaffe and the German Navy. Its sole purpose should be to provide the coup de grace, if it should still be necessary, to a country whose war economy is already paralyzed and whose air force is no longer capable of action.

This situation, Jodl considered, would not occur before the end of August or the beginning of September. He anticipated having to deal with an opposition of about twenty English divisions so that at least thirty German divisions would have to be embarked. The invasion nevertheless must be prepared in all details as a last resort.[10]

Thus, with uncanny symmetry, at the highest levels in the opposing militaries, the invasion was seen as the least favourable option, and by Jodl as the last resort. That qualification was constantly to recur but, through the course of the battle to come, Germans sought to implement all three options. Most times it was "pick and mix". Their problem – and possibly even the reason for their downfall – was that they failed to concentrate forces on any one. At times, it seems as if they themselves did not know precisely what they were intending. Different parts of their famed – but actually quite chaotic – war machine were at odds with each other. Even at this early stage of the war, military (to say nothing of political) incompetence was by no means the exclusive provenance of the British.

Nevertheless, Jodl did not confine himself to military issues. "Since England can no longer fight for victory but only for the preservation of its possessions and its world prestige", he argued, "she should according to all predictions, be inclined to make peace when she learns that she can still get it now at relatively little cost." There was as strong a hint as could be made that Britain might be disposed to a peace deal, with a warning: "Against a complete destruction, England would fight to the bitter end".

On the other side of the fence, when it came to evaluating the battle to come, the British Chiefs' 25 May report was not their last word. A day later, they had produced another report, this one addressing the very specific question of whether the Navy and Air Force could resist an invasion. The short answer was "yes", but with caveats. If Germany gained complete air superiority, they thought the Navy could hold out, "but not for an indefinite period". Should German tanks and infantry gain a firm footing on our shores, British land forces would be "insufficient".[11]

But, echoing the findings of their earlier report, the Chiefs argued that if Germany attained air superiority she might attempt to subjugate Britain by air attack alone. An invasion would not be necessary. They then shifted their ground to discuss the importance of air attacks on aircraft factories, made "by day or by night". By day, the Chiefs thought we could prevent serious damage. But, they said, "We cannot be sure of protecting the large industrial centres … from serious material damage by night attack". Further, whether the attacks succeeded would depend "not only on the material damage by bombs but on the moral effect on the workpeople and their determination to carry on in the face of wholesale havoc and destruction". This was back to square one. The "real test" was "whether the morale of our fighting personnel and civil population will counterbalance the numerical and material advantages which Germany enjoys".

Whether a blockade could succeed would depend whether ships could be sunk, at a rate faster than they could be replaced. Hampering port operations and goods distribution was also part of the plan, slowing the turnaround of ships and the arrival of goods at their final destinations. Where air activity was involved, this would mostly take the form of daylight precision bombing.

As to the battlefield, the images of convoys, U-boats and escorts are all associated with the desperate Battle of the Atlantic, but they belong as much to the Battle of Britain. But the battlefield was cast much more widely than the ocean. The blockade was not only countered by military action but with the ration book, recycling and voluntary abstention. There was also the expansion of the agricultural system. From 1939 in the British Isles, the area under cultivation was to increase from just short of thirteen million acres to over nineteen by 1945, while the number of tractors on farms from 1940 to 1943 increased from 1.5 to 1.9 million. Yield per harvested acre rose by thirteen percent between 1940 and 1942 and by the same amount again by 1945. These changes were the result of an intensive programme of agricultural development which was every bit as much part of the war as running convoys across the Atlantic.[12]

A ship's worth of cargo saved was a ship that did not have to be fought through to a British port. And, to that extent, the people were as much part of the war as were the armed services and the merchant marine.

Turning to the invasion – this was perhaps the purest part of the battle, in the military sense, with the least direct civilian involvement. It comprised four components: the preliminary battle for the control of the air and sea; the assembly of an invasion fleet (including parachute aircraft and gliders); transport to the landing areas and the beach assaults; and the land battles by the invading forces. Only the first two components would be attempted.

The preliminary battle for control of air and sea would be fought on the German side mainly by the application of air power, involving the targeting of airfields, port installations, communications, warships and shore defences, all to pave the way for the landings. This would require daylight bombing, affording the accuracy needed to guarantee the destruction of specific targets.

During the day, however, British fighters could operate freely. They had to be engaged and defeated, their bases attacked and destroyed, in order to allow the bombers to do their work. One crucial tactic would be to use the bombers as bait, forcing the defending fighters up, allowing them to be shot down by the escorts. Then, immediately preceding the landings, the cities would be bombed to provoke terror and mass flight. The idea was to block the roads and railways, hampering the mobility of the defending forces, as had happened during the invasion of France. That terror bombing could be achieved by day or night, but was time-critical and dependent on shock. To have its effect, it had to be carried out only hours before an invasion.

The "Blitz" would also rely on "terror bombing", but over a longer time-span, aimed at convincing people that they should give up the fight. This was indiscriminate bombing, carried out during daylight or, if losses were too high, under the cover of darkness. With then current technology, which was beginning to master the day bomber – thus confounding Baldwin – the night bomber was unstoppable. A parallel part of this strategy, though, was continuous diplomatic pressure. The Nazis constantly tested the water to see whether the other side had had enough, constantly offering an easy way out with attractive peace terms, adjusting the military effort in an attempt to gain a political result. In psychological warfare, the Nazis, and Hitler in particular, excelled. Using such tactics, they had walked into Czechoslovakia, subdued Poland with minimal force and quelled France. Victorious troops had marched into Paris without a shot being fired. Now they were ready to take on England.[13]

However, this was by no means the full extent of this complex battle. There were two other elements. The first of these was propaganda. As well as stiffening domestic morale, this was crucial for Churchill's long-term war aim. While Hitler's was merely to neutralize Britain, his was to crush Germany. For that, he needed the USA, and not only its financial and material support, but its active participation as a fully-fledged military partner. Bringing the USA into the war would require Britain to put on "a good show". The airmen would become a vitally important part of that. Additionally, they would have a specific, short-term role in reassuring the American public and president that Britain was not about to collapse, with the risk of aid finding its way into German hands, as had happened with US materiel delivered to France.

The second of these additional elements was the domestic politics of Britain. In 1940, this was a country riven with dissent, a huge divide between the upper and lower strata of society, with what was seen as a decadent ruling class holding the line against an emerging and increasingly powerful labour movement, which was by no means enthusiastic about the war. The unions, with over five million members, represented a powerful and vocal political faction. In the context of a coalition government, they often performed the role of an extra-parliamentary opposition, and had to be kept on side.[14]

At this stage, the war was expected to be over by 1942, and Churchill, the party politician, was looking at the post-war political settlement. The labour movement was seeking to use the war as an opportunity to impose a new order, a bloodless revolution, while Churchill was seeking to maintain the *status quo* built on the foundations of empire, king and country.

This internal conflict not only shaped the Battle of Britain, the battle itself became a tool to demonstrate Churchill's prowess as war leader, to strengthen his leadership and to help reinforce his view of how the war – and the peace – should be managed and won. This made it as much a political as a military event. In this, there was never any sense from Churchill and those close to him that the outcome of the battle was ever seriously in doubt. But there was real uncertainty about the outcome of the peace. Arguably, therefore, greater stakes were being played for in the battle to shape the post-war Britain – and Empire. Albeit in a different form, that same battle continues to this day. Our politics are still being shaped by those same forces which shaped the Battle of Britain, which is why it is perhaps as relevant today as it was then.

2

Let battle begin

The avowed object of the enemy was to obtain a quick decision and to end the war by the autumn or early winter of 1940. To achieve this, an invasion of Britain was evidently thought to be essential.

The Battle of Britain, HMSO 1941

In the very first instance, there was no invasion. Outline plans were drawn up by the German Naval Staff in November 1939 and presented to Hitler on 31 May 1940. At that time, still embroiled in the subjugation of France, Hitler and the *Oberkommando des Heeres* (OKH) – the Army Chiefs of Staff – had rejected them.[1]

However, there was no shortage of threats. Hitler's air force chief, Hermann Göring, had offered on 30 December 1939 the New Year's message to the semi-official newspaper *Völksicher Beobachter* that: "The German Air Force will strike at Britain with an onslaught such as has never been known in the history of the world". Then there was Dr Paul Josef Göbbels, Germany's Minister for Propaganda and Popular Enlightenment, in full, triumphal flow: "If England will have it no other way, then she must be beaten to her knees", he wrote.[2] That had been on 25 June 1940, the day the armistice between France and Germany came into effect and fifteen days before the official start of the Battle of Britain.

Nothing is ever quite what it seems, though. Many students of the Nazis – such as the CBS Radio correspondent in Berlin, William L. Shirer – attested that they were capable of dissembling to a most extraordinary degree.[3] They lied and deceived, in the latter case not only the world but themselves. Variously, they believed their own propaganda, or some of it, which made it all the more credible to outside observers and unwary historians. But, if one can take Göbbels' words at face value, the battle was not inevitable. The *Führer* "would be agreeable to peace", he had added. "Negotiations are already under way on these issues, via Sweden for example." He then observed: "No one knows yet whether they will be successful," concluding, "We must wait".[4]

Five days later, on 30 June, Göring issued a General Directive for the "Operation of the Luftwaffe against England". He told his airmen "to seize every possible opportunity by day and by night for attacks on hostile air units while airborne or on missions". According to this directive, "So long as the enemy air force remains in being, the supreme principle of warfare must be to attack it at every possible opportunity by day and by night, in the air and on the ground".[5] That looked firm enough and it certainly led to hostile air action being taken against Britain, including the attack on the anti-aircraft ship HMS *Foyle Bank*, stationed in Portland Harbour. Following a Stuka attack on 4 July, it was sunk with the loss of 176 lives and earned Royal Navy gunner Jack Foreman Mantle a posthumous Victoria Cross. The RAF had failed to intervene.[6]

Two days after Göring's directive, on 2 July, Hitler's most senior soldier, Field Marshal Wilhelm Keitel, C-in-C of the German Armed Forces (OKW), issued a Supreme Command Directive. It was headed: "Prosecution of the war against England", the first paragraph declaring:

> Invasion of England is quite possible under certain conditions of which the most important is the gaining of air superiority. For the present, therefore, the time at which it will take place remains an open question.

Preparations were to begin immediately, although the invasion was only a "possible event" so they had to be "theoretical". The planning circle, Keitel instructed, "will be as restricted as possible".

On 7 July 1940, Hitler was visited by Italian Foreign Minister Galeazzo Ciano, son-in-law of the dictator Benito Mussolini. During discussions about the next phase of the war, the *Führer* professed himself "rather inclined" to "unleash a storm of wrath and steel upon the English". But Ciano was not convinced that Hitler was committed to this course of action. In his diary, he noted that "the final decision has not been reached". He was delaying an address to the *Reichstag*, "of which, as he himself puts it, he wants to weigh every word".[7]

From the British perspective, on the day before the official start of the Battle of Britain, Churchill was confident that the Fleet should be able to deal with what was left of the German navy – heavily damaged during the invasion of Norway two months previously – if it attempted to escort an invading force.

Unescorted convoys could be dealt with by small craft. And in any event, he felt, there was little chance of an invasion being launched from the French coast.[8]

DAY 1 – WEDNESDAY 10 JULY 1940

On the actual start date of the battle, it nevertheless looked as if the decks might have been cleared for war. The sign came from Signor Virginio Gayda, a close confident of Mussolini and editor of the influential *Giornale d'Italia*. In his newspaper he had written:

> Italy and Germany have agreed on a threefold attack against Britain. Italy's part against the British Empire will consist in immobilising in the Mediterranean, Red Sea, and Indian Ocean, a large part of the British Fleet, as well as large land forces in Egypt. The Axis Powers are determined to blockade the British Isles and to break Britain's Empire contacts. She will be defeated at home, in her imperial territories and on the sea.

Thus, the official version of history would have it that a great battle was about to begin. But the inside word was that it was to be a blockade, while peace feelers were already in progress. There were even numerous reports to that effect in the American media. *United Press* reported that Germany might embark on a "peace offensive", while conveying a report that the RAF had found little along Norwegian, Dutch Belgian and French coasts to indicate any unusual troops or transport concentration such as would be needed for an attempted invasion. The British aviators, therefore, were actually set to fight off an invasion that had no formal or physical existence. Success was thereby assured, but only in the same sense that Lambeth Council had succeeded in keeping rogue elephants off its High Street.

Like elephants, invasion fleets are not easy to conceal. Following on from his discussion at the War Cabinet, Churchill noted as much in a secret minute on 10 July, exactly as *United Press* (*UP*) had openly reported.[9] Its distribution included the C-in-C Home Southern Forces, the recently promoted General Sir Alan Brooke, in charge of the Army's defence of the south coast. In the absence of any evidence of a conventional invasion fleet, it had recently been hypothesized that the Germans could be preparing a secret, unconventional fleet, comprising fast motorboats each capable of carrying a tank. But Churchill was not convinced, hence his minute, in which he stated: "I find it very difficult to visualise the kind of invasion all along the coast by troops carried in small craft, and even in boats," then adding:

> I have not seen any serious evidence of large masses of this class of craft being assembled, and, except in very narrow waters, it would be a most hazardous and even suicidal operation to commit a large army to the accidents of the sea in the teeth of our very numerous armed patrolling forces.

With over 1,000 armed patrol vessels at the Navy's disposal, he went on to repeat the very obvious point: a surprise crossing should be impossible. In the broader parts of the North Sea the invaders should be an easy prey, as part of their voyage would be made in daylight. Churchill did not believe a German invasion was imminent – and nor did he believe one could be successful.

But there were other good reasons why Churchill need not fear an immediate invasion. From two different directions, British diplomats had received strong and credible approaches from high-level personages, putting out peace feelers on behalf of the Nazis. And in an area replete with rumours of conspiracy, underhand dealings and even treachery, there was absolutely nothing untoward about the way these approaches were handled. Both were reported to, and discussed by, the War Cabinet on this day.[10]

The first approach was to Sir Samuel Hoare, Britain's ambassador to Spain – by the Spanish Foreign Minister. That was highly significant as Hoare had been one of Chamberlain's staunchest political allies and a strong supporter of appeasement. Ousted from the Cabinet by Churchill, he had wanted the post of Viceroy of India but had been prevailed upon to take the Spanish post. In moving him to Madrid, where Pétain had been ambassador and where peace talks between France and Germany had so recently been recently brokered by the Spanish Government, the Germans believed Churchill was quite deliberately keeping the door open to peace talks.

Now, the Spanish Foreign Minister had been discussing with Hoare the possibility of Franco acting as an intermediary between belligerents. According to the German Foreign Ministry which was rapidly appraised of the meeting, Hoare had agreed that "it is possible that it will some time come to that".[11]

The second approach was to Sir David Kelly, the British Minister (Ambassador) in Switzerland, resident in Berne. As a result, on 8 July, he had telegraphed to London a lengthy, encrypted despatch. It detailed a meeting with Dr Carl

Burckhardt, Acting President of the Red Cross. The two-page telegram had been received the following day, decrypted and then rushed to the first possible War Cabinet meeting.[12]

Burckhardt had just returned from a visit to Berlin on the "flimsy pretext" of discussing Red Cross relief for refugees in France. He had stayed for three days with Baron Ernst von Weizsäcker, a German Foreign Service official second only in ranking to Foreign Minister Joachim von Ribbentrop. After the war, Weizsäcker claimed to be a member of the Nazi resistance, but at this time, he had arranged long, individual conversations with two Nazi *Gauleiters* and a general, all three unnamed. The four, including Weizsäcker, affirmed that Hitler was hesitating to attack England because he still clung to the hope of developing a working arrangement with the British Empire. The General said that, while the Germans were confident of their ability to defeat England, they realized that it might involve much greater sacrifices than had the defeat of the French army. They were thus willing to call off an attack, if they could do so without the loss of face.

Burckhardt had passed the substance of these discussions to Kelly, with the clear hint that the Germans would be willing to negotiate a peace settlement. This had not been the first time he and Kelly had met on such a matter, and nor was it the first approach of this nature that had been made to him by a Nazi intermediary. Starting in late June, under the aegis of Monsieur Charles Paravicini, the former Swiss Ambassador to London, he had had several meetings with Prince Max Hohenlohe, a minor but immensely rich European noble who had acted for the Nazis. "The message he professed to bring from Hitler was always the same, though with an increasing note of urgency", wrote Kelly in his autobiography. The crux was a promise that Britain would be left untouched and the Empire would not be fragmented, with Hitler asking nothing more than to be given a free hand in Europe.[13]

According to historian Andrew Roberts, the pair had "regular meetings" near Geneva at "a very quiet little fish restaurant on the borders of the lake".[14] They also served who sat and ate, it would appear. However, Kelly himself refers to only one meeting in this restaurant, which was "well away from town". This was their third, and a family affair "with our wives and his [Hohenlohe's] daughter". There was much more formality to other meetings. The second took place in the Spanish Legation in Berne, having been arranged through a man who was later to become Spanish Ambassador in London.

In the first meeting between Kelly and Burckhardt, the diplomat had pointed out that British distrust was "a fatal obstacle to any peace". This he did again in the first of the July sequence of meetings but, in his telegram to London, he had suggested a new line of action. There was no thought of compromising Burckhardt by publicizing the contact. But, instead of "a flat negative", Kelly proposed that he should be left "without instructions". That way, the Germans would be left guessing as to whether His Majesty's Government were taking their talk seriously or not. "So long as secrecy is maintained, complete silence on our part can in no way weaken our war effort while it may weaken that of the enemy by causing hesitation", Kelly advised.

The Cabinet, on the advice of Foreign Secretary Lord Halifax, agreed with this line. Kelly was given a free hand. He was later to write that "it was obvious that every day gained for the production of Spitfires and the training of crews was priceless". Knowing the vital importance of gaining time, he had "made a show of interest", while keeping London informed. He never received any comment on, or acknowledgement of, his unofficial reports, so there was never any question of discussion and still less of negotiation. On 7 January 1941, however, he was to receive a personal telegram from Churchill, with the cryptic note: "All your work excellent and messages deeply informative".[15]

Thus, to a muted and distant drumbeat, the Battle of Britain started: a vital and barely appreciated – and most often misrepresented – part of the battle was British diplomats buying time for their country to prepare for war.

Despite that, a fly on the wall in Supreme Command (OKW) in Berlin would have seen Keitel do something that might have caused Churchill some worry. He instructed "strong artillery support" to be provided to cover the front and flanks of a future crossing and landing.[16] Huge guns were to be installed on the coast from Calais (Cap Gris Nez) to Boulogne, the first by 22 July. The programme was complete by 31 August. These guns, however, could be used against shipping, helping to close the Straits to British traffic. This had the approval of Grand Admiral Räder. He had consistently opposed an invasion and fully supported Führer Directive No. 9. Through his pressure, on 17 August 1940 it was to become established as a "total blockade" – a term which had special significance under international law, allowing unrestricted warfare against shipping.

In media terms, the start of the battle was downbeat. Middle England's newspaper, then the best-selling *Daily Express*, was concerned with "seavacu-ation", the evacuation of children overseas, mainly to the USA or Canada, and a hugely controversial issue. All sections of society were represented in the evacuation scheme, but the aristocracy and moneyed classes were particularly in evidence. Lord Mountbatten sent his wife and children. The Countess de Borchgrave, Lady Margaret Barry, Lord Radnor, Viscount Bayham, the Earl of March and Viscount Bethell all sent their children. Many of the Guinness family, City magnates like the four Rothschild families and Sir Charles Hambro dispatched theirs.[17]

Some were later to attract political fame: Paul Channon, destined to be Mrs Thatcher's Minister of Transport; Jeremy Thorpe, to lead the Liberal Party; and Shirley Williams, to become a Labour cabinet minister. In all, an estimated 17,000 children were sent out of the country – more than 11,000 privately funded. Predictably, the high proportion of the wealthy taking advantage of the scheme turned it into a *cause célèbre*. On 1 July, the *Express* had urged the government to act, fearing that it was "going to have a bad effect on the nation". But it was already having that effect, and was soon to have a powerful impact on Information Minister Duff Cooper. He was the man responsible for maintaining the morale of the people, and had packed his son, John Julius Norwich, off to New York.

As to the air war, waiting for the Germans were Fighter Command's three – soon to become four Groups. In the north and Scotland was No. 13. Watching over Yorkshire and Lancashire, the Midlands and part of East Anglia, was No. 12. Covering the south and south-east, including London, was No. 11. In the south-west, No. 10 was in the process of being set up. Much of today's action was going to be in No. 11 area, under the command of New Zealander, Air Vice-Marshal Sir Keith Park – effectively Dowding's right-hand man. He operated out of a deep bunker in the grounds of Hillingdon House in Uxbridge, on the western outskirts of London. From there, information was fed to his eight sector airfields which had direct control of the squadrons. Park took day-to-day control of the entire air battle over the south-east of England.

On this day, the action started early and was focused on a convoy of small ships rounding North Foreland in Kent, codenamed "Bread". Convoy attacks were to be a feature of the early action, a phase which the Germans called *Kanalkampf*. The ships had been detected by a German Dornier Do 17, a twin-engined bomber converted to reconnaissance duty. The RAF attempted to shoot down the spy with six Spitfires, led by a soon-to-be "ace", Flight Lieutenant Adolf "Sailor" Malan. But they found themselves outnumbered by more than twenty Messerschmitt 109 single-engined fighters. Despite a spirited fight, the Spitfires were unable to bring down the Dornier. A free fight between Spitfires and Me 109s over Dover then cost the Fighter Command an aircraft, with no loss to the *Luftwaffe*.[18]

The action that followed was on such an unusually large scale that it provided the basis for claiming the Battle of Britain had started. Nearly thirty Dornier bombers, escorted by as many Me 110s twin-engined fighters, and nearly twenty Me 109s, flew towards the convoy. One flight of six Hurricanes was guarding it, a further sixteen were on their way and eight Spitfires from RAF Manston piled in. With more than a hundred aircraft aloft, a huge dogfight broke out. One Hurricane shed a wing after colliding with a Dornier. Its pilot, Flying Officer T. P. K. Higgs, baled out. His body was eventually washed up at Noordwijk, Holland. The Dornier was also downed, while another was so badly damaged that it crashed on its return to Cherbourg. For all the activity, though, the only shipping casualty was the Dutch steamer *Bill S*, sinking six miles off Dungeness.

This, then, was the shooting war – or part of it. But what now evident was how the fighting – or the narrative describing it – was becoming the raw material for the propaganda effort which was going to feed the battle for public morale. As importantly, it was serving the British propaganda counteroffensive aimed at undermining German military and civilian confidence. Duff Cooper was to say that propaganda had an important part to play in defeating Germany, declaring: "It is, in fact, an essential element in the strategy of total warfare".[19] Propaganda was not an optional extra. It was an important weapon in its own right, designed to have both psychological and military effects, either or both potentially war-winning.

With Churchill also determined to present a brave face to the USA, it was inevitable that the air battles of the south-east would be given a high profile, even though they represented a fraction of the overall activity. This day was a case in point. The convoy action was highly publicized, despite there being significant action elsewhere, which lacked high profile (or any, in some cases) reporting. For instance, a train near Newhaven was attacked – the driver was killed and the guard injured. Further north, the SS *Waterloo*, sailing from Yarmouth, was sunk by remarkably accurate high-level bombing. To the west, a total of sixty-three, ultra-modern, twin-engined Junkers 88 bombers mounted a series of attacks. In the very first air raid in Swansea, one dropped four bombs on the docks. With no air-raid warning, surprised workers were caught in the open. Twelve were killed outright and a further twenty-six injured. Sheds and workshops were extensively damaged.

Nearly 300 miles to the west of Dover, out of sight of the London media, other aircraft attacked Falmouth Harbour. Falmouth was then a very substantial port. Shipping which used to discharge cargo in eastern ports had been re-routed there to avoid the air threat. Additionally, a large number of ships which had escaped occupied countries were berthed there. And the raid, on people who had yet to become accustomed to the ferocity of aerial bombing, was both spectacular and devastating. The British tanker *Tascalusa* was sunk. Alongside her was the 6,000ton Greek steamer SS *Marie Chandris*. She was set on fire by the tanker. Another British tanker, the *British Chancellor* was hit and badly damaged. The Dutch salvage tug *Zwarte Zee* was damaged by splinters from the blast and later sank. The wharf caught fire and dozens of men had to be rescued by launches and tugs. It was a desperate, frantic endeavour which saved them.[20]

Not far from Falmouth as the Junkers flies, the Royal Ordnance factory at Pembury was hit and seventeen bombs fell on Martlesham. One aircraft flew over Pembroke Docks where one of the largest Admiralty oil depots in the country was sited. That was an ominous sign, but there was no attack. That was to come. However, summing up the flying activity of the day, the German purpose seemed very clear. This was Directive No. 9 in action, imposing the blockade.

On the British side, for the day's activity, there was to be a highly publicized "score". This became a prominent feature of the air battle. On each and every day, the number of British fighters lost was compared with the number of German aircraft downed – of all types. The result was to be seen on the *Daily Express* front page the next day. Its lurid, triumphal tone was taken from the official communiqués: "37 German raiders down," it proclaimed. "Three Spitfires attack fifty and win!" The strap read: "Germans make their greatest raid – and the RAF secure their greatest victory". A "day of glorious deeds" readers were told. Only two British fighters had been lost, but the pilot of one was "safe".

The damaging attacks on Falmouth and Swansea – and elsewhere – were barely mentioned, even in official reports. "At a South-West Coast port fires were caused," was the only reference to Falmouth. The selective reporting thus distorted perceptions – as was intended. The Dover action was presented as a challenge to Fighter Command, representing the start of an offensive that had a single, focused aim – the destruction of British air power. But it was framed in terms of a challenge that the RAF could meet and overcome.

Right here, in the reports of the first day of the battle were the beginnings of the myth. The reality was the actual "score". Based on post-war records, the RAF lost two fighters, and seven other aircraft. Six of those were twin-engined Blenheim bombers, and five of those were from No. 107 Sqn. Therein lay a tragic tale, the like of which was to be repeated many times.

While *Luftwaffe* bombers were attacking Britain, a total of forty RAF Blenheims were carrying out daylight bombing raids on targets as far apart as Stavenger in Norway, the Rhur, the docks at Bremen, St Omer and the airfield at Glissy, near Armiens. The bombing of Glissy was allocated to six Blenheim Mk IV bombers. On arrival over their target, their formation had been broken apart by heavy flak, whence they were set upon by nine Me 109s. Only one Blenheim survived.[21] That brought the RAF losses on the day to the nine. Against that, the Germans actually lost just ten aircraft. This was most emphatically not the great victory claimed. More to the point, the *Luftwaffe* was teaching the RAF the lesson that daylight bombing against defended targets, without fighter escort, was suicide. This was a lesson the RAF would be slow to learn, but was in turn to teach the *Luftwaffe*.

DAY 2 – THURSDAY 11 JULY 1940

On this day, at a *Führer* conference in Hitler's Berghof retreat, Admiral Räder discussed moves against England. Wholly against the idea of an invasion, he was convinced that U-boat and air attacks on convoys, and bombing centres of industry, were enough. A landing should be a last resort, reserved to make England ready to sue for peace. He set out the great difficulties and risks involved in a landing. In particular, he doubted whether an area free of mines could be cleared close to the enemy coast, and he pointed out that the route taken by the invasion fleet would have to be protected by its own minefields.[22]

Even while this meeting was under way, there was another air attack on a British convoy. As had been the case during the previous day's fighting, this was quite obviously the Germans executing Führer Directive No. 9 once more. But its contribution to the British propaganda war was greater. It was portrayed the following day as another great air battle, the *Daily Express* proclaiming: "And 22 more – big raids are smashed again".

Compared with what was to come, the fighting was still small scale, making the propaganda the dominant element, as the daily loss figures became a weapon of war. Released daily throughout the battle, they presented enemy losses of roughly double the actual level. The Germans were doing much the same, but there was a further distortion on the British side. For comparison purposes, the Air Ministry only counted the fighters downed. Yet Bomber and Coastal Commands were part of the battle and taking casualties. On many days, when the losses from these Commands were added, the British totals exceeded those of the Germans.

Even without these curious omissions, so gross were the recording errors that one might have thought two sets of books were being kept, one correct and the other for public consumption. This was not the case. Each side fiddled the figures and then believed its own propaganda. This was far more damaging to the Germans, as they ended up vastly underestimating RAF strength. The British, who had initially exaggerated the size of German forces, continued to do so throughout the battle, despite the inflated kills. Their tactics, therefore, were unaffected.[23]

Appreciation of the strategic position in the British camp was mixed. Guy Liddell, MI5's director of counter-intelligence, found the German air attacks "rather difficult to understand". It was difficult to see why, if as many as a hundred planes came over here, they did not drop their bombs to some purpose, he wrote in his diary. If they take the risk of coming over here at all they might as well do as much damage as possible. Liddell's explanation was that the German pilots were "not very efficient and/or rather frightened".[24]

Harold Nicolson, a former diplomat and currently parliamentary secretary to Duff Cooper in the Ministry of Information, wrote that the German bombing raids of our ports "are already pretty bad", but added: "God knows what they will be when they start full out". As to the bigger picture, he wrote: "our morale is perfect. I am cocky about the war". Significantly, he then wrote: "All our reports show that Hitler funks invading us, yet is pledged to do so. They expect an invasion this weekend. That is Hitler's last horoscope date. After that the stars are against him".[25]

Nicolson had his own department to keep him informed and one mechanism was a daily "Home intelligence" report, compiled from sources throughout the country and collated by his department in London.[26] It was giving him some very important information about the state of morale. "The public is cheerful," it said, "but there is evidence that the cheerfulness is superficial":

> People are disinterested in the general war situation and its international implications, and Hitler's failure to arrive is promoting an apprehensive feeling that "he must have something very unpleasant in store for us". Determination to meet the challenge is widespread and confidence in the Navy is at a high level. "The Navy will win the war for us in the end."

Despite the efforts of the Air Ministry publicity team, the RAF featured poorly in public consciousness, although in areas which had been heavily bombed, there was a demand for "further reprisals" – a theme which was to become a constant. Thus, aggressive RAF action was "strongly applauded". But what must have been worrying was the finding that, "People are disinterested in the general war situation". The government needed the population actively engaged, committed to the fight and thus willing to provide the labour and the fighting men. Indifference could so easily turn to resentment and then to rebellion as the hardship and dangers started to bite. The clue to getting popular attention and commitment was in the report. The utility of talking up RAF successes was self-evident.

There was also a warning that poor information management incurred penalties. For instance, the policy on reporting enemy raids was to prohibit identification of locations. The legends "somewhere in England", a "north western town" and a "town on the south coast" thus became familiar. But this led to some absurd situations where local newspapers could not report the location of raids on their doorsteps. It was also policy to prohibit the release of casualty figures, with only vague statements made about deaths and injuries. Home Intelligence noted that this was bringing "suspicion on other official communiqués and on the honesty of official news as a whole" – as well as some resentment over the emphasis on London and the south-east.[27]

With next to no publicity for the Falmouth raid, similarly there was virtually nothing publicly written about an attack on the Yorkshire port town of Bridlington this day, when HE bombs fell in a goods yard, setting fire to kerosene tanks and a van loaded with shells, some of which exploded, the fire being brought under control after about three-quarters of an hour of difficult and dangerous fire fighting. And, at Portsmouth, there was another dangerous situation on the same date when a gasometer was fired by a bomb attack.[28]

As for the air war, the Channel was overcast with a cloud base at 5,000 ft. Weather still had a huge influence on the conduct of the battle. One pervasive myth, though, is that the summer of 1940 was long and hot. But until September, when there was an unseasonably warm, clear spell, the weather was mostly cool with frequent rainy periods.[29]

That was the case on this day, although it was good enough to permit attacks on Channel convoys, with an incursion off the Suffolk coast by a single Dornier. As this aircraft was heading for Cromer, it was picked up by radar and allocated to No. 242 Sqn based at Coltishall. But for the defenders, the conditions were less favourable. A blanket of cloud sagged over the airfield, grounding the squadron. The squadron commander volunteered to go aloft, piloting a Hurricane in near-zero visibility and driving rain. Flying towards Cromer at about 1,000 ft above the cloud, he spotted the Dornier and caught up with it, firing two long bursts before the aircraft plunged into cloud. It was later seen diving into the sea. Squadron Leader Douglas Bader, Commanding Officer (CO) of No. 242 Sqn, and the man who famously had lost his legs in a flying accident before the war yet had come back to fly again, had scored his first kill of the battle.[30]

In the better weather further south, action had started earlier. Two German formations operating out of Cherbourg had been detected making for a convoy in Lyme Bay. That there should be attacks on two successive days was unusual, perhaps signalling that the Germans were about to increase the tempo of the fighting. What was to become a classic pattern was developing, with Spitfires and Hurricanes scrambled, intercepting Stuka dive bombers, in this case, escorted by Me 109s. The action cost Fighter Command three aircraft, but the Stuka attack was disrupted and no ships were sunk.

Portland Harbour, meanwhile, was being attacked by a force of about fifty aircraft, one of the bigger *Luftwaffe* formations to date. Mixing it with the bombers was Squadron Leader Peter Townsend, commander of No. 85 Sqn based at Martlesham, flying his Hurricane. Picking off a Dornier, he raked the bomber with his eight Browning machine guns but, unlike Bader's victim, the crew lived to tell the tale, recording 220 hits when they got back to their base. The Hurricane, on the other hand, had a smashed coolant system. Its engine stopped when still twenty miles from the English coast. Townsend baled out and was fortunate enough to be rescued by a trawler.[31]

Embedded here is another narrative, one the RAF is less keen on retailing – the story about how pilots were treated and how little their lives were really valued. This is typified by the fate of another airman to end up in the sea that day. He was Sergeant (Sgt) F. J. P. Dixon who, like many before and afterwards, baled out successfully over Portland Bill, only to be drowned before he could be rescued.[32]

Almost the same fate attended Squadron Leader John Peel, CO of No. 145 Sqn. He parted company with his Hurricane over Selsey Bill, but luck favoured him. The coastguards saw his parachute and the Selsey lifeboat was launched. There was a strong breeze and a moderate swell but within the hour the crew had spotted him. He was pulled from the sea semi-conscious and exhausted. Peel later wrote to his rescuers, telling them: "When you arrived I had almost given up hope and I doubt I could have lasted more than a few minutes". It was six days before he was fit to return to the battle.[33]

Almost exactly a year later, on 9 July 1941, Peel was again shot down over the Channel. This time he had a dinghy, into which he climbed. An Air Sea Rescue Lysander was scrambled from Hawkinge, spotted him and directed a Royal Navy patrol boat and RAF launch to his location, whence he was picked up, despite enemy attempts to interfere. He was back flying the next day. The remarkable difference is that, in mid-1940, there was no organized air-sea rescue service. A year later, a service was being developed, which was to save the lives of thousands of aircrew. The traditional Battle of Britain narrative stresses how Fighter Command was desperately short of pilots, to the extent that the success depended on its ability to keep up numbers. Yet, through unnecessary losses arising from the lack of rescue services, this was to a very great extent, a self-inflicted wound.

Back in July 1940, during the night there was activity over south-west England, East Anglia, the Yorkshire coast and Portsmouth. By day, the British steamer *Hornchurch* was sunk by German bombing off Aldeburgh Light Vessel.

The steamer *Josewyn* was damaged near St Catherine's Point, off the Isle of Wight. There was a scrap over the Channel when a German He 59 rescue seaplane had been seen. Two Spitfires were shot down and the seaplane forced to land. There were Stuka raids on Portland, at which the RAF was late in arriving, the radar having given false (low) estimates of strength, although a later raid on Portsmouth was well and truly carved up.

One other narrative emerges here, the often-told story about the chain of technologically advanced radar stations which served to detect the German intruders and give the fighters vital warning, avoiding the need to mount costly standing patrols. Yet Britain's technical lead in radar is yet another myth of the battle. So powerful is it that it has tended to obscure other achievements. In the technology, the Germans were far ahead of the British who, in adopting their cumbersome, low frequency "Chain High" system of 300-foot non-rotating transmitter masts, and a separate receiving array, had gone down a techno-logical cul de sac. The poor performance of the system, effective only over water, led to many difficulties.[34]

The great achievement of the British was not so much the technology but the integration of the radar with other intelligence inputs – such as radio inter-cepts from the assembling air fleets and sightings from the expanded Observer Corps. These were fed into a sophisticated command and control system, at the heart of which was the "filter room", located at Bentley Priory, on the outskirts of London. A former stately home, one-time hotel and then girls' boarding school, it had been acquired by the RAF in 1926. There, intelligence was sorted and processed to give a best estimate of enemy strengths and intentions, whence it was passed rapidly to the operations room where it guided decision-making.[35]

Despite this, the technology had a long way to go. When the *Luftwaffe* mounted a massive night bombing campaign against the UK, there was little effective defence. Guns, without the radar directors which only came very much later, were next to useless. They were fired largely to bolster civilian morale, giving the impression that countermeasures were being taken. Sometimes, only blanks were fired, turning the guns into noise-makers. These at least had the merit of reducing the cascade of damaging and sometimes lethal shrapnel produced by exploding anti-aircraft shells, and the number of misfires.[36]

Similarly, pilots flying night sorties in aircraft designed and equipped only for day fighting, without accurate radar direction, were largely useless.

Their main concession to the night-fighting role was that they were painted black, and even that had little value when the unshielded exhausts of the day fighters produced beacons of flame which alerted the German bombers to their presence. Accidents killed far more aircrew than did the *Luftwaffe*, and continued to do so long after the senior ranks of the RAF were aware of the perils and the uselessness of the endeavours. That night, in a raid on Portsmouth by thirty bombers, nine civilians were killed and fifty were injured. In Yorkshire, five people were killed in an incident in Bridlington. The *Luftwaffe* suffered no casualties.

Throughout this period though, whenever weather permitted, the RAF was active in what was called the counteroffensive, conducted by Bomber Command, together with Coastal Command and Fleet Air Arm aircraft. This night, two Blenheims had been sent out to search for E-boats in the Channel. They had encountered a Dornier and attacked it, leaving it with extensive tail damage and trailing smoke from both engines.[37]

At the end of this day, the *Luftwaffe* lost eighteen aircraft but no Me 109 pilots. Fighter Command lost seven aircraft in the course of 432 sorties. Three pilots were dead. Bomber and Coastal Command had lost between them six aircraft, bringing the RAF "score" to thirteen aircraft down, with the *Luftwaffe* eighteen – a "win" for the home team, but again no great victory.

The difference in presentation between the claimed scores and the reality emphasized just how important the clerks and the statisticians were. In effect, they were more powerful than the warriors. Their manipulation of the figures could achieve something mere bullets could not. It could turn a narrow win into a major success, or a defeat into victory – after the event. In a war where the ability to continue to fight was dependent almost entirely on how the battle was perceived, a paper win had the same value as the real thing. The bizarre thing is that anyone could now think that the information produced at the time was not in some way tainted.

There was a less creative aspect to the propaganda – an attempt through censorship, encouragement and sanctions, to control popular sentiment. Leading this endeavour was Duff Cooper. A close personal friend of Churchill, his political ally during the days of Munich and anti-appeasement, he had been rewarded with this key post of Minister of Information. Unashamedly upper class and very active in "high society", with his famously glamorous wife, the

Lady Diana, he revelled in his notoriety as a playboy, although this was leavened by his undisputed talent as a writer and razor-sharp wit. But even his best friends struggled to argue that he was a success as Information Minister. And this day he was addressing the nation, courtesy of the BBC, to launch a new campaign.

Beaverbrook, as the new minister for production and still the proprietor of the *Daily Express*, had the day before launched his own campaign, an ill-judged attempt to bolster aircraft production by enjoining housewives to donate their aluminium pots and pans. As the stockpiles grew, embarrassed officials had to concede that the scrap was of little value for aircraft production. Most of the highly publicized heaps were buried in holes in the ground.[38]

Cooper's effort was different, if no less ill-considered. Ostensibly aimed at countering "defeatism" and preventing the spread of "alarm and despondency" – which was a criminal offence under emergency powers regulation – his brain-child was the "Silent Column". This was a development of the "careless talk costs lives" campaign, and described by the *Glasgow Herald* as a "campaign to kill rumour". Cooper appealed for recruits to "an imaginary regiment – the silent column" composed of men and women resolved "to say nothing that can help the enemy".

The nub of the campaign was to invite "sensible people" to shame figures, such as "Miss Leaky Mouth" and "Mr Glumpot". To reinforce the message, three cinema adverts had been produced, a deluge of new coloured posters were issued, and quarter-page adverts were placed in 108 newspapers and 72 magazines. But there was a fist of steel inside the patronizing glove, the threat of criminal sanctions. Through these, unwittingly, Cooper was unleashing a war against his own people. The campaign brought out the worst of the "tittle-tattle" elements of British society, redolent of Gestapo informers – with whom comparisons were made. Magistrates and judges took their lead from the campaign and, in a week, had imprisoned seventeen of their fellow citizens, sentencing them to a total of 123 weeks, with fines of £162 – in the days when £3 was a weekly wage.

One of the first was Harry Blessingdon, a young engineer overheard in a hotel lobby proudly telling a Church of England Canon about his airfield-building work. That cost him three months' imprisonment and a £60 fine. William Garbett, a Birmingham clerk, was heard saying in a public restaurant:

"It will be a good job when the British Empire is finished" – one year's imprisonment. Leicester schoolteacher, Kathleen Bursnall, got two months and was fined £20 for saying to soldiers: "You are bloody fools to wear that uniform".[39]

Cases like these crystallized resentment against Cooper, his Ministry and the entire government, with the media very quickly turning against them. Comparing the hyperactivity of the Ministry in pursuing this campaign, with its inefficiency in getting information to the media, the *Daily Mail* remarked sourly: "If the Minister of Information is to kill rumour he must put something in its place". Thus, if propaganda could win or lose the war, Cooper was doing his best to lose it.

DAY 3 – FRIDAY 12 JULY 1940

The British Government, on the other hand, was fully aware of Germany's use of propaganda as a weapon. Its next initiative on the horizon was a "European economic system", which would "sweep away the customs barriers, quotas, currency restrictions, wastefulness and inefficiency of an anachronistic capitalist system".[40]

Hitler had in mind a sort of proto European Union and it was obvious, said Churchill in a "most secret" telegram sent this day to the governments of Canada, Australia, New Zealand and South Africa, that he could make great play with all this. He could pose as the regenerator of a decadent European system.[41] As master of Europe, he could afford to restore the semblance of freedom to his victims in a scenario where Britain was cast as the warmonger, "demonstrably bent on reducing the greater part of the world to ruin". The Prime Minister of South Africa, Jan Smuts, was to respond with a long telegram, offering his own ideas for a post-war settlement.[42]

Throughout this whole period, Hitler had openly declared his reluctance to make war with Britain. Whether this was a tactical ploy, or genuinely meant, is not known. Possibly, it was both. No student of politics can be unaware that part of the skill set of any successful politician is the ability to hold and affirm entirely different and contradictory principles – sometimes simultaneously. And Hitler was the consummate politician.

To demonstrate his good faith, Hitler on 13 June had granted unprecedented access to Karl von Wiegand, a Hearst Newspapers journalist, for a prolonged interview. Von Wiegand was chief European correspondent for the *New York Journal American*, the principal isolationist newspaper in the Hearst stable. To him, Hitler had denied wanting to destroy the British Empire. "On the contrary," he had told Wiegand, "just before the outbreak of this war ... I submitted a proposal to the British Government wherein I went to the length of offering armed assistance of the Reich for safeguarding British Empire." The published interview transcript was circulated to the War Cabinet on 15 June – rather bizarrely marked "secret".[43]

Less secret, but in the longer term almost as problematical for Churchill was the issue of what had become known as "war aims". Throughout the early part of the war, there had been considerable pressure for an open statement, and events this day were shaping up to increase that pressure.

The source was Harold Nicolson, who had brought up the matter at the policy committee of which he was a member. Writing in his diary, he confided that there were two issues. On the one hand, there was the possibility of Hitler calling a European Economic Conference, announcing the economic consolidation of Europe. On the other, when the bombing began on a large scale, people would ask, "What are we fighting for?" In order to combat the first, Nicolson wrote, we needed free trade and pooled resources. For the second, we needed socialism. With his committee, he agreed to draft in leaflet form a manifesto promising the world free trade, and in Britain "equality of opportunity". But, he wrote, "Would it be difficult to get Duff Cooper to put it to the War Cabinet? Will it not be felt that we had better leave this sleeping tiger to sleep in its own way?"[44]

In the air fighting, a pattern was now beginning to emerge, plus a degree of continuity that marked it out as a battle, rather than a series of disjointed actions. So it was that, after fog in the Channel had cleared, radar picked up aircraft heading for convoys "Agent" off North Foreland and "Booty", twelve miles north-east of Orfordness. The heavier attack was aimed at "Booty". Sections from six squadrons were scrambled but they were unable to stop the destroyer *Vanessa* being disabled by near misses from German bombs. Meanwhile, the RAF was taking the fight to the enemy. Blenheims were sent out for a search-and-destroy mission of enemy aircraft. One was attacked by twelve Me 109s. The crew made it back to their base on Thorney Island where their aircraft crashed on landing.

The publicity continued to give the impression that action was confined to the south-east and Home Counties, stoking up fears of an invasion. But there is a major and serious gap in most popular narratives. This day and throughout the battle, the Germans were carrying out "nuisance" raids all over the country, some by day but mostly by night. Never at any time was the entire resource of the *Luftwaffe* focused on a single, strategic objective, and never was there one localized battle.

County Durham, for instance, saw a large number of incendiary bombs dropped on railway lines leading to a small village with the unlikely name of Seaton Snooks. Others fell in West Hartlepool. Incendiary bombs fell in a village near Consett. In an almost comedic incident, a cow was killed and a house slightly damaged by fire.[45] There was nothing in the least bit amusing when Aberdeen was raided, though. The single He 111 was shot down, but not before it had killed twenty-six and injured seventy-nine, and caused considerable damage. The day became known locally as "Black Friday".[46]

At "the end of play", the "cricket score" was rushed out with a speed that did not permit reflection or accuracy. Once published, it was difficult to correct results without loss of face, especially if adjustments had to be substantially downwards. Fighter Command admitted to four lost, in 670 sorties, and claimed twenty-two Germans downed. The actual figures were nine and eight-respectively. With a Coastal Command Blenheim and a Whitley bomber also lost, the day brought eleven losses to the RAF, putting the Germans ahead. A combat exchange rate of more than 5:1 was being claimed, when the ratio was closer to 1:1. Furthermore, five British fighter pilots had been killed, one reported "believed drowned". Cumulative fighter pilot losses in three days stood at ten, almost enough to man a squadron.

This day being a Friday, a weekly résumé on the naval military and air situation had been sent to the War Cabinet. Throughout the war, a secret appraisal was sent every Friday.[47] This one covered the period from noon on 4 July to noon on 11 July. It conveyed the sense of an escalating air war, noting more operations by the German long-range bomber force. Ports on the south coast and shipping in the North Sea had become important targets. While U-boat activity had decreased, enemy aircraft had inflicted considerable damage on shipping in the Channel.

General Alan Brooke, in an entry in his diary, wrote that: "This was supposed to be a probable day for an invasion!" He had spent the day in the office.[48] Also recording an entry on the invasion was another diarist and a vital witness in the ongoing narrative. This was 25-year-old John "Jock" Colville, Churchill's private secretary. He heard Churchill talking with two of his generals, Paget and Auchinleck, referring to "the great invasion scare". This, Churchill had said, was serving a most useful purpose. It was well on its way "to providing us with the finest offensive army we have ever possessed and it is keeping every man and woman tuned to a high pitch of readiness". Churchill had doubts on whether it was a "serious menace", although he intended to give precisely the opposite impression, and to talk about "long and dangerous vigils, etc.", when he broadcast two days hence.[49] The threat was to be exploited as a unifying and motivational force.

What may have triggered the discussion was that the Prime Minister had received a response to his memorandum of 10 July on the invasion. It had come from the First Sea Lord, Admiral Dudley Pound, who told him: "[W]e have to take into account the characteristics of the Hitler regime". Complete disregard of losses could be expected if this would help gain the objectives. It could not be assumed that "past military rules" could be relied upon. Under certain conditions, the Germans might be able to land as many as 100,000 troops on British soil, without being intercepted by naval forces. The real question was whether they could be kept supplied. Unless the German air force had overcome both our air force and our navy, Pound wrote, this "seems practically impossible".[50]

As to the invasion of England, the German military had been studying the problem. It was now in the hands of Colonel General Alfred Jodl, twice-wounded veteran of the First World War who had celebrated his fiftieth birthday on 10 May as German tanks had rolled towards France. Now Chief of Operation Staff of the OKW, he was the German military's most senior war planner. With the approval of the Supreme Commander and his immediate boss, Field Marshal Keitel, Jodl had on this day finalized a document entitled *First Thoughts on a Landing in England*.[51]

This was the first serious attempt to consider the practical implications of the invasion. Jodl had no illusions. There were the three important difficulties: Britain's command of the sea; the mobility of her Army, which could move rapidly to the landing areas; and the impossibility of achieving strategic surprise. As Churchill had earlier surmised, shipping concentrations in the ports of northern France could not be concealed.

The first problem Jodl believed could be circumvented by a landing on the south coast where the crossing was short, and by substituting command of the air for the naval supremacy which the Germans did not possess. To cope with the lack of strategic surprise and the anticipated mobility of British forces, he proposed that the landing should "take place in the form of a river crossing in force on a broad front". In other words, he anticipated multiple, simultaneous landings, over such a wide front that the enemy could not concentrate its forces against any one spearhead, without another breaking through.

The role of artillery would fall to the *Luftwaffe*; the first wave of landing troops had to be very strong; in place of bridging operations, a sea lane completely secure from naval attacks would be established in the Dover Straits. He suggested that the fighting troops of seven divisions should land between Dover and Bournemouth, under the command of General Gerd von Rundstedt, then Commander of Army Group A. And the operation had a name: *Lion*. It was shortly afterwards changed to *Sealion* (*Seelöwe*), a strangely unthreatening name for an operation which had the potential to change the world.

3.

War of the people

This is no war of chieftains or of princes, of dynasties or national ambition; it is a war of peoples and of causes. There are vast numbers, not only in this Island but in every land, who will render faithful service in this war, but whose names will never be known, whose deeds will never be recorded. This is a War of the Unknown Warriors.

Winston Churchill, BBC broadcast, 14 July 1940[1]

In 1940, the British people were reluctant warriors. Memories of the previous war, the General Strike in 1926 and the ongoing class struggle were in the consciousness of many. Churchill himself was not universally popular, and the labour unions were flexing their muscles, refusing to back a war simply to create profits for capitalists. They wanted recognition that this was a war of the people – a political agenda which then conferred rights in determining the shape of the peace. Churchill appeared willing to talk, and Hitler still appeared to be looking for peace.

DAY 4 – SATURDAY 13 JULY 1940

As the pilots of Fighter Command took to the skies, the country's most popular tabloid, the *Daily Mirror*, on its front page was lauding the heroism of the RAF. But the plaudits were for Bomber Command. The media had not yet caught up with the narrative. This became something of an interesting phenomenon. From an outsider's perspective, there appeared to be a significant element of competition between the Commands, and there was certainly no public perception of a coherent battle developing.

However, the Germans were getting more organized. Under General Albert Kesselring, commanding the Second Air Fleet, *Kommodore* Johannes Fink had been appointed *Kanalkampführer* to take charge of attacking shipping in the

Channel area. He set up his headquarters in an old bus near the statue of Louis Blériot on top of the cliffs at Cap Blanc Nez. Under his direction, there were two sharp engagements off Dover. But once again, the action was not confined to the south-east. There were also attacks on two convoys off Harwich, carried out by aircraft of the Fifth Air Fleet, commanded by General Hans-Jürgen Stumpff. They were operating out of Dutch, Danish and Norwegian airfields. Then, during the night, there was airborne minelaying in the Thames Estuary. Once again, the *Luftwaffe* was most definitely fulfilling Directive No. 9 objectives. This could not be characterized as a battle devoted to breaking down the strength of the RAF, which was said to be the German aim in the official Battle of Britain narrative.

Furthermore, only part of the British effort involved fighters. On this day, Blenheim bombers were sent to strike against barges moored in canals near Bruges. The action cost three aircraft. When Coastal Command losses were added to the five from Fighter Command, the RAF was ten down against six lost to the *Luftwaffe*. In the more important metric of fighter pilots, the British lost four, two over the Channel, bringing the cumulative total to fourteen since 10 July. The *Luftwaffe* had lost two Me 109 pilots in the same period. Fighter Command was losing the battle.

DAY 5 – SUNDAY 14 JULY 1940

Despite the censorship, commentary on the fighting was still permitted. Thus, Major (Maj) Oliver Stewart, air correspondent of the *Observer* noted a change in German strategy. "Air blockade has been the enemy's objective during the past week", he wrote. There had been increased aerial effort but it had been diverted from land targets to shipping. The main forces "would seem to have been concentrated against our convoys". The official view was not dissimilar, but Stewart reinforced it and made it public. This was a German campaign against shipping, not the RAF – and obviously so.

The attacks on the day were also against Channel shipping, the same that the BBC's Charles Gardner had come to watch. By night, there was the dispersal of effort. Heinkel bombers attacked oil tanks at Avonmouth, to the south of Bristol. RAF Bomber Command was also out. Six Blenheims attacked oil and petrol storage tanks on the Ghent–Selzaette Canal. One was lost and another badly damaged by four Me 109s. On the day, Fighter Command lost one aircraft and one pilot. Bomber Command brought the total RAF losses to three, against the *Luftwaffe's* three. Since 10 July, fifteen single-seat RAF fighter pilots had been lost.

In London, Colville recorded speculation that *der tag* (the invasion of Britain) might be imminent. Churchill was saying that an invasion was "highly probable", repeating to himself: "Hitler must invade or fail. If he fails he is bound to go East and fail he will". Churchill, with his grasp of history, may have been thinking of Napoleon. But it was rather surprising that – after his confident performance in the War Cabinet only days previously, when he had held that an imminent invasion was unlikely – he should have changed his mind. It turns out that the source of this short-lived "scare" was a party of three Dutch naval officers who had recently escaped from Holland in a small boat. They had arrived saying that the Germans were talking about 11 July being *der tag*.[2]

Another factor undoubtedly weighing on Churchill's mind was the speech he was about to broadcast. This was one of his lesser-known efforts, labelled: "War of the unknown warriors". In front of the microphone that evening, he noted that it had been "a great week" for the RAF and Fighter Command. He was not to know that, in the five days of fighting just finished, losses were exactly at parity, at forty-six each.

"We await undismayed the impending assault", Churchill told his listeners. "Perhaps it will come tonight. Perhaps it will come next week. Perhaps it will never come. "We must show ourselves equally capable of meeting a sudden violent shock or – what is perhaps a harder test – a prolonged vigil. But be the ordeal sharp or long, or both, we shall seek no terms, we shall tolerate no parley; we may show mercy – we shall ask for none".[3]

The Prime Minister made it clear what would happen should the invader come to Britain. There would be "no placid lying down of the people in submission". We would "defend every village, every town, and every city. The vast mass of London itself, fought street by street, could easily devour an entire hostile army. We would rather see London laid in ruins and ashes than that it should be tamely and abjectly enslaved". Then, in a marked change of mood, making a statement that he would subsequently contradict, he concluded:

This is no war of chieftains or of princes, of dynasties or national ambition; it is a war of peoples and of causes. There are vast numbers, not only in this Island but in every land, who will render faithful service in this war, but whose names will never be known, whose deeds will never be recorded. This is a War of the Unknown Warriors; but let all strive without failing in faith or in duty, and the dark curse of Hitler will be lifted from our age.

At this moment, the conflict had become a "war of peoples". On 20 August, it would become the war of the "few".

Another broadcaster that day was Yorkshire writer and playwright, J. B. Priestley, hired by the BBC to deliver a series of talks under the generic title: *Postscript*. In philosophical terms, he was Churchill's opposite. Hailing from Bradford in West Yorkshire, from an "ultra-respectable" middle-class background, he was grammar school educated and now a successful writer and social commentator. Although he lived in the south, he never lost his Yorkshire accent. Sometimes described as a Fabian socialist, his philosophy was actually his own. His trademark was the People's War concept, putting him at odds with the jingoistic, flag-waving patriotism that was so much Churchill's stock-in-trade.

His slot had been after the nine o'clock news, the talk ostensibly about Margate and the war's effect on the all but deserted holiday town. But Priestley's technique was to use homespun stories as platforms for his message. The war was not merely a means of defeating fascism, he said. It was an opportunity to radically reform British society. Thus, only an hour or so after Churchill had addressed the nation, Priestley was telling largely the same audience:

> The Margate I saw was saddened and hateful; but its new silence and desolation should be thought of as a bridge leading to a better Margate and a better England in a nobler world. We're not fighting to restore the past; it was the past which brought us to this heavy hour; but we are fighting to rid ourselves and the world of the evil encumbrance of these Nazis so that we can plan and create a noble future for all our species.[4]

Priestley's message was anathema to Churchill and especially to the Tory right wing, which was continually irked by his broadcasts. While fully supportive of Churchill the war leader, Priestley differed profoundly about how people should be motivated to fight and how the peace should be managed. Over a series of broadcasts, he was gradually to set out his thesis that the common man was entitled to a say in creating the peace. But, in lauding the "many" on this one day, Churchill and Priestley were at one. It was not to last.

DAY 6 – MONDAY 15 JULY 1940

Another common distortion in the Battle of Britain narrative is the suggestion that the air fighting was centre-stage, the nation transfixed by the action as it unfolded. But, at this stage, that was very far from the case. For most people, the air battle was "noises off", small-scale, localized and rarely seen. Even domestic politics continued as before.

For example, union conferences continued. Speaking at the Mineworkers' Federation Conference in Blackpool was Alexander Sloan MP. A time would come, he said, when ordinary people would have to say that the war should end. It would be brought to an end not when politicians or militarists decided, but when there was a rising of the common people to say that it should cease.[5] This was the nightmare which haunted Churchill. Before his election, Sloane had been the miners' union agent in Ayrshire. In 1921, he had been imprisoned in Barlinnie, Glasgow, for standing up to strike-breaking coal owners. A working-class "hero", in many ways he represented the authentic voice of the Left. People like him were potentially dangerous – they could mobilize the people.

That speech got little coverage, but not so Duff Cooper. He had become the story as the press picked up the arrival in New York of his 9-year-old son aboard the liner SS *Washington*, a beneficiary of the seavacuation scheme. No better example could have been found to illustrate the class divide in Britain. The following day, *Daily Mirror* journalist William Connor, writing under the pseudonym *Cassandra*, caustically welcomed the safe arrivals, then adding:

> I was disgusted and angered that millions of ordinary kids, without wealth, without fame, without rank, title, or influence, have been left here without a hope in hell of getting out of range of Hitler's bombers. And since the Minister of Information is as keen as anyone to keep up the morale of this great country of ours, I'll tell him that the spectacle of the children of powerful politicians and rich peers getting to safety, while the humble multitude of the ordinary people's children are left, is deplorable. It is exactly the type of thing that should NOT happen.

This was extremely damaging to a government seeking to represent the war as an egalitarian struggle against the forces of evil. It was doubly damaging for Duff Cooper, who was charged with maintaining public morale. And, for him personally, things were to get worse. But alongside Cooper's "outing", Signor

Virginio Gayda was again causing a stir. Britain, he wrote, was about to be served with an ultimatum by Germany and Italy:

> Preparations will be completed in a very few days, and Britain will have to settle its last account. It will have to chose between submission to the renovating, restorative forces of Europe and an extremely violent war in which inexorable destruction, the fateful precipitous step towards the final overthrow will be measured not by years or weeks of which Mr Churchill spoke but by days and hours.

Watching events from the heart of Berlin was US correspondent William L. Shirer. As an American neutral, but sympathetic to the British, his insights from the heart of the enemy capital were invaluable. Now, he had picked up from the German press that German troops of all arms "stand ready for the attack on Britain". The date of the attack would be decided by the *Führer* alone. One hears, Shirer said, that the High Command is not keen about it, but that Hitler insists.[6]

This was a classic example of the "fog of war", with different stories and opinions circulating at the same time. The military correspondent of *La Stampa* wrote of German military authorities discussing the question of where to land troops. The Germans, this correspondent maintained, were convinced that Britain would be forced to surrender within four weeks. The attack would start at several points at once, beginning with the bombardment of London, coinciding with mass attacks on the RAF. The German High Command was contemplating landing 25 divisions comprising 500,000 men.

The *Associated Press* (*AP*), on the other hand, thought that the German High Command had not finalized the plan to conquer Britain and the RAF was adding to their difficulties. Germany's need for a quick war was as great if not greater than ever. Its leaders were anxious to make the grand assault on Britain. But the more realistic High Command had counselled caution, realizing the stupendous difficulties with which they had to contend. It also reported that there had been a "lull" in the battle. Back in London, that was certainly how Chamberlain saw it. Reflecting the observation of Guy Liddell a few days earlier, he wrote to his friend Samuel Hoare in Madrid telling him that the air raids so far were "not the real thing". Little damage had been done to life or property.[7]

Whatever else, though, something was clearly stirring at the highest level. But it was not to the German Navy C-in-C's liking. It was four days since Räder had told Hitler of his reservations about an invasion. Now Supreme

Headquarters was saying that the *Führer* wanted preparations for a launch, any time from 15 August onwards. The Grand Admiral's worst fears seemed to be realized. Nevertheless, a diplomatic response was called for, and the Navy noted that: "operations and landings which had previously seemed impossible were now feasible, thanks to the superior leadership and to the exceptional moral and offensive power of the Armed Forces".[8]

Churchill this day was completing his exchange of memorandums on the likelihood of invasion, responding to Pound's intervention of 12 July. He expressed his personal belief that the Admiralty would "be better than their word", and would exact losses in transit from any invader, which would further reduce the scale of attack the Germans could mount. He also thought the British Army should be able to deal with a dispersed force of 200,000 men, but stressed that the greatest precautions must be taken in the south, given the "sovereign importance of London". From this time, many of the naval assets which would otherwise be used to escort merchant convoys on the North-Western Approaches would be tied up on anti-invasion duties in the south and east.[9]

As for the propaganda war, the Air Ministry "cricket score" was evident, especially on the *Express* front page. There had been 206 German "planes" lost in attacks on Britain since the start of the war and 130 "since the Battle *for* Britain began on June 18". Elsewhere, Bomber and Coastal Commands were sinking "invasion" barges – an activity that was to become a media staple. But, as with the fighter "scores", these reports had to be treated with caution. Poor weather had been hampering operations and, on that day, there had only been eleven Blenheims flying. Their war loads were minute – typically four 250lb bombs – and they had also been instructed to hit oil and petrol storage tanks on the Ghent–Selzaette Canal. The amount of damage they could have done was extremely limited.

Possibly of greater long-term importance, a Hudson bomber had attacked two German minesweepers off the German island of Terschelling. This illustrated the vulnerability of minesweepers in open seas yet, if the Germans were to shepherd an invasion fleet safely to England, the *Kreigsmarine* needed a week or two to sweep the Channel. If the safety of minesweepers could not even be guaranteed in home waters, Channel operations were going to be extremely hazardous.

In the air war, the pattern established in the last few days was continuing. To the Channel area, alerted by reconnaissance aircraft to intense shipping movement, the *Luftwaffe* sent fifteen Dorniers to brave the low cloud. The bombers reached a convoy but were thwarted by Fighter Command Hurricanes. A small force of bombers also crept inland to the Westland factory at Yeovil, plus other targets in the west of England and Wales. Overall, though, it was a very light day for the air war. Fighter Command flew 449 sorties, losing four Hurricanes and one pilot. The Germans lost four machines.

Nevertheless, this early stage of the Battle of Britain was as much if not more a running sea battle, with far more sailors than airmen actively engaged. And casualties were very much higher. In the Merchant Navy alone, an estimated 1,730 seamen serving in British-registered vessels died through the official battle period, compared with 544 Fighter Command aircrew.[10]

On this day, the 3,000-ton SS *Heworth* was damaged by German aircraft near the Aldeburgh Light Vessel. Ten miles south, the Polish steamer *Zbaraz* was so badly damaged by bombing that she foundered. And the steamer *Bellerock* was sunk by a mine in the Bristol Channel. Seventeen crew members were lost. The *City of Limerick* was bombed and sunk in the Bay of Biscay. Two crew members were killed. German bombers then sunk the Panamanian steamer *Fossoula*, 40 miles from Cape Finisterre. Four crew members went missing. The Portuguese steamer *Alpha* was sunk 100 miles south-west of Land's End.

Suffering from wholly inadequate air-sea rescue services, Fighter Command was also having problems with this hostile environment. Too often, when airmen were forced to bale out or ditch, the sea was proving lethal, a direct consequence of the lack of thought given to preserving one of Fighter Command's most important assets. The RAF had assumed that, in the crowded waters of the British Isles, downed pilots would be spotted and picked up by commercial shipping, naval patrols or civilian lifeboats. The Germans, by contrast, relied on a specialized fleet of some thirty rescue seaplanes, mainly Heinkel 59s. Additionally, crewmen were issued with inflatable dinghies as well as their life jackets, and had fluorescent dye to stain the water and make them more visible. The British fighter pilots had neither dinghies nor dye. The Germans plucked over four hundred and some British aircrew from the seas in their rescue aircraft.[11]

Conscious of the inadequacy of its arrangements, the Air Ministry asked the

Admiralty to move motorboat patrols close inshore during air combat. The RAF also moved five of its own high speed launches (HSLs) into the No. 11 Group area. But the need was for aircraft, preferably amphibians or floatplanes that could co-operate with rescue launches and act as their eyes.

Remarkably, some were being provided unofficially by Flight Lieutenant "Digger" Aitken, a New Zealand-born career officer.[12] He had joined the RAF in 1937 and in January 1939 – in the days when the naval air was part of the RAF – had suffered an engine failure in the Hawker Osprey he was delivering to the carrier *Ark Royal*. Forced to ditch in the chilly waters of the Channel, it had been a while before he had been rescued. In June 1940 he had been an instructor on Walrus amphibious flying boats, stationed at Gosport. Concerned at the number of pilots ending up in the sea, and remembering his own experience, he "borrowed" his unit's aircraft and began rescue operations off the Isle of Wight.

Walruses from RNAS Ford joined in but, in late August, Aitken's base at Gosport had been bombed. When Ford was also attacked, the Walrus fleet was dispersed. Some aircraft went to Yeovil and thence to Wales, others to Scotland and still others to Trinidad. Aitkin was transferred to No. 3 Hurricane Sqn, a squadron he was shortly to lead. Despite having, in a few months saved thirty-five British and German airmen, it was to be October 1941 before Walrus amphibians were used as RAF rescue aircraft. In the meantime, the British Government decided that He 59 rescue seaplanes were being used to report the movements of shipping convoys and, despite their Red Cross markings, ordered them to be shot down.

DAY 7 – TUESDAY 16 JULY 1940

Hitler issued a formal, written directive, ordering preparations for an invasion. This was Directive No. 16, the preamble of which boldly stated:

> Since England, in spite of her militarily hopeless position, shows no sign of coming to terms, I have decided to prepare a landing operation against England, and if necessary to carry it out.[13]

The aim was to eliminate the English homeland as a base for the carrying on of the war against Germany, and preparations were to be completed by mid-August. The first essential condition for the plan was "that the English Air

Force must morally and actually be so far overcome that it does not any longer show any considerable aggressive force against the German attack". Completely unaware of this but with almost perfect asymmetry, across the Channel, Dewitt Mackenzie of the *AP* wrote: "the Nazis would be just as happy if they didn't have on their hands the job of making good their threat to invade England and annihilate that island kingdom". A month since the fall of France, he stated:

> the conquering Germans are still withholding the blow of their upraised fist. And now diplomatic quarters in Rome say Fascist Foreign Minister Ciano intends to go to Berlin tomorrow to consult with Hitler about a speech in which the Führer might offer England a chance to surrender. The alternative would be a smashing attack.

The *AP* was also reporting that an "apparent trial balloon" peace offer was being floated in Rome, with an alternative threat of a full-blown assault on the British Isles. For the Swiss newspaper *Le Petit Dauphinois*, though, the invasion was already a done deal. An expeditionary force of 600,000 men and hundreds of ships was ready to attack Great Britain.

But, while the newspaper was right about ships being plentiful, this was to be an opposed landing and the German High Command expected no ports to be available in southern England. Most, if not all, would be blockaded and mined, the facilities destroyed. Troops and equipment would have to be discharged directly onto the beaches – as they were in 1944 by the Allies. And the German Navy had no dedicated landing craft – none at all. Nor was there time to design and build them. The process had started but the first craft would not come off the blocks until early 1941, and then not in sufficient numbers to support a major landing.

The Navy, therefore, had to requisition and convert hundreds of river barges (*prahms*). It set the requirement at 1,700 craft. Many would be Rhine barges. All would have limited seagoing capabilities. Some would be "dumb" – i.e., without engines, requiring tugs to tow them across the Channel and manoeuvre them onto the beaches. Others were self-propelled, but equipped mainly for river waters, with a maximum speed in choppier coastal waters of four knots or less – slower than the tidal races they were supposed to navigate. They would need assistance to negotiate the tidal streams and currents of the Channel.

Even when converted, they were not assault craft in the style of Normandy, June 1944. They lacked the quickly activated drop-down ramps. Instead, their bows had been cut away and replaced with heavy timber slats. Each slat had to be lifted out and then heavy ramps had manually to be run out and positioned. Unloading equipment was a slow and labour-intensive business, hardly ideal on an invasion beach, beset by obstacles and under fire. Many period photographs show the barges moored with tethering ropes, to keep the vessels from broaching and their ramps firmly in place.[14]

For the initial assault phase, however, the Germans planned to use a fleet of 1,161 motorboats. Some were *sturmboots*, high-powered motorboats specifically designed for river crossings under fire. Capacities varied between five and about twenty troops and they had been used with great effect during the *Blitzkrieg*. But there were not enough of them. Boats had to be requisitioned from the lakes and rivers of Europe. Many were recreational craft, built for inland waters and quite unseaworthy. They were, however, to be augmented by submersible tanks, lowered into the water from specially adapted barges, supplied with air through umbilical hoses. So-called Seibel ferries, catamarans constructed from linked pontoons, were to provide anti-aircraft gun platforms for local defence. Substantial numbers of parachute and glider troops were supposed to protecting the landing zones, provided by Göring's *Luftwaffe*, of which they were part.[15]

Ships were another matter. In 1944, the Allies had dedicated landing ships fitted with huge clamshell doors and internal ramps. They could discharge tanks and all manner of equipment straight onto the beaches. But the Nazis lacked any such provision. Without port facilities, their ships could only anchor offshore and laboriously unload their cargoes, using their own davits, into waiting barges. Or they could be beached, but again unloading was perilously slow. Using davits to transfer cargo and the many horses (50,000 were needed in the first wave), the Naval Staff estimated thirty-six hours would be needed to unload each ship.

As to the shooting war on this day, the weather was poor. Fog straddled the north of France, the Straits of Dover and south-east England. There were thunderstorms in many other districts. Most of the *Luftwaffe* stayed at home, with only a few light attacks on shipping and some night activity. Fighter Command flew 313 sorties and lost no aircraft. Bomber Command lost two Blenheims. German losses totalled three. In seven days of desultory, small-scale fighting, the *Luftwaffe* had not sought to force the issue, losing fifty-three aircraft to the RAF's fifty-two. A reason for the low intensity of the battle was offered by Dewitt Mackenzie of the *AP*. He reported that Hitler still thought he could make peace with Britain. He was not ready to launch a major offensive.

Duff Cooper, on the other hand, was picking a fight with the media, triggered when Labour MP Manny Shinwell let slip that opinion as well as news content might be censored. The *Daily Mirror* thought it "incredible" that Cooper should seek to remove the "safety valve of rational criticism". But that was already the case for the public. "Defeatism" was a criminal offence and, in conjunction with the "Silent Column" campaign, draconian penalties were being applied. George Alderson had been the latest victim, fined £50 by Carlisle magistrates for offences which included his declaring that Hitler's flag would be flying over Buckingham Palace within the fortnight. Home Intelligence reports were now picking up serious public unease. Many people thought grumbling was a British tradition.

On a more positive note, Nicolson had a long discussion with Duff Cooper about the "war aims" leaflet he was producing. Cooper agreed that "nothing will prove an alternative to Hitler's total programme except a pledge of federalism abroad and Socialism at home". Cooper, however, feared that this was "too much of an apple of discord to throw into a Coalition Cabinet". Nevertheless, he asked Nicolson to draft a memorandum for the Cabinet, putting the thing as tactfully as he could.[16]

Jock Colville was "rather depressed", having read a note from Dowding on vulnerability to night bombing. The RAF was "almost certain" to evolve an effective technique for intercepting bombers by night, but there was no night fighter capable of making use of this invention. Even if we had one, its effect would be "limited". Sooner or later, Dowding had concluded, each side must begin a race for the destruction of the other's aircraft industry. This would mean bombing the civilian population. Then, wrote Colville, "the real test will begin: have we or the Germans the sterner civilian morale?"

This was harping back to the views of the British Chiefs of Staff on 25 May, and subsequently – the sentiment shared by Räder, by Jodl, by much of the German High Command and even by Hitler himself. Seven days into what Dowding believed to be the decisive battle, both sides were convinced that the war would be decided by the civilian population's ability to withstand the effects of mass bombing.

DAY 8 – WEDNESDAY 17 JULY 1940

On this day the newspapers were not following that war in any great detail. They were complaining about proposals for new administrative courts. These were to be without juries yet would have the power to hand down death sentences. As the enabling measure went before parliament, the *Daily Mirror* published a lament that would not look out of place today:

> Many MPs, appointed as guardians of the people's liberties, did not bother to attend the House when this measure, gravely affecting the liberty of the subject, was debated. Until the debate was ending, there were never more than fifty or sixty members in the Chamber. At times, even when vital points were being discussed, the number fell to barely thirty.

Meanwhile, for "indiscreet repetition of unfounded rumours" that British troops had fired on refugees at Boulogne to prevent them boarding ships transporting troops to England, labourer John Dodd was imprisoned for three months. Such prosecutions, according to Home Intelligence, were now being widely criticized. "Informed circles" were nervous about the way the law was being interpreted and working-class people were "suspicious and afraid". "We are fighting for freedom but losing what freedom we've got" was one comment.

Beaverbrook's *Express* joined the chorus of criticism, declaring: "[A]lready there are many prosecutions of a rather foolish kind directed against talk liable to cause alarm and despondency". It added: "Aged and silly people are being sent to prison for offences which could in the first instance be met by a good talking to and a warning. The difficult task of police and magistrates must be done with level-headed common sense".

In the evening, the government tried to stoke up public interest in the air war, with a broadcast by Air Minister, Sir Archibald Sinclair. Another of Churchill's appointees, he warned listeners of a "great onslaught" to be launched within the next month, by land, sea and air simultaneously. Colville wrote of it being "expected daily now", adding that it might be "followed perhaps by a peace offensive rather than by an invasion". There again was another hint that Hitler might want to make peace. Of any air offensive, Colville noted that, since St Swithin's Day, it had rained and blown ceaselessly, "so we may expect a respite until the sun shines again".

Certainly, there was very little happening on the air front. Dull weather and occasional rain limited activity to the occasional raider as far apart as Dundee and Cornwall. The focus again had been on shipping. Overnight, aircraft were out laying mines in the Thames Estuary and between Middlesbrough and the Wash. The Bristol Channel and Severn Estuary were mined by Heinkel 111s. Fighter Command flew 253 sorties, losing one Spitfire. Bomber Command lost a Blenheim. The *Luftwaffe* lost four aircraft. It was low intensity warfare.

For the German General Staff, though, it had been a busy day; it had issued an order allocating forces for *Sealion*, instructing thirteen divisions to move to the coast for use as first-wave troops. Six divisions of General Busch's 16th Army were to depart from the Pas de Calais and land between Ramsgate and Bexhill. Four divisions of General Strauss's 9th Army, embarking in the area of Le Havre, would land between Brighton and the Isle of Wight. Three divisions of General Reichenau's 6th Army, leaving from the Cherbourg peninsula, would land in Lyme Bay between Weymouth and Lyme Regis. Some 90,000 men would be put ashore in the initial assault. Numbers would increase by the third day to 260,000.[17]

This was the "broad front" strategy, first outlined by Jodl. But Räder believed its risks were so great that he feared the entire invading forces could be lost. Unequivocally, he refused to guarantee the safety of the transports if the crossing stretched from Ramsgate to the Isle of Wight. As Navy chief he could not, of course, override Army decisions. Thus he told the Commander in Chief of the Army, Colonel-General Walther von Brauchitsch, that he intended to appeal directly to Hitler to get the plan changed.[18]

DAY 9 – THURSDAY 18 JULY 1940

While a major dispute was brewing between the heads of his Army and Navy, Hitler had something else on his mind. The clue was in despatches from Spanish correspondents in Berlin. They were affirming he would make a peace offer to Britain at the end of this week. A rejection of the offer, they said, would probably be followed immediately by an attack. *Reuters* noted that a meeting of the *Reichstag* to hear a statement by Hitler "may be announced in Berlin tomorrow". No announcement was made. *Reichsführer* Heinrich Himmler was afraid the British bombers might come over.[19]

But there was definitely to be a meeting on the Friday. "There is some speculation whether it will be ... an occasion to announce a new Blitzkrieg – this time against Britain – or an offer of peace", said *Reuters*. One can easily sense the tension, the feeling that momentous events were about to unfold, the dark, brooding presence of Nazi Germany poised to rip Britain apart, but for the *Führer* desperate to give her one last chance to come to terms.

On the other side of the Channel, however, there was no such sense of foreboding. The *Express* had a banner headline which proclaimed: "Don't muzzle free speech". In a commentary on the train wreck of Cooper's "Silent Column" campaign, it reported that Ministers were "perturbed at the way in which their exhortations to exercise discretion in speech are being interpreted". Reports were being sent to Whitehall for examination of recent cases in which minor offences had been visited with heavy punishment by magistrates. And Cooper had had to write to his "Sensible Persons" all over the country, telling them that the idea was certainly not to make people frightened to open their mouths – that there was no intention to stifle criticism.

Oblivious to such assurances, British authorities were throwing people in jail with undiminished enthusiasm. Thomas Graham, aged 50, was sentenced to three months' imprisonment for telling an LDV platoon commander and three of his men that what they were doing was "a lot of rot". John O'Hara, aged 58, an Irishman, of no fixed abode, got fourteen days hard labour for saying in a pub: "The English are a lot of traitors". Preston Percy Cockburn, a 42-year-old aircraft fitter, was remanded for a week after telling his landlady that a north-eastern town had been "bombed to hell", and that "the Government dare not publish it".

Not only was Cooper's policy being criticized. MPs were not happy to learn that he had sent his son abroad to safety. Labour MP Jim Griffiths demanded equality. Ministers who had sent their children to the USA were "showing an example which is resented and which makes the people think that after all this is the old class Britain". Nor was this the only discomfort for Cooper. Commander Sir Archibald Southby, MP for Epsom, challenged him over apparent favouritism to the BBC. Censors were permitting it to broadcast material which had not been cleared to the press. The hapless Cooper was forced to admit that the BBC was not censored by his department. The newspapers made a meal of this, also citing occasions when clearance by the censor had been slow and inefficient.

That was the public face of the war in Britain. Behind the scenes, in Whitehall, Lord Halifax had in front of him a report from an official by the name of Frank Roberts who had been reviewing the diverse peace feelers. Among those he reviewed were approaches from the Papal Nuncio in Berne, the Portuguese Dictator Dr Salazar in his capital, Lisbon, the Finish Prime Minister, Max Hohenlohe, via Sir David Kelly and also Birger Dahlerus. Roberts took the view that the Nazi feelers were calculated to lull the British into a false sense of security and to divide opinion in the country. Hitler was also seeking to strengthen his hand in negotiations with Spain, France and even Japan, all of which countries he was hoping would go to war against Britain.[20]

The day itself was most definitely not part of the long hot summer. Generally cool, there was occasional rain in southern districts and the Straits of Dover were cloudy. The Germans used the cloud to sneak a group of thirty Me 109s over the Channel. It adopted a standard bomber formation to fool the radar, and when an unsuspecting British fighter squadron tried to intercept, it lost a Spitfire. The raiders escaped unharmed. German aircraft then bombed a coastguard station and sunk the East Goodwin Light Vessel. The day was then marked by a series of small actions, all over the country, some against shipping, others inland. Most caused little damage and few casualties. In the Govan and Scotstoun area of Glasgow, however, a mid-morning raid saw eight bombs dropped near the Royal Ordnance factory. Only slight damage was caused to it, but a number of nearby tenements were seriously damaged and an occupied communal shelter was blown up.

At the close of play, Fighter Command had lost three Spitfires, one in a collision with a Miles Master trainer, with one pilot killed. Three Blenheim fighters had been lost, and three bomber versions had also been downed. A Wellington had failed to return from a raid on Bremen. That brought total RAF losses to ten. The *Luftwaffe* lost five aircraft. No fighters or their crews were lost.

DAY 10 – FRIDAY 19 JULY 1940

For much of the British public, their day had started with a rationed breakfast and the daily newspaper. Some would have been reading *Mirror* journalist

William Connor, still writing under the pseudonym *Cassandra*. He declared that Cooper's campaign had reached "preposterous proportions":

> You just daren't open your trap. Ordinary sensible criticism has become something like verbal treason and harmless decent citizens are being clapped in jug before they can say "God Save the King!" For instance, a court the other day was invited to decide whether calling a Cabinet Minister a fool was defeatist talk.

"Well, I mean to say …", Connor added wryly. Even the *Guardian* had noticed something amiss. The campaign, it intoned,

> [was] certainly never intended to encourage a sort of amateur Gestapo movement in which a few people with nothing better to do would use a lull in the actual operations of war in order to foment baseless suspicions against their neighbours.

The Daily Express reported on William Garbett, a 25-year-old Birmingham clerk, who was jailed for a year on the charge of making a seditious speech. He had said in a Cardigan café: "I see we are being beaten. It will be a good job when the British Empire is finished. We are fighting to provide dividends for the ruling classes". A 50-year-old artist, Bernard Wardle, from East Dulwich, was jailed for three months for telling two Canadian soldiers not to fight for England. "The whole Government is rotten to the core", he had said.

Taking time from the greater affairs of state, it was this to which Churchill had to give priority. "I have noticed lately," he wrote to the Home Secretary, "very many sentences imposed for indiscretion by magistrates' and other courts throughout the country in their execution of recent legislation and regulation." It was time for action: "All the cases should be reviewed by the Home Office, and His Majesty moved to remit the sentence where there was no malice or serious injury to the State", Churchill instructed.[21]

The Chiefs of Staff's Friday résumé was in front of the British War Cabinet, to which was appended a secret commentary on "German Air Force tactical policy". This revealed the British perception of the battle. It was seen as a preliminary phase. The two protagonists were sizing each other up, testing each other and getting ready for a major offensive. The "variegated pattern of tactics" showed that there was "no settled policy". The Germans, it was thought, were experimenting to devise the best tactics.

Despite this, with nine British convoys at sea, Fighter Command was expecting heavy raids – and it got them. The day started with Stuka attacks on Portland and Dover. These were driven away but British fighters encountered stiff German resistance.

Then a notable disaster started to unfold. Just past midday, No. 141 Sqn had been moved forward and ordered to patrol over Folkestone. The squadron had formed a month previously and had only recently arrived in the No. 11 Group area, a squadron with no combat experience. Worse still, it was equipped with the Boulton Paul Defiant "turret fighter", armed only with four .303 machine guns in an electrically-powered turret abaft the pilot. The aircraft had been designed to attack bombers and was not equipped to take on conventional fighters. Its deployment was based on the assumption that the *Luftwaffe* would be unable to escort bombers on raids to Britain. However, even though the fall of France had changed that, the Air Ministry kept the aircraft in service since they had enjoyed limited success – mainly when mistaken for Hurricanes and attacked from the rear.

This fateful sortie started badly when three pilots had to abort with engine faults. Thus, by one o'clock there were nine Defiants patrolling in the middle of the Channel. Completely unaware of their peril, they were bounced by twenty Me 109s, flying "up sun". Four Defiants were shot down immediately, the remaining five desperately trying to evade their attackers as the Me 109s pressed home their attack. Two more were shot down and the remaining three badly damaged. Those escaped only after the intervention of Hurricanes from No. 111 Sqn. In 15 minutes, six machines had been destroyed and ten men killed. One Me 109 had been severely damaged and crashed back at its base. No. 141 Sqn was withdrawn from the battle. Its partner No. 264 Sqn was soon to follow.[22]

Dover now took its usual pasting. The port had been designated the anti-invasion base for the 1st Destroyer Flotilla – the first naval line of defence if the Germans came. And the destroyers got plenty of attention. During the day's raids, HMS *Griffin* was slightly damaged by near misses but sustained no casualties. HMS *Beagle, en route* from Dover to Devonport, suffered slight damage from near misses. There were no casualties there either. Fleet oiler *War Sepoy* was not so lucky. Damaged beyond repair, she was later broken in two and used as a block-ship to seal off the western entrance of Dover Harbour to keep out E-boats. Minesweeping trawler *Crestflower* was badly damaged by bombs, foundering off Portsmouth. Two ratings were killed.

Anti-Aircraft Command had better luck. A Condor was brought down by its guns during a minelaying sortie and crashed into the North Sea between Hartlepool and Sunderland. There were two survivors.

Illustrating the breadth of the battle, in the morning, four Dorniers had arrived over Glasgow and bombed the Rolls Royce works, causing heavy damage and casualties. In Berwick upon Tweed, four bombs were dropped on a field east of the town wall. One demolished an empty army air raid shelter. In Sunderland, the first enemy bomb fell – also in a field. At about six in the morning, bombs were dropped on the aerodrome at Norwich causing some damage, followed by Milton Aerodrome near Pembroke taking a hit. In the early evening, a boy's school on the coast at Polruan, twenty miles west of Plymouth, was demolished. Just before midnight, RAF Manston was hit. No damage was reported.

Fighter Command flew over 700 sorties, losing ten aircraft. Five pilots had been killed and one rendered *hors de combat* with serious burns. Bomber Command lost three aircraft. The *Luftwaffe* only lost five. A triumphant Göring called his crews together to praise their actions. As for the mood in Berlin:

> there was an air of sombre expectation among the people of that great city still unharmed by bombs. The light summer evening of Northern Europe lay over the dark shadows of its massive Wilhelmian apartment houses. The pale rays of the sinking sun painted the wide avenues through which Hitler's cortège drove to the Kroll Opera House, for a great Reichstag session. Around the entrance there was a multitude of fanioned automobiles, a commotion of uniforms, a sense of self-conscious importance. "Tonight," Göbbels said excitedly, "the fate of England will be decided".

The speech started a few minutes after seven, an hour ahead of British time. Arrangements had been made for the text to be transmitted to London piecemeal, with segments being translated and sent to the prime minister's office at roughly five-minute intervals.[23]

This was Hitler's "Last appeal to reason". Opening with a history of recent events, which he described as the "most daring undertaking in the history of German warfare", the bulk of the speech was addressed to the British people – his attempt to bypass the British Government. "If this struggle continues," he warned, "it can only end in the annihilation of one of us. Mr Churchill thinks it will be Germany. I know it will be Britain. I am not the vanquished, begging for mercy. I speak as a victor". Echoing the words of his 11 June interview with Wiegand, he declared: "Mr. Churchill ought perhaps, for once, to believe me when I prophesy that a great empire will be destroyed – an empire which it was never my intention to destroy or harm".[24]

The BBC devoted six minutes to the speech on the nine o'clock news and, on its own initiative, issued a rejection. Insulting in tone, it was delivered in German by Sefton Delmer, former Berlin bureau chief for the *Daily Express* and still its roving correspondent. Shirer found the Germans unable to understand the rebuff. "They want peace", he wrote in his diary.

Anticipating the "last appeal", the German chargé d'affaires in Washington had already sent a message to the British Ambassador, Lord Lothian. It stated that "if desired", details of peace terms could be obtained from Berlin. Lothian, a figure around whom rumours of conspiracy swirled, was said to be in touch with "dissidents in the war cabinet", who would be prepared to negotiate. An important figure here was Lord Halifax.

The fourth son of the 2nd Viscount Halifax, this tall, angular Englishman had been born on 16 April 1881 with an atrophied left arm that had no hand. His family had been visited by tragedy, his three elder brothers having died before he had reached the age of nine. He became heir to the title and great estates in Yorkshire. Serving as Foreign Secretary for Chamberlain, he had been one of the primary architects of the appeasement policy, and had met most of the top Nazi leaders. He had openly expressed his admiration for the Nazi regime, and especially its robust stance against the Communists.[25]

Lothian, as Ambassador to the USA, reported directly to Halifax, who asked him to discover what terms Hitler had in mind. Churchill, learning of this, intervened and forbade further contact – an injunction with which Lothian did not immediately comply.[26] But this was far from the only contact. The capitals of Europe, and indeed Washington, were awash with rumours of meetings and deals, with Madrid, the Vatican, Berne and Stockholm variously mentioned as centres of negotiation. And although Halifax was accused of plotting against Churchill, never was there any good evidence to suggest that he was ever anything but a loyal member of the government. Insofar as he was seen to be entertaining Nazi peace offers, he – like his minister in Switzerland,

Sir David Kelly – may have been playing for time, running a skilled disinformation operation which fooled that Nazis into thinking that a peace deal was a possibility.[27]

What was then equally important is that, on this very day, the German Naval Staff was to set in motion a process which was to give the British the very time they needed. Recorded in the Naval War Diary were its reservations on *Sealion*, which were to lead to a delay in the planned implementation of the operation and then contribute to its postponement and cancellation.

Specifically, the Staff thought the task allocated to the Navy was out of all proportion to its strength and bore no relation to the tasks set for the Army and Air Force. Troops had to be carried from extensively damaged harbour installations and adjacent inland waterways, which were of limited capacity. Transport routes lay in a sea area in which weather, fog, current, tides and the state of the sea could present the greatest difficulties, not only at the first crossing but also on reaching the enemy coast and during resupply.[28]

The first wave would have to be landed on open beaches. "This imposes severe limitations in tonnage and draught of the selected ships", the Staff said. Landing barges had to be adapted "by means of specially constructed ramps" to put troops ashore. The construction programme was under way, but only minimal alterations could be made in the time. The great navigational difficulties, the Staff added, were "obvious", noting also the absence of information on the position on mines. An adequate safety margin as regard mines would not be obtainable, it said, in spite of the use of all resources. Furthermore, the British were in a position, at short notice and at the last moment, to lay minefields to protect the beaches.[29]

These were no trifling points. Collectively, they showed that the Staff understood completely that the invasion would be very dangerous, with very small chance of success, even without bringing in the small matter of air superiority.

4.

War and peace

Either the invasion will take place and be defeated or else it will be indefinitely postponed. In either case there will be a reaction of opinion and people will begin to ask themselves the question "What next?"

Duff Cooper, memorandum to the War Cabinet, 20 July 1940[1]

After Hitler's "peace offer", there followed a short period when there were two conflicting initiatives. One was devoted to exploring the possibility of immediate peace. The other, rejecting any peace deal, focused on developing "war aims" to motivate the people and engage them fully in fighting the war, and thereby help them resist Hitler's blandishments.

DAY 11 – SATURDAY 20 JULY 1940

Hitler, according to Ciano, was genuinely disappointed by the reaction to his speech. The Italian Foreign Minister recorded him being concerned that war with the English would be "hard and bloody", and that people everywhere today were "averse to bloodshed". He might have been more disappointed by the reaction of Duff Cooper. He had submitted a memorandum to the War Cabinet entitled, "Propaganda for the future". The title was misleading – perhaps deliberately so – but he had anticipated the peace offer, setting out ideas for a new political order in post-war Europe. This, heavily disguised, was the Nicolson "war aims" proposal. Cooper started with an upbeat message:

The morale of the people of Great Britain at the present time is excellent. Their mood is one of expectancy and confidence. They are awaiting an invasion and have no doubts as to their ability to repel it. But no moods endure indefinitely, and from the point of view of propaganda it is important that we should prepare for what is to come.

The invasion would take place and be defeated or else it would be indefinitely postponed, he said. He had no doubts. The prospect of defeat did not merit discussion. His concern was that a peace "offensive" from Germany "would be more dangerous than any invasion". It would have a very wide appeal and to those suffering from war-weariness and lack of vision would seem eminently fair and reasonable.

Nazism and Fascism appealed to millions of young people in Europe, said Cooper, but while Britain was fighting for survival, they would not infect "our people". When the menace to the island had been withdrawn, though, something else had to be put in its place "to stimulate the temper of the nation". If the fighting was merely to restore the Europe of Versailles and the England of the last two decades, people would not be convinced of the justice of their cause. Since Hitler was introducing his new order and uniting Europe. Britain had to do the same, offering a Europe "united by goodwill and in friendship, not by force and in terrors". It would be a Europe based upon some federal system. Armaments would be pooled and trade barriers broken down. Each nation would be allowed to conduct its own affairs in its own way with the same kind of freedom as each state in the American Union.

This was a template for a federal Europe, one which was to dominate the political debate after the war and still raise the temperature seventy years later. It was remarkable that, with the dictator across the water threatening annihilation, the British propaganda chief was calmly considering the shape of post-war Europe.

As for Hitler's speech, the media played down the "peace offer". It did not go so far as to consider what the terms might be. The *Express* presented it as a blustering threat. The *Mirror* bluntly headlined: "Hitler says submit". Britain had been given an ultimatum: "Talk peace or I destroy you. Hitler piled threat on threat and called it his final appeal to reason". *Reuters* suggested that nobody believed that Britain would entertain a peace offer. The *New York Times* recorded British officials taking the speech as an indication that the long anticipated and long delayed Battle for Britain may not be far off. Harold Nicolson, expecting an imminent invasion, wrote of "a sort of exhilaration in the air", expressing pride in being "the people who will not give way".

Home Intelligence found public opinion largely following the newspapers. But rather than the invasion threat, the "most serious cause of tension", it reported, "are (sic) the prosecutions for spreading rumours". There was alarm at the coincidence of measures which appear to be aimed at the freedom of the civilian. One respondent complained: "It's the Gestapo over here", adding a rebellious note: "They can prevent us talking but they can't prevent us thinking".

The latest to be prosecuted was Victor Muff, reigning Bradford billiards champion. He was fined £10 by Huddersfield magistrates for making a whole list of allegations: we could not possibly win the war; old-age pensioners would receive more under Hitler; Churchill had caused miners to be shot; that he had caused many lives to be lost at Gallipoli; and the government, had they any sense, would accept any terms Hitler offered. Considering how much more others had been fined – for saying considerably less – Muff seems to have got his money's worth.[2]

After the Defiant losses of the previous day, the Air Ministry was in "damage limitation" mode. It talked of victory and sneered at German propaganda. Taking its cue from the Ministry, the *Guardian* reported the German habit of exaggeration "is its own undoing". Only later did the Ministry come clean on its own misfortune.

With a peace deal in prospect, the *Luftwaffe* restricted its incursions inland, although it mounted coastal raids all over Britain, from Scotland to Dorset. The area off Dover was now being called "Hellfire Corner", so intense was the activity. Keeping up the pressure, the *Luftwaffe* attacked a convoy code-named "Bosom". A number of Stukas were shot down and more were severely damaged, but the SS *Pulborough* was sunk and the destroyer HMS *Brazen* had her back broken by several near misses. After another attack put a bomb directly into her engine room, she sunk in 100 ft of water. Destroyer HMS *Acheron* was damaged by near misses, ten miles off the Isle of Wight.

The result of the air fighting appeared to be a victory for the British. As well as the Stukas, five Me 109s were downed with the loss of four German pilots – the highest number lost in one day so far – bringing the total to fourteen *Luftwaffe* aircraft lost on the day. But Fighter Command lost nine aircraft overall, eight in combat, with seven pilots lost. Since the start of the battle, Fighter Command had lost thirty pilots, as against seven Me 109 pilots lost. On this day, two had successfully baled out over the sea but had drowned. Ironically, one of those had been shot down by a German He 59 rescue seaplane.

Bomber Command lost nine aircraft bringing total RAF losses for the day to eighteen, compared with the *Luftwaffe's* fourteen.

DAY 12 – SUNDAY 21 JULY 1940

Setting the tone for the treatment of the air war, the *Sunday Express* ran a front-page headline announcing: "12 German raiders shot down off our coasts". This time, the figures were not exaggerated, although the same could not be said of the narrative. The fight over the convoy had been "one of the most thrilling sky battles of the war", and though the bombers had attempted to press home their attacks with "great recklessness", the ships were unharmed. *The Observer* was more direct: "Nazi air raid on harbour fails", it reported.

The second story in the *Express* was Hitler's peace offer, with the paper reporting: "Hitler down with a bump". No one was interested. But in Berlin, there was a major debate about how long Britain should be given to respond, with Göring apparently against a rapid move. Meanwhile, German radio transmitters were pouring out a barrage of propaganda in English, attacking Britain's "ruling clique", "British warmongers", "the rotten Westminster plutocrats" and "the arch-plotter Winston Churchill". And putting the activity in context, the Swiss newspaper, *Basler Nachrichten*, wrote that the "appeal to reason" was not directed at Churchill but to a "defeatist opposition" which was believed to be strong in Britain.

A key issue for *Express* columnist John Gordon was the "Silent column" campaign. Men and women of that obnoxious type who love to pry and poke their noses into their neighbour's affairs are slinking up and down the streets with their ears flapping, he wrote, hoping to hear an incautious word of conversation so that they may run off and tell the police. As a result of this pernicious crusade, men and women are being hauled into police courts, charged with passing remarks much the same as those you can hear round any dinner table in London. Most of these people are decent, harmless citizens. Not pulling his punches, he went on to condemn "our magistrates, who can always be relied on to be stampeded into stupidities by every wave of passion". They are, he said, "inflicting sentences on these people that are nothing short of revolting cruelty".[3]

Hitler this day summoned his commanders to a conference. But his immediate priority was not the invasion of England. He was thinking of Russia.

He asked von Brauchitsch, his Army chief, to advise on the possibility of an autumn invasion, only a couple of months hence. The Army chief managed to head him away from the idea, but told General Erich Marcks, Chief of Staff of the 18th Army, to look at the problem. Seconded to the planning staff OKH, he was given until 4 August to come up with a plan.

Only two days after his speech in Berlin, the possibility of a peace deal with Britain was discussed at some length. The Naval Staff war diary recorded speculation about a "strong and influential group in England who would like to know details of the peace conditions". There were rumours of "a telegram from the Duke of Windsor to the King, advising a Cabinet reshuffle, and of an audience which Lloyd George had with the King".[4]

Turning to the invasion, Hitler stressed the need to "strive with every means to end the war in a short time and to exploit our favourable military and political situation as quickly as possible". Operation *Sealion* could be considered as "the most effective means to this end". He described it as an "exceptionally bold and daring undertaking". Even if the way was short, this was "not just a river crossing, but the crossing of a sea which is dominated by the enemy". This was not a case of a single crossing operation as in Norway; operational surprise could not be expected. Hitler did, therefore, accept that the naval difficulties were formidable and appreciated that "the most difficult part will be the continued reinforcement of equipment and stores". The operation was therefore to be undertaken "only if no other means are left for settling with Britain".

"The time of year is an important factor, since the weather in the North Sea and in the Channel is very bad during the second half of September and the fogs begin in the middle of October", Hitler said. The decisive need for the participation of the *Luftwaffe* required the main operation to be completed by 15 September. He asked Räder for a full report on how far the Navy could safeguard the crossing and when their preparations would be completed. If it was not certain that they would be ready by the beginning of September, other plans would have to be considered; and Räder's report would show whether the invasion would be carried out that autumn or postponed to the following spring. About the beginning of August he would also decide whether air and naval warfare would be intensified.[5]

Back in England, ties with the Commonwealth in 1940 were still very strong. South African, Australian, New Zealand and Canadian nationals in particular were playing an active part in the war. Of the Commonwealth leaders, South African Prime Minister Jan Smuts was a respected figure. Not only was he one of Churchill's closest personal allies, at the end of the First World War, it was his study and report which had led to the formation of an independent RAF. This day, he broadcast to the people of Great Britain and the USA.

Smuts spoke of the Allied cause being "very far from lost". It would not be until Britain itself was taken. And Britain would prove to be an "impregnable fortress" against which German might would be launched in vain. "If that attack fails, Hitler is lost and all Europe, aye the whole world, is saved", Smuts declared. Even if Hitler "did not venture to attack Britain", he was equally lost. Then, said Smuts, the same combination of sea power and air power which had baulked him at Dunkirk, and which would have saved Britain from invasion, would then be turned in a victorious offensive against Hitler. That offensive in the end "would throttle and strangle and bring down in ruins his vast land empire in Europe. For in a war of endurance," Smuts concluded, "the time factor must prove fatal to Hitler's plans".[6]

A few hours after that broadcast, J. B. Priestley took to the airwaves. His theme was to contrast himself with an "official", a "conceited, ungenerous, sterile kind of a chap". This, in the inimical Priestley style, quickly led to a wider appraisal of the war. There were two ways of looking at it, he said, the first being the "official" way, as a "terrible interruption":

> As soon as we can decently do it, we must return to what is called peace, so let's make all the munitions we can, and be ready to do some hard fighting, and then we can have done with Hitler and his Nazis and go back to where we started from, the day before war was declared.

Arguing that this "official" way was wrong, Priestley lodged the idea that we had to get rid of the "intolerable nuisances" of "Nazists and Fascists" but not so that we could go back to anything. "There's nothing that really worked that we can go back to", he said. We had to go forward "and really plan and build up a nobler world ... in which ordinary, decent folk can not only find justice and security but beauty and delight". But, said Priestley, we could not go forward and build up this new world order, and "this is our real war aim, unless we begin to think differently".[7]

As to the shooting war, after the frenetic activity of the previous day, fighting was "on a reduced scale". Raids were plotted off the Scottish, east and south coasts, apparently searching for shipping. An attack was made off Dundee. Trawlers were attacked off Beachy Head and a convoy about ten miles off the Needles was attacked by a large German formation, including Me 110s used as bombers – a tactic never seen before. Fighter Command flew 571 sorties, losing only two aircraft, with total RAF losses standing at six. Ten *Luftwaffe* aircraft were lost. For once, the British had ended up ahead. From the small scale of the fighting, though, even if it was partly imposed by the weather, one thing was clear – Hitler was staying his hand.[8]

DAY 13 – MONDAY 22 JULY 1940

Mussolini expressed an opinion on Hitler's speech. The Duce wanted war and damned it as "too cunning", fearing that the English "might find in it a pretext to begin negotiations".[9] Over the weekend, Churchill had been under considerable pressure to respond, especially as there had been diplomatic representations through Sweden and the Vatican.[10] Churchill's first thought had been to hold "a solemn and formal debate" in both Houses of Parliament, an idea he raised in the War Cabinet. His colleagues counselled that this would be making too much of the matter, "upon which we were all of one mind". The *AP* reported that hopes of British acceptance were "dwindling fast" and it appeared that the scene was being set for total war. Sources close to the Axis set 27 July as the most probable "zero hour" for an assault. But diplomatic activity continued.

In the *Frankfurter Zeitung*, editor Dr Rudolf Kircher set out "semi-official" German peace terms – they were the mix which was to become increasingly familiar. The Berlin correspondent of the Japanese *Domei* agency claimed that "a lull" was expected while Hitler watched the reaction of Britain. A definite refusal would launch the German attack on the British Isles. The general sentiment in Germany was for peace, but Churchill and his group would have to resign. A new Cabinet centred on Chamberlain, the Prime Minister of the First World War, Lloyd George and the British fascist leader Oswald Mosely – now in prison – would have to be formed. Nevertheless, it was "almost a foregone conclusion" that Britain would turn down Germany's terms.[11]

Colville, writing in his diary, thought this was "the psychological moment to define our own war aims and state our terms". They would be such that Hitler must refuse them, but in so doing would lose credit in the eyes of the outside world and also in those of his own people. But, Colville feared, "the Government lacks the imagination to make such a move". Forty-eight MPs agreed with his sentiments, having tabled a resolution calling for Churchill to state Britain's war aims. To those must be added Duff Cooper, and there was the Smuts' response to Churchill's telegraph on 12 July, with its lengthy proposal for a post-war settlement.

By coincidence, a major meeting was being held at the Reich Economic Ministry in Berlin, under the chairmanship of Minister Walther Funk, to discuss a directive issued by Göring on 22 June, concerning the organization of a Greater European economic area under German leadership. The Germans were well advanced with their plans for a post-war settlement of their own. But, indicating the uncertainty in the broader situation, the report stated:

> One difficulty of planning lay in the fact that the Führer's aims and decisions were not yet known and the military measures against Britain were not yet concluded. We therefore did not know whether the British Empire and its economic influence would remain to any extent or not. Those responsible for preliminary planning should assume that the British economy would continue to exist in some form and would affect the situation at any rate outside Europe.[12]

From the USA, there were reports in the media – relayed by J. W. T. Mason, the *United Press* "war expert", that "tentative peace suggestions" were being presented by neutral powers. But Churchill seemed to float above the fray, ignoring these and all calls to respond with a detailed alternative vision. Instead, he instructed Lord Halifax to reject Hitler's initiative. This Halifax did during a scheduled broadcast to the nation. "We shall not cease fighting," he said, "until freedom for ourselves and others is secured." Not unaware that Halifax was the man most likely to be seen as a negotiator, the *Irish Times* observed that this "may be taken as the authoritative answer to Herr Hitler's vague offer of peace. Nothing could be more definite".

Meanwhile, in the Glasgow Sheriff Court, 47-year-old Matilda Lynn was sentenced to twenty-one days imprisonment for, among other things, telling an acquaintance that docks in the south had been destroyed and that the Germans were in control there.[13] In reporting such events, though, the press was not a disinterested player. It was fighting its own battles with the Ministry of Information, and had forced what was regarded as a major U-turn, when the

Ministry announced that it would not introduce compulsory censorship. The left-wing *Daily Herald* crowed: "We have been saved from a blunder … which might have had the most evil consequences".

More softening of the official line was apparent from Harold Nicolson, who had hosted a free concert in Hendon Park, sponsored by his Ministry. With more than 10,000 attending, he announced a policy rethink. The Ministry, he said, "is not, an Ogpu[14] or a Gestapo. It does not desire to dictate to the citizens of this free country what they should think, say, feel or hear. It does not pry upon the private thoughts of the people. It does not bully and it does not sneak". He finished by saying: "We want people to be more friendly and neighbourly than they have been. Talk more than you have ever talked before," he said, "but talk of victory".[15] The *Mirror* noted, rather sourly, that Nicolson had not told his audience that the most effective way of preventing or killing rumour was speedier release of news of national importance.

The German Naval Staff was giving Hitler the bad news that invasion preparations could not be finished by the middle of August. And only when air superiority in the Channel area had been achieved could minesweeping start. Mine clearance was vital in order to permit free passage of the fleet, but it could take up to two weeks. The timetable was being stretched to the point of inelasticity. And only on this day had the Führer Directive been turned into detailed orders for action and passed down to the lower echelons, telling the various naval departments to start preparations in earnest. Merely preparing and transmitting orders to the various levels of command took time. It would not be until 25 July that the collection points for the barges would be set up.[16]

On the propaganda front, the *Daily Express* declared that the British were winning the "Battle of the coast". Twenty-one "Nazi Raiders" had been shot down over the weekend. The *Daily Telegraph* made the figure 24. The paper then ridiculed Hitler's "boast" to "starve British ports of shipping and the British people of the food and raw material they need". After a month of intensive German air attacks, he had "completely failed". But at least the paper acknowledged that the Germans were waging an "economic war", part of the blockade that was using U-boats as one of the primary weapons.

This day was a landmark of a different kind – the first time a German submarine had visited a French port, in this case Lorient. Soon, eight or nine boats would be based at the port, taking 450 miles off the route over the north of Scotland. Gradually, the network of bases was extended, taking in Brest, Cherbourg and St Nazaire.[17] The grip was tightening on Britain's supply lines and the *Express* was premature in predicting victory. It was also underestimating the deadly effect of the minelaying programme. German destroyers, E-boats and specialist minelayers, U-boats, and aircraft were encircling Britain's coast, its estuaries and ports, with deadly barriers of high explosive. And most of this action was by night.

Fighter Command, on the other hand, flew 611 daylight sorties. They lost two aircraft and downed two Germans. And the British were trying to impose their own version of a blockade. Six Swordfish carried out a minelaying sortie and raids were carried out on airfields in France and barges in Amsterdam. Another two aircraft were lost, bringing total RAF losses on the day to four, against the two to the *Luftwaffe*.

DAY 14 – TUESDAY 23 JULY 1940

Halifax's speech jolted official German circles, according to Shirer. He recorded "angry Nazi faces" at the noon press conference. A spokesman had said with a snarl: "Lord Halifax has refused to accept the peace offer of the Führer. Gentlemen, there will be war". Shirer noted that the campaign to whip the people up for a war with Britain had started with a bang that morning. Every paper in Berlin, he said, carried practically the same headline: "Churchill's answer – cowardly murdering of a defenceless population!". The story was that, since Hitler's speech, the British had increased their night attacks on helpless women and children.[18]

Hitler, however, stood aloof. He attended a performance of Wagner's *Götterdämmerung* at the *Bayreuther Festspiele* – the last time in his life he was ever to see a live performance of Wagner. Augustus Kubizek, a childhood friend, recalled the Chancellor telling him: "I am still tied up by the war. But, I hope it won't last much longer and then I'll be able to build again and to carry out what remains to be done".[19]

The *Press Association* conveyed news of a "renewed German peace drive". German radio had embarked on an intensive "peace offensive" in which Great Britain had been repeatedly urged to accept Hitler's "appeal to reason". The Bremen station was almost monopolized from 9.30 p.m. by a series of talks on the theme that this was Britain's last chance to save herself. "Unless the Führer's offer is accepted now – and as it stands – there can be no question of its acceptance at a later date, or of any negotiations at any time," one had said. "If the Führer is forced to do what he does not want to do, the order for the utter destruction of England will be finally and irrevocably given. The sad fact of the present crisis is that the views of the British people have not been heard at all".

That, of course, was the last thing the British Government wanted. William Connor, writing in his *Cassandra* slot in the *Mirror*, noted that a farmer had been fined £26 for "revealing" that Hitler had only sent over a few bombers so far, then speculating on what would happen when thousands came over. "I suppose he can count himself lucky that he wasn't clapped in the State dungeons for about half a year", wrote Connor.

Elsewhere Haydn Spenser Dunford, a 28-year-old dockyard fitter, described as a "Dunkirk hero", had been fined £50 and ordered to pay £15 15s costs by Falmouth magistrates for "trying to cause disaffection among naval men". This was a man who had been at the Dunkirk and Brest evacuations and among the first to board bombed ships. He had rescued wounded men and thrown boxes of ammunition overboard to prevent explosions. Yet he got no sympathy from the bench chairman, Mr A. W. Chard, who told him: "Only by a majority have we decided to fine you. The next offender like you will have no option to prison". Dunford's mates had a whip-round to pay the fine.[20]

The *Daily Express* this day listed five cases caught by Cooper's "Silent Column", including Phyllis Bateman, a 30-year-old Post Office clerk in Clacton, jailed for three months for suggesting to two Army sergeants – flippantly, she claimed – that if they did not agree with government policy then they should "revolt". "Why don't you start a riot or a strike?" she is alleged to have said.

Home Intelligence articulated complaints about the prosecution of a prominent South Yorkshire councillor for calling Chamberlain a traitor and criticizing him for unpreparedness. This was contrasted with Halifax's broadcast rejection of Hitler's peace offer. "We will not stop fighting till freedom for ourselves and others is secured", he had said. On another occasion, a man had been fined for saying, "this is a capitalist war in defence of dividends". This raised more than a few eyebrows. The *Daily Worker* had been openly saying much the same thing for months.

The last straw was the conviction of a vicar, on the evidence of four boys

– two aged 15 and two 16. It was alleged that in addressing about a hundred boys he had "communicated air raid information which might be useful to the enemy, and made remarks which were likely to cause alarm or despondency". In Germany, stormed the *Mirror*, children are taught to spy on adults – even on their own mothers and fathers. The British people have often been told that one of the worst features of the Gestapo system of the Nazis is the way children are encouraged to supply evidence for its prosecutions. And the British people are now being assured by their Ministry of Information that there is no intention of encouraging a "Gestapo" atmosphere here. We need more than mere assurances.

There was only one person who could now sort this – the Prime Minister. In the Commons, he was challenged by Kenneth Lindsay, MP for Kilmarnock. The policy was "well-meant in its endeavour", Churchill assured him. After the briefest of defences, Cooper's baby was passed into what was called in the USA "innocuous desuetude".[21]

The *Express* on its front page offered a story about the state of the fleet. Britain, as builder of warships for the world's navies, had been able to take over ships being built in British yards for foreign governments. This was not helpful to Churchill, who was in the process of begging fifty surplus destroyers from Roosevelt.

But the story also gave details of a massive new minefield being laid, from Cornwall to south-east Ireland, ostensibly to prevent the Germans invading Ireland. This was the lead item in *The Guardian*, which also noted that much of the French deep sea fishing fleet in the western ports had escaped to Britain. Many of the vessels had been taken over by the Royal Navy, bringing home the staggering number which were being conscripted, or "impressed" in Navy jargon. Trawlers, drifters and whalers were to form the backbone of the patrol service, providing capable warships which could spell death to any invasion fleet.

As to the air war, the *Luftwaffe* was still targeting shipping. This day it concentrated its attacks on a convoy codenamed "Pilot" steaming off the Lincolnshire coast. Two raiders were shot down by fighters. In the mid-afternoon, a lone Dornier dropped bombs on the old airship hangar at Pulham and another attempted to bomb the Vickers Armstrong aircraft factory at Weybridge. Fighter Command lost three aircraft, all to accidents. A Blenheim and a Hudson were also lost, bringing RAF losses to five, compared with six suffered by the

Luftwaffe. In two full weeks of fighting, total RAF losses stood at 110, compared with ninety-nine to the *Luftwaffe*.

One of the *Luftwaffe* losses made history in a small way when a Blenheim night fighter downed a Dornier 17 using airborne radar. But with the final stages of the kill in bright moonlit conditions, it was a long time before the success could be repeated. The *Luftwaffe* had its own successes. The cargo ship *Lady Mostyn* detonated a mine 1½ miles off the Formby Light Vessel, sinking with the loss of all seven crew. And a Dornier bomber attacked a submarine, about 150 miles east of Aberdeen. This was most likely the *Narwhal*, which had sailed from Blyth on 22 July to lay mines off the Norwegian coast. She failed to return.

DAY 15 – WEDNESDAY 24 JULY 1940

Assessing progress so far, the air fighting had started with a flurry in the Dover and south coast region, with additional attacks on the east coast. The rest of the country had suffered sporadic attacks, many by night, and a minelaying campaign was under way. From purely the operational stance, therefore, the picture had been a brief burst of activity, followed by a prolonged lull, with no major engagements other than attacks on shipping.

Only when the political dimension was added did this make sense. Without doubt, Hitler had been holding back the *Luftwaffe*, in the hope of negotiating peace. But now briefly in Berlin, he was "full of fury against London". Walther Hewel, diplomat and Nazi Party "fixer", wrote to Hohenlohe in Switzerland, instructing him to break off contact with Kelly. "The Führer does not desire further attempts made to build bridges for the British. If they crave their own destruction, they can have it", he wrote.[22] The *Mirror* ran a story headed: "Nazis cancel peace offer". It was remarkably well informed.

However, even as this was happening, Göring was starting a new – and independent – line of contact with London, through the founder of the Dutch KLM airline, Albert Plesman. The initial contact had come via a Swedish KLM pilot named Count von Rosen, who was also Göring's nephew. Göring arranged a meeting at the luxurious Karin Hall on his estate in the most beautiful part of the March of Brandenburg, forty miles from Berlin. Plesman then wrote a text which was later forwarded to London. It offered terms which were very familiar, leaving the British Empire intact, giving Germany control of the European continent and allowing the USA control of the Americas. But, in a significant addition, it also offered to remove occupation forces from Norway, Denmark, Netherlands, Belgium and France.

The document was sent to the Dutch Ambassador in Stockholm and from there to Eelco van Kleffens, the former Dutch Foreign Minister, now in London as part of the Dutch Government in exile. He in turn passed it to Lord Halifax in the Foreign Office, where it was "studied with much interest". There was communication between van Kleffens and Halifax as late as 29 August. Later, however, Plesman learned that there was "no interest in his plan", while Göring disowned it.[23]

With only tiny fragments of the frenetic diplomatic manoeuvring being reported, the main concern of the British people was budget day. Swingeing tax increases to pay for the war were being announced. There was also a historical milestone, with the start of universal "pay as you earn" (PAYE). Tax was to be deducted in instalments from wages, rather than as a lump sum at the end of the year.[24]

The war started early when a hostile aircraft appeared over Glasgow and bombed a printing works. Some windows of a Rolls Royce factory were broken and a few minor casualties were reported. Then, a few minutes before eight in the morning, an enemy formation was detected heading towards a convoy in the Thames Estuary. Fighters were scrambled but no German aircraft were shot down. At about eleven, an enemy formation threatened a convoy of small colliers. RAF fighters sent to intercept were visible from the coast, and thousands lined the shore to watch, raising the profile of Fighter Command. Elsewhere, houses were damaged in the usually quiet suburb of Walton-on-Thames and the Vickers factory in Weybridge was attacked by a solitary Dornier. Brooklands airfield was bombed by a Junkers 88 pretending to come into land. Remarkably little damage was done. This one got away, but another Junkers crashed near Brest. The aircraft was destroyed and all four crew perished.

Less visibly, shipping continued to be targeted. HMT *Rodino* was sunk off Dover, together with anti-submarine trawler *Kingston Gelena*. Twenty sailors were killed. The trawler *Fleming* was also sunk. And at sea that night, a disaster unfolded. The French liner *Meknès*, sailing from Southampton with 1,179 repatriated French naval personnel, was headed for Marseilles. Despite sailing floodlit and with prominent French markings, it was attacked and sunk by E-boat S-27. Destroyers responded to distress signals but 383 French sailors still drowned.[25]

By comparison, air losses for the day had been trivial: Fighter Command five – with 561 sorties flown; the *Luftwaffe* twelve down. No operational Bomber or Coastal Command losses were reported. The sea battle had been larger than the air component.

DAY 16 – THURSDAY 25 JULY 1940

The *AP* reported a statement by "authoritative Vatican quarters", saying the Pope had abandoned any hope of a settlement between Britain and the Axis powers, following the British Government's response to Hitler. Feelers made through the Vatican had been "negative". The Pope was expected to deliver a homily of sorrow and to ask the faithful throughout the world to pray for peace.[26]

Pam Ashworth, a Mass Observation correspondent, had a different "take". The wireless had reported the absence of raids overnight, the first time for more than a month. Conversation in her office elicited the view that, "Hitler wants to give us another chance to do the right thing".[27]

Shirer, meanwhile, wrote of receiving "a first glimpse" of Hitler's "new order", with details given by Walther Funk following the meeting of the 22 July, setting out the goals for the new European economy.[28] These had been delivered in a speech, which had had a "sensational effect", a kind of distillation of long deliberations on the economic reorganization of Europe. It was regarded as a kind of semi-official blueprint for all the occupied countries.[29]

The German Naval Staff, meanwhile, was beginning to assemble shipping for the invasion. Suitable ships were "limited" and had been reduced even further by the Norwegian operation. There were about 1.2 million tons available to German industry. Coal and ore traffic absorbed about 800,000 tons. The rest was coastal traffic. Diverting these ships would hurt the German economy, especially if they were kept for a long time. Furthermore, although ships from defeated countries could be used, they needed German crews. German ships would have to be laid up to release sailors. As for the inland waterway fleet, about a third of the German fleet would be needed. The effect on the supply of coal, ore and food would be "considerable".

The requirement for tugs could be met only if every single tug over 250 horsepower was withdrawn and all trawlers being used for deep sea and coastal fishing were requisitioned. This, said the Staff, "would practically stop the supply of fish". The motorboat quota could only be met by requisitioning craft from inland waterways. Most of these were unseaworthy.[30]

Meanwhile, ploughing down the coast of Kent was a 21-ship convoy designated CW8. As it rounded the North Foreland, the two columns or "divisions" turned towards the Channel, picking up a "snooper" in the form of a *Luftwaffe* reconnaissance aircraft. There followed a series of fighter sweeps over the Channel towards Dover in what turned out to be a ploy to clear the way for the Stukas. Instead of flying high, the Me 109s came in at sea level, forcing defending Spitfires down to meet them. Hurricanes from Biggin Hill joined in. Past midday as the fight developed, eleven Hurricanes came in to assist in the dogfight with fifty Me 109s. Short of fuel, the Messerschmitts disengaged and the British fighters withdrew.

It was now the turn of the ships. Away to port, merchant navy gunner John Gallagher on the collier *Tamworth* spotted "a swarm of bees". He was witnessing the start of a mass attack by over sixty Stukas. Spitfires, answering a frantic call for help, engaged the fighter escort. Meanwhile, the Stukas sunk three steamers, killing eight seamen. Another ship was sunk two miles off Folkestone, with the loss of one crewman. Another was sunk off Dungeness. Five more ships were damaged.

Three E-boats then slipped out of Calais to attack the remnants of the convoy. It was now late afternoon. Two destroyers, HMS *Boreas* and *Brilliant*, and two Norwegian motor torpedo boats (MTBs), steamed from Dover to meet them. At 35 knots, their sterns sunk low in the water and their stern-waves streaming higher than their decks, the destroyers engaged. The Germans drove though the fire but were then seen to retire at speed.

The Allied warships were now in mid-channel in broad daylight, far from the cover of Dover anti-aircraft guns. Retribution was closer. Stukas hit the *Boreas* twice on her bridge. An officer and sixteen ratings were killed outright and another five died of wounds. Twenty-five were wounded. *Brilliant* was also badly damaged, with two bomb hits to her stern. Both destroyers were towed into Dover and, with them out of the way, the German boats returned. In quick order, three steamers were sunk, with the loss of six seamen. The Germans now had virtual control of the Channel at its narrowest point.[31]

Fighter Command flew 641 sorties on the day, initially claiming thirty-nine confirmed and unconfirmed "kills", including one unknown aircraft type. This was initially recorded as a Chance Vought V 156, one of a formation pounced upon by Spitfires. Intelligence officers suggested that the Germans were so short of aircraft that they were resorting to captured French machines. The truth emerged when the Royal Navy reported the loss of a Blackburn Skua.

The revised figures had sixteen *Luftwaffe* aircraft downed, as against seven RAF fighters. Bomber and Coastal Command between them had lost eleven aircraft, at a cost of twenty-eight lives. The final score, therefore, was *Luftwaffe* sixteen, RAF eighteen, plus the Skua, bringing total British losses to nineteen. Five fighter pilots from each side were killed. But, while the balance of advantage went to the Germans, life went on regardless.

The Yorkshire Post reported how the miners of Grimethorpe Colliery had returned to work after a week-long lighting strike. The paper also reported the particularly tragic loss of the trawler *Campina*, impressed by the Navy. It had been blown apart by a mine as it had entered harbour, killing all its eleven crew – an event witnessed by two young wives of the crewmen who had been invited to join their husbands for a holiday.

DAY 17 – FRIDAY 26 JULY

Such had been the expectation of an invasion that there was now international media speculation about the lack of action. *AP* journalist, Kirke L. Simpson, in a widely syndicated piece for the US press, explored the continuing delay. "This cannot be ignored", he wrote. "Whatever the explanation, it is daily becoming an increasing threat to Hitler's prestige."

One very obvious explanation for the delay was the simple fact that the Germans were not ready. Alan Brooke, now safely installed as C-in-C Home Command, expressed his pessimism "as to our powers of meeting an invasion". But there was still no certainty that he would have to meet one. Even now, an invasion attempt was not a foregone conclusion. The apparent finality of the German responses to the Halifax speech was not what it seemed. The political correspondent of the *Glasgow Herald* was writing that "Hitler's so-called peace offer remains open because of his refusal to take Lord Halifax's 'No' for an answer".

Colville seemed aware of this. "There is some agitation for an authoritative reply to Hitler's speech, and I think Winston should make one, stating our terms and our aims subtly and clearly", he wrote. Captain M. M. Corpening, the current Berlin correspondent for the *Chicago Tribune*, confirmed that something was afoot. He had obtained details of peace terms handed to the King of Sweden by the German Government for onwards transmission to Great Britain. His dispatch was printed in his and many other leading American newspapers the following day.

The *Express* resumed its attack on Duff Cooper, having learned that the Ministry of Information was employing researchers to test public opinion and report back on morale. This, the newspaper held, was the job of MPs. Cooper was trying to bypass parliament. The Ministry of Information "began as a joke. It has always been a joke. Now it is getting beyond a joke", said the paper, dubbing its officials, "Cooper's snoopers".[32]

At the War Cabinet, Cooper was mainly concerned with his paper on post-war Europe. He had, since submitting it, become aware of General Smuts' telegram which had suggested that a "brains trust" be set up to work out an alternative plan for countering Hitler's peace movement. Churchill, however, refused to give Cooper his head. He had earlier suggested a loose free-trade arrangement with the USA and now suggested that the matter "required further study by various groups of Ministers". Cooper was asked to submit a scheme for further examination.[33]

In media terms, the war was on hold while headlines were given over to the events of 17 June and sinking of the *Lancastria* in the worst shipping disaster of the war. Then, the 16,243-ton Cunard liner, packed with an estimated 5,800 British soldiers evacuating from the port of St Nazaire, had come under attack from German aircraft. She had taken three bombs and within twenty minutes had sunk, with an estimated 4,000 drowned. This had been more lives lost than in the *Titanic* and *Lusitania* combined. It was also the largest single loss of life for British forces in the whole of the Second World War.[34]

The disaster had happened over a month previously, and the survivors had been landed at Falmouth, from where considerable rumours had been spread as to the number of casualties. British censors had forbidden any mention of it. It had taken an American newspaper to release details and only once they emerged had the British Government made a statement.

Churchill had personally blocked the news, saying at the time: "The newspapers have got enough disaster for today at least". In his book published in 1949, he claimed he had intended to release the news a few days later. But with the pressure of events, he "forgot to lift the ban". It had then been *some years* before the knowledge of this horror became public".[35] The news, though, had actually broken in less than six weeks. On 3 August, the *Illustrated London News* published many photographs of the incident.[36] The curious assertion by Churchill simply did not accord with the facts.

Home Intelligence found the public unimpressed. The long-delayed announcement, it said, "has had a bad effect on morale". The loss had been generally known in certain districts and the news had been broadcast on German radio. The lack of adequate explanation for the delay "had produced criticism and general suspicion. People wondered what else is being kept back".

Back in the war, low, dark cloud and heavy rain over Britain made flying even more difficult and dangerous than usual. But still the *Luftwaffe* came. Shipping south of the Isle of Wight provided the targets. Hurricanes shot down two bombers, at a cost of one of their own. SS *Haytor* was sunk by a mine in the North Sea, where a Fokker seaplane operated by a Dutch crew was also lost.

Hastings suffered its first air raid when a single aircraft dropped eleven bombs. Some fell on the cricket ground. Others wrecked buildings.[37] In the early evening Weymouth and Bristol were hit. Aberdeen was raided but with no serious damage this time. Gradually, though, the *Luftwaffe* was moving inland. In the north-east of London, an estimated 120 bombs fell, as well as incendiaries. A number of civilians were killed. Overnight, there was minelaying in the Thames Estuary, Norfolk and the Bristol Channel.

On the day, RAF Fighter Command mounted 581 sorties, despite the bad weather. It lost five aircraft. In addition to the Fokker, a Whitley was lost, bringing the RAF total to seven. With the *Luftwaffe* losing only two aircraft, the odds on the day again favoured the Germans. And the Admiralty decided that it could no longer take the risk of escorting ships through the Dover Straits in daylight.

DAY 18 – SATURDAY 27 JULY 1940

Luftwaffe operations started just before ten. Again shipping was the target, with an attack on a convoy off Swanage, Dorset. Simultaneously, two convoys off the estuary were bombed. From Harwich emerged a group comprising six minesweeping trawlers, with anti-aircraft protection from the destroyers *Wren* and *Montrose*. HMS *Wren* came under heavy and sustained bombing from fifteen Heinkels. She was holed below the waterline and sank with the loss of thirty-seven crewmen. *Montrose* then had her bows blown off and other major damage. Amazingly, she remained afloat and was towed back to Harwich.

Further south, in Dover Harbour, the destroyer *Codrington* was alongside the depot ship *Sandhurst* in the submarine basin. A bomb fell close to her, breaking her back and she sank in two pieces. The destroyer HMS *Walpole*, also alongside *Sandhurst*, was badly damaged as was the depot ship itself. She was to be further damaged in a raid on 29 July. The action was notable for being the first time Me 109s had carried bombs. This changed the tactical equation. Fighters could no longer be ignored while the RAF went after the bombers.

None of these events were made public at the time. The loss of the *Codrington* was not officially released until 18 May 1945. Moreover, there were other shipping losses attributable to the *Luftwaffe*. SS *Salvestria*, an 11,938-ton whale factory ship, while approaching Rosyth in Scotland, activated an acoustic mine. The *Durdham Sand Dredger* was sunk by a mine in the mouth of the Severn. HM Salvage Vessel *Tedworth* was bombed and slightly damaged off North Foreland; a convoy was bombed off the Humber; and the SS *Westavon*, in a convoy about forty miles off Orfordness, was disabled by a near miss from a bomb.

With news that the Germans were about to install heavy guns at Cap Griz Nez, the Admiralty decided to pull its warships out of the port of Dover. This was another significant victory for the Germans. They knew it – their reconnaissance photographs showed the empty berths. But the British public were not allowed to know. Censorship kept information from the public, not the enemy. Convoys would now be run as "combined naval and air operations", the number of vessels limited to twenty-five. A mobile balloon barrage was to be provided for each convoy. With such complications, it would take time to arrange the next sailing.

On this day, RAF Fighter Command lost three aircraft in 496 sorties, the RAF total reaching four when a Battle bomber exploded after a bomb fell on to the ground while it was being loaded, killing six men. The *Luftwaffe*, on the other hand, lost five aircraft. Meanwhile at Wolverhampton, William John Robson, an Air Ministry technical instructor, was fined £15 with 12s costs for "despondency" talk. Robson had said he admired Germany, that he had shaken hands with Hitler and that British troops had run away at Dunkirk.[38]

Across the Atlantic, in a widely syndicated news piece, Russian-born American aviator Major Alexander de Seversky questioned the likelihood of a German invasion of Britain.[39] Unless Germany possesses a huge secret armada of new types of fighting aircraft, of which the world has no inkling, it was not possible. "There is a great gulf between the political logic of the Führer's threats and the tactical realities of the situation", he wrote. "If victory has gone to Hitler's head and he overrides the objections of the strategists in this connection, then Germany is heading for a terrific failure." Given that, there was "room for suspicion", de Seversky thought, that the deliberate German ballyhoo was a stratagem to compel Britain to keep its men and machines at home.

DAY 19 – SUNDAY 28 JULY 1940

The correspondent for the *Chicago Tribune* was expelled from Berlin for breaking the story about Germany's peace terms. That story was even reported in the *Observer*. London denied receiving any such terms. Berlin's correspondent of the Stockholm newspaper, *Tidninger*, claimed that the German Government "fully realized" that the main obstacle to the British willingness to negotiate was disbelief in any German promises or assurances. To counter this, Germany was willing to make "concrete" guarantees. Coming from Berlin, that was felt to be "a remarkable German admission".

Otto D. Tolischus, Pulitzer prize-winner and Berlin correspondent for the *New York Times* until he had been expelled in March, was now writing for the paper from Stockholm. The German peace offensive was being driven home with a worldwide drumbeat of totalitarian propaganda, he observed. But, inasmuch as Churchill had already anticipated Hitler's "peace" offer with a categorical "no" and Lord Halifax had repeated it after the offer had been made, foreign observers (in Stockholm) were puzzling over why the Germans were persisting with it. Tolischus explained:

> First, if it fails, it is designed to undermine British fighting morale, as did Hitler's constant "peace" offers to France and his insistence that he did not want to fight France undermined French morale. Second, if it succeeds, it has assured a German "political" victory over Britain. There is no doubt here that Hitler would prefer the latter result. The latest private advices from Berlin, coming through several sources, insist that the oft heralded German blitz invasion of England has been called off or indefinitely postponed, because the entire military staff is against it and only Joachim von Ribbentrop and Heinrich Himmler are for it.

Tolischus thereby, in a few deft sentences, clarified what has since evaded generations of historians. The Germans were using diplomacy as a weapon of war – it was an integral part of the battle. As to the invasion, "The military staff are reported to be against it," Tolischus said, "because it would be very costly and the result is highly uncertain." Yet George Axelsson, his replacement in Berlin thought that the process of "softening up" Britain had begun in earnest. After an order in France freezing road and rail traffic, a landing attempt, he said, "may be a matter of days if not hours". Confusingly, the same newspaper cited the Italian *Telegrafo*. It claimed that the systematic bombing of British harbours, railway centres and war plants was a "new tactic" that was aimed at "starving the British", and in particular isolating the seven million people of London from their food supplies.

London-based "aeronautical experts" cited by the Australian newspaper, the *Age*, seemed to agree with the *Telegrafo*. In order to starve Britain, they said, Hitler must prevent ships from the Atlantic using four great waterways: Southampton water; Bristol water; the Mersey; and the Clyde. Heavy attacks on ships at sea and approaching the two southerly ports was probably Hitler's immediate plan. The second stage would be to demoralize the half-starved civilian population by a general and intense bombing. The third would be the final blow, landing troops at several points, hoping that the confusion throughout the country would enable success.

In Britain, the morning saw attacks in Cornwall, Cardiff and Newport. In the early afternoon, a sizeable force of forty bombers escorted by Me 109s headed for Dover. Aircraft from four squadrons broke up the raid. There was also a raid in Newcastle, Twenty-five high explosive bombs were dropped almost in a straight line across the city. There was considerable damage, three women were killed, one woman and two men were injured. The *Newcastle Evening Chronicle* the next day was not allowed to reveal the location of events on its own doorstep, having to write about "a town in north-east".

Attacks on shipping continued. The Belfast registered MV *Orlock Head*, was bombed, sinking in the Pentland Firth. In the Thames Estuary, the armed trawler *Staunton* was presumed blown up by a magnetic mine. All thirteen crew were lost. And there had been very active minelaying during the night. As to the air casualties, Fighter Command on the day flew 758 sorties with a loss of five aircraft. Bomber Command lost three. Ten *Luftwaffe* aircraft were lost.

As this was Sunday, J. B. Priestley gave one of his *Postscript* talks. This time he used for his foil RAF pilots. "In return for their skill, devotion, endurance and self-sacrifice, what are we civilians prepared to do?" Priestley asked. At the very least, we could "give our minds honestly, sincerely and without immediate self-interest, to the task of preparing a world really fit for them and their kind – to arrange for them a final 'happy landing'". He stressed the virtues of co-operation, as practised by RAF pilots, rather than the competitiveness which they experienced in business life, where the watchword was "survival of the slickest".[40]

5.

Closing the door

Before however any such requests or proposals could even be considered it would be necessary that effective guarantees by deeds, not words, should be forthcoming from Germany ...

Winston Churchill, 3 August 1940. Response to German peace feelers sent via the King of Sweden[1]

In the following six days, history was made. To a counterpoint of threats from Göring and continued fighting, peace diplomacy continued. Meanwhile, a different question was being explored – what was to be the shape of Britain, Europe and even the world, after the war? Even in the darkest days of the war, these questions were being considered, the answers thought vitally necessary if people were to resist the blandishments of Hitler and his new order. Churchill, however, wanted to get on with the war. He would have to wait. The German Naval Staff was still looking at the problem of invading England.

DAY 20 – MONDAY 29 JULY 1940

The *Express*, following on from the *New York Times*, was talking up the invasion threat. But it also tapped into the *New York Sun*, retailing the details of another exclusive interview by Karl von Wiegand, this time with Herman Göring. The *Luftwaffe* chief had told him: "My air force is completely prepared and all set for the signal of command from the Führer to do our part in the general attack". He had added ominously, "I can assure you our attacks on England so far have been merely armed reconnaissances". There was some recognition of this in Britain.

The Foreign Office Permanent Secretary, Alexander Cadogan, wrote in his diary of "half-hearted air raids". Despite "various good indications" that the Germans were going to attack, they had not done so. The British War Cabinet,

meanwhile, was being appraised of a telegram sent by the Ambassador at
Angora on 16 July, reporting that the German Military Attaché had stated that
the invasion of Great Britain had been postponed until the first week in August,
and that he intended to go to Germany to follow events. On the 27 July the
Ambassador had reported that the German Attaché had left Istanbul on the
previous day, for Belgrade.[2]

The Cabinet could hardly have known that Göring was pursuing his peace
initiatives and the Naval Staff had only just completed their feasibility study
into *Sealion*. From the latter came a memorandum initialled by Admirals Otto
Schniewind and Kurt Fricke, two key members of the planning staff. They
stated that the landing could only be towards the end of September, which
meant the weather would be "a source of great difficulty", particularly during
the supply phases of the operation. Worse still, they did not think the German
navy could stop the Royal Navy breaking into the crossing area. They thus
advised against an invasion in 1940. If the air war and the naval blockade did
not induce the enemy to make peace, the invasion could be considered in May
1941 or thereafter, they suggested.[3]

To this Schniewind added a note confirming that the navy could not take
responsibility for the landing in the current year. Carrying out the operation at
all appeared "extremely doubtful". With this, Räder was in full agreement. He
felt that the only possible way of carrying out the operation would be to reduce
the crossing area to the Dover Straits, thus dropping the other two crossing
zones. He intended to tell the *Führer* this, without delay.

In the Dover Straits this day, the weather was fine with light, north-westerly
winds and haze. Two sizeable convoys were on the move and an early morning
raid was brewing. Just after seven, however, it became apparent that the ships
were not the target. The raid was heading for the harbour. Air Vice-Marshal
Park, from his bunker in Hillingdon, was now under considerable pressure
from the Admiralty to protect the port. He and Dowding both preferred to
hold back the fighters to deal with intruders further inland. But, nevertheless,
he released a squadron of Spitfires and one of Hurricanes.

These fighters met what turned out to be twenty Stukas supported by about
fifty Me 109s. As the waters of the harbour erupted under a storm of bombs,
four Stukas were shot down. But the Me 109s had the advantage of height and
extracted a toll of five British fighters, killing one pilot. The ferocious fighting

was made all the more hazardous for the RAF by the enthusiastic participation of anti-aircraft gunners.

This was the first of two attacks. By the end of the second, SS *Grondland*, which had been damaged on July 25, had been sunk. Nineteen crewmen were killed. Patrol yacht *Gulzar* was sunk in the submarine basin.[4] The depot ship HMS *Sandhurst* – damaged two days previously – was set on fire.[5] With the half-submerged wreck of the *Codrington* still alongside, her substantial stores of fuel and explosives threatened to devastate the town. Again and again, personnel from Dover Fire Brigade and the Auxiliary Fire Service forced their way into the burning ship. Despite thick black smoke creating a pyre visible for miles, they stayed in place as the bombers returned. The fire was extinguished and the town saved. Three senior fire officers were awarded the George Medal: Ernest Harmer, Cyril Brown and Alexander Edmund Campbell. Six firemen were commended.[6]

In Portland, the Royal Navy lost its fourth destroyer in a month. This was HMS *Delight*, escorting a Channel convoy. She had sailed from Rosyth, through the English Channel and had stopped at Portland on the way, departing on July 29. In contravention of local orders and placing herself at considerable risk, she was sailing in daylight. After leaving the harbour, German radar at Cherbourg picked her up and directed aircraft to attack her. Some twenty miles off Portland Bill by then, she put up a spirited fight but a bomb on her fo'c'sle ended it, causing a major fire and explosion. She managed to limp towards Portland Harbour but sunk early the next morning, having lost six of her company.[7]

This was not the end of the fighting. A heavy raid on Harwich by Heinkels and Dorniers developed, but was beaten off by elements of three squadrons. They downed three Heinkels. Steamers *Clan Monro* and *Moidart* were sunk by mines in the same area. The mine was turning out to be a potent weapon.[8] SS *Ousebridge* found one in Queen's Channel, Liverpool. Her bow was blown off and back broken. Two of her crew were killed.

Raids were seen in Wales, with incendiaries and explosive bombs dropped in three locations, including Port Talbot. In the early morning, bombs had been dropped at Altcar (Lancashire), near Crewe, in Essex, Gloucestershire, Cheshire, Midlothian and Berwickshire, causing little or no damage. Bombs were also dropped near the aerodromes at Yatesbury and Hawarden. During the early hours of the morning, a Heinkel *en route* to bomb the Bristol works at Filton was downed by anti-aircraft fire. The crew baled out. Two were at large for some 48 hours, but one crew member wandered abroad for nine days, believed to be the longest period a German airman was at large before capture.

For Fighter Command, the day had seen 758 sorties, for the loss of four aircraft. One Blenheim bomber was lost. Total *Luftwaffe* losses were thirteen across the whole country, although the RAF claimed "17 of 80 raiders" shot down in thirty minutes in the Dover action. In later news bulletins, the censor permitted Dover to be named – the first permitted mention of a place name.

DAY 21 – TUESDAY 30 JULY 1940

Unusually, the account of the previous day's air action was relegated to the back page of the *Express*. One of its staff reporters had watched the battle and, on this day, the newspaper crossed the line. Responding to censorship by omitting details of events was one thing. But the reporter wrote: "I saw how bad the bombers' aim was. Ships in the harbour had bombs scattered around them, but they were not hit. Five trawlers had narrow escapes".

On 9 August, *War Illustrated* was to repeat the claims that nothing had been hit, showing "during and after" photographs of ships in outer harbour. With thick, black smoke pouring from the stricken *Sandhurst* in the naval basin, no one within miles could have been unaware that the *Luftwaffe* had scored a hit, not counting the sinking of the SS *Grondland* and the patrol yacht *Gulzar*. Nevertheless, *War Illustrated* headed its article, "This Battle of Dover was won in the sky". There was a line between omitting material on the instructions of the censor, and actively telling lies. On this occasion, the press crossed it.

By now, German planning for *Sealion* was gathering momentum. But the Naval Staff stuck to its view that the operation could not be carried out until after 15 September. Even if the transportation of the first wave succeeded through exceptionally fine weather, there could be no guarantee that further waves could be successfully transported. The operation was suicide.

Thus, the Naval Operations Division added its voice to calls for a postponement. Nevertheless, it suggested preparations should continue. Unrestricted air warfare together with naval measures "should cause the enemy to negotiate with the Führer on the latter's terms". As an alternative, they argued for a major German front in the Mediterranean, launching an operation through Spain against Gibraltar. They wanted armoured troops to be sent to support the Italian offensive against Egypt and the Suez Canal, attacking the British in Haifa in order to deprive them of vital oil supplies, and to incite the Russians to sweep southward to the Persian Gulf.

Another key man in the invasion planning process was recently promoted Colonel-General Franz Halder, Chief of Staff of the OKH. This Bavarian Catholic, from an old military family, recorded seeing the Navy memorandum on 28 July. He observed that it "upsets all previous calculations about the crossing". Halder sent Colonel Greiffenberg, Chief of the OKH Operations Branch, from his office in Fontainebleau to the naval headquarters in Berlin to get more detail. He returned with "much depressing information". As a result, the Army was resigned to prospect that "the Navy in all probability will not provide us this autumn with the means for a successful invasion of England".[9]

Führer Headquarters (HQ), meanwhile, sent a signal to C-in-C Air Force ordering preparations for the "great air offensive" to be "accelerated to the utmost" so that the operation could begin within twelve hours of the issue of the executive order.[10]

So went the war. This day was marked by unsettled weather, low cloud and drizzle. Although flying was heavily restricted, the *Luftwaffe* was still out hunting in the Channel and North Sea. A group of Ju 88s attacked a convoy off the Suffolk coast – without success. Overnight, the Bay of Liverpool was mined heavily. Bombing in ten separate areas in Wales was reported. He 111s visited the Filton aircraft factory and the oil tanks at Avonmouth. On the other side of the country, bombs were dropped on Hull, with some damage to shops.

For the port city of Hull, bombing was by no means a novelty. The first raid had been on 19 June and raids continued until 1945, making it one of the most heavily bombed British cities of the war. Close to 1,200 people were killed and 3,000 injured. The city spent more than 1,000 hours under alert, suffering 86,715 buildings damaged and 95 percent of houses damaged or destroyed. Of a population of around 320,000 at the beginning of the war, approximately 192,000 were made homeless. Much of the city centre was completely destroyed and heavy damage was inflicted on residential areas, industry, the railways and the docks. Yet the port continued to function throughout the war.[11]

The censors would not allow Hull to be identified by name. The media thus referred to a "North-East" town or "northern coastal town", when it referred to it at all, which was not very often. Consequently, it has only been in more recent years that its plight has been recognized. Perversely, at this time, Churchill was headed north for a visit to the north-east. He inspected the Home Guard, coastal and other defences, including those near Hartlepool, returning to London on 31 July.[12]

Back to this dog-end day of July, Fighter Command flew 688 sorties for two aircraft lost, against seven Germans claimed, including a Heinkel off Montrose and an Me 100 off Southwold. Bomber Command lost one Blenheim. The RAF was meanwhile asserting that its night bombing of Germany was "most effective" and was worrying the German High Command. Intelligence reports, it said, indicated that its raids were causing serious damage. This was despite the whole British nation getting a tutorial on the effect of bombing on national morale and industrial production, and the resilience of populations and industrial systems. The RAF chiefs, however, seemed to be out of the room.

DAY 22 – WEDNESDAY 31 JULY

As July drew to a close, diverse reports in the Axis press were suggesting that preparations for an invasion were nearly complete. German and Italian travellers in Spain claimed that Franco intended to mount an attack on Gibraltar to coincide with an invasion.

The official German news agency rejected any idea that "the war against England is being waged only half-heartedly". Since the fall of France, it said, purely military considerations had been eclipsed by politics. But Germany was now waging war against England with as much determination and certainty of victory as she had against Poland and France. Such stories got little coverage in the British media. Home Intelligence observed that they aroused only "limited" public interest.

The preparations, though, were far from complete. In a bid to speed things up, Hitler had summoned a meeting at his Berghof mountain retreat in Austria. This was to be a key moment. Head of the Army, Walther von Brauchitsch, was there; so was his number two, Franz Halder. Räder was there to represent the Navy and the conference began with his report. All preparations, the Grand Admiral said, were in full swing. Granted air superiority and favourable weather, minesweeping, which had already begun, would take three weeks.

Minelaying could only then begin at the end of August. He thus confirmed to Hitler's face what his Naval Staff had told him. The Navy could not be ready until after 15 September.[13]

As to the exact date of the invasion, there were technical requirements which had to be satisfied. First, the Army insisted on a landing at dawn, which meant that last part of the crossing would be at night. To enable the fleet to be manoeuvred and controlled, a half moon rising about 11 p.m. was essential. Then, the landing had to take place about two hours after high tide, when the ebbing sea would enable the barges to be firmly run ashore. This fixed the landing to between 19 and 26 September.

This late start was likely to create weather difficulties, especially during the supply phase of the operation. Even if it was fine for the first wave, there was no guarantee that it would stay that way. "Weather conditions," Räder pointed out, "are of the utmost importance." Not least, the sea had to be calm enough for the barges to cross and be beached safely. In heavy seas, it would be impossible to transfer loads from steamers into barges lying alongside. Then Räder addressed the contentious issue. Going over the heads of the Army and the Supreme Command, he appealed directly to Hitler for a landing on a narrow front, crossing at the narrowest parts of the Dover Straits. To finish off, Räder pleaded for May 1941 as a better time.

In a curiously anodyne response, Hitler began by observing that nothing could be done about weather conditions, though he recognized that storm tides must be borne in mind. But his inclination was to seize the moment. Delay would only make things more difficult. The British Army, still in a poor condition, would by spring have a formidable force of 30–35 divisions. The strength of the *Kriegsmarine* relative to the Royal Navy would not have improved by then.

Aware of the potential advantages to accrue from his Axis ally drawing troops away from the UK, Hitler was nevertheless dismissive of the staying power of the Italians, especially in East Africa. Pondering over a postponement, he reviewed the options of using air and submarine warfare. Although this might decide the war, it would take from one to two years. He spoke of an operation against Gibraltar which was dependent on the attitude adopted by Spain. When von Brauchitsch proposed the dispatch of two armoured divisions to support the forthcoming Italian offensive on Egypt, he said "this diversion manoeuvre" should be studied. But, he concluded, "a positively decisive result can only be achieved by an attack on England".[14]

Hitler therefore decided that the air war should start immediately. If the results were not satisfactory, invasion preparations would be stopped. But, he said, "If we gain the impression that the English are being crushed and that the air war is, after a certain time, taking effect, then we shall attack". An attempt had to be made to prepare the operation for 15 September. But, as to the all-important question of the narrow front, Hitler was silent. He simply did not comment.

Instead, he went on to look at the bigger picture. Britain, he said, was reliant on Russia and the USA. If Russia dropped out of the picture, this would tremendously increase Japan's power in the Far East, forcing the US to focus its attention and resources there. By this means, America would be lost to Britain. Russia's destruction, therefore, had to be made a part of this struggle. Spring 1941 was the time to take on Russia, with the state "shattered to its roots with one blow". Hitler's words were later summarized by Franz Halder: "Russia is the factor by which England sets the greatest store ... If Russia is beaten, England's last hope is gone. Germany is then master of Europe and the Balkans ... Decision: As a result of this argument, Russia must be dealt with. Spring 1941".

By way of complete contrast, *AP* writer Kirke L. Simpson was looking at the war from a transatlantic perspective, telling his US audiences about the "sudden concentration of German air attacks on Dover". They had stirred worldwide conjecture that Britain's hour of ultimate trial had come, with Dover as a prospective bridgehead. Yet, Simpson thought, the circumstances of the Nazi bombardment sharply conflicted with that impression.

There then followed an appreciation of the difficulties facing the Germans. The British could deny the enemy use of the sheltered waters of Dover or any other narrow-mouthed harbour on the English Channel, but a landing on England's open beaches would be even more difficult, unsheltered as they were from the swells of the shallow Channel and North Sea. Weather would be crucial. Any signs of a prolonged spell of calm would raise greater fears in Britain than the intensified air bombardment of Dover and its vicinity. Nevertheless, Simpson noted that a worldwide propaganda exercise was underway. The Germans were doing their best to convince everybody that the assault on England would be over and another smashing Nazi victory recorded by 1 October or thereabouts.

Reflecting more closely the decisions of the Hitler conference, Virginio Gayda was again in *Il Giornale D'Italia*, this time stating that the invasion of the British Isles would not be "a simple military advance". England would probably not be invaded until the British people had been weakened by bombs and blockade. The tactics of attrition must be used, he wrote: constant air attacks to demoralize the population and destroy the island defences; attacks on ships bringing supplies to England, and a strong submarine blockade and a weakening of empire defences in the Mediterranean.

In England, a warm summer's day with clear skies made it perfect for an invasion – or spending a day by the seaside. For a brief moment, holiday-makers had more in common with Hitler than their own government, with access denied to their favourite beaches. That morning, a Sunderland of No. 10 Sqn Royal Australian Air Force, based at Mount Batten, was escorting the merchant cruiser *Moolton* out from Plymouth after a refit. Three and a half hours into his patrol, pilot, Flight Lieutenant Bill Garing sighted a formation of five Ju 88 bombers heading for his charge. He flew his heavy flying boat at them aggressively and, faced with an aircraft nicknamed the "flying porcupine", the Germans retired. Garing was awarded a DFC.[15]

The only other fighting in the morning was over the Channel at 11 a.m., when Stukas attacked some small convoys. In the afternoon, Dover enjoyed the attention of ten Me 109s which had been patrolling the Calais area. Of particular note was No. 41 Sqn, which claimed it had destroyed an aircraft identified as a Heinkel 113. The kill was later confirmed.

Bomber Command despatched 28 Blenheims to carry out daylight raids on enemy airfields and industrial targets in Germany. Because of the lack of suitable cloud cover, which the aircraft relied upon for protection, only eleven actually bombed. One failed to return. Six Battles were detailed to attack invasion ports. On their return, one was shot down by an RAF night fighter and crashed into the sea off Skegness. A Hudson and two Hampdens were also lost.

On the day, Fighter Command flew only 365 sorties, losing five machines. With Bomber Command, RAF losses amounted to ten, against three Germans. In the twenty-two days of the battle, Fighter Command had lost 101 aircraft. Total RAF losses stood at 172 against 167 Germans lost. Furthermore, British losses to air action included eighteen merchant vessels and four destroyers. Ten merchantmen had been sunk by mines, some of which may have been laid by aircraft. Thirty-eight were damaged and three destroyers sustained serious damage, plus a depot ship. Three armed trawlers had been lost to direct air action, and another two to mines. In all respects, the *Luftwaffe* was well ahead.

DAY 23 – THURSDAY 1 AUGUST 1940

Despite the war, the *Daily Mirror* chose to attack the Ministry of Information, its columnist John Harper calling for its abolition. The news section conveyed a report of Commons criticism the previous day of "nosey parkers" employed by Cooper's department "to make a personal canvass of householders".[16] Cooper himself had then been questioned about the delay on releasing news of the sinking of the *Lancastria*.

Loyally, the Minister had had to take responsibility for the delay, unable to reveal that Churchill himself had forbidden publication.[17] The *Mirror* gave no quarter: "Mr Cooper was in an apologetic and fumbling state of mind. And well he might be, for clearly his explanation did not convince even himself that he had behaved with other than his usual weakness". His explanation had been "an insult to both the dead and living whose heroism Mr Cooper deliberately suppressed for five weeks". Only one man stopped the publicity it deserved, the paper said. He "probably thinks any publicity – even publicity given to gallantry – is rather vulgar. It is time he retired into obscurity himself, and gave way to a Minister of Information who will tell the public the truth".[18]

There was also an attack on Home Secretary John Anderson, targeting the emergency powers he was laying before parliament. They would enable the Executive to prevent the expression of any kind of opinion in any newspaper at all, giving the Minister complete power over the press and placing him in a position "no whit inferior" to that occupied by Dr Göbbels in Germany.

Anderson was a key character in government line-up. Under Chamberlain, he had been Lord Privy Seal, then responsible for devising the government's "shelter policy". On the outbreak of that war, he had been appointed Home Secretary and Minister of Home Security. It was no coincidence that the two portfolios had been combined. The latter was charged with civil defence – then called Air Raid Precautions, or ARP – responsible as the name would imply, for protecting people. But the Home Secretary was in charge of maintaining law and order. He was the man who would have to deal with the panic and the collapse of law and order, should the terror bombers have their intended effect.

However, the man who held both the stick and shield was not even a politician, in any real sense. He had qualified as a mathematician and studied chemistry in the University of Leipzig – producing a brilliant dissertation on uranium – but had then decided to become a civil servant, with a score in his entrance examination setting a new record. By 1937, he had been for five years the Governor of Bengal, only latterly being put up for election in the safe seat of the Combined Universities in Glasgow, in order to take up a post as minister. It was said of him that, in an age before the computer was invented, he was a tolerable substitute for one, failing to infuse his departments with any "warmth, humour or general sympathy".[19] When it came to using the stick or the shield, few had any doubt which he would prefer.

While the press was fulminating about Anderson, Virginio Gayda was ramping up his rhetoric, declaring that a lightning victory against Britain was now impossible. Britain would be "worn down in a war of attrition". In the *Daily Express*, he was cited as saying:

> The last phase of the war cannot proceed in a manner similar to that which struck down France, not only because Britain is an island, militarily well defended, but also because Britain has an Empire which extends to all continents and which is taking part with imposing forces in the war. The war must rather be one of continual hammering and attrition. This is just what Italy and Germany are doing now.

With his close association with Mussolini, Gayda had built an impressive record for reliability. *AP* elaborated on his report, citing the German High Command. This stated that Britain would be brought down by bombing and "blockage", announcing that there would be "night raids … against ships and facilities in southern English ports, as well as searchlight positions". Military observers in Germany had emphasized the point of "making English ports useless for receiving war supplies".

Back in Germany, Keitel noted the Navy's concerns about meeting the 15 September deadline. With the details of Hitler's conference to hand, he issued orders that the preparations should continue, but "will cease" on the 15th. After eight days, or at the most, fifteen, after the start of the "great air attack", the *Führer* would decide whether *Sealion* would go ahead. If it did not, preparations would resume but "in a form which will avoid the severe damage to the economic situation by the crippling of internal shipping traffic". However, Räder, assuming that Hitler's silence on the issue of the narrow front had meant that he had agreed with the Navy view, issued his own orders for the naval preparations to be carried out on the basis of the narrow front. A profound misunderstanding was now in the making.

Plans for the air war were about to change as well. Since 19 July, Hitler's peace offer had been on the table and only a small fraction of German air strength had been committed to the battle. Most of it was confined to attacks against shipping and ports. But, with the deposed King of England, the Duke of Windsor, sailing for the Bahamas, Hitler evidently concluded that his attempts to drag Britain to the negotiating table were not going to meet with immediate success.[20] He thus issued Führer Directive No. 17: "In order to establish the necessary conditions for the final conquest of England," he declared, "I intend to intensify air and sea warfare against the English homeland". Once again, he ordered the *Luftwaffe* to overpower the RAF "with all the forces at its command" in the shortest possible time. Attacks were to be against aircraft, ground installations, supply organizations and also against the aircraft industry and manufacturers of anti-aircraft equipment. Crucially, written into the directive was the provision that, after achieving temporary or local air superiority, the air war was to be continued against the ports, in particular against food stores, and also against stores of provisions in the interior of the country.[21]

This was not a plan devoted to invasion preparations, but a template for strategic bombing. The directive allowed for attacks on the ports, to be made "on the smallest scale" in view of the forthcoming operations, but it also stated that attacks on warships and merchant ships could be "reduced". The *Luftwaffe* had to give "adequate support" to naval operations and *be ready* to take part in *Sealion*, but it was not required to direct its strength to invasion preparations. And "terror attacks as measures of reprisal" were reserved specifically to Hitler.[22]

Also, and significantly, the attack was to be delayed. It was not to begin until "on or after 5 August". As the British Government was still mulling over the peace offer made through the Swedish King – an initiative that may have been brought about by Göring himself, via Birger Dahlerus – it is not untoward to suggest that, even at this late hour, the full might of the *Luftwaffe* was being held back for just a few days more, until an answer had been received.[23]

Daily operations, meanwhile, continued at their usual tempo. With heavy mist over the Channel, action was mainly targeted against shipping off the Yorkshire coast. But in the mid-afternoon, a single raider dropped bombs on the largest factory complex in Norwich, the Boulton and Paul Riverside works, where the Defiant fighter was made. In BBC and press reports, Norwich was identified. With the exception of an air attack on Dover Harbour, this was the first time naming had been permitted, most certainly because of William Joyce (Lord Haw-Haw), a Irish national who broadcast in English from Hamburg, who had already identified to location of the attack. According to BBC figures, at least half the country listened occasionally his programme *Germany Calling*, a third regularly. Details were even listed in *The Times*. So inadequate was the official news that people were turning to the enemy for information. His jeering about this raid had prompted the fuller disclosure.

On the naval front, the steamer *City of Canberra*, heading for London, was damaged by a mine about ten miles from Aldeburgh. German bombing damaged the SS *Kerry Head* close to the Old Head of Kinsale, and the tanker *Gothic*, twelve miles from Flamborough Head. The coast off East Anglia was getting a dangerous place to be.

In 659 sorties, Fighter Command lost of two fighters. Four Blenheims and a Hudson were also lost, but two Blenheims made a surprise attack on Leeuwarden airfield, destroying four Me 109s. These brought *Luftwaffe* losses to seventeen.

In a highly revealing episode, *Luftwaffe* aircraft dropped reprints of Hitler's "last appeal to reason" speech over the West Country and East Anglia. Four He 111s were engaged on this activity in the Bristol area alone. Some leaflets were collected up and sold the next day with the proceeds going to charity. Many fell on empty countryside. Others were hastily gathered up by officials and destroyed. Few understood the significance. The Germans were still trying to bypass the British Government and appeal directly to the people. It was too little, too late. But it suggested that the peace initiative was still alive, albeit in its final throes.

DAY 24 – FRIDAY 2 AUGUST 1940

In Stockholm, the *Svenska Dagbladet* newspaper reported that "well-informed circles" were saying that the Axis powers were continuing their peace efforts, not wanting to try an invasion of England, the success of which was doubtful. In London, the *Express* based a leader on Gayda's most recent intervention. "Hitler has had a triumph already with his invasion propaganda", it intoned:

> in spite of the many voices which he uses. He says one day through the voice of Göering that invasion is coming at any moment. The next day he uses the mouthpiece to explain why it has not come yet. Hitler's method is always the same: Propaganda first, fighting afterwards. Words before deeds. Creating confusion and striking at morale in advance.

There is no evidence that Gayda ever spoke for anyone but Mussolini, and the *Führer* and the *Duce* did not always sing from the same hymn sheet. What the newspaper did not know (or chose not to acknowledge) was that Hitler still seemed to believe there was a possibility of a peace deal. Over southern England that night, bombers dropped more reprints of his speech.

This seemed to be of little interest to the British media. Instead, the smouldering discontent with Duff Cooper erupted. The proximate cause was the Ministry of Information conducting door-to-door surveys on morale – the "Cooper's snoopers" issue that had already attracted some notoriety. This had the *Guardian* referring to the "ill-starred ministry". But Cooper had made a counter-attack in the Commons the previous day and the *Daily Express* devoting its front-page banner headline to it.

This was a most extraordinary situation. The nation was, by all accounts, locked into a life and death struggle – on the cusp between peace and total war, with millions of lives in the balance. Yet the papers were more concerned with a debate in the House of Commons triggered by Conservative MP Sir Archibald Southby. And never mind the German invasion. This was about public opinion surveys, which were being branded "an invasion of privacy", the Ministry of Information (MoI) being comparing with the Gestapo. Cooper lashed out at his tormentors. The usefulness of MPs was "limited" in wartime, he declared. Furthermore, the Press "had proved themselves unworthy of being trusted with any important matter".

In the German camp, preparations for *Sealion* were continuing apace. Von Brauchitsch, Halder and Räder were in Sylt, a town on the west coast of Denmark, watching a beach assault demonstration. Unloading the barges proved problematical and Halder was critical of the high angle of descent of the ramps, declaring the design "unsatisfactory".[24] Von Rundstedt was not there, and strategic issues were not discussed. Furthermore, Göring was working separately on his air offensive. He had decided to call it *Eagle Attack* (*Adlerangriff*), to be launched on 11 August with *Eagle Day* (*Adlertag*). His force would consist of almost 1,700 aircraft. Field Marshal Kesselring, based in France at the head of the Second Air Fleet, was to play the major role. His bases were closest to England. In support was to be Field Marshal Sperrle's Third Air Fleet in north-west France. General Stumpff's Fifth Air Fleet would operate from bases in Norway, Denmark and Holland, against the Midlands and the north of England.

The main target was the RAF although, as events would demonstrate, *Luftwaffe* strength would be widely dissipated. For all that, Göring estimated that it would take him only three days of good weather to destroy British air power. Against him, as of 2 August, were 63 Blenheim fighters, 238 Spitfires, 352 Hurricanes and 22 Defiants, totalling 675 aircraft.

The British public, meanwhile, was being briefly entertained by the Hull registered steamer *Highlander*. It had claimed two bombers shot down and had steamed into Leith Harbour with the remains of one, a Heinkel 115 seaplane, draped across her stern. The *Luftwaffe* responded by attacking a convoy off Harwich and sinking the armed trawler, *Cape Finisterre*. One man was killed. In the Thames Estuary, the Ellerman Lines cargo ship *City of Brisbane* was attacked and set on fire. Her master ran her aground and she was still burning three days later, a total loss. Minelayers were active overnight and there were raids on the RAF technical college at Halton, the airfields at Catterick, Farnborough and "Romford" and the Forth Bridge area.

That day, Fighter Command put up 477 sorties. None of its aircraft were lost to enemy action, although two were lost in accidents, one during a night take-off. Bomber Command lost six. The Germans had lost five, one shot down by the *Highlander*. Not only the airmen exaggerated their kills.

DAY 25 – SATURDAY 3 AUGUST 1940

The *Guardian* reported on Duff Cooper's performance in parliament. He had revealed his real weakness when he had lost his temper, the paper said. The *Mirror* joined the fray, remarkably giving a front-page slot to *Cassandra* under the headline "the crazy gang", a lengthy, sarcastic diatribe against Cooper's department. Jock Colville was less than sympathetic: Cooper had "not produced many results as Minister of Information". Nicolson, the loyal deputy, was feeling "very depressed". The whole press, "plus certain pro-Munich conservatives, have planned and banded together to pull Cooper down". He nevertheless thought that his boss might survive for a few weeks "with Winston's support".[25]

This passed by most of the public. The spat was seen as a dispute between the Press and the minister. Home Intelligence reported growing confidence in the defence of "our island fortress". On this Saturday though, the big news – for the *Daily Express*, at least – was that its proprietor, Lord Beaverbrook, had been appointed to the War Cabinet. He was to remain minister of aircraft production.

The invasion temperature appeared to be rising. The next day was the anniversary of the start of the First World War. The Monday was the start of a brief period when the tides would be at their highest and thus believed to be the most favourable for an invasion. This was enough to ramp up the "scare". It was then intensified by reports in the French media of Nazis "concentrating troops all the way from the Spanish border to the Belgian frontier". The irony was unrecognized – this was the very antithesis of concentration. Nevertheless, in Rome, the *Corriere Padano* newspaper said that the "zero hour" for a concerted Axis attack against Britain was "about to strike".

Bombs fell on the outskirts of Swansea and a few fell into the waters of Swansea Bay. No casualties were reported. In and among 415 sorties, Fighter Command intercepted five raids in the south-west, without loss, but six other RAF aircraft were downed, against four *Luftwaffe* losses. Naval Albacores were in operation against invasion targets in Dutch ports. SS *Wychwood* was sunk by a mine off Aldeburgh. The steamer *Statira*, sailing in convoy for London, was badly damaged by German bombing near Stornoway. Overnight, the *Luftwaffe* continued its minelaying.

However, the most important event of the day, if not the battle so far, was to remain secret for many years. Churchill later described it as the day when the King of Sweden "thought fit to address us on the subject" of Hitler's peace offer. The reference is disingenuous. The US media had known about it and had been reporting on it for well over a week. The offer itself was the culmination of continuous diplomatic activity since before 19 July. This the Prime Minister himself acknowledged. He admitted that after Hitler's speech there had been "days" of diplomatic representations through Sweden, the USA and the Vatican. Even then, there was no mention of Berne.[26]

Churchill now had in front of him a draft Foreign Office response. He thought it was "trying to be too clever", entering into "refinements of policy unsuited to the tragic simplicity and grandeur of the times and the issues at stake". He suggested demanding "effective guarantees by deeds, not words", amounting to complete German withdrawal for all her occupied territories, and guarantees of security. These were conditions Hitler would never accept. The quadrille appeared to be at an end.

Churchill also sent what appeared to be a coded signal via the press, the effect being to emphasize his rejection of the offer. "The Prime Minister wishes it to be known," he said, "that the possibility of German attempts at invasion has by no means passed away … Our sense of growing strength and preparedness must not lead to the slightest relaxation or moral alertness". The British Prime Minister had closed the door to peace and cleared the decks for war.

Churchill was ready and waiting, apparently spoiling for a fight. In his memoirs, then Free French leader, General Charles de Gaulle recalls seeing the British Prime Minister at Chequers, one August day, raising his fists towards the sky. He cried, "So they won't come!" De Gaulle had said to him, "Are you in such a hurry to see your towns smashed to bits?" Churchill had replied that the bombing of Oxford, Coventry and Canterbury "will cause such a wave of indignation in the United States that they'll come into the war".

6

War drums

Don't be deceived by this lull before the storm, because, although there is still the chance of peace, Hitler is aware of the political and economic confusion in England, and is only waiting for the right moment. Then, when his moment comes, he will strike, and strike hard.

William Joyce (Lord Haw-Haw), Radio Hamburg broadcast, 6 August 1940

Had this been an epic Hollywood Western, native scouts would have been anxiously scanning the horizon, listening to distant war drums beating with ever-greater intensity. In rock gullies, murderous struggles would be being played out, as outriders clashed with Indian war parties. Back at the fort, the music would be playing as elegant officers danced with their costumed wives.

DAY 26 – SUNDAY 4 AUGUST 1940

August was holiday time, and this was supposed to be Bank Holiday weekend – except that it had been cancelled. Nevertheless, where access to beaches was still permitted, large crowds congregated. The Home Intelligence report for the day identified "continued indifference to international affairs" and the war in general. Altogether, there was a lack of focus as people relegated the hostilities to lower down their lists of concerns.

The papers carried Churchill's invasion warning, taking it largely at face value. The *Sunday Express* put the key quote on the front page, with the words in capitals. Alongside the warning, the *Observer* invoked the anniversary of the start of the First World War, but the newspaper was not alone in referring to it. J. B. Priestley did so as well. Himself a veteran who had had a torrid time in the trenches, he referred to it when he broadcast another of his evening *Postscript* talks on the BBC.

He was attracting audiences of over ten million, perhaps the only speaker who could challenge Churchill's growing popularity. His talks were being reported by newspapers, increasing the size of his audience. And this Sunday's effort was one of his most controversial. "We must not only summon our armed forces," he said, "wave our flags and sing our national anthems, but we must go deeper and by an almost mystical act of will, hold to our faith and hope." He continued:

> We have to fight this great battle not only with guns in daylight, but alone in the night, communing with our souls, strengthening our faith that in common men everywhere there is a spring of innocent aspiration and good will that cannot be sealed.

His appeal to the "common man" attracted many complaints, notably from the government chief whip, Captain David Margesson, acting on behalf of a group of right-wing Tories.

It was not only Priestley's broadcasts that were getting the attention though. In the *Sunday Express* he had been interviewed by resident columnist, Peter Howard, in a feature entitled "People I meet". Priestley, he wrote, "believes that the common people of England must have a greater share in running the country". Nazism was evil, but the force behind it was good – it was the despair and dissatisfaction of the people with the world as it is. "In our new world," he said, "there must be an outlet for young men of energy. In the old England there was no part for energetic young men to play. That is half the secret of these Nazi and Fascist successes."

Through the day, there was little air activity. Two British bombers were lost. Fighter Command flew a "mere" 261 sorties, losing one Spitfire which crashed in a practice dogfight. Its pilot was killed. A Blenheim fighter and a Defiant were also lost, bringing total RAF losses to five. The *Luftwaffe* lost six aircraft.

Action at sea was particularly bloody. Heroes of the action were the armed trawlers. Designated Her Majesty's Trawlers (HMT), they were manned by reserve officers and conscripted crews, some of them civilians who had never before been to sea. Mostly, but not always, they were unloved, unsung and unrewarded. By the war end, nearly 500 of them had been lost.

This day, anti-submarine trawler *Kingston Chrysoberyl*, engaged a German E-boat off St Catherine. Minesweeping trawler *Drummer* was sunk by a mine off Brightlingsea, Essex. Two ratings were lost. Minesweeping trawler *Marsona* was sunk on a mine off Cromarty. An officer and ten ratings were killed. Minesweeping trawler *Oswaldian* was sunk on a mine in the Bristol Channel. Twelve ratings were lost. Also, the steamer *White Crest* was damaged by German bombing off Cape Wrath. Even in the air, the Navy was taking losses. In a raid on oil tanks and barges at Rotterdam, two officers were killed when their Swordfish was shot down.

Understandably, the Senior Service was not always impressed by its junior upstarts. In their tiny warships there was danger, little glamour and precious little recognition. But this was not sour grapes over disproportionate publicity for the air war. Overall, the effect was to perpetuate the distorted impression of fighting intensity and skew resource priorities. Despite apparently preparing for an invasion, the Germans were themselves committing substantial resources to the blockade.

Churchill himself was less than sanguine about the situation. This day – before even the extent of the losses was known to him – he had sent a minute to Admiral Pound, and the First Lord of the Admiralty, noting that the losses on the North-Western Approaches were "most grievous", asking to be "assured" that the problems were being grappled with. He did concede, however, that the "great falling off in the control" was largely due to "the shortage of destroyers through invasion precautions". He wanted a "protective concentration", based on a new headquarters in Liverpool, then complaining about the delays in moving command operations north from Plymouth.[1]

DAY 27 – MONDAY 5 AUGUST 1940

Hitler's thoughts this day were on the plan to invade Russia, delivered by General Erich Marcks. With the outline in his hands, he set the time for the spring of 1941. Jodl was having to deal with more immediate concerns. Hader, the Army Chief of Staff, had caught up with Räder's assumption that the narrow front was now policy. Von Brauchitsch was involved and tensions were building between the two services.

In an attempt to smooth over the dispute, Jodl got an agreement between the parties that the Navy chief had misunderstood Hitler who, while appearing to support the Army, had not actually committed to a broad front. Räder accepted this, but insisted that the issue had to be resolved. It was thus arranged with von

Brauchitsch that Halder, and the Navy senior planner, Admiral Schniewind, would meet in Fontainebleau to see if a solution could be agreed.

Almost on autopilot, the *Luftwaffe* continued attacking shipping in the Straits of Dover. A raid on Norwich, however, caused considerable alarm. The bomber was identified as a Blenheim, raising speculation that the Germans were using captured machines. This was taken seriously enough for the Air Ministry to order all British aircraft to change their markings, leading to some potentially fatal incidents when aircraft with old-style markings were challenged by fighters.

On the day the *Luftwaffe* lost three aircraft, against three RAF fighters, with Fighter Command flying 402 sorties. Bomber Command was building its strength and the scale of operations, with eighty-five sorties flown. Through this day and night, there had been considerable activity. Coastal Command aircraft had been busy as well, taking part in forty-nine sorties, losing one Hudson. On the naval front, trawlers south of Selsey Bill were attacked early in the morning. RAF fighters failed to intercept. Another minesweeping trawler, this one the *River Clyde*, was sunk by a mine off Aldeburgh Light Float. Eleven ratings were killed immediately and one died of wounds.

DAY 28 – TUESDAY 6 AUGUST 1940

The morning headline from the *Daily Mirror* sought to explain "Why Hitler has waited so long". It was talking about air raids, not an invasion. The reason was that the *Luftwaffe* was not quite ready. Crews needed additional training. Readers were warned to expect not fifty or a hundred machines in an attack, but hundreds. With extraordinary prescience, the paper forecast extensive night raids, and told its readers: "this must be remembered: neither the Germans nor ourselves have yet solved the problem of intercepting bombers at night. In any raid, a number of planes are sure to get through the defences".

In terms of the bigger picture, Home Intelligence was reporting that "there are many in authority who feel that the present lull should have been used (and might still be used) for a clear statement of a constructive peace policy on our part".[2]

As to the air war, the weather was cloudy and windy – not ideal for operations. The *Luftwaffe* was still operating on a small scale, and still mounting attacks against ports, shipping and airfields. It lost three aircraft on this day. Bomber Command lost a Hampden. Fighter Command lost five aircraft, all to accidents, including two at night. One pilot was killed. Accidents were the hidden toll exacted by air warfare. Pilot Officer H. W. A. Britton, serving with No. 17 Sqn, had taken off in a Hurricane on a routine air test. His aircraft crashed shortly afterwards, caught fire and was destroyed. Britton was killed. The cause of the crash was unknown.

For all that there was killing on an industrial scale, war occasionally took on a human face. Henry Wilfred Arthur Britton, known as "Billie", was born at Crowborough, Sussex, on 8 July 1921, son of a major in the Royal Corps of Signals. He was an "Army brat", educated at Army schools in Egypt, Aldershot and Catterick before attending state schools in Bedford and Edinburgh. He joined the RAF on a short-service commission in May 1939. After training at Perth and Brize Norton, he was posted to 12 Group Pool on 23 February 1940 where he converted to Hurricanes. A posting to No. 17 Sqn at Martlesham Heath followed in March. He was 19 years old when he died, his career as a front-line pilot lasting less than five months.[3]

Meanwhile, Göring had called a meeting in his Karin Hall base to brief his commanders on *Eagle Attack*.[4] William Joyce (Lord Haw-Haw) ramped up his rhetoric, through *Germany Calling*.[5] This day he told his British audience:

> I make no apology for saying again that invasion is certainly coming soon, but what I want to impress upon you is that while you must feverishly take every conceivable precaution, nothing that you or the Government can do is really of the slightest use. Don't be deceived by this lull before the storm, because, although there is still the chance of peace, Hitler is aware of the political and economic confusion in England, and is only waiting for the right moment. Then, when his moment comes, he will strike, and strike hard.

It was a risky, even foolhardy strategy, threatening something that might not happen, a huge bluff that would spell ruin if called. However, the regional *Yorkshire Post* reported that well-informed quarters in London believed an air *Blitzkrieg* would be launched soon. The RAF was closely watching for signs of a German invasion of this country, reassuringly certain that it would be able to give due warning of its launch.

Kirke L. Simpson, for the *AP*, explained to his American readers some of the background.[6] His was a long article headed: "Nazis may delay invasion attempt". If the week passed without invasion, he concluded: "it would go far toward convincing the world that whatever his own desire, Hitler's generals had ruled out invasion as too risky until England has been 'softened' by blockade".

This view was shared by the US military and naval establishments. General Pershing, former commander of the American Expeditionary Force, wrote that England had most to fear from the German air and sea blockade, not the invasion. He thought that a *Blitzkrieg* against England, if attempted during this week of high tides and dark nights, would be beaten off.

Simpson reminded his readers that Hitler had recently told the *Reichstag* that the German invasion of Norway had been the most "daring" military adventure in history. Attempting an invasion of England, unless Britons had been brought close to despair by bombing and starvation, would make the Norwegian campaign a minor operation by contrast. The elements argue for it, he wrote. Every rule of military prudence is against it. In his final passage, however, Simpson noted that:

> unlikely though the prospect of invasion might be, the British authorities are doing nothing to contradict the suggestion that the Germans are coming. The threat of invasion is a unifying force. Possibly, it is of greater value to the British government than it is to the Germans. For the best of all possible reasons, the British nation is being put through an elaborate charade.

At this point, however, there was no way of telling whether Hitler was going through the motions. Only he could tell whether he was truly committed to the operation, and he never shared his innermost thoughts.

DAY 29 – WEDNESDAY 7 AUGUST 1940

In June, when the Germans had been least prepared to invade, British "invasion fever" had been at its highest. Now, with invasion preparations more advanced than they had ever been, Home Intelligence reported "growing confidence" that any German invasion would be repelled. Despite Churchill's attempts and the increasing stridency of German propaganda, some respondents were expressing the view that the danger of invasion was "remote". The war was "somewhat in the background" and those who could were trying to get on their holidays.

Good weather and the "holiday spirit" had made a valuable contribution to continued cheerfulness.

In Berlin, a clue as to the thinking of the High Command came when Keitel issued a new order entitled: "Directive on deceptive measures to maintain appearance of constant threat of invasion of UK". This started in a curious fashion, stating "whether or not we invade England" the constant menace of invasion must be maintained against the English people and the armed forces. But the thrust was to ask for proposals to make the main operation appear to be an invasion of the east coast as well as Ireland. "Individuals below a specified grade of the High Command who are concerned with the preparations are not to be informed that their tasks are aimed at deception", the directive instructed.

In Fontainebleau, Halder and Schniewind, accompanied by Admiral Fricke, met for informal discussions – Army *versus* Navy. Halder did not meet the pair in his office, but in his special train, which then headed for Normandy where Halder was to watch demonstrations of landing craft in action.[7] During the meeting, there was a "strong clash of opinion". The Army Chief of Staff rejected out of hand the concept of the "narrow front" landing in the Dover area. The hinterland was "extremely unsuitable" for a frontal attack, while the area was too constrained. The Army needed to land ten divisions in four days, and that could not be done from a single, narrow beachhead.

Faced with Schniewind's insistence on the narrow front, Halder declared that, "I utterly reject the Navy's proposal; from the point of view of the Army, I regard their proposal as complete suicide. I might just as well put the troops that have landed straight through a sausage machine". Schniewind retorted that the broad front was not only suicidal, but "a sacrifice of troops on their way to land". There was no possibility of reconciliation. The issue would have to be decided by Hitler.[8]

The media in Britain were covering the invasion story in their own way. A down-page item in the *Express* reported that German Army leave had been stopped and that "Hitler is hourly intensifying his invasion campaign of nerves against Britain". The report retailed a quote from *Luftwaffe* General Sanders, who threatened "complete destruction of London docks and Birmingham". He added:

I cannot tell you when the attack will come or how, but I can say it will not come in the form in which it is anticipated in England. The German Air Force is ready to strike now.

It has already made all preparations; planes have been overhauled and pilots rested. Mr Churchill was quite right when he said that in our attacks on England we have up to date only been taking England's measure. We have not started to cut the cloth. The attacks will be directed against docks and industrial centres.

At a press conference the previous day, Ribbentrop, the foreign minister, had declared that "England will be forced to accept peace terms this year". In Spain, said the *Express* correspondent on the Franco–Spanish frontier, it was firmly believed that, with all communications between occupied and unoccupied France severed, the German invasion of Britain was imminent. All roads and railways in northern France were strictly reserved for German troops. It was thought the Germans would make a double attack, one from western France directed against south-west England and Ireland, and the other from northern France, directed against the Kentish and Essex coasts.

Yet in the skies over Britain, the day was widely regarded as "quiet". Fighter Command lost five aircraft, two others bringing total RAF losses to seven. The *Luftwaffe* lost five.

In terms of action, a convoy off Cromer was attacked, probably FS 44 – six vessels on the run that stretched from Methil, the sheltered anchorage in Largo Bay in the Forth Estuary, all the way to Southend. This one was due on 8 August. From there, the vessels would either join another convoy or make their way independently to the port of London or another destination close by. Sometimes the convoys started on the Tyne, as this one did. Most did so from September 1939 up to the end of August 1940. From then, the starting point had been Largo Bay, watched over by the RAF as it became a prime target for the *Luftwaffe*. Altogether, the FS series ran until May 1945, comprising 1,778 convoys which passed through 18,448 shipping movements, carrying well over 20 million tons of cargo. The route was protected by defensive minefields but was vulnerable to attacks by U-boat, E-boat, aircraft and mines.[9]

The convoy system was a vital link in the chain between the coalfields of the north-east and the south. Even without enemy action, there would have been problems. Through the brutally cold winter of 1939–40, there had been a desperate crisis. Snow and freezing conditions in January and February had brought the rail system to a halt and coal distribution had virtually ceased. Emergency stocks had been depleted and some areas ran out of coal completely.

The winter had been the coldest since 1895 and the January the coldest since 1838. The Thames had frozen in the upper reaches, ice interfered with shipping in the estuary, and even the sea froze in Morecambe Bay. The lowest temperature was 10 degrees below zero (Fahrenheit), recorded at Rhayader, Radnorshire, on 21 January. More insurance claims for cars with engines split by frost were recorded in January than in the whole of any one winter. Trains took a week to get from London to Glasgow, the passengers sleeping at wayside stations unable even to reach a road, which in any case they would have found blocked.

Factory workers in East London were unable to go home for two days and stayed in the factory hostel. Snowdrifts 16 ft deep were reported in outer London areas. This weather, which began before Christmas, lasted until March. It included Britain's worst ice storm, which was hailed as a thaw and proved to be a frost. The rain came down and as it fell into the lower atmosphere it froze. Nearly the whole country was covered with ice for two days, and transport was stopped.

For almost three weeks traffic in the Humber had been suspended by ice. A ship specially strengthened for ice-breaking failed to force a passage out of Goole, and an attempt to break up the ice with an empty collier of 1,500 tons resulted only in her riding up on the ice and remaining there.[10]

Now, the transportation stresses were intensifying. The inland system, and especially the rail network, was not coping. And London needed coal, 30,000 tons every week just to feed the electricity power stations, to keep the trains on the move – most of them coal-fired – and for much of the heat for domestic cooking and hot water, as well as for making the town gas. The south of England, in total, required 275,000 tons a month to be delivered by sea.

Len Deighton, in his book, was caustic about what he termed the "official stupidity" of sending domestic cargoes through dangerous coastal waters. He argued that they should have been sent by rail, as they were later.[11] But it was not that simple. The fall of France had seriously disrupted traditional patterns of trade. Much of the ocean-going trade had been diverted to the west coast to keep it away from the *Luftwaffe*. This required a major re-orientation of rail traffic. While there were plenty of locomotives and trucks, the loading and unloading facilities did not exist on the scale required, in the places they were now needed. Marshalling yards were inadequate; there were bottlenecks throughout the system, especially at junctions on lines where there had been significant routing changes. Storage depots were in the wrong places and local distribution was not fully (or at all in many cases) integrated with the rail system.

War production was also imposing additional loads on transport, as were the joint requirements of civilian evacuation from major cities, and troop movements. Operation Pied Piper, in the first week of the war had relocated three million people – nearly a quarter of the population of England – creating massive disruption. With the Phony War, where the expected bombing had not occurred, many had drifted back, only for there to be a second, more measured evacuation as the bombs began to fall. This had imposed further burdens on the rail system. Both mobilization and evacuation meant that there were more people away from home, creating more demand for long-distance transport as people returned home to visit friends and relatives. The population had become far more mobile than it ever had been. This created additional competition for track space – even more with petrol rationing and restrictions on road transport.

To make matters worse, the rail system was in private hands. Routes were regionally delimited and rolling-stock inventories were owned by regional companies. There was no provision for pooling stock, apportioning it nationally according to need and then tracking and accounting for the new patterns of usage, so that stock could be returned to where it was most needed. There simply was not the unified management – nor even the statistical information – which would permit central planning and control of what had to become a national rail system for it to function effectively.

On top of that, there were the effects of the blackout – especially on marshalling yards and goods depots, which needed high intensity illumination to work efficiently in the hours of darkness. Air-raid warnings which forced workers to take cover, and then actual bombing damage, all had significant effects on goods movements – which were set to increase. Thus, while there was – in theory – sufficient rail capacity to cope with extra traffic generated by closing down the coastal shipping trade, the system was not up to the task. It would never catch up. By the time changes had been made, the rail infrastructure had deteriorated, rolling stock had worn out and the whole system could only be kept running by offering a vastly poorer service to passengers, itself creating huge problems and enormous aggravation.

Furthermore, if there was stupidity, it was not necessarily confined to officials. Pre-war, the Ministry of Transport to a certain extent foresaw that there would be difficulties "in placing a sudden demand on the railways for greatly increased traffic in unfamiliar channels". It was the railway companies which proved to be the obstacle, displaying unwarranted optimism about their ability to cope, based on flawed planning assumptions, not the least of which being that passenger traffic could be drastically cut.

In the meantime, to keep London and the southern towns supplied, there was no alternative but to use the colliers, plying from the coalfields of the north. Had they not sailed, London would have gone dangerously short of coal – even more so than it actually did. And coal-fired steam pumps pushed water through the mains which fed the fire hydrants. Without coal, the story of the Blitz could have been very different indeed.[12]

Thus, with their escorts – many of them armed trawlers – these small ships traversed the dangerous waters of the east coast and the Channel. Their crews did so uncomplainingly – badly paid, with no pensions, no holiday or sick pay or even injury compensation. If their ships were sunk from under them, their pay ended the moment the water lapped over their boots. They faced appalling dangers and suffered a far greater number of casualties than did "the few" who were to capture the nation's imagination.[13] Their largely unrecognized heroism gave the planners a breathing space, time to resolve some of the problems of adjustment, the like of which had never before been experienced and for which the country was singularly ill-prepared.

But, if the heroism of the "Coal Scuttle brigade" as it came to be called was unrecognized, fighting yet another unrecognized aspect of the war was J. B. Priestley. To his campaign, a reference was made in William Hickey's column in the *Express*. Sixteen editors, war correspondents and columnists had dined with Duff Cooper, the meeting chaired by Priestley. He had been particularly interested in discussing the government's definition of "peace aims", constantly bringing the talk back to the "new Europe" that we must be supposed to be fighting for. He and others urged that the government should define the sort of new world order they wanted. He spoke of the need to counter the Nazi claim that they were fighting for a new order, "we merely for the *status quo*".

Priestley said he spoke for the thoughtful younger generation, in the Forces and out, who were asking the question, troubled by the government's apparent lack of a programme and adherence to old ways. He built up a glowing picture of the alert, politically educated young British public, absorbed in world affairs. Hickey demurred. Priestley, whom he described as "an earnest Liberal", was taking an unrealistically optimistic view. "There are, thank heaven", Hickey continued, thousands of these "young intelligents" (chiefly in the working classes) but they are still in a small minority. Priestley "was probably making the amateur's mistake of thinking those who write letters to him were representative". The real man-in-the-street rarely wrote letters; more rarely still intelligent or "progressive" ones.

DAY 30 – THURSDAY 8 AUGUST 1940

The shooting war erupted – the sea and air together to make for the biggest fight yet. So many aircraft were involved, and so vicious was the fighting, that some regard 8 August as the true beginning of the Battle of Britain or, variously, the start of the second phase. Even then, the main action was against shipping, specifically Convoy CW9, codenamed "Peewit", routed from Southend to the Yarmouth Roads off the Isle of Wight.

The convoy was the first attempt to run the Straits after it had been closed by the *Luftwaffe*. Briefing the convoy skippers, an unnamed Royal Navy Reserve (RNR) commander told them that keeping the route open was a matter of "prestige". "We don't give a damn about your coal … we'll send you empty if we have to", he was reported to have said. And so, with twenty-five merchant ships and nine escorts, the convoy had weighed anchor at 7 a.m. on the morning of August 7.[14]

Some reports have it that the convoy was picked up by radar, but there was no need for high technology. The convoy could be seen by shore observers sailing through the Straits in daylight. The Germans then only had to wait for darkness and lie in wait further down the Channel, listening for the approach of the ships. That is what they did. That night, four E-boats lay in the water, engines throttled back, rocking in the swell. At two in the morning, the quiet was broken only by the thumping rhythm of gliding ships and the wash and suck of water. Then they struck. There was the snarl of high-powered diesels kicking into life, the ghastly green glow of a star shell punched into the sky by a destroyer escort, and the night ripped apart by the slam of gunfire, escorts and convoy blazing away with everything they had.[15]

The coaster *Holme Force* and her 1,000-ton cargo of coke was the first to go down, torpedoed off Newhaven. The *Fife Coast* followed, ten to fifteen miles west of Beachy Head. Eleven lives were lost. The steamer *Ouse* was sunk in the confusion. She collided with the steamer *Rye* while avoiding a torpedo from one of the E-boats. Twenty-three survivors were rescued from her. Steamers *John M*, ten miles south of The Needles, and *Polly M*, fifteen miles from Cape Wrath, were damaged.

Daylight brought the Stukas, in the first of three major attacks of the day. SS *Coquetdale* was the first casualty. The *Empire Crusader* followed, sunk fifteen miles west of St Catherine's Point, with the loss of her master, two crew and two naval gunners. The Dutch steamer *Ajax* was sunk fifteen miles west of St Catherine's Point, with the loss of four crewmen. Three other Dutch steamers, *Veenenburg*, *Omlandia* and *Surte* were damaged, as were British steamers *Scheldt* and *Balhama*. The Norwegian *Tres* was damaged so badly she later sank in St Helen's Bay. Two anti-submarine yachts and four anti-submarine trawlers were also damaged. HMS *Borealis*, serving as a barrage balloon vessel, was sunk 4.5 miles from St Catherine's Lighthouse.

Against all that, Fighter Command lost twenty-one aircraft, claiming in total the destruction of sixty-six, as against twenty-one *Luftwaffe* aircraft actually destroyed – although many more were damaged. Two RAF bombers lost put the *Luftwaffe* ahead, with twenty-three British losses to twenty-one German. More dangerously, eighteen Fighter Command airmen were lost – including three from a Blenheim F1. Fifteen were lost at sea. One, Flight Lieutenant "Henry" Hall, crashed off Dover. His friend and fellow pilot, Johnnie Kent, later observed that these early combats had been "the most deadly of all". Many a good fighter pilot lost would have been invaluable in the days that followed.

Fighting over England, Kent observed, one would come down on land where medical attention, if required, could rapidly be obtained. Over the sea it was different. "The chances of being picked up during a convoy attack were very remote and this may well have happened to Henry as it did to so many others", he wrote. Hall had commanded a flight in No. 257 Sqn but had previously been a test pilot at Farnborough. He was exactly the sort of experienced pilot the British could ill-afford to lose.[16]

Despite all this, and solely on the basis of the grossly inflated tally that actually concealed a small net loss and a disastrous loss of experienced pilots,

Churchill was moved to direct a congratulatory message to be sent by the War Cabinet to the Secretary of State for Air and the Chief of the Air Staff. Such was the power of statistics in willing hands.[17]

No similar message was sent to the Admiralty, or even to the Shipping Minister congratulating the merchantmen who had taken such risks. Instead, the Navy received a sharp memorandum from the Prime Minister to Admiral Pound. "Since we are using the convoys as decoys," he wrote, "surely they should creep in along the shore a good deal more than they do." Churchill also complained that there were too many convoys running. There had been four working at the same time. Only one should be run every four or five days, he said. No thought was given to the need to move goods.[18]

By the end of the evening, Jock Colville was thinking about greater events. He believed "personally" that the invasion would not be delayed much longer: Germany was probably gathering herself for a formidable blow. However, he confided that he had been comforted by the views of an "eminent German", whom he did not name. This person had opined that Germany's position was "splendid but hopeless".[19]

DAY 31 – FRIDAY 9 AUGUST 1940

No doubt with huge relief, the Ministry of Information announced the newer, bigger and better RAF victories, the *Daily Mirror* and the *Daily Express* both recording fifty-three victories for the loss of sixteen RAF fighters. Not everyone was convinced. George Orwell was one of the more prominent sceptics and there were enough of them to invoke a rebuke from Ernest Bevin via the *Mirror*. "If we let cynicism and bitterness get into the hearts of the people we shall (blank, blank) lose the war", he complained. Asking what could best cheer the people, the paper suggested: "News of a victory". Defensive talk, it averred, makes for cynicism. And what does not make for cynicism? The paper's answer was: "This sort of thing – we shot down 53 enemy aircraft yesterday".

The media was certainly entering into the spirit of things, treating their readers to a diet of excited reports from towns "somewhere on the South-east coast", where Spitfires "roared", while cannon and the machine guns provided "an almost continuous chorus". Typical of the genre was copy from George Fyfe in the *Daily Telegraph*. He had written:

The battle scene changed swiftly from one part of the sky to another in a highly
exciting game of hide-and-seek. Pilots who had lost their adversaries in the mist would
suddenly re-establish contact and in wonderful displays of aerobatics begin blazing
away at one another with all their guns.

Later in the same piece, he wrote of a Messerschmitt which had "raced away"
from the scene, followed by two Spitfires, which "streaked through the sky in
thrilling pursuit". But this was not an action game for the entertainment of the
watchers. The "highly exciting game of hide-and-seek" cost No. 145 Sqn five
pilots in three actions that day, although it in turn claimed an inflated seventeen
enemy aircraft destroyed. This had Keith Park rushing to the squadron to
congratulate the survivors on "their magnificent efforts". Archie Sinclair sent
a telegram of congratulations to CO, Squadron Leader John Peel. But the
squadron was falling apart. After taking three more casualties, it was withdrawn
from the line on 14 August and sent to Drem, in Scotland.[20]

In the air on this day, there were no great battles. There was activity on the
East Coast, with occasional forays over Dover and Plymouth. One Heinkel
bombed properties in Sunderland. Four people were killed and seventy-eight
injured. The aircraft was shot down and crashed into the sea off Whitburn. In
South Shields, a bomb fell in a garden in a residential area. Four people in an
Anderson Shelter, 10 ft from the crater, were uninjured. One Home Guard was
killed by machine-gun fire. A Heinkel was shot down by AA gunfire during
operations near Flamborough Head.

Overnight, a lone bomber, thought to be searching for Fort Dunlop or the
Castle Bromwich Spitfire factory, released its bombs over suburban Birmingham.
The very first bomb on the city severely damaged two houses and killed an
18-year-old cinema projectionist. Several others caused slight damage.[21] A stick
of five fell on a house in the Prenton district of Birkenhead, across the water
from Liverpool, claiming the life of a maid, 30-year-old Johanna Mandale.[22]
She was the first of 442 to be killed in the town, with 606 injured. On the day,
Fighter Command flew 409 sorties, losing two aircraft. Bomber Command lost
a Blenheim and Coastal Command an Anson. The *Luftwaffe* lost four aircraft.

At Chequers that evening, Churchill discussed the attack on the "Peewit"
convoy with Minister of War, Anthony Eden, and a group of his senior military
staff, including the First Sea Lord, Admiral Pound. He approved of the idea
of using the convoys as "bait", although he acknowledged that "surviving bait

are getting fed up". In drawing the Germans into battle, Churchill asserted, we stood to lose little. Pound stated that there was a surplus of coastal vessels, while the air battles demonstrated to the world that we were superior to the Germans. The enemy must be less powerful in the air than we supposed, he mused, for if their strength was as great as we believed, they would have come again today and would be bombing our ports incessantly.

Colville retailed how Eden could not understand why the Germans expended so great an effort against "comparatively unimportant objects". It was suggested to him that they still thought they could starve us out and did not understand "the unimportance of these coastal convoys". They seemed to know less of the importance of their own coastal trade than did the Germans. But the very fact that so much effort was being expended on non-military targets hardly suggested a commitment to an imminent invasion.[23]

DAY 32 – SATURDAY 10 AUGUST 1940

It was a cloudy day with some rain. Göring decided to wait before launching his grand offensive. *Eagle Attack* was postponed for three days. Fighter Command, therefore, experienced "exceptionally light" enemy activity. For longer than some could remember, there were no losses. Nevertheless, there was action over the Channel and Me 110 pilots attempted a surprise evening strike on Norwich. A lone Dornier put eleven bombs close to RAF West Malling.

The German Naval High Command was concerned about further slippage in *Sealion*. The war diary noted that mine clearance is being affected by the inactivity of the *Luftwaffe* "which is at present prevented from operating by the bad weather". The diary added that "for reasons not known to the Naval Staff", the *Luftwaffe* had also missed opportunities afforded by the very recent good weather. Here, the German Navy was focusing on the issues on which a successful invasion would depend. The Air Force had been attacking "Peewit" and other non-invasion related targets. And the Army, after the abortive discussions between Halder and Schniewind, was appealing to higher authority. In a memorandum to the Supreme Command, the General Staff reiterated its demands for a broad front landing.[24]

During the night, the *Luftwaffe* attacked Bristol Docks and leaflets were dropped over Bristol. Bombs fell for the first time on Abergavenny, Rochester and Wallasey, along with heavy raids on Weymouth. Serious damage was done to the Llandore GWR (Great Western Railway) viaduct near Swansea where a direct hit on a shelter killed five. He 111s hit Swansea itself and fifteen people were killed. It was difficult to see the relevance of these targets to an invasion in southern England. As for the "score", no fighters but three British bombers were lost, against two *Luftwaffe* losses, one a take-off accident in a Me 109, when the pilot was killed.

Despite the overarching threat of invasion, many people were far more concerned about the damage being caused by German air activity. Much dissatisfaction was being expressed at the lack of protection, with complaints of insufficient numbers of barrage balloons and anti-aircraft guns. These complaints were passed to the Air Ministry, which had Air Vice-Marshal Peck warning, in particular, of the lack of public protection in Swansea, where there was a major refinery.[25]

The Air Ministry, meanwhile, was "correcting" the previous day's score, adding seven further kills to bring the total number of aircraft lost by the Germans on the day to sixty. The War Cabinet had been told that fifty-two enemy aircraft had been shot down. A further fourteen were "unconfirmed". It was also told that British casualties amounted to seenteen fighters and a Blenheim "engaged on a training flight". With the actual casualty rate standing at twenty-one, this was close to the number actually lost. The claim then that "several of our pilots have been rescued", was less candid. A more truthful statement might have been: "very few of our pilots have been rescued".

There was also a certain stridency with which the government insisted its figures were correct. After an air battle, it asserted: "RAF crews engaged made reports which are carefully compiled, together with pictures taken by the camera gun carried on every British fighter".[26] This "gun", it was claimed, registered a picture with every burst of machine-gun fire, and also recorded the time. However, few cameras were fitted to RAF fighters before September 1940, and then mainly as training aids.[27]

As to the shipping losses, the official British claim was "three small ships" sunk by the E-boats, totalling 2,500 tons. That was accurate, although an E-boat was claimed destroyed, with a second one badly damaged, which was not true. And no mention was made of the two ships damaged. The air attack toll was similarly distorted. The British claimed two ships lost, totalling another 2,500 tons, and seven damaged. In fact, five ships had been sunk, totalling just short of 5,000 tons. Five merchantmen had been damaged, plus two anti-submarine yachts and four anti-submarine trawlers. Neither the British nor the Germans, who claimed fifteen ships and 72,000 tons, produced reliable figures.

DAY 33 – SUNDAY 11 AUGUST 1940

Readers of the *Sunday Express* were greeted with a detailed map on the front page, identifying towns and cities which had suffered bombing from the Germans. Places such as Swansea, Pembroke, Exeter and even Dumbarton in Scotland were identified. It had been compiled by *Time* magazine, reliant entirely on German sources, but it was uncannily accurate. And the title to the map was: "Battle of Britain: Bombings June 18 to July 21".

A narrative on the previous day's raids was consigned to the back page, where the headline, "Biggest day of raids: 7 hit by bullets" covered a story with remarkably little detail. The censor had been at work and the locations described were all vague, such as a "south-east town" and the "north-east". In the former, workers had been attacked by a Dornier, and then machine-gunned.

There was a brief reference to an attack on a hospital and then, from another south-east district, there was the almost obligatory account of how a family had been saved by their shelter. "I scoffed at Anderson shelters till now," said a Mr A. White, standing amid the wreckage of his home, "but ours saved the lives of my wife and two daughters." However, the impact, so to speak, of this account was somewhat diminished by the experience of a Mrs Thornley, whose house had been wrecked by a bomb and she had been buried in the debris. When extricated, she had been found to be "practically unhurt". She had been in the bath when the bomb had fallen.

This day, a Sunday, was supposedly a day of rest. But for many, it was another day of life-and-death struggle. The air war started early when at 7.30 a.m., Me 109s and 110s attacked Dover. Spitfires roared in to intercept.

About this time, alarmed by the growing toll of pilots lost at sea, Keith Park succeeded in borrowing some Lysander aircraft to work systematically with rescue launches and other craft, a step towards building an air-sea rescue service.[28] How much they were needed was highlighted by the "not unrepresentative" experience of Pilot Officer Stevenson sent to intercept the Dover

raid.[29] After mixing it with a group of Me 109s and being forced to bale out at
high altitude (23,000 ft), Stevenson had drifted eleven miles out to sea on his
parachute before hitting the water. He then recalled:

> One string of my parachute did not come undone, and I was dragged along by my left
> leg at ten miles an hour with my head underneath the water. After three minutes I was
> almost unconscious, when the string came undone. I got my breath back and started
> swimming. There was a heavy sea running. After one and a half hours an MTB came
> to look for me. I fired my revolver at it. It went out of sight, but came back. I changed
> magazines and fired all my shots over it. It heard my shots and I kicked up a foam in
> the water, and it saw me. It then picked me up and took me to Dover.

With Stevenson yet to receive his chilling baptism, the Dover attack was done.
But it was a mere prelude. A formation of 165 bombers and Me 110s, escorted
by fighters, was on its way from the Cherbourg area to attack the Portland naval
base and Weymouth. This was the largest single raid so far. Nine squadrons
raced to intercept, only to become tangled in a massive dogfight that spread
across the entire width of Weymouth Bay at heights up to 23,000 ft. The
bombers ran in at 15,000 ft to drop their bombs, setting naval oil tanks on fire.
HMS *Scimitar* was damaged by near misses, and the destroyer HMS *Skate* took
numerous near misses which wrecked her bridge.

Pilot Officer J. S. B. Jones was one of those shot down. He baled out and
landed in the Channel. Three Spitfires, supported by Blenheim fighters, were
ordered up to look for him. They came across an He 59 riding on the sea thirty
miles off Cherbourg, recovering *Luftwaffe* airmen, protected by six circling
Me 109s. The Spitfires held off the fighters while the Blenheims destroyed the
seaplane. When another He 59, from Calais, flew into the area, it was shot down
as well, but two Spitfires were downed by the German escorts, killing their
pilots. Neither Jones nor his parachute was seen. His body was later recovered
and buried in France.

Others were still fighting for their lives. Among them was the crew of the
destroyer HMS *Windsor*, damaged by German bombing off the Botany Buoy in
the Thames Estuary. Destroyer HMS *Esk* was lightly damaged at Harwich. An
armed trawler, HMT *Edwardian*, hit by a bomb, had to be run aground at North
Foreland. The trawler *Peter Carey* took a hit but her crew managed to save her.
Elsewhere, the steamer *Kirnwood* was damaged by bombing, as was the tanker
Oil Trader.

On the day, Fighter Command lost thirty-one aircraft. A Royal Navy Fulmar was lost near Aberdour and an Anson failed to return after a patrol. Bomber Command lost five aircraft, bringing British losses to thirty-eight. The *Luftwaffe* lost thirty-six. Of the thirty-one single-seat RAF fighters downed, twenty-five pilots had been killed. The Germans had lost nine Me 109 pilots, including one taken prisoner. Two had been rescued unhurt and one had crashed on home territory. The British were exchanging nearly three fighter pilots for every German.

In propaganda terms, however, this had been a clear win for the British. The RAF claimed fifty "kills", a figure which was rapidly inflated to sixty – against twenty-four losses. Duff Cooper was jubilant. He predicted that Britain would soon establish air superiority. "Just as we retain command of the seas," he said, "so we are rapidly assuming command of the air".[30] Leo Amery, the Secretary for India, delivered a similar buoyant message in a speech at Blackpool.[31]

Churchill shared the optimistic mood. "I do not think the German Air Force has the numbers or quality to overpower our Air defences", he wrote to Robert Menzies and Peter Frazer, the prime ministers of Australia and New Zealand. Furthermore, the Navy was increasing in strength each month, and he expected over 500 new vessels to have joined the fleet in the period from June to December. He told his prime ministerial colleagues:

[t]o try to transport a large army, as would now be needed for success, across the seas virtually without Naval escort in the face of our Navy and Air Force, only to meet our powerful military force on the shore, still less to maintain such an army and nourish its lodgements with munitions and supplies, would be a very unreasonable act.

"On the other hand," he mused, "if Hitler fails to invade and conquer Britain before the weather breaks, he has received his first and probably his fatal check." With that, the Prime Minister conveyed a "sober and growing conviction of our power to persevere through the year or two that may be necessary to gain victory".[32]

DAY 34 – MONDAY 12 AUGUST 1940

This was the day when it became a criminal offence to feed the ducks in Regents Park. So said the *Daily Express*, which sternly warned that, under defence regulations, "wilful waste of food fit for human consumption" was now prohibited, on pain of a £500 penalty. Presumably by way of balance, the British papers offered news of unremitting victory: "60 of 400 raiders shot down", blared the *Daily Telegraph*. It told of the *Luftwaffe* suffering "another humiliating defeat". For the second time in four days, "60 German bombers and fighters were shot down". The triumphal cry of the *Daily Express* was more succinct: "Again!" Again the propaganda was concealing a small net loss.

The news was not accepted uncritically. Running at this time was a controversy about the use of a photograph claimed to have been taken on 8 August, purporting to show five German aircraft shot down, plunging into the sea. Among those newspapers which had carried the photograph was the *Yorkshire Post*, on the front page of its 9 August edition. But the picture was a fake and the papers had to carry corrections, conveying a statement from the Air Ministry denying that it had been an official photograph, a correction which had also been broadcast by the BBC. As recorded by Home Intelligence, this episode fuelled suspicions that successes were being exaggerated, adding to popular mistrust of the media.[33]

The *Daily Express* was moved to observe that the great trouble was that the defence departments did not take the people into their confidence sufficiently. They did not trust the people to take a realistic view of the facts. They held back items of good news, perhaps for fear the public's hopes were raised too high. They held back items of bad news, perhaps for fear the public's hopes should sink too low.

Mixed messages were also coming from the German High Command. Although, ostensibly, the invasion of Britain was still on, Keitel sent a signal to all three of the armed forces' chiefs. On the supposition, he wrote, that *Sealion* could not be carried out this year, and that the Italian offensive against the Suez Canal did not succeed, the possibility had to be faced that the *Führer* may decide to transfer German forces to the Italians.[34]

With startling prescience, the *Daily Express* editorial this day repeated Churchill's warning of the previous week that the danger of invasion had not passed, and that Britain was "not out of the wood", then saying that "the wood" was not just the British Empire. It extended over many parts of the British Empire. Therefore, the Battle for Britain, the paper said, "may be fought around the region of the Suez Canal".

The next day, the delayed *Eagle Attack* was due to start. This was viewed by historians as the worst period for the RAF, when the *Luftwaffe* focused its attacks on airfields and infrastructure. But there was some relief to be gained from the shift in focus. The previous day had not only seen a high loss rate, 83 percent of RAF fighter pilots shot down had been killed. At that rate, there would no longer be a viable force within the month. For the Germans to move inland would be a blessing in disguise for the RAF. Their aircraft losses might increase, but more pilots would be saved.

This day was going to be a busy for the Germans. There were preliminaries to be sorted before the big show got under way. The message had finally dawned on the *Luftwaffe*, though, that radar was playing a part in warning RAF pilots. Thus, for the first time, radar stations were deliberately targeted. Soon after dawn, in bright, clear weather, a raid developed over the Channel. British controllers delayed scrambling fighters, wary of a feint. When Spitfires were put up, it became clear that the German move was indeed designed to draw off the fighters – a tactic implemented so successfully on 25 July and many times since. But, by nine o'clock, five radar stations were under attack. The airfield at Lympne was also bombed.

Next, a formation of Stukas attacked convoys "Arena" and "Agent" in the Thames Estuary. HMTs *Tamarisk* and *Pyrope* were sunk. Twelve men were killed and four wounded. Simultaneously, an attack was mounted on "Snail" and "Cable" convoys. However, the main target was Portsmouth naval base. When the German bombers had finished, the harbour railway station had been destroyed, the pier demolished and a pontoon dock holed. Fires had broken out in several buildings including a brewery and a furniture store in the old town. Casualties were initially reported as 8 killed and 75 injured, although the final toll was 29 killed and 126 injured.[35]

While Portsmouth was being hit, the Chain Home radar station in Ventnor, Isle of Wight, was knocked out by a number of well-placed bombs. British deception techniques concealed the extent of the damage, convincing the Germans that their attacks had been unsuccessful.

By now, the focus was moving to RAF Manston. Numerous hits rendered it non-operational until the next day. Hawkinge was given some detailed attention and Lympne, which had already received 141 bombs, got another 100 which knocked it out of the action. The remainder of the attack force bombed Hastings and Dover, leaving jubilant *Luftwaffe* crews to celebrate a claimed seventy-one RAF aircraft destroyed. The success was illusory. Fighter Command had managed 732 sorties with the loss of twenty-three fighters, against the *Luftwaffe's* actual twenty-eight losses, including eleven Me 109s and ten pilots. Bomber Command lost five – making the two sides exactly equal.[36]

It was a day to remember for Flight Lieutenant R. A. B. Learoyd, who gained a Victoria Cross – the first for Bomber Command – after bombing the Dortmund–Ems Canal in a Hampden. This raid was to have a significant effect. Causing a blockage of the canal, movement of motorboats from the Rhineland was held up, setting back invasion plans.[37] As for those standing out under the night sky listening, something had changed. The drums had stopped.

7

Eagle Attack

From now till early next year, England's will to resist must be broken, if not by a landing then by every other means. This most important task will take precedence over everything else. We are now entering into the decisive battle against England.

Generaloberst Alfred Jodl, Chief of Operation Staff OKW, 15 August 1940[1]

With the peace initiatives apparently at an end, the preparations done and the waiting over, now came the battle. But this was not a normal joust, with clear objectives, a defined battlefield and a visible winner. In the shifting sky, not the generals but the clerks and statisticians decided the victors.

DAY 35 – TUESDAY 13 AUGUST 1940

This day was marked by the *Daily Telegraph* and *Daily Express* offering a similar diet of distortion and exaggeration, but with a new twist. Upping the "kill" to thirty-nine – as against the actual of twenty-eight – Fighter Command losses had been heavily discounted, from twenty-nine to nine. The statisticians had won another victory. George Orwell noted: "if the reports are true, the British always score heavily". He wished he could talk to some RAF officer "and get some kind of idea whether these reports are truthful".[2]

The papers were also full of accounts from the previous day's bombing. Unusually, the locations were named, with the fate of Portsmouth prominent in reports. The *Express* claimed: "Dockyard attack has little success". But it noted that some houses and commercial properties were also hit. It told its readers: "Casualties in this area were very light, although several cases of fatal injury have been reported". The *Daily Mirror* was more forthright, writing: "Two women – Mrs Robertson and her married daughter, Mrs Mann – were killed when their Anderson shelter was blown out of the ground".

This rare mention of casualties associated with an Anderson shelter contrasted with a report in the *Yorkshire Post* on a raid in "another South-East Coast town" (probably Gosport). Bombs wrecked a dance hall, a private garage and three cottages and a joinery works, said the paper, adding: "A man named Smith sheltering in a public building was killed. Eight people in an Anderson shelter in a garden where a bomb wrecked an outhouse escaped unharmed".

While the British public was digesting the morning news, two important events were under way. First, Göring launched his long-awaited *Eagle Day*. Secondly, considering his presence necessary for the opening of the air offensive, Hitler returned from his retreat in the Berghof to Berlin. He was to confer in the afternoon with Räder, who was insistent that the dispute over the invasion plan had to be resolved.[3]

The launch of *Eagle Day*, meanwhile, was going badly awry, partly through incompetence, and partly through the unexpectedly poor weather which ruined any chance of a successful early start. But not until the first aircraft were airborne did Göring postpone the operation. Three bomber units missed the recall and ploughed on without their Me 110 escorts. In two separate formations, one was headed for the Coastal Command airfield at Eastchurch, the other for Odiham. A third element provided a diversion off Portland.

Poor data from radar and the lack of strength confirmation from the Observer Corps led to insufficient fighters being scrambled. Eastchurch suffered as a result, very heavy bombing, causing considerable damage and destroying five Blenheims on the ground. Twelve personnel were killed and forty injured. Fighters then caught up with the Dorniers, shooting down four and damaging another four. To the west, the other bomber group, comprising Ju 88s, was engaged by fighters from three squadrons. The Germans never reached their targets. Neither did the Portland raid, which had kept its escort. It was inter-cepted with the loss of six, all within five minutes – a disaster on the scale of the loss of the RAF's Defiants.

But a greater disaster had befallen the RAF, a repeat of No. 107 Sqn's grief. At half past eight that morning, twelve Blenheim IVs of No. 82 Sqn had taken off from RAF Watton in Norfork, headed for Aalborg airfield in northern Jutland. One turned back, reporting technical problems, leaving eleven to fly on at 8,000 ft in clear skies and brilliant sunshine, with no fighter escort. Through poor navigation, they made landfall thirty-five miles further south than intended, crossing over at Søndervig where they were instantly registered by German observers. The response was twenty-five Me 109s. When they had finished, flak took over. In minutes, the squadron had ceased to exist – its aircraft either smouldering debris or sunken wrecks. The damage to Aalborg airfield was negligible.[4]

Into the afternoon, the weather had improved over England. *Eagle Day* was reinstated. Large-scale attacks were launched against Portland, Southampton, Portsmouth, Kent and the Thames Estuary. RAF fighters dealt with the first wave of Stukas but a formation of Ju 88s broke through to Southampton, causing serious damage and starting large fires in warehouses and docks. A small force of Ju 88s attempting to bomb Portland was thwarted by other fighters. Escorting Me 109s were put to rout, with three shot down.

On the coast near Lyme Regis, a gaggle of Stukas headed for RAF Middle Wallop. It had become routine to send in Me 109s to flush out the fighters, but this went fatally wrong. The Messerschmitts had already turned back short of fuel, setting up another "Defiant moment". Six out of nine Stukas were shot down, one was damaged and the rest forced to turn back.

Other Stukas, failing to find RAF Warmwell, dropped their bombs on the Dorset countryside. Two *staffel* of Ju 88s searching for Middle Wallop had better luck. They happened on RAF Andover, HQ of Maintenance Command. Twelve bombs were dropped, damaging the station headquarters and officers' quarters. One aircraft on the ground was damaged. Two people were killed. A force of Stukas then headed for the airfield at Rochester, where another failure of navigation had the landscape paying the penalty.

A separate group of forty Stukas made for RAF Detling, about three miles north-east of Maidstone. They found it. No warning was given and surprised airmen failed to take cover. The CO and sixty-seven airmen were killed, the operations block was demolished, hangars were set on fire and other buildings destroying. Services were knocked out. Twenty-two aircraft were totally destroyed, some of them Blenheims bombed up ready for a mission.

Through this period, the meeting between Räder and Hitler had gone ahead. The Grand Admiral said he recognized the justice of the Army's demands, but could not meet them. The supply of reinforcements could not be accelerated, as further transports could neither be assembled nor accommodated in the invasion ports; and it was certainly not possible to provide additional transports for the landings in the Brighton sector and Lyme Bay. *Sealion*, he repeated, should only be attempted as a last resort if Britain could not be made to sue for peace in any other way. Hitler added to this: "An abortive venture would mean a great gain in prestige for England. One would have to wait and see precisely what effect intensive battles in the air would have on England".[5]

Meanwhile, to sow fear and apprehension, the German aircraft scattered 45 parachutes in various districts, including Scotland, Derbyshire, Staffordshire and Yorkshire. Two parachutists were reported to have been captured, one in civilian clothing. Eventually, the drops were found to be a "crude hoax", calculated to cause alarm. The captured parachutists were spies.[6]

By the end of the day, in its bid to make the invasion unnecessary, the *Luftwaffe* had flown 1,485 sorties over England, its largest number yet. It claimed seventy Spitfires and Hurricanes destroyed, plus eighteen Blenheims. Actual Fighter Command losses were fourteen, including one destroyed on the ground at Eastchurch, with 700 sorties flown. In total, including all Bomber Command casualties, losses numbered fifty. The *Luftwaffe* lost forty-seven. In terms of aircraft, the *Luftwaffe* came off slightly better. But the British had at least contained their losses to three pilots killed out of thirteen fighters shot down, although two more had been seriously burned and were out of the fight. Five Me 109 pilots had been lost. Neither side had achieved a knock-out blow.

Before the day was out though, the RAF was to add what many regarded as another "own goal", losing a Spitfire pilot on night flying practice. The use of Spitfires or Hurricanes as night fighters was proving fruitless. The handful of enemy destroyed was far exceeded by the accidental losses. In the dark, Defiants were better platforms. Blenheims were better than nothing, pending the arrival of Beaufighters. On the other hand, both Blenheim and Defiant were near useless during the day, yet were still used to fly day missions. Somebody was not thinking straight.[7]

DAY 36 – WEDNESDAY 14 AUGUST 1940

The previous evening, the *London Evening News* had reported on "one of the greatest aerial battles ever to take place", its location "off the southeast and southern coasts". There were fears that this was the opening stage of the invasion. But "well informed experts" had their doubts. Aware that the *Luftwaffe* was still only deploying a fraction of its strength, they believed the "change in tactics" was an attempt to "reconnoitre the strength of the RAF" before mounting even more vigorous air attacks. The *Daily Telegraph* conveyed the opinion of "authoritative quarters in London", which said much the same thing.

Harold Nicolson was not so sure. "We do not understand what is happening", he confided to his diary. "The German attacks are more serious than mere reconnaissance, but not serious enough to justify the heavy losses they receive." He was troubled by the German losses of "more than 100 pilots" the previous day. This was unsustainable, and they, "our experts", no more than Nicolson, could make it out.[8]

Not everyone was so gullible. Christopher Tomlin, another Mass Observation correspondent, wrote of his father being "dubious about RAF claims". It is easy for a pilot to think he's sent a machine down; the authorities only have the pilot's figures to rely on. If the figures are true, Germany will soon stop sending bombers here as she can't afford to lose them at that rate.[9]

The *Daily Express* ran an article from Hubert Knickerbocker, star correspondent of the US-based INS agency. "Is it invasion or blockade?" he asked. "With 400 or 500 of his bombers and fighters attacking all along the Channel south coast of Britain today," he wrote, "Hitler gave some evidence that he is trying, by his three-to-one superiority of numbers, to knock out the RAF before he attempts invasion." But the star was not convinced. "There is plenty of other evidence that the current operations represent another step in the attempted blockade of these isles", he suggested. "Today's observed results do not encourage the belief that the Germans are going soon to be able to attain sufficient superiority in the air to attempt to launch vast landing parties from troop-carrying airplanes, gliders and parachutes."

To muddy the waters further, the paper had its own air correspondent, Basil Cardew, argue that the invasion "may come soon now". In his view, there would be fighting on these shores, "maybe in quite short a time". Cardew added: "The Germans know that the North Sea becomes too rough at the end of August for their shallow boats and in their neck-or-nothing gamble, they may be forced to act quickly".

The man on the spot was William L. Shirer. He was travelling courtesy of the *Luftwaffe* from Berlin to Ghent. His pilot had a little difficulty finding the camouflaged landing field. From the air, it looked "just like any other place in the landscape, with paths cutting across it irregularly as if it were farmland". Aircraft were also hidden in camouflaged tents. So skilful was their construction, Shirer wrote, "that I doubt if you could distinguish one from above a thousand feet". Arriving in Ostend, he looked in vain for the kind of barges and ships needed for an invasion. There were none in the harbour and only a few barges in the canals behind the town.[10]

Coastal Command photographic reconnaissance aircraft and naval patrols had brought back the same detail as Shirer.[11] Hiding aircraft at the edges of airfields was one thing. Concealing a 3,000-strong invasion fleet was quite another. An invasion was not imminent.

In a move, the relevance of which was only later fully to emerge, the Naval Staff war diary recorded a conversation between Göring and Räder on the difficulties involved in a broad-front landing, and agreed between them that the landing should be restricted to the Dover Straits. The pair had met in Berlin in the Reich Chancellery, after a ceremony where Hitler was handing out the batons to his newly appointed field marshals.

Hitler now seemed to be expressing open doubts about *Sealion*. Räder noted that he "does not propose to carry out an operation whose risk is too great: he advocates the view that the aim of defeating Britain is not dependent on the landing alone, but can be achieved in a different way". Regardless of the final decision, Räder also noted, Hitler wished to keep up the *threat* of an invasion. Preparations, therefore, had to continue. After the formal conference, the Naval Staff sent a suggestion to Jodl to the effect that, if Hitler did not want to go ahead with the invasion, but wanted to keep up the fiction, "the retreat should be sounded" and a special deception operation set up.

The Navy had not yet got its way. Far from any agreement having been reached over the dispositions of forces, von Brauchitsch had been assured that "sufficient" forces would be landed in the disputed Brighton sector. But Hitler was wavering. He ordered Jodl to examine the possibility of landing those forces without heavy equipment, just in case a full landing could not be protected.[12]

However, a record of the *Führer's* political thoughts had also been kept by Field Marshal Wilhelm von Leeb, the general who had commanded Army Group C and broken through the Maginot line. In his diary, von Leeb had Hitler ruminating about the reasons why Britain would not make peace. Probably, there were two, he said. First, she hopes for US aid, but the USA cannot start major arms deliveries until 1941. Secondly, she hopes to play Russia off against Germany.

But, he continued, Germany was not aiming at the destruction of England. Germany's victory would make the situation more difficult for England, benefiting Japan in East Asia, Russia in India, Italy in the Mediterranean and America in world trade. This was why peace was possible with Britain – but not while Churchill was prime minister. Therefore, Hitler said, we must wait for results from the *Luftwaffe*, and possible new elections.[13] He was banking on regime change to pave the way for peace negotiations.

The public, of course, had no means of knowing what was going on – any more than did the militaries on either side, sometimes even about the dispositions of their own forces. But ordinary people were also being fed a daily diet of propaganda. For instance, as regards the air war, the *Daily Express* had told its readers that sixty-nine enemy aircraft had been downed the previous day. It also told them that thirty German airfields had been hit. There was not the slightest hint of the disaster at Aalborg. The airfield was claimed as one of the successful targets.

Silence had not been an option. Lord Haw-Haw had already announced the loss of No. 82 Sqn. Damage limitation demanded a response, and it was skilfully done. And there was evidence that it was working. Home Intelligence was finding that the equivocation and indifference of early July had gone. The upbeat news of the exploits of the RAF and its "successes" was strengthening public confidence. Morale was high.

After its efforts of the previous day, the *Luftwaffe* flew just a third the number of sorties, putting up 91 bombers and 398 fighters. Even then, the raids were slow to start and, when they did, the focus was again on Dover and Kent airfields. Just after midday, 80 Stukas flew towards Dover, escorted by as many Me 109s. Four squadrons of British fighters intercepted and, for a short while, there were over 200 aircraft fighting over Dover. The Stukas sunk the Goodwin lightship and the Messerschmitts shot down nine of Dover's barrage balloons. Two British pilots were lost in the Channel.

While the Dover scrap was going on, a dozen Me 110 fighter bombers slipped through to attack RAF Manston, demolishing four hangars and destroying three Blenheims on the ground. Revenge was swift. Squadron personnel shot down a raider with a Hispano 20mm cannon. Another was brought down by a Bofors gun manned by Anti–Aircraft Command. At Middle Wallop, Heinkels bombed a hangar and offices. Three airman ran to close the hangar door in an attempt to protect the Spitfires inside. They were caught by a 500kg bomb which brought the massive doors down on them, killing them outright. Two Spitfires managed to take off and shoot down one of the intruders.

RAF Andover was attacked again. About fifteen bombs were dropped. A transmitter was destroyed, killing a civilian radio operator. Corporal Josephine Robins, a Women's Auxiliary Air Force (WAAF) telephone operator, was in a dug-out which took a direct hit, killing two men and injuring others. Despite dust and fumes filling the shelter, she calmly gave first aid to the injured and helped with their evacuation. She was awarded a Military Medal, one of only six WAAFs to be so honoured.

In the two days of *Eagle Attack*, Fighter Command had lost ten front-line fighter pilots. And this day saw No. 145 Sqn relieved and moved to Drem, in Scotland. From May, only six of the original pilots had survived. The squadron was down to its last eight serviceable aircraft. Fighter Command had lost eight aircraft on the day, plus the three Blenheims on the ground. Bomber Command lost a Hudson, three Blenheims and two Whitleys bringing the total RAF losses to seventeen, as against *Luftwaffe's* twenty-two.

Before the close of play, however, the Germans had been given another message – this one from Secretary of War, Anthony Eden. Although overshadowed by Churchill, who had taken the Defence Minister portfolio, Eden nevertheless made his own contributions. Now, broadcasting on the BBC, he said that the real war had hardly begun. It would begin "when we take the offensive and strike home at the enemy. That is the way wars are won, and that is what we mean to do", he said. Countries at present under the Nazi heel will be "like ghosts arising from the dead".[14]

DAY 37 – THURSDAY 15 AUGUST 1940

The *Daily Mirror* reported that some observers were convinced that the air fights of the previous three days were a prelude to the full "Battle of Britain". Supposedly with just over a month to go to the invasion, Jodl circulated a "summary of the situation referring to invasion of UK". He stressed that the landing operation "must not founder under any circumstances". Failure, he wrote, can have political repercussions far outweighing the military setback.

He confronted the irreconcilable positions between the Navy and the Army, agreeing that the landing should extend from Brighton to Folkestone. He endorsed the plan for ten divisions to be landed within the first four days, reinforced by another three during the next four, with airborne troops reinforcing the troops landed in the west. "Should these conditions not be fulfilled," he asserted, "I consider the landing to be an act of desperation which would have to be attempted in a desperate manner, but which we have at this stage no reason whatever to contemplate." He added tersely, "England can be brought to her knees in other ways".

One of the "other ways" Jodl had in mind was the economic destruction of southern England. He also pushed the idea of stepping up U-boat warfare from French ports. But there were the other elements which were being seen more and more frequently: taking Egypt, if necessary with Italian help, and taking Gibraltar, with Spanish and Italian agreement, thus creating a second front. Nevertheless, Jodl cautioned against undertaking military operations which were not necessary for the conquering of England. "We should fight for victory and not just conduct operations on military objectives", he said, adding:

> From now till early next year, England's will to resist must be broken, if not by a landing then by every other means. This most important task will take precedence over every-thing else. We are now entering into the decisive battle against England. Therewith within our coalition the general principles of war will remain valid – to concentrate all strength in the decisive undertaking – that is air and U-boat warfare against England.[15]

Jodl was expecting a long campaign – six months or more. His emphasis was on the blockade and industrial disruption, with little reliance on an invasion.

Against this background, the *Luftwaffe* launched phase two of *Eagle Attack*, a deliberate attempt to saturate the British defences, synchronizing the attacks from the two French-based air fleets with General Hans-Jeurgen Stumpff's Fifth Air Fleet. This had never been tried before. Now, Stumpff had orders to attack airfields near Newcastle and in Yorkshire. Based on the intensity of fighting in the south and the *Luftwaffe's* estimate of the RAF's strength, it was assumed that the north had been denuded of fighters. Little opposition was expected.

Opposing Stumpff was Air Vice-Marshal R. E. Saul, commanding No. 13 Group from his headquarters in Newcastle. He had elements of six Spitfire squadrons, four Hurricane squadrons, the remnants of No. 141 Defiant Sqn and a Blenheim fighter squadron. In the two sectors which covered the north of England – his domain covering southern Scotland and Northern Ireland – he had three squadrons of Spitfires, one of Hurricanes and one of Blenheims. He was also able to rely on fully operational radar, reaching out over the North Sea, offering far more notice of an attack than the southern system. By coincidence, it was already on full alert to cover the departure of a convoy leaving Hull that morning.

For insurance, *Luftwaffe* planners had set up a feint to draw off fighters, comprising two *staffeln* of He 115s seaplanes from the Norwegian coast. Unfortunately, a navigational error put the main force on almost the same track as the seaplanes. No sooner had the radar began to pick up the seaplanes, they turned back and were replaced by the bombers. The only effect of the feint was to extend the already lengthy period of warning.

Confronted by alert British forces, the bombers of the main force jettisoned most of their bombs in the sea. Of a total of about a hundred, eight bombers and seven Me 110s were destroyed and several more damaged, without British loss. Further south, a separate force of Ju 88s, heading for the bomber base at Driffield, evaded a blocking force by splitting into eight sections. It destroyed twelve Whitley bombers and killed seventeen personnel. The airfield was non-operational for the rest of the year. Nevertheless, six Ju 88s were shot down, representing about 10 per cent of the aircraft deployed. In all, the northern attackers lost sixteen bombers out of the 123, and seven fighters of the thirty-four available.

On the day as a whole, Fighter Command lost thirty-three aircraft (thirty of them in the air), with many more damaged. Bomber Command losses on the ground, plus others on operations, brought total losses to forty-nine. By contrast, the Germans actually lost seventy-one aircraft to all causes, giving the RAF a clear victory. Nevertheless, the Air Ministry claimed 144 – slightly more than twice the actual figure. This was yet another victory for the clerks and statisticians.

While the RAF – with the full support of the British Government and the approval of the Ministry of Information – chose to make this a numbers game, the numbers that mattered were not aircraft downed, but pilot losses, in particular single-seater fighter pilots. Eleven had been killed and three taken prisoner: two crash-landed in France and one plucked from the sea by German rescuers. Thus, from twenty-nine fighters shot down, fourteen – nearly half (48.3 per cent) – had been lost. Even if this was nowhere near the 83 per cent suffered on 8 August, it was still serious. Comparing like-for-like, the Germans had lost six Me 109s, with four pilots dead or missing – less than a third of the RAF loss. In three days of *Eagle Attack*, Fighter Command had lost twenty-four pilots, plus a few more injured and out of play – more than two squadrons. This was not sustainable.

But this was actually a battle of perception. On paper the RAF had scored a great victory and Harold Nicolson, in the embattled Ministry of Information, was ecstatic. "Everyone is in high spirits about our air triumphs", he wrote. "In fact the superiority shown by our men is a miracle … Our triumph today was superb."

The King captured the mood with a message to the Archie Sinclair. "Please convey my warmest congratulations to the Fighter squadrons who, in recent days, have been so heavily engaged in the defence of our country", he wrote. "I, like all their compatriots have read with ever increasing admiration the story of their daily victories. I wish them continued success and the best of luck." The mood was contagious. Home Intelligence the next day reported that "confidence and cheerfulness prevail". It added: "Intensified raids are everywhere received with calmness, the results with jubilation". There was the living evidence that perception engendered by statistical manipulation mattered more than reality, and of the powerful effect of exaggerated victories.

DAY 38 – FRIDAY 16 AUGUST 1940

The newspapers were quick to applaud the RAF's "triumph", printing uncritically the latest scores. Gone was the rancour between the press and the Ministry of Information. The air battle was at last taking centre stage.

With full details as yet unknown, as much attention was given to a night raid which had targeted Croydon aerodrome – the closest yet to London. Of the battle as a whole, "This was no preliminary", said the *Daily Express*. "This was no skirmish. This was the real thing. Yesterday, Goering threw his air force against Britain. … They came in their hordes and they went home again humbled." And now, the paper said, in a separate editorial piece, the people join in the battle. They become part of the front line of the defence of Britain. The people of

Britain who stay on the ground, who have nothing to strike back with – whose only weapons are their discipline, their calmness, their presence of mind, they also serve.

However, the greatest of the battles of the previous day had taken place over the sea and in the sparsely populated East Riding. The victory had become a media event but it was the *news* of it, rather than the actuality, that had had a "stimulating effect on public opinion". And, as Home Intelligence noted, it "more than counteracts the effects of disturbed nights in raided areas". On 17 August, two days after the victory, it wrote: "the air battles are everywhere regarded as encouraging victories". There was reference to confidence increasing "a feeling of growing exhilaration". The attitude to the war was "stiffening", with "less tendency to compare it with a sporting event".

To *Flight* magazine, sporting events were exactly how the battles were being seen. "Day by day the British public waits anxiously for the half-time scores and the close-of-play scores, as if Hutton were batting against Australia; and very disappointed is that public if a century is not scored." The first century, it went on, produced rather delighted surprise, but now we have come to reckon on one as a right. Oh a dull day, when a mere seventy-five or so raiders are shot down, the public attitude is that "Jerry is bowling for safety, and won't give our bats a chance". But *Flight* also had other points to make. In common with many others, it asked: "What is Göring trying to do?"

> The raids on Dover, Portsmouth, and Southampton can be understood, and so can the attacks on our aerodromes. But what profit do the Germans expect from bombing and machine-gunning suburbs? They can have no hope of beating this country to its knees by sheer terrorism, and the price which they pay in aeroplanes and air crews is high.

Thus did the magazine conclude that more and heavier attacks should be expected, until it began to dawn on the German High Command that the game was not worth the candle. In the meantime our fighter pilots were "not weary in well-doing".

Another viewpoint came from Devon Francis, the *AP* aviation editor. He had filed a widely syndicated report entitled "Furious air attacks may mean Hitler has dropped plans for land invasion". "Germany will try to bring the British to their knees by air attacks alone", Francis wrote. Having "borrowed liberally" from the Douhet doctrine, if the Germans could inflict enough damage on

England by air, no invasion would be necessary. Francis noted that the primary purpose of warfare was not to take and hold ground but only to destroy an enemy's will to resist. He recalled that during the 1914–18 war Germany itself scarcely felt the tread of an enemy soldier's boot, yet the German will to resist had been broken.

Here were the two approaches being discussed – one where the focus was on physical and the other on moral dominance. But the very fact that different commentators were drawing different conclusions betrayed difficulties in interpreting the German intent. On the receiving end, it was impossible to tell what they were. Shirer, on the other hand, was better positioned to divine what was going on. Still in northern France as guest of the Germans, he had been continuing his tour, then writing in his diary:

> In a couple of fields along the way this afternoon, we saw what looked under the camouflage like barges and pontoons loaded with artillery and tanks. But there was certainly not enough to begin an invasion of England with. However, two or three Germans in our party keep emphasising what we saw and hinting that there is much more that we didn't see. Maybe. But I'm suspicious. I think the Germans want to launch a scare story about an imminent invasion of Britain.[16]

It is unlikely to be a coincidence that, at the same time, General Halder was also in the area, making a tour of inspection. Possibly, that was the reason why Shirer was there, although he made no reference to Halder's presence. And the General was not impressed with what he saw. Travelling down the coast from Ostend, to Dunkirk, Calais, Boulogne and finally Dieppe, he noted that many of the approaches to the harbours were badly blocked, with sunken vessels obstructing the harbour basins. There were no ramps to load the barges and cranes would be needed, but many of these had been destroyed by the fleeing British. There was no evidence of repair work being carried out.[17]

Furthermore, the controversy over the invasion planning, precipitated on 12 July, was continuing. Having touched the very highest ranks in the German military, and engaged the *Führer* himself it had been triggered by Jodl. It was now addressed by his superior, Field Marshal Keitel, on Hitler's orders. Preparations for a landing in Lyme Bay "will be suspended in default of sufficient possibilities for protection", he ordered, although he then opened up a "possibility" of a crossing in the direction of Brighton, without heavy equipment. The issue still had not been resolved.[18]

Blockade activities continued. The Irish-owned cattle carrier *Lady Meath*, from Dublin *en route* Birkenhead, paused briefly off Holyhead to embark a Royal Navy team from the inspection vessel HMS *Manx Lad*. Both ships were ripped apart by an acoustic mine. This was the second such incident and marked another step in the use of so-called "influence" mines. Another type, the magnetic mine, had been deployed in British waters since November 1939. By a happy accident, one had been dropped on the mud flats at Shoeburyness on the night of 23 November. It had been successfully defused by Lieutenant Commander Ouvery and his Royal Navy team, allowing countermeasures to be developed. Now, a new threat had to be dealt with.

Against this background, the air war was being played out. The Germans, undeterred by their losses the previous day and buoyed by their own propaganda, were preparing to deliver what they believed to be the killer blow. Early morning mists shrouding the Channel, however, ensured it got off to a slow start. Not until nearly 11 a.m. was the first sign of a raid noted. Very quickly afterwards, attacks developed against Norfolk, Kent and the London area. Once again, airfields were the main targets, with Manston and West Malling hit. The latter took loads from eighteen bombers and was knocked out for four days.

Less than half an hour after these raids had withdrawn, giving scarcely time for the fighters to return and refuel, large formations were reported crossing the south and south-east coasts. With an estimated 300 enemy aircraft inbound, a total of 86 fighters were scrambled. The main raid, flying up the Thames Estuary apparently headed for Hornchurch, was blocked by Spitfires and harried all the way back to the French coast. For a while, all three southern groups of Fighter Command were engaged. Nevertheless, weight of numbers drove other enemy aircraft through. Their scattered bombing caused considerable damage. Among the areas hit were several London suburbs. Gravesend and Tilbury were attacked. Raiders also dropped bombs on Harwell and Farnborough airfields. In these raids, fifteen civilians were killed and another fifty-one injured.

At times, RAF fighters had difficulty containing the raids. In one episode near Deal, five British fighters were shot down. Worse was to follow. At exactly one o'clock, another large *Luftwaffe* formation crossed the eastern end of the Isle of Wight. On a signal from the lead aircraft, it split into four, the largest group heading for RAF Tangmere. The station's two Hurricane squadrons were scrambled, but they failed to prevent a "textbook assault" by a large group of

Stukas. Massive fires broke out and, in the midst of the mayhem, PO "Billy" Fiske – the first US volunteer to fly for the RAF – tried to nurse his damaged Hurricane onto the strip. The target for several strafing runs, his aircraft caught fire and only by tremendous feats of gallantry was the badly burned man extricated from his cockpit. He died the next day.

Six Blenheims were destroyed on the ground and four damaged, plus one Spitfire was written off. Seven Hurricanes were badly damaged and later also written off. A newly delivered Beaufighter, yet to be equipped with top secret radar for night interception, was slightly damaged. Fourteen servicemen and six civilians were killed. Forty-one were severely injured. The Stukas paid for their insolence, losing seven of their number, with three damaged. Other Stukas, however, broke through to the Ventnor Chain Home (CH) radar and further damaged the equipment. Another section attacked the naval station at Lee-on-Solent, destroying six naval aircraft and three hangars. Two Fleet Air Arm Blackburn Rocs were damaged.

Over the eastern outskirts of Southampton, three Hurricanes picked up these raiders. Led by Flight Lieutenant James Nicholson, the flight was bounced by a *staffel* of Me 109s leaving all three crippled. Nicholson remained with his burning aircraft long enough to shoot down an Me 110, only then baling out. Badly burned he took fire from Home Guard volunteers before landing, whence he was rushed to hospital. He later made a full recovery, but not before becoming Fighter Command's first and only Victoria Cross winner.

There were three more raids to come. These included a strafing run by Me 109s over Manston and attacks on Heathrow, Heston and Feltham airfields by a total of seventy-five Heinkels. More importantly, in terms of effect, was an attack by two bombers on Brize Norton. Using the now classic *ruse de guerre*, two Ju 88s joined the circuit with their wheels down as if to land, only cleaning up as they reached the perimeter of the airfield. They made for the hangars, dropping thirty-two bombs which destroyed forty-six fully fuelled Oxford trainers and damaged six others. Eleven Hurricanes in another hangar were also damaged.

Visiting No. 11 Group's operations room at Uxbridge was Churchill. He was able to watch the drama as it unfolded. On the receiving end of the attack, with only limited information, no one could possibly have fully evaluated or understood what was going on. But Churchill the showman was in charge. On leaving the operations room he told his military advisor, Major General Hastings Ismay,

"Don't speak to me. I have never been so moved". After several minutes of silence, he said: "Never in the field of human conflict has so much been owed by so many to so few". In four days time, that sentence was to be repeated in the House of Commons and relayed to the world.[19]

That day, by the Chiefs of Staff, Churchill was told that intelligence pointed to the continuance of preparations for invasion. But it was thought "probable" that Germany would not finally decide upon an invasion until the results of the present air attacks upon the United Kingdom had been appreciated.[20]

For the day, Fighter Command had good enough reason to be pleased. It had lost twenty-nine aircraft, some destroyed on the ground. But only twenty-three had actually been shot down. The *Luftwaffe* had lost forty-seven. In total, although the RAF had only written off thirty-eight combat aircraft, putting it ahead, the destroyed Oxfords brought the total to eighty-four, almost twice the *Luftwaffe* losses.

The pilot situation was not so good either. Since 10 July, Fighter Command had lost well over 200 front-line pilots, enough to fly most of the serviceable Spitfire inventory on any one day. The *Luftwaffe* had lost about a third the number of Me 109 pilots, with 46 lost in that most recent eight-day period. The exchange ratio was improving.

DAY 39 – SATURDAY 17 AUGUST 1940

General Halder, still in northern France, had been joined by Army chief von Brauchitsch for a staff conference, then to watch the first demonstration of beach assault craft, with a landing at Le Touquet carried out at regimental strength. Halder thought it went well, even though barge unloading had been "painfully slow", the beaches had been too soft, the barges had grounded too far out and there had been problems with the ramps.[21]

The morning fare for the British public was the previous day's aerial victories. The *Guardian* announced: "71 more raiders" knocked out. The *Express* claimed sixty-nine, with a loss of eighteen RAF fighters. Tellingly, the newspaper called the fighting round two of the "Air Battle of Britain", an acknowledgement that the air effort was only part of the show.

The *Daily Mirror* highlighted the raids on the London suburbs, as did Harold

Nicolson in his diary, noting that eighteen had been killed in Wimbledon. To the RAF, he awarded a "bag" of 75, and confided that:

for the moment everything is overshadowed by what seems to be the failure of the German air offensive against this island. They have done some damage here and there: they have killed and wounded many people, but they have not dealt us a really serious blow and our confidence rises.

However, Hitler was focusing on another aspect of the war. He pronounced a total blockade of the British Isles. "Today the fortress besieged is no longer Germany, but the British Isles", he wrote. "The failed British hunger blockade against German women and children is now opposed by Germany's total blockade of the British Isles which is herewith announced." This, Hitler added, represented "a further decisive step towards ending the war and eliminating the British rulers responsible for it". In the waters off England, the war at sea had "now begun in full violence".[22]

For all that, in the shooting war department, after the drama of the previous day, it was relatively quiet. One RAF Blenheim fighter was lost on a night landing accident and a Hurricane crashed after a fire in the air. Two Blenheims and a photo-reconnaissance Spitfire were lost. The Germans had a single-engined Arado 196 floatplane shot down by a British merchantman.

For small bands of men down on the ground, it was not going to be quiet for some time. They were the bomb disposal teams, who became a vital part of the battle. Their task was clearing up the ordnance that had failed to explode or where delayed action fuses had been fitted, sometimes in a deliberate attempt to kill those dealing with them. On this day, a team led by Lieutenant (Lt) Edward Reynolds had been called to deal with a 250kg unexploded bomb 17 ft down in the garden of a council house in the south of Bristol. The bomb had a new type of fuse and there were no details on how to neutralize it. Traffic was stopped and local residents evacuated. Reynolds got into the pit and removed the fuse. His actions "were risky and the merit of his actions was all the greater for the lack of exact knowledge of this type of fuse", said the citation for his George Cross.[23]

Completely invigorated by the upsurge in fighting, Duff Cooper addressed the nation after the BBC nine o'clock news. "This was to have been the week of the German victory", he crowed. "It has been the week of British victory instead." He also challenged Hitler to "keep his promise" on the invasion. "We should not have liked him to [come] before we were ready to receive him," Cooper said, "but we are quite ready to receive him now and we really shall be very disappointed if he does not turn up".

He was at pains to build on the myth of the "few", even though this group had yet to be defined by Churchill. "There is no terror in Great Britain today", he said. "Rather there is a longing that they [*Luftwaffe* bombers] shall come again in greater numbers in order that we may continue to take the fearful toll of them that we have already taken. If these air raids increasing in frequency and numbers are the prelude to invasion, then we can only say that the prelude has been a melancholy failure." Cooper went on to say:

> The day may come – and it may not be too far distant – when we as spectators shall again applaud the victory march through our streets of those who saved the world. The British people will have cheers for all as they march by – soldiers, sailors and civilians. But it may be that, when the survivors of the Royal Air Force come along, the cheers will be choked in the throats of the most enthusiastic; and remembering those who have not survived, and all we owe them, we shall fall in thankfulness upon our knees.[24]

With access to a comfortable and safe air-raid shelter, Cooper was in a good position to be so defiant. Others were less so. And as for the "survivors of the Royal Air Force", the High Command seemed bent on ensuring that they were kept to a minimum. This day saw the end of a drama which marked the first use of a Dornier 24 by the German air-sea rescue services. Produced under licence in Holland, the production line had been captured during the occupation and the aircraft had been requisitioned. On the previous day, an He 59 had gone to the aid of the crew of an He 111 downed in the North Sea, only itself to be shot down by an RAF Blenheim. In a Force 6 sea, the Do 24 was the only type that could attempt a landing to effect a rescue, which it did. Badly damaged and unable to take off again, it still managed to recover the other crews. It finally sank under tow as it approached its base – but not before all personnel had scrambled to safety.[25]

These events highlighted that strange lacuna in British planning. RAF pilots were not going to see dedicated rescue amphibians for at least a year. Many were to drown for the lack of them.

DAY 40 – SUNDAY 18 AUGUST 1940

The *Sunday Express* was celebrating "twelve hours without a single air raider", its front page recording an Air Ministry communiqué which had announced the previous night, "no enemy attacks were made in the country in the twelve hours from sunrise today (5.50 am)". It was the calm before the storm. On this day, 2,200 *Luftwaffe* aircrew were to fly 850 sorties. The RAF was to respond by having 600 airmen fly 927 sorties.

But, before even a shot had been fired on this day, the paper had decided that 11–18 August was the "First week of Blitzkrieg". We have had just a week of it. It is not new to us – in theory. We saw it on the screen in *The Shape of Things to Come*, heard it from the stage in *Dark Horizon*, newspapers told us what it was like in Shanghai, the newsreels showed us it in Barcelona. Now it is here (remember though) eleven months later than we expected it. Sunday, 11 August 1940 is the date historians will mark down as the beginning of the *Blitzkrieg* over Britain. And Britain had a triple defence to meet it: "a superb Air Force, a powerful artillery to clear the skies, a people ready to suffer everything".

With considerable prescience, the paper then explored the date options for the invasion. The attempt, the paper argued, would most likely be made with barges and lighters towed by suitable craft, so it was "imperative" that the sea should be calm. The best combination of tides and moon fell between 18 and 23 September, when it thought the invasion should fall.

The air action of Britain this day started with a morning reconnaissance flight. Spitfires shot it down. From then on, it was a day of massed formations. At one time every serviceable Spitfire and Hurricane in No. 11 Group area was either flying or at readiness. It was subsequently to be called "the hardest day" and gave some credence to the assertions that the RAF was being specifically targeted.[26]

The first wave of attacks was directed at Biggin Hill and Kenley airfields. German tactics comprised simultaneous high and low-level attacks, escorted by Me 109s to draw away the RAF fighters. Among those sent aloft to meet this threat were Hurricanes from No. 501 Sqn but before they had a chance to intercept the raiders, they were bounced by Me 109s led by ace Gerhard Schopfel. Five were disposed of. Famously, Schopfel shot down four of them.

In order to raid Biggin Hill, nine low-level Do 17s should have met up with thirty Ju 88s bombing from high level, but the formations missed a rendezvous over France. Thus, the Dorniers had forged on alone, to be met by Hurricanes from No 32 Sqn and Spitfires from No. 610 Sqn. For the Germans, it was not a happy meeting. Two went down immediately, two crashed into the Channel (although their crews were rescued) and three had to force land in France. Of the two that actually got back to base, one carried its dead pilot and was flown by the flight engineer. The damage done to Biggin Hill was slight.

The raid on Kenley was more successful as the high-low combination came together. Fighters were up to intercept both, although No. 111 Sqn was unable to engage until the low-flying Dorniers had cleared the airfield. Bombs destroyed hangars, the equipment stores, ten Hurricanes and two Blenheims. Communications and services were cut. Twelve personnel were killed and another twenty injured. Several raiders made for Croydon, only minutes away as the Dornier flies, bombing a hangar, destroying one Hurricane and damaging another. Other aircraft bombed West Malling, hitting two hangars and destroying three Lysanders.

Disrupted communications created serious problems for No. 11 Group controllers, who lost track of their own aircraft for about two hours. Fortunately, the focus of the action was moving westwards. Eighty-five Stukas, plus a separate raid of twenty-five Ju 88s, approached the Isle of Wight, escorted by 157 Me 109s. Fearing that their fighters might be caught on the ground, controllers ordered all southern sector aircraft to take off and orbit their airfields. The effect was to allow the bombers free access to their targets, the naval air stations at Ford and Gosport, the Coastal Command airfield at Thorney Island and the radar site at Poling, near Littlehampton.

The Ju 88s caused considerable damage at Ford and Gosport. But Stukas forming up for an attack on the Poling radar were picked off by Hurricanes which caught them at their most vulnerable point, as they entered their dives. Survivors formed up with the Stukas that had attacked Ford and Thorney Island. They were savaged by Hurricanes and Spitfires from three squadrons, while other Spitfires held escorting Me 109s at bay. Some sixteen Stukas were shot down. Two crashed on their way home and two more were damaged. Elsewhere, a further seventeen had been lost and five more damaged, mostly to the guns of fighters. This was a decisive defeat for the Stuka.

Some mystery attended the reasons for the *Luftwaffe* attacking the airfields they did. None were operational fighter stations and it was assumed that they were the targets. However, there is evidence that bomber and other stations were deliberately targeted, the former in an attempt to reduce RAF "nuisance" raids on *Luftwaffe* airfields. Unwittingly at Ford, though, the Germans had knocked out part of the "Digger" Aitken unofficial air-sea rescue service. The station was home to the Walrus amphibians of No. 751 Naval Air Sqn. Already in the process of "dispersal", the squadron was moved to Scotland to protect it from the bombing, making the aircraft unavailable for Channel rescues.[27]

Still the action was not over. At three-thirty, a dozen Me 109s strafed Manston destroying two Spitfires, killing one man and injuring fifteen Then, near five o'clock in the evening, eight raids comprising about two hundred and fifty aircraft crossed the Essex coast via the Blackwater and Thames Estuaries, headed for the airfields at North Weald and Hornchurch. With No. 12 Group providing four squadrons to patrol their bases, Park alerted thirteen of his own squadrons and sent up four to meet the enemy. Spirited fighting failed to stop the bombers. Soon, over sixty Hurricanes were engaged, backed by more to the south. Fate then intervened. Dense, low cloud forced the Germans to retire. The daylight battle was over.

That same weather system kept most of Bomber Command home that night. But it did not stop the *Luftwaffe* mounting raids in South Wales, RAF Sealand (Chester), Birmingham and Wolverhampton. An unexploded bomb at Hook, Hampshire, blew up, killing five members of a bomb disposal squad.

For the Germans in particular, it had been a long and dangerous day. Fighters had not been their only hazard. This was no longer the beginning of June, when the Anti-Aircraft Command's only contribution had been to shoot down a lone Battle, killing two of its crew. Anti-Aircraft Command was now a major player. The Command was acquiring new equipment and capabilities. Defending Kenley had been experimental rocket launchers, known as Parachute and Cable (PAC) launchers.[28] Together with the guns, these were said to have accounted for two Dorniers, although one had probably been brought down by an ancient Lewis gun. Nevertheless, countrywide, the day had proved the best so far for the Command.

Nor was this a static situation. Kenley would by October have acquired four three-inch guns to add to its four modern Bofors guns. Nationally, the stock of

Bofors would increase by 70 per cent through the course of the battle, to 466 by the first week in September. A quarter of all those guns would stretch in a belt from Sussex to Surrey. Improvements in detection, prediction and fire control – and ammunition – were making anti-aircraft artillery a formidable daylight weapon.[29]

As for Fighter Command, it had lost forty-three aircraft, including those destroyed on the ground and one tragically shot down by anti-aircraft fire at Kenley. A further twenty-nine, none of them fighters, had been destroyed on the ground during attacks on Gosport, Ford and Thorney Island, bringing the total British losses to seventy-nine. With those lost at Croydon and West Malling, the number reached seventy-six. The *Luftwaffe* had lost sixty. It would be difficult to argue that this had been a victory for the RAF.

DAY 41 – MONDAY 19 AUGUST 1940

Doubtless unaware of the real situation, the media had a field day. "At least 115 more!" the *Daily Express* crowed, the headline spread across its front page. It claimed a mere sixteen RAF fighters lost, with eight of the pilots safe. The *Daily Mirror* was claiming 140 enemy aircraft down, also to sixteen lost. The exaggeration was so extreme as to demonstrate vividly that the propaganda had become a central part of the battle.

Inside Lord Beaverbrook's *Express*, however, the editorial was complaining about Duff Cooper again, and more censorship. "How long is this gagging to go on?" it asked. The grief this time was US correspondents having their cables held up, supposedly to prevent the news getting back to Germany via New York that "the sirens were sounding in London". As a result, American editors were being forced to use German propaganda. Said the *Express*: "It is vitally important to the future of our cause that the Americans hear how we fare now. The reporters should be given full liberty to send descriptive material without delay".

Cooper seemed undisturbed by this latest attack, and more interested in his ideas for a future world. His paper had been reviewed by the War Cabinet on 26 July. He had discussed it further with colleagues and now he was suggesting a Committee of Ministers to take his ideas further. With himself in the chair, it would look at the possibility of setting up a post-war "international system in Europe", based upon the principle of federation. It would also look at social reform in the UK.[30]

As to the shooting war, a frontal system was moving in from the Atlantic, across the British Isles and into Europe. The bad weather that had closed down operations in the early evening of the previous day was going to dominate for some days. There was going to be no serious flying for a while. Fighter Command still lost six aircraft, though, and Bomber Command nine. With RAF losses totalling fifteen, the *Luftwaffe* suffered eight.

Stocktaking and retrenchment were the order of the day. But the style and mood of the opposing sides was very different. Göring summoned his commanders to Karin Hall. Adolf Galland, a fighter ace heavily involved in the battle, was ordered to attend. To him, the estate presented "a picture of peaceful serenity". He also noticed that the war had hardly made any difference to daily life at home. Having come straight out of a battle for life and death, he was not best pleased with the, "could-not-care-less" attitude at home and the general lack of interest in the war. He "guessed fairly accurately" that the battle on the Channel was of decisive importance to the continuance and the final outcome of the struggle, although he conceded: "Naturally we had no insight into the ramifications of this war".

Galland and another "ace", Werner Mölders, were given their own *Gruppen* (equivalent to an RAF wing) to command. But there was no praise. The *Reichsmarschall* was convinced that his fighter pilots' lack of commitment was robbing him of success. Nevertheless, he accepted a reduced role for Stukas and the Me 110s. And he had news of a new strategy. The costly daylight attacks were to be replaced by night raids. In daylight, bombers were to be used as "bait", sent up in just sufficient numbers to draw fighters into battle. Restrictions on bombing civilian targets – except London and Liverpool, which required Göring's personal permission – were to be lifted. The absolute priority was to damage Fighter Command.

Reflecting on the battle, Galland in his autobiography referred to the third phase fought between 8 August and 7 September. In this action the bombers returned to the task allocated to them by Douhet: the enemy air force must be wiped out while still grounded. But Douhet, he said, envisaged for this task waves and waves of bombers, darkening the sky with their multitudes. He would have been gravely disappointed to see the realization of his strategic dream as it was put into practice over England at the time.[31]

The commander with the most immediate responsibility for frustrating Göring's ambitions was Keith Park. His meeting was in the austere surrounds of Hillingdon House. The contrast could not be more extreme. At the very centre of events, fighting the battle day-on-day, Park was the self-contained professional. "Survival is everything", he told his controllers. The battle would be won if Fighter Command could stay in being until the autumn, when it would be too late for the Germans to invade. But he was worried about the number of pilots being lost over the sea in hot pursuit of retreating aircraft. Pilots were to be vectored to large enemy formations over land or within gliding distance of the coast – except for shipping and convoy protection in the Thames Estuary.[32]

One crucial issue emerging at this time was that fighter losses could no longer be made good from production. The combined weekly output of single-engined types was a little over a hundred. The RAF was eating into its reserves. A potential pilot shortage, though, was a bigger problem. With over 200 pilots lost from the start of the battle, replacements had numbered about 60. These newcomers, "though of equal spirit, as yet possessed only a tithe of the fighting skill of their predecessors". Volunteers from Lysander and Battle Squadrons, from Allied Forces, and those about to embark on the final stages of bomber and coastal training, were rushed through specially shortened fighter courses.

There was also the strain on those who survived: the long hours at dispersal, the constant flying at high altitudes (two or three sorties a day was normal, six or seven not uncommon), the repeated combats, the parachute descents, the forced landings. The tiredness of those who had been most actively engaged was a factor which could be neglected no more than the casualties.

General Sir Hugh Elles of the Ministry of Home Security seemed unconcerned with these details. He had spent some of his valuable time responding to the concerns of the citizens and burghers of Swansea about air raids, drafting a carefully phrased letter to Hugh Dowding, as the person in charge of the air defences. He referred to the importance of the docks in Swansea and "the great refinery of Llandarcy" close by. He also asked for the installation of more barrage balloons on South Wales, "more for psychological reasons than anything else". In a dusty response, Dowding was to tell Elles: "I have no balloons for psychological use and am having to refuse physiological claims".[33]

That very afternoon in South Wales, three Ju 88s sped low-level across the coast. Roaring up the Milford Sound, they lobbed their bombs into an oil depot.

This was not Llandarcy. Its turn was to come. This was the Pembroke Docks complex, the largest Admiralty fuel storage site in Britain. Two tanks received direct hits and eight of the fifteen on the site exploded and burst into a flaming inferno.

In the immediate locality, there was chaos. Shrieking mothers, some hysterical, were frantically looking for children. From a pig farm close to the depot, terrified pigs fled squealing down the road. Firemen, soon on the scene, found jet black smoke churning across the carriageway in such dense clouds it was impossible to see. The blaze was creating a deafening roaring noise. Fire fighters had to "shield their faces from the scorching heat".

The conflagration became the largest "single-seat" fire the UK has ever known – even to this day. In the three weeks before it was finally extinguished, it consumed 33 million gallons of fuel oil, during which time 650 firemen were engaged. On 22 August, 5 firemen from Cardiff were killed in an explosion while fighting the fire. Twenty-eight were injured. Of those who were about to become "the few", there had been so sign. The depot had been completely undefended.[34]

8.

Redefining the war

In the last war millions of men fought by hurling enormous masses of steel at one another. "Men and shells" was the cry, and prodigious slaughter was the consequence. In this war nothing of this kind has yet appeared. It is a conflict of strategy, of organisation, of technical apparatus, of science, mechanics, and morale.

Winston Churchill, House of Commons, 20 August 1940[1]

What started off as a "war of peoples" was now to be redefined by Churchill as the war of the "few", a war fought by a technocratic élite, to whom the many owed "so much". The idea of setting out "war aims" was then rejected by the Prime Minister. His emphasis was on breaking the Nazi tyranny. Concealed by the censor's crayon, however, the war was being redefined in other ways, while events were leading inexorably to the Blitz.

DAY 42 – TUESDAY 20 AUGUST 1940

Despite the bad weather, Heinkels bombed Liverpool. At least 30 tracks were reported over Lincolnshire and Nottingham and a number of RAF bomber airfields were attacked as they lit flarepaths for returning aircraft. Sheffield, Nottingham, Hull, Derby and Leicester were raided by small numbers of bombers, causing 112 casualties.

Seven Fairey Battles of No. 12 Sqn had also been out, attacking invasion shipping in Boulogne. Had they each delivered their 1,500lb bomb load, this would still have been a light raid. As it was, because of the haze, the glare of the German searchlights and the heavy anti-aircraft fire, four aircraft failed to find suitable targets. One returned with engine trouble and another with a bomb-rack snag. Yet another was shot down, the crew taken prisoner. Despite this, readers of the morning's *Express* were regaled with the squadron's exploits.

Astute readers might have wondered why it was still making attacks. A raid the previous Saturday had "virtually completed the destruction of the commercial port". Naval and air bases had been left in flames.

It was Churchill's big day in the Commons. But in a remarkable contrast with the extravagant ceremony attendant on Hitler's speaking engagements, he had to wait his turn in an unadorned debating chamber. There were oral questions. Sir William Davison asked why there was still a great shortage of coal in many provincial towns. The Mines Secretary, David Grenfell, wearily answered that, in view of the heavy demand for coal stocking, some delays were inevitable.[2] The crisis of the previous winter was still casting its shadow.

When he stood up to speak, Churchill ruminated on the nature of the war. But no longer was it his "war of peoples" of 14 July. After his visits to Fighter Command HQ, having been immersed in the technology, the planning and the statistics, it had become "a conflict of strategy, of organisation, of technical apparatus, of science, mechanics", and only then of morale. He talked about the "great air battle" in progress, telling the House that it was too soon "to attempt to assign limits either to its scale or to its duration". The Prime Minister also asserted that, in France, British fighter aircraft had been inflicting a loss of "two or three to one" on the Germans. At Dunkirk, this had been about three or four to one. In this current battle a larger ratio was expected, and that expectation "has certainly come true". It must also be remembered, he said:

> that all the enemy machines and pilots which are shot down over our island, or over the seas which surround it, are either destroyed or captured; whereas a considerable proportion of our machines, and also of our pilots, are saved, and soon again in many cases come into action.

These two last assertions illustrated the fragility of the Prime Minister's grasp of events. His exchange ratios were based on inflated kill figures, ignoring the Bomber and Coastal Command losses, and aircraft destroyed on the ground. But the figures for losses, from the start of the battle to the end of this day, adding two RAF and four *Luftwaffe* losses for the day, gave a total of 602 British aircraft lost, with the German figure standing at 585. As to pilots being "saved", only the previous day Park had expressed his concern at the number of pilots being lost. Dowding was later to write:

It might also be assumed that all German crews who were in aircraft brought down during the Battle were permanently lost to the Luftwaffe because the fighting took place on our side of the Channel. Such an assumption would not be literally true, because the Germans succeeded in rescuing a proportion of their crews from the sea by means of rescue boats, floats and aircraft.[3]

Churchill was considerably less knowledgeable about some technical aspects of the campaign than one might imagine. Lord Halifax, in his dealings with the Prime Minister often described him as talking "rot".

Nevertheless, Churchill was extremely well informed about aircraft recovery, which he described as a "vast and admirable system of salvage". He was referring to the Civilian Repair Organization (CRO), set up by his friend Lord Beaverbrook. This was indeed a superb system, which could take aircraft normally considered beyond repair and ensure their "speediest return" to the fighting line. In July 1940, 40 per cent of aircraft reaching fighter squadrons had come from this source.[4] And it was such considerations that brought Churchill to the best-remembered part of his speech, when he said:

> The gratitude of every home in our Island, in our Empire, and indeed throughout the world, except in the abodes of the guilty, goes out to the British airmen who, undaunted by odds, unwearied in their constant challenge and mortal danger, are turning the tide of the world war by their prowess and by their devotion. Never in the field of human conflict was so much owed by so many to so few.

Crucially, Churchill did not refer here to Fighter Command, or even pilots. He spoke of "British airmen". Only then did he declare: "All hearts go out to the fighter pilots, whose brilliant actions we see with our own eyes day after day". But, he added:

> we must never forget that all the time, night after night, month after month, our bomber squadrons travel far into Germany, find their targets in the darkness by the highest navigational skill, aim their attacks, often under the heaviest fire, often with serious loss, with deliberate careful discrimination, and inflict shattering blows upon the whole of the technical and war-making structure of the Nazi power. On no part of the Royal Air Force does the weight of the war fall more heavily than on the daylight bombers who will play an invaluable part in the case of invasion and whose unflinching zeal it has been necessary in the meanwhile on numerous occasions to restrain.

Not in any way could Churchill's "few" be taken to be an exclusive celebration of fighter pilots. The passage gave far more credit to the bombing effort. It afforded one "of the most certain, if not the shortest of all the roads to victory". Nor was this the speech of a prime minister expecting imminent invasion, leading a nation fighting for its life, its very survival apparently hanging on the slender thread of a few squadrons of Spitfires and Hurricanes.

Thus, time and again the actions, the demeanour, do not match the words. And behind the scenes, R. A. Butler, under-secretary at the Foreign Office, was briefing newspaperman Cecil King, telling him that the invasion was "hooey". There had never been, he said, sufficient concentrations of troops in northern France. Hitler's troops were going east. They were going to attack Russia.[5]

The war, of course, had not stopped for Churchill's speech. A bomber formation was intercepted over the Thames Estuary and a spirited fight developed late in the day when Polish fliers from the newly commissioned No. 302 Sqn shot down a Ju 88 off the Yorkshire coast at Withernsea. The evening saw a raid on Newton Abbot. This small Devon town just north of the naval base of Plymouth was regarded by the Germans as an important strategic railway junction. Three aircraft bombed the station and the streets surrounding it. Then they strafed the area and attacked a Plymouth train. Severe damage was caused to the station with fifteen locomotives, fifty-two coaches and twenty-two goods wagons damaged. Fifteen people were killed and sixty were seriously injured. Chased by two Hurricanes, the attacking aircraft fled, flying so low that they had to climb to clear the river bridge as they made their escape.[6]

The day saw two Fighter Command aircraft lost, and eight *Luftwaffe* losses, including a seaplane lost in a storm and a Condor which went missing during a sortie to Northern Ireland.

DAY 43 – WEDNESDAY 21 AUGUST 1940

The newspapers gave Churchill's speech prominent coverage, but the *Daily Mirror* homed in on his admission that he had been asked for a better definition of Britain's war aims. He had told the Commons that while the battle raged and the war was still perhaps in its earlier stage, he did not think it wise, "to embark upon elaborate speculations about the future shape which should be given to Europe or the new securities which must be arranged to spare mankind the miseries of a third World War".

The ground, said Churchill, was not new. It had been frequently traversed and explored, and many ideas were held about it in common by all good men, and all free men. "But before we can undertake the task of rebuilding we have not only to be convinced ourselves, but we have to convince all other countries that the Nazi tyranny is going to be finally broken." To Priestley, and for that matter Duff Cooper, this was a snub. But there was something else. Having shared with Priestley the "war of peoples" concept, Churchill had turned his back on it and redefined the war. It had become, after all, a war of princes, of technocratic élites.

In an implied rebuke to the Prime Minister, though, "George" Strube in the *Express* political cartoon depicted his trademark "little man" holding a large bunch of flowers, labelled "bouquet". Surrounded by a circle of eleven men, each in different guises – from airman to anti-aircraft gunner and ARP warden – he was puzzling who to give it to. And well he might. Each man was pointing his neighbour. So much for "the few" – here was a graphic depiction of the many.

Churchill had other things on his mind by now, having been made aware of growing US scepticism about the scale of the RAF victories. Writing to Archie Sinclair, he told him, "The important thing is to bring the German aircraft down and win the battle". American correspondents and the American public "will find out soon enough when the German air attack is plainly shown to be repulsed". Separately, he wrote to General Ismay, commenting that "The prospects of invasion are rapidly receding".[7]

Air activity, hampered by poor weather, was relatively light. And the *Luftwaffe* was undergoing a reorganization, transfering Me 109s from Cherbourg to the Pas de Calais where their short range could be better exploited. Göring visited the headquarters of the Second Air Fleet for the first time. While he was there, a convoy running the Straits was shelled by the newly installed heavy guns at Cap Gris Nez. Sixteen aircraft then attacked the convoy. No losses or damage were recorded, although the attrition of the merchant fleet continued elsewhere. The British steamer *Letty* was lost *en route* to Ireland, from an "unknown agent". In a raid on Southampton Dock, the hulk *Kendal* was sunk, together with a hopper barge. The net layer *Kylemore* was sunk by German bombing off Harwich, the steamer *Alacrity* was damaged at Falmouth and the trawler *Wolseley* off the Pembrokeshire coast.

On the domestic front, Home Intelligence found that the Prime Minister's speech had been extremely well received. In London, where morale was said to be "excellent", it was thought to be "completely right", particularly "his reference to the RAF". It "epitomizes the feeling of the country", one respondent had said. Confidence had greatly increased since the beginning of the war.

And that war went on. Ju 88s machine-gunned firemen battling the fire at Pembroke Docks, now in its third day. At RAF St Eval, the sector station for Cornwall, three intruders dropped bombs and incendiaries, and then machine-gunned dispersed aircraft. Five Junkers Ju 88s then bombed the Radio Direction Finding station on St Mary's, Isles of Scilly. On the east coast, a formation of Dorniers was spotted. Intercepting aircraft claimed several kills. The former Butlin's holiday camp at Skegness, requisitioned by the Royal Navy, was bombed. There were injuries and a new recruit was killed. The mood was lightened, however, when German radio claimed that HMS *Royal Arthur*, the official name for the camp, had been sunk with great loss of life.[8]

In 599 sorties, Fighter Command lost four aircraft, three destroyed on the ground at St Eval. A Hampden lost on operations brought the RAF total losses to five, against the *Luftwaffe* loss of thirteen bombers.

DAY 44 – THURSDAY 22 AUGUST 1940

Air Secretary Archibald Sinclair made the pages of the *Daily Mirror* with an explanation of how enemy air losses were computed "so that public confidence in the British announcements may be maintained". Having so done, he declared that "It could be asserted with confidence that the reports of our pilots tended to err on the side of understatement. They were on their honour".

The *Daily Express* carried a large advert for War Bonds, with a pull-quote from the Prime Minister: "Never in the field of human conflict … ". Said the copy: "You can back our airmen by buying … ".

Paul Mallon, a widely syndicated Washington columnist, found his way into several US newspapers with yet more rumours of Nazi peace offers. To the latest were attached "surprisingly moderate" terms, he wrote: Churchill was to be replaced by Beaverbrook, and the UK would join in an economic alliance with Germany, against Russia and Japan.[9]

The *Luftwaffe* attacked more convoys in the Straits of Dover. Bombs were again augmented by the shore batteries. When they failed to hit any ships, they shelled the town. This would be the start of a four-year bombardment which recorded 2,226 shells landing within the town boundaries. Many more fell in the surrounding countryside, the harbour waters and the Straits. Essentially a front-line town, the civilian population dropped from 40,500 in early 1939 to an estimated 12,000.

Dover was not alone in its torment. During the day, there were more raids on RAF Manston, this coastal station being attacked so frequently that it was in the process of being abandoned. That night, Aberdeen, sites in Yorkshire, Hampshire, South Wales and Bristol were hit. Filton airfield was also bombed, as raiders targeted the Bristol Aircraft Company works. And despite Sinclair's defence of the scoring system, the British claimed seven enemy aircraft downed, for the loss of two of their own. The actual figures were four – against nine RAF aircraft lost. Ironically, on this one day, the Germans did not exaggerate. They claimed seven RAF aircraft for the loss of six of theirs.[10]

As the toll of RAF pilots and other aircrew lost at sea steadily mounted, belated moves were made to improve air–sea rescue. Then Deputy Chief of the Air Staff, Air Vice-Marshal Harris (in time, to take over Bomber Command), chaired an Air Ministry meeting with a view to setting up a formal service. The "skeleton" Coastal Command service would be combined with the boats of the Auxiliary Naval Patrol. RAF launches would be placed under the operational control of the navy, while the RAF would control air searches. The twelve Lysanders supposedly borrowed from Army Co-operation Command were kept on.[11]

In Paris, German Army chief von Brauchitsch was still fighting his corner for a broad-front landing. He was trying to broker an agreement that an assault unit of about 7,000 men should be conveyed to the Brighton area in 200 fast motorboats and 100 motor sailing vessels. Support would be given by 4,500 men of the 7th Parachute Division, who were to take up blocking positions on the South Downs against expected British counterattacks.[12]

DAY 45 – FRIDAY 23 AUGUST 1940

Catching up on recent events, the *War Illustrated* magazine published a feature on what it described as the "first phase" of the "Air Battle of Britain". This was taken to be 8–13 August, the opening shot being the attack on the "Peewit" convoy. The qualifier "Air" was still in common use, even by Churchill, acknowledging that the air fighting was only part of the wider battle.

The *Daily Express* reported the bombardment of Dover. As German guns had fired, RAF bombers had roared into action. The paper's reporter had seen "great red glows in the sky then, low down on the water line, fires that lit the French coastline". Watching every flash over there, he wrote, "We decided the RAF boys were having a successful trip". But no gun was ever damaged in an air raid. The bombing was singularly ineffective, while the guns proved virtually useless as anti-shipping weapons. Both sides overstated the capabilities of their weapons.

A far greater cause of alarm in official circles was an attack on Convoy OA 203 in the Moray Firth, when the steamers *Llanishen* and *Makalla* were sunk by air-dropped torpedoes. When the New Zealand-owned RMS *Remuera* was also torpedoed three days later, the worst fears were realized. The Germans had developed a reliable air-launched weapon. No details of it were released to the media. Not even the War Cabinet was told.[13]

In the War Cabinet this day, Duff Cooper made some progress in getting his "war aims" committee approved. The Cabinet agreed that there was a growing demand for "some statement of what we were fighting for". We must make our aims clear, not merely to our own people, but also to the peoples of Europe whom we were trying to free. A time would come, members said, to "put across" our conception of the "new Europe".

Unusually, Churchill spoke to the item and his comments were also recorded in detail. Some of the points he thought should be included were that, in addition to the five Great Powers of Europe, there should be three groups of smaller states – in northern Europe, in middle Europe, and in the Balkans. He wanted them "linked together in some kind of Council of Europe". There should be a court to which all justiciable disputes should be referred. Remarkably, he also suggested the establishment of an international air force.[14]

Outside, one particular national air force continued its activities. Explosive and incendiary bombs, it was claimed, were dropped for the first time in the London area. There was some confusion about this as the main casualty was the Alcazar cinema in lower Edmonton. This was regarded as North London, but was administratively part of the Middlesex county area.[15]

The *Luftwaffe* also mounted small-scale raids elsewhere. Single aircraft were sometimes deployed. This had the effect of keeping the RAF unsettled, forcing

Fighter Command to fly 482 sorties for very little reward. After nightfall, twenty-two inland raids were counted, mainly directed at South Wales, Bristol, Birmingham and the north. In Bridlington, a café was hit trapping the people inside. Five German losses were recorded. One Hurricane was written off in a night raid on Croydon. Two others were slightly damaged. Bomber Command lost one aircraft as well.

DAY 46 – SATURDAY 24 AUGUST 1940

The weather had finally cleared enough to permit a relatively high level of air operations, although a morning haze delayed flying in some areas. It did not stop an early raid on Great Yarmouth.

As so often, though, the Channel area became the focus of intensive activity. First, compact enemy formations, comprising some forty Dorniers and Ju 88s, bombed the residential area of Dover. As this was happening, another five formations – none of them less than twenty aircraft – crossed the coast at different points, intercepted only by two British aircraft. The raiders limited themselves to deep reconnaissance, dropping only a small number of bombs near Canterbury. Then another formation began to head towards the English coast. The main force, comprising more than twenty He 111s, skirted Dover, bombing Ramsgate and the local airport heavily. It was the town's heaviest raid of the war, killing twenty-nine and injuring over fifty, ten seriously.[16]

In what some say was a separate raid, RAF Manston was hit by about twenty Junkers bombers protected by a similar number of fighters. The airfield was badly damaged. Living quarters were wrecked, all communications were cut and a large number of unexploded bombs made the administration areas unusable. Effectively, the station had been rendered useless for operations other than serving as a forward refuelling airfield and an emergency landing ground.

One of the units deployed from Manston was No. 264 Sqn, flying Defiants. By the end of the day, it had lost five aircraft with another seriously damaged. Three complete crews had been killed. One gunner died from his wounds. The squadron's major losses occurred fending off a raid at their home base which, with North Weald, also received attention from the *Luftwaffe*. Concurrently with the south coast attacks, a large raid was despatched to targets north of the estuary. North Weald took 150–200 bombs from nearly fifty Dorniers and

Heinkels, escorted by Me 110s. Living quarters were badly damaged, the boiler room was knocked out and nine people were killed. Ten were wounded.

In what was to have serious long-term repercussions, squadrons from No. 12 Group, under the command of Air Vice-Marshal Trafford Leigh-Mallory, had been called upon to provide cover. But what became known as the Duxford Wing – comprising multiple squadrons assembled into one formation before being committed to battle – arrived too late to have any useful effect. The performance of the wing, and the very concept, was to fuel acrimonious and prolonged disputes in Fighter Command.[17]

While sector stations were being attacked, an estimated at "fifty plus" raiders approached from the Cherbourg area. The main force skirted the Isle of Wight and made for Portsmouth at about 15,000, evading the British fighters ordered up to intercept. They had been wrongly positioned by their controllers.

In the Prince's Theatre, close to the centre of town, scores of children were settling down to a matinee. Tragically, the information provided by the radar station at Ventnor on the Isle of Wight had degraded, so the destination of the raid was not picked up and no warning was given. In the space of five minutes, the Germans dropped sixty-five 250kg and 500kg bombs. The theatre was all but reduced to rubble. Eight children were killed and seventeen were injured. Bombs fell indiscriminately on shops and houses across the southern half of the city. Many people were caught in the open unable to reach shelter. Several Anderson shelters were blown apart by the force of the explosions. A number of trench shelters suffered near-misses, and collapsed despite being reinforced with concrete slabs.[18]

Then the bombers targeted the dockyard. The destroyer *Acheron* had her stern blown off. Two ratings were killed and three were wounded. The destroyer *Bulldog*, moored alongside, was damaged by splinters. Her commanding officer was mortally wounded. The French torpedo boat *Flore* suffered severe damage to its bridge from falling masonry. HMS *Vernon*, the Navy's mine and torpedo centre, was badly damaged. By now, many had reached shelter – and did not get a chance to regret it. An air-raid shelter took a direct hit, killing 24 and wounding 42 dockyard workers. In all, from this raid, 143 city residents and workers died.

Rumours about the widespread loss of life in the city and dockyards led to a belief, absurd though it might have been, that German aircrews were

deliberately aiming their bombs at individual shelters. For some time afterwards, people were afraid to go into the shelters during alerts. [19]

With nightfall, areas in London and suburbs were attacked. Bombing was
also reported in Cannonbury Park, Highbury Park, Leyton, Wood Green,
Stepney, Islington, Enfield, Hampton Court, Millwall and others. The bomb in
the Hampton Court area completely destroyed a house. For the first time, the
City of London was bombed. St Giles' Church in Cripplegate, at the heart of the
City, took a bomb in the forecourt. It did little damage but knocked the statue
of Milton off its plinth. The poet was buried in the church and this event roused
indignation worldwide.

A large fire was started at Fore Street spreading to London Wall. Neill
Warehouse, West India Dock was badly damaged by fire. In the early hours, the
Imperial Tobacco factory and Carter Patterson's works in Goswell Road were
also fired. Two hundred pumps were mobilized but, with several unexploded
bombs reported, the area had to be evacuated and kept clear until midday on
25 August.

Seemingly at random, other suburbs were raided: Malden, Coulsdon,
Feltham, Kingston, Banstead and Epsom. In Birmingham, the Nuffield and
Dunlop Factories were bombed just after midnight. The Castle Bromwich
Spitfire factory at Erdington was hit, and so was the Moss Gear Company. The
main railway line was knocked out between Cardiff and west Wales after a train
was bombed at Cardiff. A gun site at Datchet, Buckinghamshire, was bombed
and ammunition blown up. Residential areas in Hull were hit and RAF Driffield
was bombed again. Further north still, bombers hit Leeds. Two houses were
wrecked and a Sunday school damaged. Bombs were also dropped in nine
north-eastern locations, including Newcastle and West Hartlepool. Minelaying
was reported off Flamborough Head.

This day was regarded by many as the start of the third phase of the
Battle of Britain, when the *Luftwaffe* concentrated on eliminating Fighter
Command. Between 24 August and 6 September, the "scales tilted against
Fighter Command", Churchill later wrote: "During these crucial days the
Germans had continuously applied powerful forces against the airfields of
South and South-east England. Their object was to break down the day fighter
defence of the capital, which they were impatient to attack".[20]

Fighter Command lost twenty-three aircraft on the day, including two

Hurricanes shot down by "friendly" anti-aircraft fire. Remarkably, only four pilots were killed or missing. Two were seriously injured. Four "twins" were lost, bringing total losses to twenty-seven. The *Luftwaffe* lost thirty-two aircraft, including twenty-four Me 109s. Twelve of their single-engined fighter pilots were killed, missing or taken captive. The balance of advantage went to the RAF. But for the Defiant losses, it would have been even more favourable. However, for two air armies supposedly locked in a fight to the death, the losses were not extravagant.

DAY 47 – SUNDAY 25 AUGUST 1940

"The City Bombed" blared the banner headline in the *Sunday Express*. In a "midnight raid" the sky over London had been "lit up by fire". The thud of a "screaming bomb" had been heard by watchers round St Paul's. The papers also recorded, "500 raiders attack Portsmouth", alongside the other Sundays, most of which retailed the Air Ministry claim that forty-five *Luftwaffe* aircraft had been downed. The *New York Times* argued that an invasion was less likely now, "particularly in view of the approach of autumn weather". That paper held that the results of months campaigning were inconclusive but it seemed "probable" that the Germans had lost a lot more aircraft than the British – perhaps in the ratio of two or even more to one.

Express columnist George Slocum had interviewed a neutral diplomat, just back from Vichy France – giving a valuable insight into enemy perceptions. The diplomat had expected to find the skies over Britain black with German warplanes, with his aircraft from Lisbon landing at an airport completely destroyed. He been told before he had left that Britain was starving, that the Navy had been sunk, the Air Force obliterated and the factories in flames. Panic was supposed to reign in the country and Britain was on the point of surrender.[21]

Meanwhile, another newspaper carried a large advert for War Bonds, with the pull-quote from the Prime Minister: "Never in the field of human conflict …".[22] A legend was in the making.

Raids on this day targeted RAF Warmwell, Weymouth and the naval base at Portland, with a sizeable raid developing over Kent around six in the evening. One of the day's losers was Sgt Mervyn Sprague, a No. 602 Sqn Spitfire pilot – one of two from the squadron shot down by Me 110s. Both were unhurt but

Sprague had the distinction of being rescued from the sea by a Walrus aircraft. This was almost certainly one of "Digger" Aitkin's rescues, and probably one of his last. Sprague was not to be so lucky next time.[23]

As the sun went down, the minelayers came out to seed coastal waters with their deadly loads. The bomber fleets thundered inland, and over sixty-five individual raids were plotted. Bombs fell in forty places, including Coventry. The most significant raid was on Britain's second city, Birmingham. The bombers targeted the Market Hall in the area now known as the Bull Ring. About 145 high explosive (HE) bombs were dropped (56 unexploded), with at least 110 incendiaries. Numerous districts were hit. Twenty-nine people were killed, six of them workmen repairing a gas main when a delayed action bomb exploded. Several factories suffered direct hits and severe damage was caused. The ICI Witton plant was damaged, as was a printing works and shops, together with an engineering works and many residential properties.

The prohibition on naming bombed cities was still holding, and certainly in the case of Birmingham. Press reports referred to a "Midland Town" which, combined with the deliberate policy of talking down the damage, kept this major raid out of the public consciousness. That hopelessly distorted the perception of events.[24] Far from devoting most of its strength to destroying the RAF, the *Luftwaffe's* daytime activities had been relatively modest compared with the night raids. The *Luftwaffe* was moving to night bombing, with the emphasis on civilian targets, reaching inland as far as the northern city of Leeds, where three people were killed – exactly the policy Göring had announced on 19 August.[25]

Bomber Command was going in the opposite direction. Authorized personally by Churchill in retaliation for the bombing of London, it launched its first raid on Berlin. A mixed force of eighty-one aircraft took part, comprising Wellingtons, Hampdens and Whitleys. Industrial and commercial targets were specified but dense cloud hampered their accurate identification. Bombs fell on residential areas. Six Hampdens did not return. Four Blenheims had also been lost during daylight operations and Fighter Command had suffered seventeen losses. Total RAF losses for the day, therefore, amounted to twenty-seven – for the second day running – and six more than the twenty-one sustained by the *Luftwaffe*. On aggregate count, the Germans had emerged the victors.

DAY 48 – MONDAY 26 AUGUST 1940

Shirer was in Berlin to experience the RAF's work, describing it as the "first big air-raid of the war". "The concentration of anti-aircraft fire was the greatest I've ever witnessed," he wrote, "but strangely ineffective." "The Berliners are stunned," he added. "They did not think it could happen. When the war began, Göring assured them it couldn't". The Berliners are a "naïve and simple people", Shirer remarked. "They believed him".[26]

In London, despite Churchill's attempt to kick it into touch, the matter of "war aims" had not gone away. A letter signed by H. G. Wells and other notables, issued by the left-wing "Union of Democratic Control", was in circulation and the text was published in the morning's *Guardian*. The signatories did not expect a detailed peace settlement but, they said, the general principles "on which a durable peace could be founded can and should be stated".

Very few people realized quite how desperate the war at sea was becoming. The day before, the Admiralty had warned operational units of its suspicions that acoustic mines were being used. And now the Germans made a second successful airborne torpedo attack on Allied shipping, with the sinking of the *Remuera*, twelve miles north of Peterhead. That, however, was only one element of an alarming day. The *Remuera* was part of Convoy HX.65A which had already had a rough time. Attacked by U-boats the previous day, U-48 had sunk the tanker *Athelcrest* and the steamer *Empire Merlin*. U-124 then sunk the convoy commodore's ship, the *Harpalyce*, and the steamer *Firecrest*. The steamer *Stakesby* was damaged. Well over a hundred sailors lost their lives, including Commodore Washington, the convoy commander.

When the U-boats left off, the aircraft took over. The convoy was attacked by four He 115s and eight Ju 88s. Not only had they sunk the *Remuera*, the steamer *Cape York* was so badly damaged that she sunk under tow. A shattered *City of Hankow* managed to limp back to port.[27]

None of this made the newspapers, the press being dominated by the soap opera of the air war. And the major news was the overnight bombing of Berlin. The *Daily Mirror* noted the irony. While Hitler's bombers had been making another raid on the "London area", RAF bombs had been shaking the German capital. Berliners hurrying to their shelters soon after midnight heard heavy explosions as bombs burst to the north-west.

There were also reports of RAF attacks on Calais, seen from Dover Harbour. Starting about ten the previous night, German searchlights had been probing the sky. Parachute flares were dropped and orange-coloured "flaming onions" soared into the sky. The thump of bombs was heard across the stretch of twenty miles of sea – a rare occurrence. Bombing appeared exceptionally heavy.

Tiny by comparison was a report in the *Yorkshire Post*, retailing the views of H. B. Lees-Smith, the MP for the West Yorkshire mill town of Keighley. Speaking in his constituency, he suggested that the last possible day for an invasion was the equinox on 21 September. If Hitler did not beat us by physical invasion in the next month, said Lees-Smith, he would try to defeat us by his blockade, by sinking our merchant ships.

German Army chief von Brauchitsch was now relying on the Naval Staff's understanding that the invasion would only be mounted "if an especially favourable initial situation offers sure prospects of success". On this basis the Navy had agreed to keep fifty transports at Le Havre to transfer to England the four divisions based there. Twenty-five of these ships would sail directly to Brighton Bay behind motorboats in the assault wave, while the rest would go with the main crossing. Their landing zones would be allocated according to the prevailing situation. Halder was far from satisfied. The plan had "no chance of success this year". This day, therefore, von Brauchitsch had insisted on seeing Hitler personally.[28]

Air action over Britain started with the appearance of reconnaissance aircraft in the No. 11 Group area, followed by a series of raids, one of which targeted Folkestone, killing three and injuring several others. The depleted No. 264 Sqn lost three more of its Defiants after being savaged by two Me 109s – although not before claiming a number of Do 17s downed. Fighter Command overall suffered twenty-two losses. Bomber and Coastal Command lost six. A former Dutch Fokker seaplane was also downed, bringing total RAF losses to twenty-nine. The *Luftwaffe* lost thirty-eight machines, including two He 115s destroyed on the ground by RAF bombers.

Come the night, 200 *Luftwaffe* bombers were abroad, with raids on Bournemouth, Plymouth and Coventry. Birmingham had another visit, and flights were made over London, triggering air-raid warnings. Bombs were dropped in the Hendon and Edgware districts. Bombing in and around London was becoming almost routine. The first major raid in the centre had been put down to a navigational error. The *Luftwaffe* seemed to be making a lot of those errors, given that it also had radio beams to guide its bombers.

DAY 49 – TUESDAY 27 AUGUST 1940

The Battle of Britain was long past the preliminary stage, said the semi-official Berlin paper, *Dienst aus Deutschland*, characterizing all that had happened so far as "preliminaries". "Now begins the planned destruction of industrial plants essential to war", it said.

The British newspapers reported on the prolonged overnight "raid" on London, with six hours between the first warning and the "all clear". It was small beer compared with what was to come, but enough to excite the headline writers. After the hectic fighting of the day before, Fighter Command reported less business. The new Göring doctrine was taking effect. Less than fifty intruders were detected and only four bombing incidents were recorded during the daylight hours. One of those, described as "a bad air-raid", was in Plymouth. It killed twelve inmates and staff of Ford House, an old people's home. The Great Western Railway tender, the *Sir John Hawkins*, was damaged. On the day, Fighter Command lost four aircraft, Bomber Command three and the *Luftwaffe* five.

Overnight, the *Luftwaffe* was on the rampage again. Bombs were dropped on Gravesend, Calshot, Portsmouth, Southampton, the Isle of Wight, Tonbridge, Tiptree and Leighton Buzzard. In the north-east, bombing was reported at twenty different locations. There were five fatalities at Eston and three at West Hartlepool. Since June, that town had been under repeated attack. As with so many provincial towns, night after night the warning sirens had sounded. The town suffered air raids from June 1940 until March 1943, and seventy men, women and children were killed during this time. The period between July and October 1940 was the worst. During these months there were a total of 147 warnings, often several a night, lasting for hours.[29]

Dockers at Grimsby and Immingham, very much in the front line, decided on their own response. They went on a two-day strike, demanding "risk money", plus extra for working in the black-out, and for the arduous nature of their work.

For the hard-pressed public, the shift to night bombing became the main topic of conversation and concern. The disturbance and uncertainty was causing serious problems for a population under stress. But also causing considerable concern, according to Home Intelligence, were the erratic signals given by the air-raid warning sirens. They seemed to bear no relation to the level of threat. Bombs were just as likely to drop after the "all clear" as during the warning period. Increasingly, the public was losing confidence in the system.

Ordinary people might have been even more concerned if they had been aware of the lack of harmony and focus in the higher reaches of the RAF. The Fighter Command brass hats were addressing their real enemies – each other. Keith Park was trying to sort out the behaviour of Air Officer Commanding (AOC) No. 12 Group, Leigh-Mallory, and his promotion of the "big wing" concept. This issue has been rehearsed endlessly, but the spat must be seen against a background of a nation supposedly on the brink of an invasion, fighting for its survival. Throughout the campaign, its senior leaders seemed to be devoting most of their energies to plotting against each other, while Dowding sat in his garret in Stanmore, apparently ignorant of the proceedings, or so he later claimed – himself the subject of greater plots.[30]

In Germany, the tension was between the Army and Navy. The long-running dispute over the width of the *Sealion* landing front was finally coming to a head. Despite von Brauchitsch's direct approach to him the previous day, Hitler had decided that the Army had to face the realities of Germany's limited naval power. Under the signature of Keitel, once more, Hitler ordered that, "Naval operations will be adapted to fit in with the given facts in relation to the available tonnage and cover for embarkation and crossing".[31] This was the final word. It was to be a neither a narrow front, nor a broad front, but an ugly compromise. It gave up Ramsgate at the eastern extreme and Lyme Bay at the other, but still leaving a front of eighty miles, far wider than the Navy thought safe. The Army General Staff had no choice but to accept this decision. But the attitude to the operation changed. It was now considered to be only the *coup de grace*, its object to land troops after the battle had already been won.[32]

DAY 50 – WEDNESDAY 28 AUGUST 1940

The lead editorial of the *Yorkshire Post* this day noted that the Germans were turning from day raids to night raids. To its rhetorical "why?", it answered: "One prime reason and a very encouraging reason for us is the failure of their big daylight offensive a fortnight ago". And the result got front-page treatment in the *Daily Mirror*, with the banner headline: "Nazis over London, 21 towns". This was coverage of the night of raids, and graphic testament to the way the *Luftwaffe* was progressively converting to a night bombing force.

In a separate item, the *Mirror* reported that "for the first time in the history of any nation, ordinary working people – Britons – are recognised by the State as standing in the front line of the war". That story announced official compensation arrangements – the lack of which had been a highly contentious issue in the First World War bombing raids. No one needed any reminding of their status, though. A large photograph showed a wrecked Anderson shelter and a 30ft deep bomb crater, in a "household garden near London". The occupants had survived, their survival being given considerable prominence in the press, adding to a growing body of reports detailing positive experiences with Anderson shelters.[33]

The *Guardian* returned to the matter of "peace aims and war aims". It noted that the demand for "a definite and detailed statement" united the pessimists who suspected that a British Government would make a bad peace, and the optimists who expected it to make a good one. The paper observed that the Nazis had their own scheme for a new order in Europe. Therefore, it was not enough "to answer Hitler by saying that we want to restore a Europe of free peoples". The paper wanted "ideas for the co-operation of those free peoples in an economic order" that would "save Europe from the calamities that followed that last war and ruined the last attempt to unify Europe by means of the League of Nations".

Italian Foreign Minister, Galeazzo Ciano, met Hitler at the Berchtesgaden, and recorded an explanation that the failure to attack Britain was "due to bad weather". He would need at least two weeks of good weather to overcome British naval superiority. Ciano came away with the impression that there had been a definite postponement of the assault. Nevertheless, he wrote, "Hitler seems resolved to go to the limit because, he tells me, he has rejected an attempt at mediation made by the King of Sweden".[34]

In the shooting war, there were only so many variations on a theme the *Luftwaffe* could offer. At first sight, the day looked to be a repeat of earlier efforts when, about 8.30 a.m., aircraft started to assemble over Cap Gris Nez. This was the classic pattern, with which RAF radar operators were very familiar.

It soon became clear, however, that the Germans knew their movements were being tracked. They were now practising a studied deception programme, assembling aircraft *en masse* and only splitting them up into different raids once they were past the radar and closer to their targets. The radar, in any case, could still only give limited information on formation sizes, heights and composition, so controllers were vitally dependent on the network of observer stations to give more detail. But with several raids going over together, this confused the reporting system, markedly degraded the value of the radar and made more difficult the task of vectoring the right number of fighters to the right places at the right times.[35]

So it was in this case. The bomber element of this force was two groups of Dorniers. They were escorted by fighters, the total force amounting to 100-plus aircraft. Crossing the Channel, one section – led by twenty Dorniers – headed for Eastchurch. That left twenty-plus Dorniers to fly on to Rochford, home of Short Bros, and the manufacturing site for the new, four-engined Stirling bomber. Four RAF squadrons put up to block the raid were unable to penetrate the defensive screen. They lost eight aircraft and six pilots trying. Four aircraft were from the ill-fated No. 264 Sqn flying Defiants, which were shot down by a *gruppe* of Me 109s as they went into the attack. Only eight aircraft returned to their home base at Hornchurch and only three of those were serviceable.

Thus did Eastchurch suffer yet another attack, losing two Battles destroyed on the ground. The German bombers were nevertheless deterred by spirited flak. Airfields were now benefiting from a new policy implemented by General Pile, concentrating anti-aircraft resources on them. The Germans did no lasting damage and the station remained operational, albeit restricted to daylight flying. The second raid, headed for Rochford, again met with stiff fighter opposition. Elements of thirteen squadrons attempted to head it off. As before, the fighters failed to penetrate the defensive screen and the station took the hit – but suffered only minor damage.

Churchill, meanwhile, was on the coast, seeing for himself the state of defences. While he was thus engaged, a third attack developed. This one comprised a large fighter sweep over Kent and the estuary at 25,000 ft. It was precisely the formation Park wanted his own pilots to avoid but they attempted to take it on, losing nine aircraft in the process. On the day, Fighter Command lost eighteen aircraft in all, with others bringing losses up to twenty-one. For those, the *Luftwaffe* traded twenty-eight. Fifteen were Me 109s.

Come the night, came the bombers. Avonmouth Docks were bombed, with high explosives falling on the Shell Mex can factory. HE and incendiaries fell near the plant belonging to the National Smelting Company. Bombs were dropped on the factory of Messrs S. Smith and Sons at Cricklewood. A new type of incendiary bomb was reported to have been dropped at Ulceby. A thirty-minute raid on Coventry around ten in the evening caused considerable damage to thirty-one houses and minor damage to other shops and houses. Water and gas services were affected.

The sirens sounded in Altrincham, in Cheshire, at 10.39 p.m. Forty-one high explosive bombs and one incendiary fell, one bomb hitting a petrol storage tank at O'Briens Oil works next to the canal. Two tanks each containing 25,000 gallons of fuel, were set on fire. Houses and other buildings were hit. Churchdown in Gloucestershire was bombed just before midnight, when an important water main was damaged, seriously affecting Gloucester city and a nearby RAF station.[36]

At two in the morning, several bombs were dropped on Liverpool, when some houses were demolished. Damage was caused to electricity and water mains. Fires were started but were soon brought under control. The main Liverpool–Exeter railway line was damaged, making it necessary to suspend traffic. As to London, in what was described as the "most prolonged attack of the war", over 1,000 incendiaries and some high explosives were dropped on areas in the city, with aircraft circling for seven hours. Many fires and explosions were reported.

DAY 51 – THURSDAY 29 AUGUST 1940

A secret memorandum from the Naval Staff reached the War Cabinet this day, with a covering note from the First Lord of the Admiralty, Labour Co-operative MP Albert Victor Alexander – a political appointee, his title not to be confused with the First Sea Lord, Albert Admiral Pound. AV, as he had been known since childhood, had been First Lord for two years in the 1929 Labour Government. A critic of appeasement and a supporter of Churchill as war leader, his reward had been another chance at First Lord. Despite that, he had been kept out of the

Prime Minister's inner circle and excluded from the War Room. Now, though, he was sounding the alarm, forwarding to his Cabinet colleagues a paper entitled: "Merchant shipping casualties", written by the Naval Staff. In introducing the paper, AV was blunt: "A most serious situation has arisen," he wrote:

> [t]he enemy is concentrating a heavy attack on trade with submarines and aircraft, and in addition there has been a small but steady loss due to raiders. The latter may increase as, owing to the large number of troop movements requiring escort, we are unable to release cruisers and armed merchant cruisers to hunt raiders.

In the eight weeks up to 25 August, 143 ships had been lost, amounting to 564,000 tons. A number of ships had been damaged. The losses sustained during the most recent six days had been extremely serious – 15 ships totalling 92,000 tons sunk and 12 ships totalling 42,000 tons damaged. AV surmised that Hitler might be making this attack on shipping his main offensive, instead of an invasion. The Staff made numerous recommendations, including strengthening Coastal Command patrols.[37]

Even as AV was raising the alarm, though, on the other side of the Channel Keitel was instructing the Admiral in charge of naval forces in France to make arrangements to convoy the vessels needed for *Sealion* to their assembly points at their launch harbours. The Admiral was also to provide the "necessary protection" through mined waters.

As the barges and transports started their laborious passages, observers reading the British media might have been forgiven for thinking that they were reading the chronicles of the "Battle of London and the Home Counties" – or the "Battle of London" as Churchill was to call it. Coventry had yet to be permitted its walk-on part. Most provincial raids, under the baleful grip of the censor, got little press coverage. Even the still blazing fire in Pembroke Docks got short shrift, despite the smoke towering over 1,000 ft in the air, visible for 100 miles. And this night was a reminder that the Germans were attacking the whole of Britain.

The Midlands and points north were raided by a force of about 150 bombers. The raid was the heaviest yet in Britain, with widespread damage caused in Liverpool's dockland and city. More than 470 casualties were reported. Other bombers, at one or two *staffel* strength, raided Birmingham, Bristol, Coventry, Manchester and Sheffield.

Losses on the day amounted to nine Fighter Command aircraft, and three RAF bombers. The *Luftwaffe* lost seventeen. Following the course of the battle from the most notable current texts, one also has to do a double-take, wondering whether the same war was being reported. The preferred narrative is that the battle at this time was dominated by the *Luftwaffe* attacks on the RAF, a desperate bid to break the power of Fighter Command in order to meet the *Führer's* timetable for the invasion of England. In fact, RAF airfields were only occasional targets and represented only a fraction of the effort expended. In those terms, they could not be defined as the *schwerpunkt*, the main point of attack.

At the time, even the *New York Times* was reporting the intensifying night-time bombing campaign. The British public was only too conscious of it. Home Intelligence was made fully aware of the change, reporting with detectable relief that there was "no noticeable decline in morale although in London particularly there is some depression mainly brought by lack of sleep". There was some "nervousness" in the south, about stories of attacks on Birmingham, Coventry and Portsmouth. But morale was highest in the areas which had been most heavily bombed.

If the invasion was just over two weeks away, there was no sense of it in the British media. The man in charge of Britain's land defences, General Alan Brooke, also seemed unconcerned. He had just spent a day in north Scotland, watching Army exercises and was to go to the furthest, western reaches of Wales the next day.[38] These were not the actions of a man expecting jackboots on the Brighton shingle. More problematical was the growing shipping crisis, unseen and unreported by the media, but potentially more deadly than the entire air war. And, as the days grew shorter, the civilian population was increasingly exposed to the terrors of night bombing. It is impossible to characterize this period merely as a joust between Fighter Command and the *Luftwaffe*.

9.

Countdown to the Blitz

When they declare they will attack our cities in great measure, we will erase their cities. The hour will come when one of us will break – and it will not be National Socialist Germany!

Adolph Hitler, 4 September 1940, Berlin.

The conventional narrative has this as the critical period of the battle, when Hitler turned the full might of *Luftwaffe* against Fighter Command airfields, seeking to crush the only force standing in the way of his invasion fleet, which was poised to conquer the British Isles in another lighting war.

DAY 52 – FRIDAY 30 AUGUST 1940

The *Kriegsmarine* had things to do, essential tasks to complete before the invasion could go ahead – if it was going ahead. Not least, the shipping routes had to be swept of mines, and new minefields had to be laid to protect the flanks of the invasion route. For that, air cover was needed, and the Navy was not getting it. As a result, the Naval Staff informed Supreme Command that it could not meet the 15 September deadline for the completion of preparations. It complained:

> The elimination by the *Luftwaffe* of activity by enemy sea and air forces in the Channel and along the embarkation coasts has not yet materialised, and there is no early prospect of improvement while the *Luftwaffe* pursues its present operational objectives.

One can imagine the pursed lips and the frowns of disapproval.

Within the optimal period of 19–26 September, a provisional date for *Sealion* of 20 September had been decided upon, but the Naval Staff said even that could not be guaranteed. It depended on the *Luftwaffe's* ability to eliminate enemy air *and* sea forces.

Von Brauchitsch, showing far more enthusiasm than the Navy, circulated his *Instruction for the Preparation of Operation Sea Lion*, stating that the task of the Army was to effect a "landing in force". The aim of the attack was "to eliminate the Mother Country as a base for continuing the war against Germany". Only if necessary was there to be a complete occupation. Significantly, the issue of the executive order depended on "the political situation".[1] Halder's view of the operation had firmed up. A military operation on the front now ordered could not be undertaken on the scale originally intended. Its only purpose could be to finish off (*den Fangstoß zu geben*) an enemy already defeated by the air war.[2]

In London, the British Chiefs of Staff had sent their usual weekly résumé to the War Cabinet. Enemy tactics, they said, had undergone a considerable change. No short-range dive-bombers had been seen. Even the Ju 88 had not been used for dive-bombing. The Chiefs also confirmed that which had become only too evident. The long-range bomber force was being increasingly employed and night attacks had intensified. The raids, they said, had mainly been directed against aerodromes and ports, but industrial plants and the aircraft industry had also received considerable attention.[3]

Other raids had been carried out against aerodromes and oil storage, and a considerable amount of indiscriminate bombing had been included in the operations. The heaviest daylight attacks of the week had been made on Portsmouth and Ramsgate – neither of these RAF airfields. At night industrial areas in the Midlands had been the principal objectives, although aircraft had flown over London on several nights and bombs had been dropped in the City and suburbs.

Enemy aircraft engaged in daylight operations had varied between 200 and 500 in number each day, except on 23 and 27 August, when activity had been limited to reconnaissance flights and to a few individual attacks involving not more than 75 aircraft. The heaviest attacks had developed from the south-east, and large formations of bombers escorted by fighters had been intercepted and dispersed by RAF fighters. Fighter aerodromes seemed to have been the principal objectives, but damage had been "relatively small" in view of the threatened weight of the attacks.

Focusing on the air war, the War Cabinet was this day considering a memorandum from Churchill. "The air battle now proceeding over Great

Britain may be a decisive event in the war and must dominate all other consid-erations", he had written. But this dramatic statement, written four days earlier, was merely to open a discussion on pilot training. The item under consideration was no more urgent than the relocation of a large part of the training establish-ments to Canada and South Africa.[4]

The RAF was particularly keen on the idea, but the Prime Minister was against it. "Until the issue of this battle becomes clear it would not be right to separate any large portion of our reserve of pilots or of potentially operational machines from the fighting strength of the RAF in this country", he said, recom-mending a three-month postponement. But there was no specific mention of fighter pilot training. Churchill's idea of "reserves" extended to anti-invasion measures which included 350 Tiger Moth elementary trainers. Each had been equipped with bomb racks for eight 20lb anti-personnel bombs. Once the Germans had landed, an operation code-named "Banquet Lights" would come into force, with the aircraft flying to an advanced landing ground near the coast, where the bombs would be loaded and they would then fly on to the beaches and bomb the invading troops.[5]

The War Cabinet, having agreed with Churchill to hold off moving the training facilities, also looked at shipping losses highlighted by the Naval Staff memorandum deposited the previous day. But they did not have much to offer. And in response to the plea for the urgent provision of more patrol aircraft, the Chief of the Air Staff could only say that the Air Ministry would "do their best", but he could not promise anything "in the near future".[6]

On the home front, there was little appreciation of the gravity of this building crisis. More prosaically, there was "some slight resentment" in the provinces at the way London air-raid news was being highlighted. This was due in part, said the day's Home Intelligence report, to the fact that many provincial towns, unlike London, had not been named. This caused a good deal of uncertainty over which targets had been hit. Londoners, on the other hand, were "more cheerful". They were getting used to the idea of night raids, and were sleeping in their shelters instead of going to them when the sirens sounded. Once again, there was a distinction between those who had experienced bombing and those who were new to it. In the provinces, where warnings and raids had been suffered for some time, morale was higher than in London, where people had been showing "considerable apprehension".

Not so George Orwell. He recorded in his diary that air-raid warnings, "of which there are now half a dozen or thereabouts every 24 hours", are "becoming a great bore". Opinion was spreading rapidly, he said, that "one ought simply to disregard the raids except when they are known to be big-scale ones and in one's own area. Of the people strolling in Regent's Park, I should say at least half pay no attention to a raid-warning". He recalled the previous night "a pretty heavy explosion" just as he was going to bed. Later in the night he had been woken up by "a tremendous crash", said to be caused by a bomb in Maida Vale. His only comment was on the loudness, before falling asleep again.[7]

The pilots of Kesselring's Second Air Fleet did not have the luxury of a great deal of sleep. They started flying just after dawn, their first target a north-bound convoy in the Thames Estuary. Then three waves all heading for Kent, targeted Park's sector stations at Kenley and Biggin Hill. Successive waves of bombers and fighters, roughly at twenty-minute intervals came over until about four in the afternoon. Then, over the following two hours, the enemy poured in over Kent and the Thames Estuary. They targeted North Weald, Kenley and especially Biggin Hill where serious damage was done.

But airfields were by no means the only targets. Luton, Radlet, Oxford and Slough were also on the list. The raid on Luton targeted the Vauxhall plant, where there were 113 casualties, including fifty-three killed. Areas of the town were also bombed – the bus depot was one of the buildings hit and badly damaged. The larger part of the formation continued on to bomb Radlet, targeting the new Halifax bomber factory. No substantial damage was done, and production was not interrupted.

The day proved the most intensive of the battle for Fighter Command. It had flown 1,054 sorties and lost twenty-three aircraft with eight pilots killed. Seven bombers had also been lost, bringing the RAF total to thirty, against thirty-nine *Luftwaffe* losses. Only fourteen were Me 109s. Nevertheless, twelve valuable single-engined fighter pilots had been lost, either killed or taken prisoner.

DAY 53 – SATURDAY 31 AUGUST 1940

The *Daily Express* – along with most of the other London-based national media – was proclaiming great victories in the air over southern England and London:

"Four raids in nine hours – but Goering's latest Blitzkrieg is smashed!" The cross-page banner headline read: "59 DOWN – TEN IN LONDON".

Then, with the legend "mass attacks – mass defeats", readers were told of the "great news" from the Air Ministry that the number of German aircraft destroyed over Britain this month "now exceeds 1,000". The actual number for the whole month was 657, with the total number destroyed since the start of battle standing at 826. For that, Fighter Command had traded 418 fighters during the month, and 519 since the start of the battle. Overall on the month, the RAF (and Royal Navy) had lost 641 aircraft. Since the beginning of the battle, against 826 *Luftwaffe* losses, British losses came to 813. To all intents and purposes, the two sides were at parity.

An RAF photograph taken over Pembroke showed that the oil tanks were still burning, twelve days after the raid. Residents from a hundred miles around already knew this, as did the Germans. A very similar photograph had been published in *Der Adler*, the official magazine of the *Luftwaffe*. But newspapers could only refer to "a dock in South Wales". Spitfires went up and anti-aircraft batteries had gone into action, readers were told. But there had been no guns. There were only three anti-aircraft batteries in the whole of South Wales. The lack of fighter cover had also been fiercely criticized. Echoing the words of the troops at Dunkirk, locals and firemen alike were asking, "Where was the RAF?"[8]

Home Intelligence was finding that the fear of invasion was on the wane. Reports from Cardiff and Leeds particularly stressed this. There was resentment at the "excessive" publicity given to the London air raids and "jealousy" was reported from Southampton, Portsmouth and other places. However, air raids were being "borne patiently" and in some regions the public were "agreeably surprised" that so little damage was being done.

In the claustrophobic world of Fighter Command, there was very little agreeable about the day. Göring's reorganization on 19 August was yielding dividends. More than 80 per cent of the Me 109s in northern Europe were concentrated in the Pas de Calais, and Kesselring was making good use of them. Just before eight in the morning, the operations room at Bentley Priory plotted four waves of enemy aircraft, one heading for Dover and the others flying up the Thames Estuary. Again it was left to the Observer Corps to identify the intruders. The Dover post reported Me 109s. To avoid wasteful combat between fighters, controllers attempted to pull their people out. They were not quite fast enough. The Messerschmitts shot down three aircraft and entertained themselves shooting down all the barrage balloons in Dover Harbour.

This was the start of a series of raids which culminated in attacks on North Weald, Duxford and Debden, among others which included Detling, and then Croydon. Biggin Hill once more was heavily damaged, undoing repairs of the previous day and destroying its land communications again. There were some attacks on radar stations, and then a strong attack on Hornchurch which cratered runways and perimeter tracks, and destroyed two Spitfires.

These raids, ostensibly aimed at the military, also damaged civilian targets. One saw bombs fall on Colchester and, during a raid on Duxford, bombs were dropped on eight villages to the south of Cambridge. For all that, the greater effort was expended through the night. The *Luftwaffe* was completing its transition to a night bombing force, where it could range freely with very little opposition – in some cases with strategic effect. The battleship *Prince of Wales*, being built at Birkenhead, was damaged by a near miss from a heavy bomb.

For a time during the day, No. 11 Group had the Prime Minister as guest. He had found it "very instructive" to watch officers deploying their forces and building up a front at the threatened points.[9] On the day, Fighter Command as a whole lost thirty-eight aircraft, with eight pilots killed and as many badly injured. Bomber Command lost three aircraft and a Navy Swordfish brought British losses to forty-two. The *Luftwaffe* was close, again at thirty-nine. Twenty-two had been Me 109s, reflecting the huge numbers of these fighters in play. Sixteen Me 109 pilots were dead, missing or prisoner. In aircraft numbers, the *Luftwaffe* had come out on top.

After dinner that evening, the First Sea Lord placed an urgent telephone call with No. 10. Enemy vessels, a large number of them, had been spotted by a patrol aircraft, steering westwards from Terschelling – they could be on the Norfolk coast by morning. An invasion could be in the offing. All naval ships on the east and south-east coasts were ordered to raise steam and others ordered to special patrol positions. Five destroyers on minelaying duties were told to jettison their loads and to locate and attack the enemy. By cruel fate, they had happened upon a German minelaying operation – and the *Kriegsmarine* had got there first. Three of five of these destroyers detonated mines. The *Esk* was sunk and the *Ivanhoe* so seriously damaged that she had to be abandoned and sunk. HMS *Express*, with her bows blown off, was towed to Harwich. Ninety casualties were landed by the destroyer *Vortigen*.[10]

The North Sea was a dangerous place for British ships. But the *Kriegsmarine*, with significantly fewer ships, would face exactly the same perils in supporting an invasion. With belts of mines on both sides of the Channel, weeks of preparatory work were needed before this stretch of water could be cleared for an invasion fleet – given no intervention by British forces.

Back in Britain, Beaverbrook was convinced that the heavy air attacks must mean that the Germans were trying to reach a conclusion. There were more signs of concentrations of German shipping. Jock Colville was not convinced these presented a significant threat. A serious invasion depended on the ability of the German Air Force to obtain mastery of the air, he mused. And that seemed more than doubtful.[11]

DAY 54 – SUNDAY 1 SEPTEMBER 1940

In what were clear signs of the tempo speeding up, the *Sunday Express* featured the raids on its front page, with another banner headline, this one reading: "Hitler throws fiercest air attack against us". Stung apparently by the most terrific air raid Berlin has ever experienced, the narrative ran, Hitler yesterday "disregarding all losses, started a series of heavy raids from the coast towards London".

But the bombing was not being confined to the south-east. And, with the invasion supposedly about three weeks away weather permitting, the Germans had to achieve the crucially important tasks of neutralizing enemy air power and infrastructure, degrading the land defences and knocking out road and rail links to isolate the battlefield and prevent reinforcement.

Given the short timescale and barely sufficient resources to mount a successful invasion, it did not then seem logical for the *Luftwaffe* to send 160 bombers to hit random targets in the north of England and elsewhere. Certainly, sending in the early hours of this Sunday morning a number of aircraft to Bradford, in the centre of the West Riding, to destroy the one of the largest department stores, to make a big hole in the local cinema and to knock out the local fruit market, did not seem calculated to facilitate the invasion of southern England.[12] Nor, as Leeds suffered its second raid, did the *Luftwaffe* appear to have invasion in mind. Marsh Lane goods station and yet more residential properties were damaged. A bomb was dropped on the York to Leeds arterial road.

Nor could it be said that the considerable aerial activity all over the north-east had any great relevance to the invasion. Little could be gained from the raids on Durham, Wallsend and Sunderland, especially as only slight damage was caused and there were few casualties. Other places bombed included Rotherhithe, Portsmouth, Manchester and Stockport, together with the rural havens of Gloucester, Hereford and Worcester. The only relevant target was Portsmouth.

Similarly, attacks on Liverpool – the fourth night in succession – with some bombers dropping their loads on Bristol as an alternative – did not seem to be geared specifically to furthering the success of an invasion. In Liverpool, a shelter was destroyed killing twenty people and there were many other casualties. Bombs fell in the Nelson and Clarence Docks, a trawler being hit while in the latter. Birkenhead was hit, these two communities on opposite sides of the Mersey now locked into a nightmare of several years' duration.

By the time the nightmare had finished, Liverpudlians were mourning the deaths of 2,000 of their own. Many more had been badly injured and the city centre was left looking like a moonscape. This was yet to come. Crucially, the port city was the gateway to the USA and Canada. Had it ceased to function, the war machine would have faltered. Britain might have starved. It kept going. Never in the field of human conflict had so much been owed by so many to so few – the dockers of Liverpool.

The *Sunday Express* chose this day to address its editorial to precisely the people who were to suffer so much. Under a heading "Up to you!" it asked, "Can we lose this war?" And the answer was stark: "We cannot lose the war unless our civilian population lose their nerve. That is the only way in which Hitler can gain the say and darken the earth for a generation". It went on, emphasizing the message in italics and then capitals:

"*This is a People's War*" – that is no longer merely a phrase. The words have taken on the shape of reality. Hitler is sending his bombers to terrify YOU. By numbing YOUR activities, wearing YOUR nerves and slowing up YOUR contribution to the national effort he hopes to beat civilisation into submission.

Almost as if in response, in area after area in Britain, people were picking themselves up and dusting themselves off. Some 44 civilians had been killed the previous day, with 250 injured. The larger numbers of 110 killed and 585 injured were recorded on this day. By contrast, the RAF lost 3 with 11 injured. Exceptionally, the previous day – with the Biggin Hill raid – 40 had been killed and 28 ground staff injured. The RAF though, was in the front line. The civilians were supposed to be the "many" who owed so much to the "few".

One of those "few", Sgt William Rolls of No. 72 Sqn, experienced his first scramble from Biggin Hill on this day. No contact was made with the enemy and the squadron was relocated to Croydon Airport to relieve pressure on the station. At 5.30 p.m., a small group of Dorniers, under the cover of a fighter sweep bombed Biggin Hill for the second time that day. Two WAAF telephone operators remained at their posts when a 250kg bomb brought down the heavy concrete ceiling above them. The raid had destroyed communications though. Post Office engineers worked late into the night, in constant danger from further bombs and in craters filled with water and escaping gas, to restore telephones. These men, Mason concedes, as much as any wearing uniform, contributed to the survival of Dowding's fighter forces.

Meanwhile, at his new home, Sgt Rolls was disconcerted to find that dispersal consisted of large bell tents and that the lounges and bars of what had been London Airport were available only to officers. His quarters, with the other non-commissioned officers (NCOs), were two semi-detached houses bordering the airfield – no furniture and only old iron bedsteads with straw palliasses. Breakfast was brought to them in the tents. And while the officers had the use of the restaurant, the NCOs were restricted to the canteen. The tragedy was almost overwhelming.[13]

Nevertheless, Rolls had a point. From his lumpy palliasse that evening, he might have been slightly comforted by the words of J. B. Priestley drifting from the radio – had he been given one. "The true heroes and heroines of this war, whose courage, patience and good humour stand like a rock above the morass of treachery, cowardice and panic, are the ordinary British folk", said the Yorkshire sage. This was the first opportunity Priestley had had to respond to Churchill's "few" speech.

Certainly, the airmen had not delivered anything by way of spectacular victories this day. In a day of scrappy fighting, Fighter Command had lost sixteen aircraft, including a Hurricane destroyed by a direct hit while on the ground at Biggin Hill. Bomber and Coastal Command between them lost six aircraft, including two Wellingtons, bringing total losses to twenty-two. The *Luftwaffe* loss returns for this day were incomplete. Nine were officially reported but at least seven Dorniers were shot down in southern England, and an Me-109 was also lost, none of which appear in the official returns. On balance though, the *Luftwaffe* might have come out ahead, with seventeen losses.

DAY 55 – MONDAY 2 SEPTEMBER 1940

Despite the previous day's losses, the *Daily Express* was still in triumphal mood, devoting another front-page banner headline to RAF successes. This time it was the proclamation: "WE'RE WINNING IN THE AIR". The RAF, it added, was "mastering [the] Nazi criminals". This was actually a message from Churchill, crafted on the instructions of the War Cabinet and released to the press. But, while Fighter Command was battling for supremacy of the skies, the message was addressed to Bomber Command and its then Air Officer Commanding, Air Marshal Sir Charles Portal.

The specific purpose of the exercise, the *Express* told its readers, was to congratulate the bomber squadrons "who have been engaged in the recent long-distant attacks on military objectives in Germany and Italy". It was "very satisfactory", wrote Churchill, "that so many tons of British bombs have been discharged with such precision in difficult conditions and at such great distances and that so many important military objectives in Germany and Italy have been so sharply smitten".

Privately, the record of his separate communication marked "Secret", Churchill told the War Cabinet of his exploits at No. 11 Group HQ on 31 August. He then reviewed the results of the last month of hard air fighting. "We had every right to be satisfied," he said, "our own Air Force was stronger than ever and there was every reason to be optimistic about the 1940 Air Battle of Britain".[14]

Nearly nine years later, this same man was to write of the events of this period: "In the life or death struggle of the two Air Forces this was a decisive phase". He continued: "We never thought of the struggle in terms of the defence of London or any other place, but only who won the air". Then did Churchill convey that "[t]here was much anxiety at Fighter Headquarters at Stanmore, and particularly at the Headquarters of No. 11 Fighter Group at Uxbridge".[15] This, he had not said at the time – not to the War Cabinet, at any rate. "Our own

Air Force was stronger than ever", he had said on this day, then going on to ask for – and get – permission to tell parliament on 5 September that the results of the air battle were "generally satisfactory".

This was the day, however, that Hitler issued orders that "retaliatory attacks" should be carried out against London, whenever weather conditions permitted it.[16] Hitler and Göring had already conferred on this, and by the end of August, *Grossangriff auf London* was common gossip, the operation to be named *Loge* (the German for theatre box). Even while Plesman was still pursuing his peace initiative, *Luftwaffe* bombers were ordered to move to advanced bases in northern France.[17] Something of this was picked up by the British, Colville writing that the movements were thought to indicate an intensification of air attack towards the end of the week. "It is already on a sufficiently large scale!" he added.[18]

For the moment, though, there were the more immediate dangers of the sea war, the *Express* also carrying news of a ship, which it did not name, being torpedoed on its way to Canada, carrying 321 children. This was the SS *Volendam*, which had been hit on 30 August. All had been saved.

Throughout the previous month, the Ministry of Information had been encouraging wall-to-wall media coverage of RAF exploits. But, at this "decisive phase" in "the life or death struggle of the two Air Forces" the *Daily Mirror* ran the SS *Volendam* as its lead story and devoted its political cartoon from Zec to a spontaneous tribute to the Royal Navy. On this day alone, sailors had far more contact with the enemy than the RAF. Notably, HM Submarine *Sturgeon* had a singular success, torpedoing the German steamer *Pionier* fifteen nautical miles north-east of Skagen, in between Denmark and Norway. The ship was heavily laden with a "mystery cargo". It had 753 men aboard, many of them troops on their way to posts in Norway. Some sources suggested 230 had been lost – others claimed that nearly everyone on board had perished.[19]

Sturgeon was not the only submarine in action. HM Submarine *Tigris* was another, although less lucky when she unsuccessfully attacked U-58. And the Fleet Air Arm was active over Flushing. An Albacore of No. 826 Sqn from RNAS *Peregrine* was shot down. Three crewmen were captured. In a separate action, U-46 sunk the steamers *Thornlea*, with three survivors, and *Bibury* with the loss of all hands. Canadian destroyer *Skeena* and Norwegian steamer *Hild* rescued the *Thornlea* survivors. U-47 then sunk Belgian steamer *Ville de Mons*.

The entire crew was rescued. The battle with the *Luftwaffe* also continued. German bombers attacked convoy WN 12. The steamer *Lagosian* was damaged thirteen miles east-south-east of Peterhead. Her survivors were rescued by anti-submarine trawler *Southen Gem*, steamer *Ashby* and the Dutch *Delftdijk*, both off Rattray Head. Destroyers *Duncan* and *Holderness* provided further anti-aircraft protection.

And, after so many apparently pointless raids of the previous day, the *Luftwaffe* targeted the oil tanks at the Anglo-Iranian Oil Company refinery in Llandarcy near Swansea. Overnight, five tanks, each holding 10,000 tons of petroleum products, were hit. So intense were the fires that they were left to burn out. The refinery works were closed down because of unexploded bombs. Lt Bertram Archer of the Royal Engineers defused the most dangerous, despite explosions and blazing oil. He was later awarded the George Cross.[20]

The bombers also hit the town's shopping centre in what was a major raid for the period. They killed thirty-three people and injured 115 in a blitz which lasted several hours. Some 251 bombs and over 1,000 incendiaries were dropped. The deadly mixture caused a red glare in the sky as a number of buildings burned to destruction. One shopping street in particular was badly damaged and other buildings were gutted. Parachute flares silently and menacingly hung in the area lighting the devastation for miles around. Rescue efforts were carried out using torchlight only to avoid further targeting. The new Great Western Railway station was seriously damaged, necessitating the diversion of traffic. Four wheat warehouses were damaged. Two were completely gutted with a loss of 8,000 tons of stock. Incendiary bombs also fell on the ICI factory at Upper Bank. Production was held up for twelve hours.

As people found their way into work that day, they were confronted with broken or charred ruins instead of familiar places of business or pleasure. Debris and rubble cluttered the streets, broken furniture and damp and peeling wallpaper stared forlornly from the wrecks of houses. As the Llandarcy refinery spewed out a huge column of smoke by day and red flame by night, people became concerned that it would act as a beacon for further attacks. This led to a form of "public nervousness" known as *trekking*, the nightly migration from the centre of the town to nearby rural areas. The village of Mumbles and the rural Gower peninsular, visited for pleasure in pre-war days, now provided a place of refuge as people slept in tents or huts around Gower Bay and in parked cars or lorries on open land around Swansea.[21]

As for the day as a whole, even the *New York Times* referred to a "familiar pattern" of attacks as it reviewed the activities, churning out the propaganda figures produced by the British Government. Fighter Command losses were put at thirteen instead of the actual twenty-three. Forty-two enemy were claimed downed, as opposed to the thirty actually lost by the *Luftwaffe*, a figure that included several accidents. Thus, the combat losses for each side were close. By the time the Swordfish and seven Bomber and Coastal Command losses – which included two expensive Sunderland flying boats – had been factored in, the Germans were actually ahead.

DAY 56 – TUESDAY 3 SEPTEMBER 1940

Overnight, the *Luftwaffe* visited Bristol, Cardiff, Monmouth, Birmingham and close by Castle Bromwich. Liverpool once again was hit, and so was Manchester and Sheffield. Bombs were dropped on Shilbottle, Ancroft, Blyth, South Newsham and Broomhill in Northumberland, Bishopton and Elwick in Co Durham and Hull in Yorkshire. Even then, air activity had finished relatively early, in the early hours of the morning. The *Daily Mirror* claimed that the anti-aircraft guns guarding London reached a "new high pitch of power and efficiency" overnight, "as they helped RAF fighters smash German mass raiders". The *Daily Express* had a banner headline, proclaiming "Night fighters hunt raiders", with roof-top watchers asserting that there seemed to be more RAF fighters up in the air than on any previous night alarms. This was Britain's answer to the "nuisance" raiders.

It was the first anniversary of the war. The *Guardian* thought the British people could look forward to a second year with "greater confidence than almost any of us could have thought possible two months ago". Keitel issued a directive setting out the timetable for *Sealion*. The 20 September was now to become the earliest date for the departure of the transport fleet, which put the actual landing – S-day – on 21 September. The launch order would be given on S minus ten, probably on 11 September. The final order would follow at the latest by S minus three, at noon.[22]

Meanwhile, British photographic intelligence was picking up "sudden and startling" increases in the number of barges in the Channel ports. And four Dutch spies landed in a boat from Dungeness with instructions to report to the Germans on British defensive measures and on army reserve formations. They were quickly picked up and under interrogation spoke of a concentration of mounted troops equipped with mules at Le Touquet. They also said they had been told that an invasion would take place before the middle of September. They had been given no contacts in this country and were singularly badly directed. To anybody with any knowledge of conditions in this country it should have been apparent that none of these people could hope to succeed.[23]

Göring was in The Hague, meeting with his Air Fleet commanders, Kesselring and Sperrle, to discuss the air assault on London. In the absence of approval from Hitler to carry out "terror raids", it was then that the decision was made to target the docklands.[24] Albert Plesman, who was still pursuing the idea of a peace deal that had been initiated on 24 July, learned of the plan and tried to argue against it. He was informed that the matter was out of Göring's hands as the *Führer* had made up his mind.[25] For the moment, any idea of peace negotiations seemed to be on hold – although others were to emerge.

George Orwell on this day recorded a conversation with a "Mrs C" who had recently come back from Cardiff. She had told him that air raids there had been "almost continuous". To avoid disruption, therefore, it had been decided that work in the docks must continue, raids or no raids. Almost immediately afterwards, said Mrs C, a German aircraft had dropped a bomb straight into the hold of a ship. The remains of seven men working there "had to be brought up in pails". Predictably, there had been a strike. The practice of taking cover had been restored.

This, wrote Orwell, was the sort of thing that did not get into the papers – and indeed it did not. There were occasional reports of tension between employers who were losing production, and workers who were concerned with their own safety. But since strikes were theoretically illegal, they were rarely reported. Moreover, Orwell asserted that casualties in the most recent raids, e.g., at Ramsgate, had been officially minimized, a policy which was acknowledged by Home Intelligence. But it continued to incense locals, who did not like to read about "negligible damage" when large numbers of people had been killed. Such was the distrust of official figures that exaggerated accounts of air-raid deaths tended to circulate.[26]

More pressing issues, perforce, were preoccupying Churchill. This day he had produced for his War Cabinet colleagues a detailed memorandum on "The munitions situation".[27] It opened:

> The Navy can lose us the war, but only the Air Force can win it. Therefore our supreme effort must be to gain overwhelming mastery in the air. The Fighters are our salvation but the Bombers alone provide the means of victory. We must therefore develop the power to carry an ever–increasing volume of explosives to Germany, so as to pulverize the entire industry and scientific structure on which the war effort and economic life of the enemy depend, while holding him at arm's length from our Island. In no other way at present visible can we hope to overcome the immense military power of Germany.

With this policy, the Air Staff was in complete agreement. Their only regret was that a more powerful bombing offensive against German industry was not already under way. But Churchill had much more to say. Tucked into the text was the view that a large-scale invasion was "unlikely". To Sir John Anderson, he wrote an "action this day" minute telling him that "great effort" should be made to help people drain their Anderson shelters and to make floors for them against the winter rain. The Prime Minister took the time out to offer detailed instructions to the Home Secretary on how this could be done.[28]

And despite the Plesman brush-off, the *Chicago Daily News* had peace rumours circulating. A prominent Swede had supposedly arrived in London with a new peace offer: independence for part of Poland; autonomy for Czechoslovakia under the Reich, independence for Norway and Holland; a bigger Belgium and a smaller France; and nothing from the British Empire. An offer seemed not only possible but highly probable, the London bureau ventured. London believed there was concern in Nazi circles over the failure to eliminate the RAF. A winter of warfare was not wanted by Berlin.

The air war was again scrappy, but with a major raid on North Weald fighter station by a formation of Dorniers, which damaged hangars, messes and administrative buildings. The operations room was hit but not put out of action. Fighter Command suffered twenty losses, including two Blenheim fighters shot down by Hurricanes of No. 46 Sqn. Two Blenheim bombers and a Whitley shot down brought RAF losses to twenty-three, compared with a *Luftwaffe* total of sixteen, a clear win for the "away team".

DAY 57 – WEDNESDAY 4 SEPTEMBER 1940

The big news in Britain was the agreement between Britain and the USA on the exchange of 50 obsolete American destroyers for US bases on British territories in the Caribbean and elsewhere. Churchill had been obliged, as part of the deal, to give personal assurances to Roosevelt that, if the British Isles were overrun, the British Fleet would not be surrendered or sunk, but sent to other parts of the Empire for its defence.

Many of the public saw in the transfer of the destroyers a sign that the USA might be about to join the war on the British side. Home Intelligence found the public "still in a comparatively cheerful state of mind", largely accounted for by "the continued success of the RAF both at home and abroad".

The *Daily Express* had Hubert Knickerbocker replicating a report that had been published in New York the previous day. "Britain is bleeding, but unbowed," he wrote. "Hitler's air attacks on the south-east coast have been going on now for three weeks, and the German Press boasts that the *Luftwaffe* has utterly destroyed most of the cities and ports on this crucial stretch". But, said Knickerbocker, the fate of this island and the decision of the war depends on whether enough destruction is wrought to mean blockade. Nowhere, he stated, could I find any important damage to any important ports. Ninety-eight percent of all the damage has been done to innocent civilians and their property. The Germans have failed to blockade.

So to assert may have been premature. The blockade was a long-term option. Not so the invasion. In England, War Minister Anthony Eden had warned that it would be foolish to suppose that because the autumn approached, the threat of invasion was already past. "The contrary is the fact", he had said, his words reported by the *Daily Express*. "There is no shred of evidence to show that Hitler has abandoned his declared intention to seek to subdue this country by invasion. There is plenty of evidence to cause us to be especially watchful during these next few weeks."

He was not wrong. Across the Channel, over 4,000 craft had now been requisitioned, including 1,600 motorboats. Most had been assembled at the embarkation ports, or were on their way there. The whole fleet would be ready for use by 19 September. However, the vital minesweeping programme was well behind schedule, delayed by bad weather. The area west of the Dover–Calais line was giving some concern and doubt was being expressed as to whether the mines and obstacles close to the English coast could be located by the target date.

Captain Gustav Kleikamp had his own problems. As commander responsible for the Calais group of the transport flotilla, he was worried about the lack of large-scale exercises. The "inadequate training of personnel and deficiencies in the material assembled", he complained, could not be made good in the time available. There would have been the very greatest difficulty getting a transport fleet to the landing area, especially at night. Captain Scheurlen, commanding the Le Havre Group, was also extremely dubious about the fleet capability. Among his problems, crews of the motor sailing vessels were almost entirely boys under 17 years of age.[29]

The *Luftwaffe* was continuing its attacks on RAF airfields. Four were badly hit, including Eastchurch. But there were also raids on aircraft factories. Short Brothers at Rochester was attacked. The Vickers factory at Brooklands was bombed by Me 110s, flying in from very low level. They caused much damage. Over 80 workers were killed, with 700 casualties in all. The production of Wellingtons was halted for four days. Dowding ordered maximum air protection for Hurricane and Spitfire production centres at Kingston, Langley, Brooklands and Southampton. Among other sites bombed were Canterbury, Faversham and Reigate.

Beaverbrook was getting increasingly concerned about the effects of air-raid warnings on aircraft production. There were as problematical as the raids themselves. At the Castle Bromwich Spitfire plant in Warwickshire, he had been appalled to find that on 31 August 700 men had quit work at lunchtime without authorization, and a further 700 at five in the evening. There had been 3,500 men at work over the weekend, but there had been "a marked disinclination" to continue at work after an air-raid warning had been sounded. Production had fallen off and prompt action was necessary if the situation was not to deteriorate further. He wanted the sounding of the sirens discontinued, and asked the Cabinet to consider compulsion to keep men at work during air raids.[30]

Led by Churchill, in an evening session, the Cabinet debated the disruptive effect of air-raid warnings on war production, at some length. The meeting offered changes to the warning system, to minimize production losses. Everybody engaged in useful work, and not in a position of special danger, should continue his or her work on receipt of the "red " warning, and should not seek shelter until specific instructions were received (or until guns or bombs were heard).[31]

Fighter Command on the day flew 678 sorties, losing 19 aircraft. Three Bomber Command aircraft brought the losses to 22, with exactly the same number lost by the *Luftwaffe*, including 2 He 111s to a Blenheim night fighter, aided by searchlight batteries. By night, the Germans were back on the prowl with nearly 200 bombers in the air. Liverpool was hit again. The attack was directed mainly at Edge Hill goods station and Lister Drive power station. There was damage to surrounding houses. The Dunlop rubber works and Tunnel Road Cinema were damaged. Overnight, progressing into the next day, there was a heavy raid on Bristol, with 47 aircraft attacking.

Alternatively provoked and humiliated by Bomber Command's pinprick raids on Berlin and other German cities, Hitler made a surprise speech in the Sports Palace in Berlin. The occasion was the opening of the *Winterhilfe* – winter relief – campaign. "I have tried to spare the British", he said, then complaining that "[t]hey have replied by murdering German women and children". He taunted the "blabbering" of their leaders Churchill and Eden; Duff Cooper he ridiculed as a *"Krampfhenne"* (nervous old hen). Then he went on, referring to the RAF raids on Germany, declaring:

> And should the British Air Force drop 2000 or 3000 or 4000kg of bombs, then we will drop 150,000, 180,000, 230,000, 300,000, 400,000kg, yes, one million kilograms in a single night. And should they then declare they will greatly increase their attacks on our cities, we will erase their cities. We will put these night time pirates out of business, God help us! The hour will come when one of us will break – and it will not be National Socialist Germany![32]

William L. Shirer, commenting on the speech in his diary, wrote of it being "grim and dripping with hate" for most of the evening, but he nonetheless picked out a "humorous, jaunty" moment: "In England they're filled with curiosity and keep asking: 'Why doesn't he come?'" Said Hitler: "Be calm. He's coming! He's coming!" But it was the British who came first. RAF bombers were over Berlin just before midnight. That was also noted by Shirer, who had earlier witnessed the "hysterical applause" of Hitler's audience – mainly women nurses and social workers.[33]

The reactions of the audience lent some weight to a secret assessment written by the British Chiefs of Staff. Collapse of the German Government had been considered the means by which the war would be brought to an end. But the Chiefs were now saying that there was no likelihood of this happening. In their 74-page document, they also "assumed" that any enemy attempt to invade would fail. The best probability of success and the greatest economic advantages would arise, they argued, from a naval and air attack on shipping and ports with a view to cutting off supplies, combined with air attack on industry and morale, and an intensification of the propaganda campaign.

DAY 58 – THURSDAY 5 SEPTEMBER 1940

Less than twelve hours after Hitler's charge that the RAF had been "murdering German women and children", a *Luftwaffe* bomb hit West Hill Hospital in Dartford, Kent. It demolished the maternity ward block, killing two nurses and twenty-two new and expectant mothers, trapping many more. One of the nursing staff, Sister Mary Gantry was quickly on the scene. Still in her night-clothes with an overcoat hastily thrown over them, she crawled in and out of the wreckage, giving morphine injections to trapped women.[34]

In response to Hitler's speech, readers of the *Daily Mirror* were treated to an account of how London's anti-aircraft guns had "roared into action and flung up a wall of flame against German raiders ... only a few hours after Hitler had threatened new night after night blitzkrieg in answer to the RAF's raids".

"Hitler screams threats" was the offering from the *Daily Express*. The speech made the front page of the *New York Times*. References to Hitler dropping "hundreds of thousands of pounds" of bombs on England even found their way to New Zealand where, in the *Evening Post*, the story was given front-page lead. Closer to home, the *Irish Times* not only ran a front-page lead item, which noted that "Bombing of England to be intensified", it embedded in the story a "box" with the more or less precise quote from Hitler: "If the British attack our cities we will simply erase theirs".

The speech was covered in the *Guardian*. The two-column headers told the story: "Hitler threatens bombing night after night", followed by the line: "Revenge for RAF raids". Then there was the Hitler quote in capitals. Curiously, though, when it came to the British "paper of record", *The Times*, the Hitler speech was not the main item. It got a down-page single column headed: "Hitler's new bluster". There was no mention of the threat to eradicate British cities.

This day, Kesselring launched twenty-two raids. Biggin Hill was on the list again, but an attack around eleven in the morning did no damage. However, the main railway line between Charing Cross and the coast was blocked by a salvo of bombs at nearby Chislehurst. Oil tanks at Thameshaven were set on fire, the pyre of smoke providing a convenient navigation marker for *Luftwaffe* crews for the days to come. Already, bombers from the Fifth Air Fleet in Norway and Denmark were being moved to airfields in Holland, to maximize the impact of the attack.[35] Army High Command thought it should be coordinated with the invasion timetable, but the OKW staff conference was told that Göring was not interested in the preparations for *Sealion*, since he did not think the operation would actually be carried out.[36]

And if Göring was doing his best, in the open, to make the invasion unnecessary, behind the scenes there was another attempt to achieve the same thing, by a different route. As with Hitler's speech of 19 July, peace feelers followed the day afterwards. They came via Victor Mallet, the British Minister in Stockholm. The British Government was told when he telegraphed the Foreign Office with details of a proposal received from the President of the Swedish High Court of Appeal, Professor Lars Ekberg. He in turn had received it from Dr Ludwig Weissauer, a Berlin barrister who had come to Sweden, a man "with very important connections" and "understood to be a direct secret emissary of Hitler".[37] This would have been the basis of the *Chicago Daily News'* story. Mallet asked whether he should meet Weissauer. "I should of course say nothing to encourage him but it might be of interest to listen", he wrote.[38]

In the afternoon, Churchill had been in the Commons to give his now routine monthly "war situation" report.[39] Initially, his speech focused on the fifty geriatric destroyers from the USA. He spoke at some length about them. At last turning to the air war, he stated, "We must be prepared for heavier fighting in this month of September", then telling MPs: "The need of the enemy to obtain a decision is very great, and if he has the numbers with which we have hitherto credited him, he should be able to magnify and multiply his attacks". He did not mention Hitler's speech, but did add that "Firm confidence is felt by all the responsible officers of the Royal Air Force in our ability to withstand this largely increased scale of attack". Our Air Force to–day, he said:

> is more numerous and better equipped than it was at the outbreak of the war, or even in July, and, to the best of our belief, we are far nearer to the total of the German numerical strength, as we estimate it, than we expected to be at this period in the war.

Only then did he take on the prospect of imminent Armageddon, with a warning for his audience. "No one must suppose that the danger of invasion has passed," he said:

> I do not agree with those who assume that after the 15th September – or whatever is Herr Hitler's latest date – we shall be free from the menace of deadly attack from overseas; because winter, with its storms, its fogs, its darkness, may alter the conditions, but some of the changes cut both ways. There must not be for one moment any relaxation of effort or of wise precaution, both of which are needed to save our lives and to save our cause. I shall not, however, be giving away any military secrets if I say that we are very much better off than we were a few months ago, and that if the problem of invading Great Britain was a difficult one in June, it has become a far more difficult and a far larger problem in September.

Churchill went on to tell the House that the government had been sending a "continuous stream of convoys with reinforcements to the Middle East", including "sending some of our most powerful modern vessels" to reinforce the Mediterranean fleet. We also send war supplies to Malta, including a batch of modern anti-aircraft guns.

That day the aircraft carrier HMS *Argus* had arrived at Takoradi on the West African coast. It had on board thirty Hurricanes and their pilots, ready to fly overland to Khartoum the next day. Furthermore, the New Zealand Division, only recently arrived in England, had been earmarked for the Middle East. General Alan Brooke thought they would be "a great loss to the Home Forces".[40] Remarkably, with Fighter Command supposedly on the brink of collapse and with invasion imminent, one of the best units in the Army was on notice for deployment overseas and the government could afford to send thirty Hurricanes, with pilots, to Khartoum.

Back in the Commons, there was a debate on the coal industry.[41] Mines Secretary David Grenfell admitted there was a problem of transport, "not an easy problem". Internal consumption of coal had been very much higher than in recent years, and more had to be moved on the railways than before. There had been the restrictions on coastal shipping but a record number of trains had been sent from the extreme north to the south. Never before had so much Durham and Northumberland coal come by rail into the London area and into the south. Thus offered was a picture of a system under enormous strain. It gave adequate reason why the "Coal Scuttle" convoys could not be stopped.

In its weekly review of the air war, *Flight* magazine observed that the Germans had been changing or developing their tactics. Rather reluctantly, it would seem, "they have begun to indulge more than at first in night raiding".

That night, the *Luftwaffe* roamed freely, hitting over forty towns and cities. Shops and buildings in Clifton, Bristol, were hit and four people killed. Liverpool Docks were bombed and Dunlop's Walton works were hit. Domestic premises and shops in Bootle were damaged, and Rainhill Mental Hospital was hit. At Prescot, St Helens, four were killed in an attack. Other incidents included bombing at Wallasey and at Wigan where a Methodist church was destroyed. And the day's fighting also had the *Luftwaffe* ahead on aircraft losses, with twenty-two down, compared with the RAF's twenty-eight, including six bombers.

DAY 59 – FRIDAY 6 SEPTEMBER 1940

The air war was driven off the front pages by news of the British Navy routing the Italian fleet, before it had gone on to bombard Rhodes and other Italian naval bases. "The most brilliant action of the Mediterranean War", the *Daily Express* declared. "Fleet kick at Duce's door", announced the *Daily Mirror.*

With four days to go before the countdown for *Sealion* was due to start, Grand Admiral Räder was summoned to meet Hitler in Berlin. At the meeting were Generals Keitel and Jodl, the naval adjutant, Commander von Puttkamer, and Admiral Schniewind. The blockade was intensively discussed, whence Räder sought and got permission for the "strict execution" of submarine warfare. This entailed the removal of all previously agreed restrictions on operations. When it came to discussing *Sealion*, Räder was not encouraging. Making it clear to Hitler that he meant no criticism of Göring, he told him that weather conditions and "the situation in air warfare" had delayed the planned minesweeping. Nevertheless the new deadline of 21 September could be met. Barges were in position and the transports would be ready in time for embarkation. The invasion appeared possible, "if attended by favourable circumstances regarding air supremacy, weather, etc".[42]

Duncan Grinnell-Milne, author of *Silent Victory*, the book referred to in Chapter 2, argued that the "etc" referred to command of the sea.[43] Räder was seeking to transfer to the *Luftwaffe* the responsibility for something which could not be gained by air power alone but which the *Kriegsmarine* was incapable of achieving. In effect, despite the apparently positive note, he was actually saying in a roundabout fashion that the operation could not succeed. Emphasizing that point, he said: "The crossing itself will be very difficult. The Army cannot rely on being able to keep the divisions together".

The Grand Admiral then asked Hitler what the alternatives to *Sealion* were. At the same time, he reaffirmed his own belief that Germany should continue to give the appearance of mounting an invasion but resources should be redirected to industry through the release of personnel and shipping engaged in its preparation. His alternatives matched those offered by Jodl in mid-August – taking Gibraltar and the Suez Canal to exclude Britain from the Mediterranean area. Preparations for an assault on Gibraltar, he said, must be begun at once so that they were completed before the USA stepped in. The operation should not be considered of secondary importance, but as one of the main blows against Britain. The necessary orders to prepare for that attack were eventually formalized – in Führer Directive No. 18, issued on 12 November.

Räder later told his staff that the *Führer* had regarded a landing as the means of achieving an end to the war "at one stroke". "Yet", said the Grand Admiral, "the Führer has no thought of executing the landing if the risk of the operation is too high." His impression was that Hitler's decision to land in England was still by no means settled, as he was firmly convinced that Britain's defeat would be achieved without the landing.

Overnight, the *Luftwaffe* had about 190 bombers abroad – less than the number of aircraft that had been flying during the day. But since so many of the day formations had been fighters, the capacity to do harm during the night was greater. One small example of that occurred at precisely 1.13 a.m. Sunderland Central Station was hit by two large bombs, smashing craters 30 ft across and 15 ft deep. So violent was the blast that a carriage was lifted clear off the rails and thrown across a platform. Another part of a carriage was hurled across the street, wrecking the frontage of a toy shop. Fortunately – because of the hour – no one was injured. However, an enemy aircraft crashed on a house in Sunderland causing fires and considerable damage to the property.[44]

The Sunderland raid barely registered in the press. Home Intelligence recorded continuing complaints that "important provincial towns have to hide their identity even from themselves", while London still received "excessive publicity for its raids". That problem was about to get considerably worse when the London Blitz started. Already low profile, much of the rest of the country, its hardship and suffering, became invisible.

This night, bombers were again roaming the land. Durham and Yorkshire were among the counties paid visits. In Lincolnshire, damage to property was caused at Horncastle and many incendiaries were dropped in other parts of the county. Only speedy intervention by locals avoided serious damage. In Essex, a number of bombs and incendiaries were dropped and damage was caused to overhead electric cables. Surrey, Oxford, Bucks, Somerset, Dorset and Devon were subjected to attacks, as were areas in South Wales. The Midlands reported bombs dropped over limited areas with damage to gas, water, electricity and telephone services. Liverpool was bombed again. Some houses were demolished and water mains were severed.

Railway lines were blocked by an explosion at Spellow Station. Trains from Liverpool were delayed, adding further pressure on the transport system. Buckinghamshire got fifty incendiary bombs, dropped near a military camp at Iver. Only slight damage was reported. In Kent, mains were damaged in the early morning at Orpington and Shoreham. Worcestershire also saw damage to mains. Other property damage was reported in Dudley. In Scotland, a mine was dropped near Kinghorn, but no damage was recorded. In the south-eastern region, areas near Hastings and Brighton got the attention of the *Luftwaffe*. Wye and Ashford suffered slight damage to property and telephone wires. Other bombs were reported in parts of Sussex and Kent.

By the end of the day 58 civilians had been killed and approximately 298 injured. But still there was next to no media attention. People were being asked to "take it", but many felt their sacrifices were not being recognized.

The day had been young when the weekly secret résumé of the naval military and air situation made its way to the War Cabinet. This was the day, according to legend, that Fighter Command was on its last legs, on the point of collapse, smashed by the incessant, unrelenting attacks of the *Luftwaffe*. But, if this was the case, there was not the slightest hint of it in the résumé. It did report, however, that there had been an increase in shipping activity which could have been related to the invasion.

Photographic and other reconnaissance at Flushing had revealed an increase of barges and 12 floating bridge sections were newly arrived. A concentration of 70 small ships, average length 150 ft, had been observed on 4 September. At Delfzijl there were 100 barges in the harbour and 60 motorboats moving through the canal. At Zeebrugge there were 100 barges and a few small craft in harbour. At Ostend barges had increased to 100. But there was no concentration of barges at Boulogne, although 50 motorboats had arrived. Six torpedo boats of German T Class were at Le Havre.[45]

Elsewhere, Keith Park was preparing a "terse instruction" to his controllers, noting that, during the last major raid, only 7 out of 18 squadrons despatched had intercepted the enemy, and complaining that the majority of formations were only intercepted after they had dropped their bombs.[46] The War Cabinet was not apprised of this. Instead, it was fed a diet of false statistics which had the RAF suffer 168 losses in the week, of which 148 had been fighters, against 310 *Luftwaffe* "definites" and 128 "probables". That was a claimed exchange rate of approximately 3:1 whereas the actual rate was, by some strange coincidence, exactly even – 966 aircraft lost by both sides. The previous day, the RAF had claimed 54 raiders downed, compared with a loss of 11 of its own aircraft. This day, Fighter Command claimed 45 downed, against 19 of its own lost. The actuality was 33 *Luftwaffe* aircraft destroyed against 25 fighters lost, and 3 others, totalling 28. That put the RAF only slightly ahead on the day.

More important than the reality – which was only to emerge after the war – on 6 September 1940, by its own account, the RAF was winning the battle hands down. There was no hint of a crisis in Fighter Command and, where there was a problem, as identified by Park, it was that fighters were not being effectively deployed. Despite that, in Stockholm, British Minister Victor Mallet received a telegram from Halifax telling him not to meet Weissauer. Hitler was to be told, through him, that peace was not on the agenda.[47] The people were to bear the immediate consequences. Overnight, 68 *Luftwaffe* bombers raided London.

10.

Start of the Blitz

Now here it must be very definitely be stated that the objectives in London at which our Air Force aim are all of either military nature or of those industrial categories pertaining to England's war effort.

Hamburg broadcast, 8 September 1940[1]

The air war was about to become an end in itself. But it was not to be between opposing air fleets. Rather, it was an uneven battle between the aggressor's bombers and the British people. The crown of thorns had passed from Fighter Command to the civilian population. It had to suffer, endure and survive. This was the Blitz.

DAY 60 – SATURDAY 7 SEPTEMBER 1940

The morning was quiet. However, the Joint Intelligence Committee (JIC), keeping a close watch on German invasion preparations, had for some days been concerned about the barge movements to the Channel ports. Judging that the Germans would not bring these vessels within range of RAF attacks unless they were about to be used, it decided to warn the Chiefs of Staff that they considered an invasion "imminent".[2] Alan Brooke wrote: "All reports look like invasion getting nearer".[3] Fighter Command issued a warning to all units.

Park would normally have been at his post in his Uxbridge bunker, especially if big raids were expected, but this day he left command to his controllers. Should a raid develop, his instructions were that they should keep their fighters well back from the coast in order to guard the airfields and factories. He had then left for a meeting with Dowding to discuss pilot strengths.[4]

The quiet did not last. In France, a heavy, armoured train had rolled into the Channel coast railway station of La Boissière le Déluge, just outside Calais.

From it had emerged *Reichsmarschall* Göring. Flanked by Field Marshal Kesselring and General Loerzer, commander of II Air Corps, he made his way to the cliffs and stood there as his air fleets thundered overhead on their way to London.

Just before 5 p.m., 348 bombers, Heinkels, Dorniers and Junkers, escorted by 617 Messerschmitt fighters, converged on London in three deadly waves. As they merged, they formed a 20-mile wide block, filling 800 square miles of sky. It was undoubtedly the most concentrated assault against Britain since the Spanish Armada. On this day of all days, there were no clues as to its destination until it had almost arrived, by which time the fighter squadrons were poorly placed to intercept. The Observer Corps did not realize what was happening until the leading edge of the raid had reached its destination.

Even so, the RAF was able to bring down some German aircraft. But the defence was very limited. There was very little anti-aircraft fire as guns had been sent to protect the airfields. There were only ninety-two "heavies" available for the defence of the capital. Most of the raiders had come in between Dungeness and the Isle of Wight. Sound-locators, largely concentrated along the estuary approach, were either outflanked or swamped by the large number of aircraft. In addition communications failed between many of the vital points, and many of the guns did not go into action at all.[5]

As the reports from his bomber crews came in, a triumphant Göring rushed to a specially equipped mobile studio and broadcast to the German nation on this "historic" moment. "As a result of the provocative British attacks on Berlin on recent nights," he said, "the Führer has decided to order a mighty blow to be struck in revenge against the capital of the British Empire". Making clear his role, he declared: "I personally have assumed leadership of this attack, and today have heard above me the roaring of the victorious German squadrons which now, for the first time, are driving towards the heart of the enemy in full daylight, accompanied by countless fighter squadrons".[6]

Shocked and frightened East Enders voted with their feet. There was a mass exodus in two directions. Some went eastwards to Epping Forest and the open country of Essex, where thousands camped out in makeshift shelters. Others headed west, towards the centre of London, where it was believed shelters were deep and safe and the bombing less severe. In dangerously overcrowded Tube stations, individual displays of leadership, such as from an anonymous railway porter at Monument Station, kept the crowds moving. One group which emerged at Oxford Circus made for the shelter in Dickins and Jones, one of the larger department stores. Police attempted to prevent people queuing for shelter. Firmly, but without violence, they were brushed aside. The police returned, then to organize the queue people had formed. Their endeavours were punctuated by occasional flashes of humour which undoubtedly relieved the tension.[7]

What made events almost surreal – certainly for those who were there – was that "Black Saturday" had started off as such a beautiful day. Rarely for London at the time, the temperature had been in the 90s. And although everyone knew bombs might fall, there was no awareness that there would be a seismic shift in the course of the war on that day. This made it a day not only for death and destruction, but one for mystery and conspiracy. Early press reports, in the *New York Times* for instance, noted that "the all-out aerial warfare threatened by Hitler the previous week appeared to be in full swing as his bombers raided England by day and by night". The link between his speech on 4 September and the raid seemed obvious – and Göring had declared as much. This was Hitler's revenge.

On the ground, the results were inevitable. One reporter and novelist, Mea Allen wrote in a letter: "You felt you really were walking with death – death in front of you and death hovering in the skies".[8] This was London's first experience of total war and, as it later emerged, there was almost a sense that it wouldn't happen – a real sense of complacency that caught the RAF, the government and the defenders napping. When the aircraft were first heard it was thought they were British – until the bombs began to fall. Len Jones, an 18-year-old in Poplar, a working-class district in London targeted because of its warehouses and gasworks, remembered his reactions. There was that sense with terror that it is not really going to happen:

> That afternoon around five o'clock, I went outside the house. I'd heard the aircraft and it was very exciting, because the first formations were coming over without any bombs dropping, but very, very majestic; terrific. And I had no thought that they were actually bombers. Then from that point on I was well aware, because bombs began to fall and shrapnel was going along King Street, dancing off the cobbles. Then the real impetus came, in so far as the suction and the compression from the high explosive blasts just pulled you and pushed you, and the whole of this atmosphere was turbulating so hard.[9]

That sense, that it was not really going to happen, a sense of disbelief, was echoed later in Home Intelligence reports. Questions were asked as to whether London's defences had been as effective "as has been supposed", with the conviction that there had been a false sense of security, buoyed by a belief in government propaganda.[10]

When the day bombers had finished, the night shift took over, feeding and extending the fires started by the first waves. Shortly after midnight, London Fire Brigade recorded 9 conflagrations needing 100 pumps, 19 fires requiring 30 pumps or more, 40 fires requiring 10 pumps each and 1,000 lesser fires. In the Surrey Commercial Docks alone were 2 fires requiring 300 pumps each and one requiring 130 pumps. In Woolwich Arsenal, 200 pumps were required. By the time the bombers had done their work, 306 lay dead in the capital, with another 1,337 seriously injured. A further 142 had been killed in the suburbs – the total only a hundred short of the number of pilots killed in combat in the entire Battle of Britain.[11]

The raids should not have come as a great surprise. Apart from being flagged up in Hitler's speech, London was Britain's premier port. Already, the *Luftwaffe* had attacked Liverpool, Bristol, Plymouth, Southampton, Dover, Hull and the north-eastern ports, right up to Aberdeen. On this day, the attack was not on London as a city but London as a port. The move had been entirely logical. Furthermore, while there was obviously and rightly much focus on the human suffering, proportionate to tonnage of bombs and the duration of the raids, the casualty rate was relatively modest. During the First World War, on 13 June 1917, 14 Gotha bombers, in their first ever daylight raid, had dropped bombs weighing 5,400kg on the East End. In all 104 people had been killed, 154 seriously injured and 269 slightly injured – some as a result of anti-aircraft shells exploding prematurely or on their return to the ground.[12]

This time round, property damage was extensive and, proportionately, casualties were lighter. The effect on port operations was serious. Few ships were sunk, one of them being the tug *Beckton*. But at least twenty-four were damaged, many badly enough to prevent them sailing. Others were to sustain repeated damaged.[13] With damage to the dock facilities, the cranes, the barges and the warehouses, the *Luftwaffe* had dealt a powerful blow to the British economy. All this had been achieved for the loss of thirty-seven aircraft. Fighter Command had lost twenty-two, and Bomber Command one. As to the morale of the population, and in particular London, that was another question. Over the next few days, engineering a collapse seemed, for the Germans, the most promising way of ending the war quickly.

On the receiving end, things looked ominous. As bombers were pummelling London, the coded warning "Cromwell" was sent to Army and some Home Guard Units. Church bells were rung, some bridges were blown up and forces throughout the south-east went on high alert. Many Home Guard units spent an anxious and uncomfortable night, expecting by morning to see grey-uniformed soldiers storming up the beaches. They did not come.

DAY 61 – SUNDAY 8 SEPTEMBER 1940

The residents of East London emerged from their shelters – those that had access to them – dazed and shattered, some of them later to see Churchill on a carefully orchestrated tour. The Ministry of Information men had been out in force, planting the message that the prevailing mood was one of stoicism and weary resignation. With rescue workers still clawing away at the wreckage, however, the mood in some places was much uglier. People wanted revenge.[14] They wanted explanations from the government as to why they had been left so vulnerable to attack.[15]

Even as the bombs had started falling the previous day, the Conway Hall in London had been packed with people listening to the firebrand Independent Labour Party MP John McGovern. He had been telling his audience that the war was not a struggle between democracy and dictatorship. It was, he said, a capitalist-imperialist war, a fight of have-empires against have-not-empires. The man had a following – and with good cause.

Far from the cheerful "Blitz spirit" which the BBC was later so keen to foster on behalf of its Ministry of Information masters, many people felt trapped between their own government and the government of Germany. It was a "bosses' war" and they were pigs-in-the-middle.[16] F. R. Barry, a cannon of Westminster and vicar of St John's, Smith Square, was appalled at the lack of support of the people in the bombed districts. He sought an interview with Brendan Bracken (Churchill's Parliamentary Secretary), telling him that, if this continued, there would be anti-war demonstrations, which the government might not be able to contain.[17]

The more immediate problem was the need for protection. Many of the worst raids were now happening at night and once the sirens had sounded, families sought whatever shelter they could find. Public facilities remained inadequate. The so-called surface shelters not only afforded no protection from a direct hit, they were not designed for prolonged occupation, nor equipped for sleeping. At best, they were cold and draughty, and stuffy when sealed. Few were heated. In low-lying areas they were easily flooded, and many were perpetually damp. But people, either had to make do with them, or flimsy Anderson shelters which they dug themselves in their back gardens, if they had them. Failing that, many people crouched beneath kitchen tables or under the stairs.[18]

Others seemed better provided for. Those who could afford it were able to book seats in a luxury sleeper train which left a London terminus each evening and parked up in an isolated country siding, to afford its guests an uninterrupted night's sleep. Each morning, as the train returned to London, breakfast was provided – off ration – in the restaurant car.[19]

Information Minister Duff Cooper and Lady Diana were able to rent a penthouse suite in the then ultra-modern Dorchester Hotel. This gave them access to the cellars, formerly used as Turkish baths, which had been converted into a luxury shelter, known by its inhabitants as "the dorm". There was a neat row of cots, spaced 2 ft apart, each provided with "a lovely fluffy eiderdown". Nine peers also slept there each night. Lord Halifax had his own personal space reserved.[20]

Although the shelter was advertised as bomb proof, even against a direct hit, Chief of the Air Staff, then Charles Portal, discussed its safety with Robert (later Lord) Boothby. "Don't tell them," he said, referring to the well-heeled shelterers, "but in fact they are not under the hotel at all. They are one foot under the pavement outside. If a bomb falls on them, they will all be killed".[21] For the less well endowed, the Underground stations were the obvious refuge. But those seeking shelter found the entrances locked overnight, and often during air raids. Police moved people on if they attempted to shelter, and many attest to the unpleasant and unhelpful attitude of station staff and officials.[22]

US Ambassador Joseph "Joe" Kennedy was openly dismissive of Britain's chances of survival, saying that if war continued, the present capitalist system would crack. It would be better to accept a semi-defeat now than lose all later.[23] And on this very day, an enigmatic German by the name of Albrecht

Haushofer, latterly associated with the German resistance, wrote a letter to the Duke of Hamilton in Scotland, requesting a meeting "somewhere on the outskirts of Europe, perhaps in Portugal". Haushofer was a long-time acquaintance of Hitler and a close confident of Nazi Party deputy chief, Rudolf Hess, with whom he had met on the last day of August.[24] In his letter, he referred to people whom the German Government believed wanted a "German-English agreement". They included Samuel Hoare in his ambassador's residence in Madrid, and Rab Butler, both supporters of Chamberlain's appeasement policy.[25]

Some hint of how the Germans saw the situation came from the Naval Staff war diary entry of the day. It stated:

> From a series of reports, sent by the Military Attaché in Washington, on the morale of the population and the situation in London, it emerges that the will to fight of the London population is considerably affected by lack of sleep. This physical weakness is regarded as the worst danger to morale. As regards damage, he reports that twenty-four large docks were totally burnt out and four gasometers were destroyed. The stations, Sherrycross (sic) and Waterloo, and several underground stations are damaged. Of ten good airfields round London, seven are almost completely unusable.[26]

Other reports in a similar vein provided reason for the Germans to believe that Britain was being badly damaged by the air attacks. Forcing her to conclude a peace was believed to be within the realms of the possible.

Churchill was unlikely to be thinking in these terms. According to his official biographer, after he had returned from his visit to the bombed areas of London, he had been told of an Enigma decrypt which "made it clear that the German invasion plans were so ill-advanced that even the training was not complete" and that there had been no "hard and fast decision to take action in any particular direction".[27]

For the many millions of ordinary Britons not directly affected by the bombing, and without the inside track, there were the papers to read. The *Sunday Express* had a three-line banner headline across the full width of the front page. "500 Nazi bombers strike at London: train, theatre, dog track and works hit", it proclaimed. The Germans, "driven into anger by the RAF attacks on Germany, threw everything they had into the biggest air attack of the war on London yesterday and throughout the night", the story went – under the subtitle: "Fighters and guns crash 65 raiders down in flames". Thus, the report concluded, "There is no reason whatsoever for dejection or depression. The RAF is more than holding its own".

Sunday Express readers were, by coincidence to enjoy a column from J. B. Priestley, who had been given a regular slot by Beaverbrook. He chose for his title, "The two most dangerous people – those who care but don't know: those who know but don't care". The task of the people of this country, he wrote, was to destroy Nazism abroad and also to create at home a new, thorough and militant democracy. The blockage, stated explicitly, was "Tory Britain", coming into the category of "those who know but don't care". It was a mistake to think the "fifth column" is a foreigner, he wrote. It was this group, with "no particular friends anywhere, simply because it has been regarded for some time now as being short-sighted, fumbling, greedy, reactionary and about to decay".

And in the evening, Priestley was back, this time on the airwaves with another BBC *Postscript* talk. It was a pity, he said,

> that in the earlier months of this war, the authorities were so emphatic that we were civilians, a helpless passive lot, so many skins to save, so much weight of tax-paying stuff to be huddled out of harm's way. We see now, when the enemy bombers come roaring at us at all hours, and it's our nerve versus his, that we're not really civilians any longer but a mixed lot of soldiers – machine-minding soldiers, milkmen and postmen soldiers, housewives and mother soldiers – and what a gallant corps that is – even broadcasting soldiers. Now and then, we ought to be paraded, and perhaps a few medals handed out.[28]

Of course, very few of these "soldier civilians" were going to get medals, and then only under exceptional circumstances. Yet every one of the 2,937 British and Allied airmen who qualified as "the few" gained a campaign medal and the coveted Battle of Britain clasp. But the civilians were by no means the only ones to be excluded. The sailors guarding Britain's shores did not qualify for the clasp. Nevertheless, during the night when most of Dowding's airmen were safely tucked up in their beds, the Navy was out on the narrow seas.

In one action off Ostend, three MTBs damaged two ships, one of 2,000 tons and one of 1,000 tons. The light cruiser HMS *Galatea*, escorted by destroyers *Campbell*, *Garth* and *Vesper*, plus light cruiser *Aurora* with destroyers *Hambledon*, *Holderness* and *Venetia* were despatched to shell German shipping concentrations off Calais and Boulogne. In the early hours of the morning, an Anson dropped flares over both ports. No shipping was found in Calais Roads and *Galetea* did not conduct a bombardment. However, *Aurora* bombarded the Boulogne harbour area. Destroyers *Atherstone, Berkley, Bulldog, Beagle* and *Fernie* swept along the French coast from Le Touquet to the south-west up to five miles north of Cape Antifer. The cruisers arrived back at Sheerness on 9 September. On her return, *Galatea* struck a mine off Sheerness and repaired at Chatham until 8 January 1941.[29]

Fighter Command finished the day with 6 aircraft lost. Bomber Command, flying over 130 aircraft on anti-invasion raids, brought the total to 21, against 16 *Luftwaffe* losses. No less than 10 Blenheims were shot down.

DAY 62 – MONDAY 9 SEPTEMBER 1940

Londoners this morning were confronted with a savagely remodelled landscape. Familiar landmarks lay in ruins, the latest St Thomas's Hospital in Westminster. It had taken a direct hit overnight. Life nevertheless went on. It had to.

A problem for the editors of the Monday newspapers was how to deal with the great raids of the Saturday, running into the Sunday morning, with a further set of raids on the Sunday evening. The *Guardian* handled it by giving the headline lead to the events of the Sunday night but then devoting most of the copy to the Saturday raids, about which there was now considerable detail. The headlines, however, concealed the trauma. Home Intelligence reported that the strongest feeling was "one of shock amongst all classes", who have lulled themselves into a false sense of security, saying: "London is the safest place", and "they'll never get through the London defences".

Centre page in the *Guardian* spread was the tragic story of "Bomb's havoc in crowded public shelter", after a bomb had penetrated a ventilation shaft. This admitted to fourteen deaths, the location – as always – unnamed. In Whitechapel, however, a much greater tragedy had played out. One of eight blocks of flats on the Peabody estate, sandwiched between the Royal Mint and East Smithfield's Goods Station, had taken a hit. The entire building had collapsed onto the basement where tenants and their guests had been sheltering. There were no survivors. Only long after the war was it publicly acknowledged that seventy-eight people had died, when the site was marked by a memorial plaque.[30]

Nothing of this got into the media at the time, despite the knowledge of the tragedy being widely known locally. Yet the censorship could not prevent the spread of news locally. In the tight-knit community of the East End, the story of the disaster spread like wildfire. This fuelled what Home Intelligence was constantly noting – a growing cynicism over official casualty reports. That in turn fed rumours of mass casualties and exaggerated numbers of deaths.

Despite this, Home Intelligence claimed that there were "no signs of defeatism" except among a small section of elderly women in the "front line" districts such as East Ham, "who cannot stand the constant bombing". Districts sustaining only one or two shocks soon rally, said the day's report. But in Dockside areas, it said: "the population is showing visible signs of nerve cracking from constant ordeals":

> Old women and mothers are undermining morale of young women and men by their extreme nervousness and lack of resilience. Men state they cannot sleep because they must keep up the morale of their families and express strong desire to get families away from danger areas. Families clinging together, however, and any suggestion of sending children away without mothers considered without enthusiasm. People beginning to trek away from Stepney and other Dockside areas in families and small groups. Many encountered in City today with suitcases and belongings. Some make for Paddington without any idea of their destination.

It was clear that nerves were raw. There were "many expressions of bitterness" at the apparent impossibility of stopping German raiders from doing what they liked. This issue was "bewildering and frightening people", and the opinion of anti-aircraft gunfire was "astonishingly small".[31]

The newspapers were playing down the effects of the bombing. The *Guardian* noted that London as a whole had had its first big raid and had come out of it well. It could "hold its head up now with those heroic towns of the South-east which had stood up to repeated battering". A journalist who had toured the damaged areas in the East End of London claimed he had seen nothing to show that the raids had daunted the spirits of the East End. In other papers, there were laudatory accounts of the *sang froid* of the nurses at St Thomas's. A constant theme also was the promise of revenge, although the *Daily Mail* chose a curious form of words:

> We prefer to put it another way: that the British Forces, the RAF especially, will pursue

a steadily increasing campaign against Germany for set purposes to victory, and that object will in time become overwhelming.

Many authors attested that this restraint had been "guided" by the Ministry of Information's preferences on reporting the public responses to the bombing. The calls for revenge were played down. The preferred image was one of people "stoically heroic and stolidly good-humoured". This was characterized in the catchphrase, "London can take it", assiduously promoted by the Ministry of Information, later becoming the basis for a number of newsreel titles covering different towns and cities in the UK.[32]

Daylight raids continued, hitting widely dispersed targets, which included south London suburbs such as Weybridge, Kingston and Croydon. As bombers met fighters, they jettisoned their bombs. Considerable damage was done to suburban homes. Kingston and Surbiton suffered heavily. Then Southampton and Rochester were targeted again. Through the day, though, the East End was toured by the Prime Minister and the King and Queen, in an attempt to raise morale.

At six in the evening, the first of the night shift crossed the Sussex coast, headed for London, for another night of pummelling. Somerset House and the Royal Courts of Justice were among those hit. The newly completed surgical wing of Great Ormond Street Hospital was narrowly saved from complete destruction when veteran stoker William Pendle braved flooding and fire to turn off the hospital's damaged boilers before they exploded. He was awarded the George Medal.[33] By morning, three more main line stations were out of action, another 370 Londoners were dead and more than 1,400 were injured.

And, of course, the RAF's battle continued – distant noises off. Fighter Command lost twenty-one aircraft. Bomber Command added five to the toll, bringing losses to twenty-six. The *Luftwaffe* lost twenty-seven to all causes, including at least five accidents. Twelve of the losses were Me 109s, shot down during the day fighting. Bomber casualties were minimal.

Overnight, the Royal Navy sent five destroyers to sweep the French coast from St Valery north-eastwards towards Le Touquet, seeking to locate and destroy enemy small craft which had been reported on the loose. Two destroyers had proceeded towards Calais and three towards Boulogne. MTBs also had carried out a sweep between Ostend and the mouth of the Scheldt. Only one small craft was found out of harbour. Reconnaissance aircraft reported "a fair number of vessels of small size" still entering the ports of Flushing, Ostend, Calais and Boulogne.[34]

DAY 63 – TUESDAY 10 SEPTEMBER 1940

By morning, no less than 148 German bombers had visited London. Liverpool Street Station was among the stations hit and a number of other landmarks suffered. A *Luftwaffe* bomb breached the northern outfall sewer, the great work of Victorian engineer Joseph Bazalgetti, which carried the bulk of London's sewage. Freed from their bounds, the contents poured into the River Lea, adding a pungent stench to the already overloaded atmosphere. The metaphor was somewhat fitting.

The morning's headlines told the story, not that anyone in London needed telling. On the third night of the Blitz just past, the bombing had been heavier than ever. The London correspondent for the *Yorkshire Post* called it, "the worst terrorist air raid yet inflicted upon London and probably upon any part of the country".

Much was made of the royal tour, with the *Daily Express* headlining its report: "They'd lost their homes, but could still raise a cheer", marking the reaction of the locals to the visit. Yet, on this day, people had booed the royal couple as they had made their rounds.[35] Clearly, the King had been enlisted to assist with the propaganda effort, the paper having him pointing to Anderson shelters among the wreckage, and remarking on the protection they gave. Then, said the paper, "Homeless East Enders crowded round the King's car to cheer. Police had to force a path for him. But the people climbed on to the running-boards to tap the windows and wave".

A sombre War Cabinet met at the usual time, just after midday, when John Anderson had to admit to a "difficult situation" arising for the homeless in the East End. This matter, he said, had not, perhaps, been very well handled by all the local authorities. Arrangements had been made for the London County Council to take over and a special organization was also being set up in Whitehall. It was proposed to transfer the homeless to districts further west.[36]

This was going to be too late for Canning Town in the centre of the docklands area, where tragedy was to reach almost unbearable proportions. Prior to the nineteenth century, this had been largely marshland, accessible only by boat or toll bridge. The high water table was not amenable to digging shelters and, for the same reason, there were no underground railways. Now, the hundreds made homeless by the bombing had gravitated to a "rest centre" set up in the now vacated South Hallsville School. They were promised transport away from the heat of the battle.

Journalist Ritchie Calder visited the school. He described it as "a bulging dangerous ruin" which had survived the raids only by a miracle. But he was distinctly uneasy. "It was a calculable certainty" that it would be targeted again. Yet the promised transport failed to show up. According to some, it had been mistakenly diverted to Camden Town in North London. The refugees thus settled down to spend another night in the unprotected buildings – one of the most dangerous places on earth, under the flight path of German bombers making their runs on the docks. And, at 3.45 a.m., the predictable (and predicted) tragedy struck in the form of a large calibre bomb.

Rescue workers dragged seventy-three bodies from the wreckage. But as they worked, a cordon was thrown around the area to keep people from seeing what was happening. The censor, or so we are told, warned the press there were to be no reports or pictures of the tragedy, so devastating would be the effect on the morale of an already shattered population.[37] In fact, a brief report appeared in next day's *Guardian* and the incident was reported in detail by the *AP*.

Rescue was then expected to take at least twenty-four hours. The work seems to have been gone on for three days. Then, according to legend, by "government order", the origin of which is not known – the search was abandoned. The wreckage was limed and razed to the ground. Locals are convinced that the authorities concealed the full death toll, which was far higher than the official figure. Some say it might have been as high as 400 or 450. The *Guardian* of 12 September reported the casualties of Monday night for the whole area being 400 with 1,400 injured, but with "the majority of the fatalities occurring when an elementary school in the East End of London … collapsed". There was bitterness that no effort had been made to discover the identities of the many for whom this illusory refuge had been their final resting place. The incident became a festering sore in relations between the much-troubled people and the authorities.

The full horror had yet to be fully realized as this September day dawned. It revealed a blanket of low cloud across much of northern Europe. Large-scale daylight operations were out of the question. Air activity was confined to sporadic "nuisance" raids. However, across the Channel, more than 3,000 barges and other vessels had been assembled with a view to transporting a German army to England. A decision had to be made on whether they were going to be used. The weather was poor, limiting air operations over England, and the forecast for the next ten days offered unsettled conditions. Hitler decided to delay making up his mind until 14 September.[38]

The Naval Staff recorded other concerns, the diarist writing: "It would be in conformity with timetable preparations for the operation of *Sealion* if the *Luftwaffe* concentrated less on London and more on Portsmouth and Dover, as well as on the naval forces in and near the operational area, in order to eliminate the potential threats of the enemy". Nevertheless, it went on: "But the Naval Staff does not consider this a suitable moment to approach the *Luftwaffe* or the Führer with such demands". Hitler thought the major attack on London might be decisive. Thus a systematic and prolonged bombardment of London could result in the enemy adopting an attitude which would render *Sealion* superfluous. "Hence the Naval Staff will not proceed with the demand."[39]

This, effectively, acknowledged what had been the case for some time. The air operation was a strategic bombardment. Bremen Radio this day broadcast: "It is a question of time – a few short weeks, then this conflagration will reach its natural end".[40] A Nazi communiqué stated that the air offensive would be "pressed relentlessly until the British capitulate". New waves of German bombers flying against London would "carry out remorseless and relentless warfare until the smoking ruins of industrial and military objectives, decimation of the British Air Force and shattered morale of the British people bring into power a government that will accept German terms".[41]

This was a remarkably lucid declaration of the German war aims and it would have been entirely logical for the Germans also to be exploring diplomatic channels to present their terms, as they had following Hitler's peace offer on 19 July.

Thus, on this day, Karl Haushofer sent a letter to his son, Albrecht – whom we met only two days ago. He referred to "secret peace talks" which were going on with Britain. There was talk of "middlemen" such as Ian Hamilton (head of the British Legion), the Duke of Hamilton and Violet Roberts, whose nephew, Walter Roberts was a close relative of the Duke of Hamilton and was working in the political intelligence and propaganda branch of the Secret Intelligence Service. Violet was living in Lisbon. And Portugal was said to be one of the four main places where secret peace negotiations were taking place, the others being Spain, Sweden and Switzerland.[42] All these things may have been connected – and may not have been. But there is no doubt that another "peace offensive" was in progress.

In the air war of the day, the casualty rate was well down, reflecting reduced air activity. Only two Fighter Command aircraft were lost, neither to combat, plus four RAF bombers. The *Luftwaffe* lost six aircraft, including two He 111s on the ground to a bombing raid on Eindhoven. Eight more were very badly damaged. However, much of RAF Bomber Command's efforts were focused on destroying invasion barges.

DAY 64 – WEDNESDAY 11 SEPTEMBER 1940

Reported in the *Daily Mirror*, the Federation of Tenants and Residents Associations was demanding the opening of all Tube stations at night and the requisitioning for the public of all good private shelters, as a temporary measure to meet the problem arising from the wholesale bombing of London. Londoners themselves were "hopping mad", but showing no signs of defeatism, the paper also said, citing a message sent by a *United Press* correspondent to New York.

This was the day that Göbbels addressed a group of Czech "intellectual workers" and journalists who were visiting Berlin. "The greatest historical drama that history has ever known is being played out at this moment", he told them, offering them the opportunity to reorganize Europe, "at the moment when British power is collapsing."[43] Churchill, on the other hand, had been very much in evidence in the bombed areas, but he might not have learned a great deal from the crowds who followed his progress. Certainly, he felt the need for more information, sending a minute to General Ismay asking for reports on "whether any serious effects were being produced by the air attack on food supplies and distribution, and on the number of homeless".[44]

On the latter, he might well have referred to that vital asset, the daily Home Intelligence report. It noted substantial "unplanned" evacuation from the East End. Families in the Deptford area were making for the hop fields of Kent, taking with them "such of their belongings as they can carry". Others were simply making for the nearest mainline station, with no apparent destination and no objective other than to "get away from it all". Many more, especially in South London, found shelter in the chalk caves of Chiselhurst.[45]

Those who moved west became a serious problem. Towns such as Reading, Windsor and Oxford found themselves unwitting hosts to thousands of refugees who had spent their very last pennies on getting as far from the conflagrations as they could afford. Local authorities, churches and voluntary groups found them accommodation. In Oxford, the university colleges acted as clearing houses. Five hundred to a thousand people were sheltered for nearly two months in the Majestic cinema on the city's outskirts.[46]

In other areas, notably parts of Essex, residents displayed considerable hostility to the incomers. There were ugly scenes and even violence. Something had to be done. Taking the cue from J. B. Priestley, Home Intelligence advised that, as these people were being referred to as "soldiers in the front line", this sentiment should be encouraged. "It would undoubtedly help," it said, "if the public were made to feel that their friends and relations had died for their country, in the same sense as if they were sailors or airmen." The dead from air raids were soon being buried in flag-draped coffins, reflecting their status as "killed in action".

The Wednesday report told of morale being "rather more strained than the newspapers suggest". There had been an increase in the number of people listening to "Lord Haw-Haw". Rumours, mostly "exaggerated accounts of raid damage and casualties" had increased considerably.[47]

Just after midday, the War Cabinet met.[48] In a crowded session, it considered the text of telegrams exchanged with His Majesty's Minister in Stockholm, together with the note from Lord Halifax. The telegrams were to and from Victor Mallet, concerning the peace offer which had emanated from Ludwig Weissauer on 5 September. As instructed, Mallet had refused to see Weissauer. "I could see no useful purpose in the suggested meeting in view of the express views of His Majesty's Government on continuing the war", he wrote. Ekberg, the intermediary, had begged him not to refuse as it would "certainly be reported to Hitler".

Dictated on 9 September, received and deciphered in time to put in front of the Cabinet, was a further telegram from Mallet. This was the "last chance", the Minister had been told by Ekberg, at the behest of Weissauer. The alternative to

1. The myth of rescue: an RAF 100 class High Speed Launch, built by the British Power Boat Co to an Air Ministry Order issued in 1936. Originally designed as a seaplane tender, and pressed into service as an air-sea rescue launch, the launches featured prominently in contemporary propaganda, but the reality was that there were too few available to provide a comprehensive rescue service in 1940.

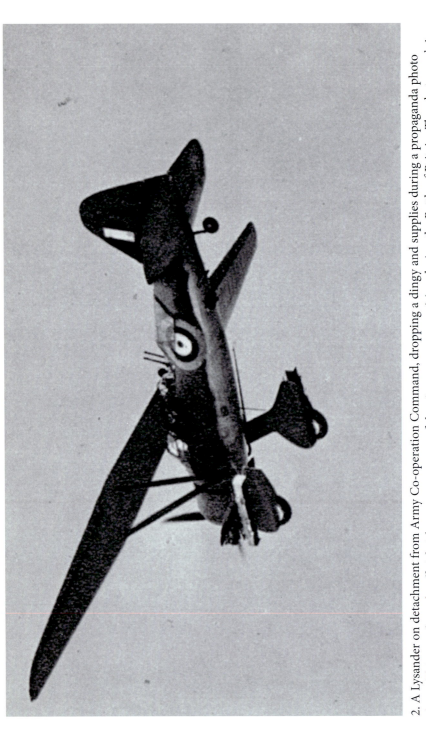

2. A Lysander on detachment from Army Co-operation Command, dropping a dingy and supplies during a propaganda photo shoot. This was the only official airborne component of the air-sea rescue provision during the Battle of Britain. The photograph is taken from a contemporary (1941) propaganda pamphlet.

3. The Supermarine Walrus – from the same stable as the Spitfire (and built in the same factory), this was originally procured for the Royal Navy as a catapult-launched spotter aircraft. Used informally in limited numbers during the summer of 1940, it was not officially taken on charge by the RAF as a rescue aircraft until 1941.

4. The Heinkel 59: used widely as a rescue craft throughout the summer of 1940, in Red Cross markings and later in Luftwaffe camouflage. This was part of the far superior German rescue system, which included inflatable rafts for fighter pilots and marker dye, neither of which was available to RAF aircrew.

5. Supermarine Spitfire 1a: the glamorous half of the Spitfire/Hurricane duo which provided the bulk of Fighter Command's day fighters. Although technically advanced, and a match for the modern Me 109 German day fighter, it was next to useless as a night fighter, allowing the Germans to circumvent the RAF with their night bombers. To that extent, Fighter Command became an airborne Maginot line.

ALL TOGETHER: "NOT ME, HE'S THE ONE."

6. An implied rebuke to the Churchill's 20 August «The Few» speech. «George» Strube in the Express political cartoon the following day depicts his trademark «little man» undecided as to whom he should award his «bouquet». The airman is only one of the many from which he has to choose. The wartime propaganda photograph depicting «The Few» showed RAF bomber aircrew.

7. The fruits of victory: a Heinkel 111 from KG55 shot down on 16 August during an attack on Feltham, near London. After it had crash landed at Annington Farm in Bramber, Sussex, local resident Gordon James took this photo as the remains were transported to a scrapyard. It was against the law to take such photos, so Mr James kept his camera hidden until after the war, when he finally had the film developed.

8. Two-way traffic: the wreck of an RAF Blenheim bomber after the disastrous raid on Aalborg airfield on 13 August 1940, when all eleven of the attacking aircraft were shot down. When Bomber and Coastal Command losses were factored in, the RAF and Luftwaffe came though the official Battle of Britain roughly at parity.

9. Propaganda: German air raid on Dover Harbour, 29 July 1940. This widely published photograph of a Stuka attack on shipping accompanied claims that no damage had been done.

10. The attack, in fact, had severely damaged and set on fire the depot ship HMS Sandhurst, laden with ammunition and fuel, threatening the town of Dover. Three firemen we to be awarded the George Medal from for their part in extinguishing the fire. Yet no details of their bravery was published. «The Few» took the accolades.

11. Despite fears of an airborne invasion, the German transport fleet had been severely depleted during the attack through the Low Country. On 10 May alone, 157 Ju 57 transports were lost, and it would be May 1941 – immediately prior to the invasion of Crete – before the fleet was back up to strength.

12. Specialist assault craft, meanwhile, were still being designed, developed and built. These Siebel ferries, for instance, were supposed to carry the anti-aircraft weapons to protect the invasion fleet. Yet they only started to come on-stream in any numbers in November 1940, after the invasion had been cancelled.

13. Spearhead German formations were being forced to rely converted assault boats (Sturmboots) designed for river crossings and barely, if at all, seaworthy.

14. Assault boats, converted barges and shipping seen here in late 1940, believed to be in Belgium during a rehearsal for the invasion. Previously unpublished, this unofficial soldier's snap shows the triumvirate, beached at low tide. Vulnerable and inflexible, this was not a credible assault force.

15. Unable to prevail against the RAF's day fighters and ill-equipped to launch an invasion, the Germans turned against the British people as their target, employing night bombing as their main tactic, the aim to force an overthrow of the government and regime change. Against them were the «many», which eventually included 300,00 men and women of the Anti-Aircraft Command.

16. Passive defence relied on civilian fortitude and largely inadequate shelters – by design. Here, wrecked Anderson shelters in the gardens of 127-129 Mapledene Road, Hackney, following an attack on the night of 9-10 October 1940. Made of curved corrugated iron bolted to strong supports, the shelters were supposed to be buried three feet underground in back gardens with eighteen inches of earth piled on top. They were small and cramped, cold, not soundproofed, and tended to flood regularly. They offered no protection against a direct hit, as this photograph illustrates.

peace was the continuance of the war on an intensified scale; special mention was made of the loss to Great Britain of Egypt, the Middle East and ultimately India. So concerned had Halifax been about the exchange that he, with his Permanent Under-Secretary Alexander Cadogan, had twice visited Churchill on 9 September. There was no disagreement between the men. It was a question not of what to, but how to reply – whether there was anything to be gained by playing for time. As a measure of how much sentiment had changed and confidence grown, the mood was for a rejection without delay.

Halifax informed his Cabinet colleagues this day that the offer was "essentially the same as that made to us recently through the King of Sweden" – to which Churchill himself had suggested a response. He proposed an immediate reply which followed the line adopted on the previous occasion: it "lies with the German Government to make proposals by which the wrongs that Germany has inflicted upon other nations may be redressed". And not only did the Cabinet approve Halifax's action, it authorized him to tell Roosevelt of the exchange, on the basis that it would score political points with the president.[49]

The Cabinet also discussed measures being taken to counter the threat of invasion, when they were told of a telegram from Hoare in Madrid, who had picked up from a German source that the real enemy objective was Egypt. From Stockholm and Madrid, therefore, sources were pointing to the Middle East. Churchill thought it "by no means impossible" that the Germans would decide not to invade, "because they were unable to obtain the domination over our fighter force".[50]

That evening, Churchill broadcast to the nation in an attempt to boost morale. "These cruel, wanton indiscriminate bombings of London are of course a part of Hitler's invasion plan," he declared. "He hopes by killing large numbers of civilians and women and children that he will terrorize and cow the people of this mighty Imperial city and make them a burden and anxiety for the Government, and thus distract our attention unduly from the ferocious onslaught he is preparing".

Churchill continued: "Little does he know the spirit of the British nation or the tough fibre of the Londoners". It was their forebears who had played "a leading part in the establishment of Parliamentary institutions and who have been bred to value freedom far above their lives". Hitler became, "This wicked man", and then: "the repository and embodiment of many forms of soul destroying hatred, this monstrous product former wrongs and shames". He had now "resolved to try to break our famous island race by a process of indiscriminate slaughter and destruction". In his finest rhetorical form, the Prime Minister then said:

> What he has done is to kindle a fire in British hearts, here and all over the world, which will glow long after all traces of the conflagrations he has caused in London have been removed. He has lighted a fire which will burn with a steady and consuming flame until the last vestiges of Nazi tyranny have been burnt out of Europe, and until the Old World and the New can join hands to rebuild the temples of man's freedom and man's honour on foundations which will not soon or easily be overthrown.[51]

In the reference to "the Old World and the New" there was a direct appeal to the USA to join the war. London's agonies were sufficient reason for this to happen. His message was spread throughout the world but, in the USAas much by the network of hundreds of "local" papers, such as the Florida-based *Sarasota Herald Tribune*. Often relying on agency or syndicated copy, their collective audience measured in tens of millions. And the message they conveyed was stark. Hitler's invasion fleet, poised on the other side of the Channel, was ready to strike.

The daily air war, however, was taking on a direction of its own. All of a sudden, there were several different wars going on – seemingly unrelated. Fighter Command was still battling away against the daylight elements of the *Luftwaffe* which, in the morning comprised one Henschel 126 on a reconnaissance mission near Dover and one machine bombing the radar station at Poling. After lunch, the Germans put up a series of raids.

The first was aimed largely at London, with bombs falling on the City, but also on the docks, Islington and Paddington. Others fell on Biggin Hill, Kenley, Brooklands and Hornchurch. A second raid, despite the best efforts of harrying fighters, managed to dump bombs on Southampton and Portsmouth. Then a force of Me 109s appeared over Dover on a barrage balloon shoot. Another force attacked a Channel convoy, disabling the escort *Atherstone*, in a throwback to an earlier phase of the fighting. While that was happening, there was a progression of single-aircraft raids heading off to bomb inland RAF aerodromes.

On the day, Fighter Command lost thirty-two aircraft, while Bomber Command again concentrated on the invasion fleet, losing five aircraft on these and other operations, bringing the total to thirty-seven. The Germans only lost twenty-six. And, after his first escape on 25 August, Sgt Mervyn Sprague was shot down again – by another Me 110. South of Selsey Bill, his Spitfire crashed into the Channel. This time there was no "Digger" Aitkin to rescue him. His body was washed ashore at Brighton on 10 October.[52]

Meanwhile, London's defences were being beefed up. On the orders of General Pile and his officers of AA Command, guns were on the move. By late afternoon of 10 September, thirty-five additional 3.7in guns were in London. By this night, more were ready – their objective less to shoot down aircraft than to worry the enemy and hearten the civilian population. When the raiders came, they threw up a barrage of 13,221 shells, an average of 378 rounds per site, with the star performer firing 805.[53]

DAY 65 – THURSDAY 12 SEPTEMBER 1940

The press majored on the overnight anti-aircraft barrage. Also reported was an attack on Buckingham Palace, front-page material but lower down, as the bomb had been delayed action, exploding in the small hours of Tuesday morning.[54] The King and Queen had been away for the night and staff were safely in shelters, well away from the spot. No one was injured.

Thus, the *Daily Express* gave more space to the raids on barge concentrations, as indeed did the *Guardian*. This was a feature of British propaganda and a measure of its skill. Some bad news, or even the potentially frightening, was allowed – but it was "offset" with the counterpoint. Thus, Hitler assembling his invasion forces was balanced by "RAF attacking". The effect was unremittingly upbeat.

In the main, it seemed to work: "In London, morale is particularly high: people are much more cheerful today", said Home Intelligence. The largely useless but noisy barrage had given Londoners great heart, an all-important sense that the nation was "fighting back". The Metropolitan Commissioner of Police also believed morale was holding up, stating: "My latest reports are that there is no sign of panic anywhere in the East End". Inhabitants were "shaken by continued lack of sleep" but there was no wish to evacuate and "no defeatist talk".[55]

George Orwell did not entirely agree. This morning he had met a youth of about twenty, in dirty overalls, perhaps a garage hand. He had been very "embittered and defeatist" about the war and horrified about the destruction he had seen in South London. He said Churchill had visited the bombed area near the Elephant [and Castle] and at a spot where twenty out of twenty-two houses had been destroyed remarked that it "was not too bad". The youth had said, "I'd have wrung his bloody neck if he'd said it to me".[56]

On the back of Churchill's speech, the *Guardian* ramped up the invasion threat. With its lead item was an analysis from Brigadier General John Charteris: "the stage is set" and "the actors are ready", he wrote. However, Hitler had failed to secure mastery of the air. The tone was not at all alarmist. And bad weather over Europe held off air operations. The RAF ended up two fighters down, both lost through accidents, while the *Luftwaffe* lost six. None of these was attributed to combat operations.

The daily Home Intelligence report did not convey wholly complimentary news. The Prime Minister's speech was generally well received, it said, but not so enthusiastically as usual. Many people "having convinced themselves that the invasion is 'off' disliked being reminded of it again".

The *Glasgow Herald* had an article based on an *AP* report, datelined Constantinople. Hitler, it said, "may make another peace offer in the next few weeks". It would be made directly or may come through intermediaries, according to "several persons recently arrived from Germany".

Hitler was extremely anxious to avoid another winter of war and a direct attack on England, "which he realised would be a risky enterprise". He still believed it was possible to defeat Britain as he had defeated France, by means of the double weapon of indiscriminate bombing coupled with intensive propaganda. Bombarding British civilians "will be continued at all costs in the hope of undermining their morale". Then he would make another "generous gesture" and offer the possibility of peace, hoping to cause dissension among the politicians of Great Britain. And the *Herald* was not alone. A very similar story was published in the *Daily Express*, attributed to *Reuters*, so this was no random piece of gossip picked up by a single correspondent.

In a telegram which the German Foreign Office received this day, the chargé d'affaires in Washington, Thomsen, referred to the "immense difficulties of life" in London, and quoted a *New York Times* correspondent who wondered "how long the nerves of a people can withstand this kind of bombardment".[57]

START OF THE BLITZ

In Germany, the war diary entry of the Naval Operations Staff for the day lamented: "[T]he air campaign is being conducted specifically as an air offensive without regard for the current requirements of naval warfare ... the fact therefore remains that chances for the execution of the landing operations have remained uninfluenced by the effects of the intensified air offensive ...". As far as the *Kriegsmarine* was concerned, the *Luftwaffe* was making no contribution to the preparations for *Sealion*. And without its full commitment, it was hard to see how any invasion could succeed.[58]

DAY 66 – FRIDAY 13 SEPTEMBER 1940

Overnight, 105 bombers had raided the capital. Casualties were said to be "relatively light", with 110 killed and 260 injured in the London area. There were harassing raids in the Home Counties and East Anglia, while four bombs fell in a "Lancashire coastal town", identified by the Germans as Liverpool. The raid killed seven, injured fifteen and destroyed ten houses.

Emerging from the night's bombing, Londoners were again regaled with stories of impending invasion, matched by tales of derring do, as Nazi convoys in the Channel had been bombed and "barge concentrations" attacked. That news, however, was two days old. The *Daily Mail* ran the banner headline, "RAF counter the invasion", while the *Glasgow Herald* had its Naval correspondent write that the Nazi leaders had hopelessly underestimated the difficulties of an invasion. Despite this, General Alan Brooke wrote in his diary, "Everything looks like an invasion starting tomorrow from the Thames to Plymouth! I wonder if we shall be hard at it by this time tomorrow".[59]

German preparations were proceeding apace, but were by no means complete. Most of the steamers needed had been transferred to the invasion ports, but there were still thirteen steamers *en route* from the French Atlantic ports.

Hitler was hosting a gala lunch for his newly promoted colonel generals, twenty of them, attended also by Keitel, Jodl, von Brauchitsch, and Göring. Expansive about the favourable air situation and fortified by the glowing reports of the devastation caused by the *Luftwaffe*, he told his generals that the invasion was no longer necessary. He agreed with von Brauchitsch that it should only go ahead as a mop-up operation, once the enemy had been "seriously damaged". But he and the High Command were also coming to the conclusion that mid-September was too soon to expect such a result. In the interim, the risks were too great to proceed.[60]

Air activity was of little strategic importance on the day. RAF and *Luftwaffe* losses were light, each force losing seven aircraft. Some damage was done to the Chatham Naval Dockyard. But there was one raid which had massive propaganda implications. With poor weather over the south-east, major daylight operations had been ruled out and *Luftwaffe* resorted to "nuisance" raids. One aircraft dropped a bomb on the garden of Downing Street and then a stick of five bombs on Buckingham Palace, damaging the Royal Chapel.

At the day's War Cabinet, the Labour Minister of Health spoke at length. This was Malcolm MacDonald, son of Ramsey – the first ever Labour prime minister. It had been an astute move of Churchill to appoint him to this key post back in May. MacDonald told his colleagues of "a remarkable improvement in the morale of the people during the preceding 36 hours". He put this down to the heavy anti-aircraft fire. Perversely, it had had the effect of slowing down the evacuation of the homeless. People who earlier had clamoured to be taken away were now reluctant to leave.

Another big problem was the fracture of the Northern Outfall. A vital part of the sewage pumping machinery had been damaged and the main sewers broken in several places. Sewage was draining into the River Lea instead of into the Thames. Repairs would take several months, it was said. And the Silvertown district, which had been at the epicentre of the bombing, had been evacuated owing to the water supply being cut off. The supply had been restored, but people would not be allowed to return.

But the far bigger problem was the shelters. People in certain parts of London were "showing reluctance" to use Anderson and street shelters. They preferred underground shelters, such as the basements of churches, schools and public buildings. These were getting overcrowded, and outbreaks of infectious disease were feared.[61] But the London *Evening Standard* reported that "hundreds of people" had used Tube stations as air-raid shelters. "From Earl's Court to Leicester square (sic), for example, every platform was lined with people sitting on newspapers and leaning against the wall". Few, the newspaper observed, appeared to make any effort to catch the trains, although the services were still running.

That brought the War Cabinet to discuss increasing the amount of air-raid shelter accommodation in London. The use of the Tubes for this purpose "was proposed", but by whom was not recorded. The Minister of Transport intervened to reject the idea. This was John, soon to become Lord, Reith. He had been first director-general of the BBC and then Minister of Information under Chamberlain, before being exiled to the transport portfolio by Churchill. He told his colleagues that he had examined the question, but agreed with the conclusions of the committee which had examined the question before the war. It was more important to keep the Tubes available for transport.

John Anderson chipped in, telling the Cabinet that the Commissioner of Police "strongly deprecated the use of the tubes as shelters". The public had been educated to use shelters and there was broadly sufficient shelter accommodation available for the majority of the population. Advice urging the public to use shelters was continually being given, and new shelters were being built as soon as material was available. Materials for air-raid shelters did not, however, enjoy a very high priority, and the supply presented some difficulty. Whatever members of the Cabinet may have privately felt, they agreed on a common line: the shelters provided, while "not affording immunity from a direct hit", offered the best protection available.[62]

The attack on Buckingham Palace then was discussed. The Cabinet rallied round to "invite" the Prime Minister to send a message on their behalf to the King. "The War Cabinet offer their hearty congratulations to their Majesties", it said, "on their providential escape from the barbarous attack made on their home and Royal Persons". The Cabinet also agreed that, "subject to His Majesty's consent", the fullest publicity should be given to their message.[63]

11

Rebellion

It is your destiny to lead Britain to victory. It is your right as citizens of the greatest city this world has ever known to show all others the way. It is not an easy way. Victory cannot be achieved by seeking safety and forgetting the rest. But the results of your endurance will be glorious. There will be a crown for your courage.

Editorial, *Daily Express*, 20 September 1940

The daylight air war was building to a climax and 15 September was to be marked as the day a victory turned the battle, later celebrated as Battle of Britain Day. Problematically, however, the night bombing continued, bringing a confrontation between the people of London and the government over air-raid shelter policy, and in particular the use of Tube stations. The government had rejected their use, triggering mass disobedience and then outright rebellion, in what may have been one of the most critical periods of the war.

DAY 67 – SATURDAY 14 SEPTEMBER 1940

Over a hundred Londoners lay dead from the latest raids, but there was no confusion in the British media about the most important story: Buckingham Palace. This was the second time the palace had been hit, but this was the incident that really made the headlines. The *Daily Mirror* splashed across its front page, "King and Queen in palace, bombed", with the *Daily Express* offering a more lurid: "Dive bombers try to kill the King and Queen". Famously, the Queen was said to have remarked that she was glad to have been bombed. She could now look the East End in the face.[1]

Under the signature of Neville Chamberlain, a more sombre report was reaching the War Cabinet, analysing the overall extent of the bombing damage to London. None of the news was good but, in particular, the authors regarded the railway situation with some anxiety. If the damage was to increase, the position might well progressively deteriorate, they wrote, and lead to serious traffic congestion in a short time. Further, the supply of coal to the south of England, which was already difficult owing to the great reduction in the seaborne coal traffic to the south coast, was bound to be aggravated. We think, they concluded, that the position on the railways is one which should be closely watched.[2]

Unsurprisingly, the "authoritative" German publication *Das Reich* – the house journal for the Nazi Party – called on "London" to surrender, or face the fate of Warsaw or Paris. Very few Londoners would have read the call, which was also published in the *New York Times*. Many more would have read the leader in the *Guardian*, which was trying to make sense of events. The attack on London was causing damage and disorganization to the daily life of the capital city, it mused, but "that can hardly be an end in itself". The paper also noted that Göring needed mastery of the air "in order to support whatever plans his Führer may have for an invasion". It then noted that "neither fires behind St Paul's nor bombs on Buckingham Palace would bring it any nearer in a military sense".

In Berlin, Hitler and Räder met. The air attacks against England, and in particular those against London, must continue without interruption, the Grand Admiral told his *Führer*. Given suitable weather conditions, the attacks should continue at the expense of the preparations for *Sealion* "because they might bring about a decision of the war". Hitler summed up the situation thus:

> Attacks to date have had enormous effects, though perhaps chiefly upon nerves. Part of that psychological effect is the fear of invasion. That anticipation of its imminence must not be removed. Even though victory in the air should not be achieved before another ten or twelve days, Britain might yet be seized by mass hysteria. If, within the coming ten or twelve days, we achieve mastery of the air over a certain area, we could, by a landing operation, compel the enemy to come out with his destroyers against our landing fleet. We could then inflict upon the enemy such losses that he would no longer be able to protect his convoys. Cancellation of our plans would not remain a secret. It would ease the strain on the enemy's nerves, and consequently must not be ordered now.

Three points emerged from this. First, the invasion threat was a psychological weapon. Secondly, Hitler expected the air offensive to succeed, but "mass hysteria" might bring an earlier collapse. Thirdly, the purpose of a landing operation would be to entice the British destroyer fleet to its own destruction, robbing the convoys of escorts. And, if the ships were sunk, Britain starved. Nevertheless, doffing his cap to the idea that the invasion could still be executed, he promised to make a final decision on whether to go ahead, in three days time – 17 September.[3]

Within the British Air Ministry, there seemed to be little concern about an invasion. More important was Dowding's failure to deal with night bombers. Having set up a powerful and well organized day fighter force, he had effectively created the airborne equivalent of the Maginot Line, which the Germans – as they had done in May 1940 with the real thing – were circumventing. A committee was set up, ostensibly to look at the problem, headed by former Chief of the Air Staff, Sir John Salmond. Called the Night Defence Committee, members included Trenchard, Air Marshals Freeman, Joubert, Tedder and Sholto Douglas. This was office politics. The outcome was already decided. It was a "get Dowding" committee which would represent the problem as his personal failure, the headline issue by which his downfall would be engineered.[4]

Meanwhile, real people were suffering. Communist councillor for Stepney, Phil Piratin, took charge of some fifty of them, including a group of what *Time* magazine called "ill-clad children". As the sirens sounded, they burst into the Savoy Hotel and occupied the basement air-raid shelter. "If it is good enough for the rich it is good enough for the Stepney workers and their families", he declared. After a tense confrontation with the police, the hotel manager allowed them to remain. Negotiation with the waiting staff produced silver trays laden with pots of tea, bread and butter, at a heavily discounted price. As the initial tension dissipated, it became a relatively good-humoured occupation and the demonstrators left when the "all clear" sounded, but not before having had a "whip round" to tip the doorman.[5]

The *Guardian* thought the occupation a symptom of the "serious deficiencies" in the help given to those affected by bombing. People, it said, should not be treated as victims of misfortune "whose adversities are to be tempered by charity" but as citizens "who happened to have received blows from a common enemy which other citizens have so far escaped". This was but one sign that the political consensus was breaking down. Labour councillors in a northern town were demanding better shelters for schoolchildren, condemning existing provisions as "totally inadequate". Elsewhere, there was concern expressed about the lack of amenities in public shelters, after women with babies, children and old people were reported coming away from them "almost on the point of collapse".

Home Intelligence thus reported, perhaps unsurprisingly: "there is little interest in the possibility of an invasion, nor does the prospect alarm people". In the regional reports, the observation from Leeds (north-east) was: "Despite warnings about invasion, it cannot be said that most people take the threat seriously". Nevertheless, Alan Brooke wrote in his diary:

> Ominous quiet! German shipping reserves greatly reduced. Have the Germans completed their preparations for invasion? Are they giving their air force a last brush and wash up? Will he start tomorrow, or is it all a bluff to pin troops down in this country while he prepares to help Italy to invade Egypt etc??[6]

For Fighter Command, this was an opportunity to rebuild its operational strength. Newly manufactured and repaired fighters replenished inventories, airfields and radar stations were restored and newly trained pilots were integrated with rested veterans. Park then paired Hurricane and Spitfire units, the one to attack bombers, the other to take on the fighters.

Just past three in the afternoon, 150 German aircraft crossed the coast headed for London. Another wave of 100 came over at six, some of them attacking airfields. Most did not get through to their primary targets, but numerous isolated incidents were reported. Despite good weather overnight, there was little bombing of London. Leicester took some hits and four houses were demolished.

Bombing reports were being presented daily to the War Cabinet. But they did not begin to confront the sheer brutality of unrestricted warfare. For instance, in the north-west town of Warrington on this fine Saturday afternoon, families were enjoying a "Spitfire gala" on Thames Board Mill's recreation ground, held to raise money for the town's Spitfire fund.

Without warning, a bomber dived down and released two bombs. One completely wrecked the light wooden clubhouse. A local newspaper reported two families "partly wiped out", members of others "lie in hospital gravely wounded". One bomb fell in the canteen and 150 people were buried in the wreckage. Of these, 14 were killed and 21 seriously injured. It was all over in seconds, leaving the dead, dying, injured and a mass of mangled debris as the Nazi bomber swept back into the skies and vanished".[7]

Hundreds of miles south, in Brighton, 11-year-old Monica Duplock and her 9-year-old brother had gone to the Odeon Kemp Town cinema to watch a matinee performance. As they sat in the cinema, a Spitfire was pursuing a Dornier bomber that had become parted from the rest of its formation. In a vain attempt to escape its pursuer, the Dornier pilot jettisoned his load. Twenty-five 100lb bombs rained down on Kemp Town. Two smashed into the cinema, killing three children outright. Monica was hit in the neck by flying shrapnel and was bleeding very badly from her wound. Her brother, in a desperate attempt to save his sister's life, carried her to the nearby Sussex County Hospital. She died there of her injuries.[8]

In the whole of the war, 198 people died in Brighton from the bombing. Including Monica, 52 died on this one day, representing over a quarter of that total. This was a day that the fine-suited gentlemen in RAF Fighter Command regarded as a "lull", recording an "unusually low" level of attacks. Flying 860 sorties, they lost fifteen aircraft, with four others destroyed, a total of nineteen against the *Luftwaffe's* nine, one of which was an He 59 rescue seaplane. Monica would have been so proud.

DAY 68 – SUNDAY 15 SEPTEMBER 1940

The Berlin correspondent of the Swiss newspaper *Basler Nachrichten* reported what he thought was a "curious change" in the utterances from Berlin regarding the conduct of the war. The Germans now say, he wrote, that the destruction of London and its industrial organization will mean the paralysis of the entire economic and financial structure of the Empire. Therefore, an invasion of Britain will not now be necessary to defeat her.

This was picked up by the *Sunday Express* and splashed on its front page, with the headline: "Is Hitler hesitating?" For the first time it is officially declared in Berlin that London's destruction is capable of bringing about England's defeat and military collapse, the paper wrote.

Inside the book, Priestley was again in full flow, sounding off once more about "the old type Conservative" and "the short-sighted fumbling and muddling of his type of mind". We who are not ripe old True Blues, wrote Priestley, "are accused, as usual, of being lost in misty illusions and pipe-dreams, but it was they who had thought that Hitler, Goering, Ribbentrop, Mussolini, Ciano and their Spanish puppets were not such bad fellows and might be won over if they were visited often enough".

The theme was: "Who are the indispensible people?" The answer was the industrial workers, the "genuine backbone" of the country, the class without which we could not possibly survive either in peace or war. If the industrial workers disappeared, "we should lose the war. Yes, in a week", he wrote. And with the defeat of Nazism and Fascism must also go the defeat of "injustice and treachery to the human spirit" which prevented the working class seeking a better life.

Meanwhile, buoyed by the tardy response to its raid on 7 September, believing its own propaganda about kill rates and vastly underestimating the UK's aircraft production and repair capacity, the *Luftwaffe* mounted a daylight spectacular on London. The aircrews found themselves flying into strong headwinds, slowing the ground speed of the formations and giving RAF controllers ample time to send up squadrons to intercept. Even the "big wing" managed to put up something of a show.

The star of the action was Ray "Arty" Holmes, who in his Hurricane rammed a Dornier over central London before baling out. The tail-less Hun, captured on grainy newsreel footage, smashed in the forecourt of Victoria Station and demolished a number of shops. As firemen tackled the blaze, this provided yet more entertainment for the crowd which had gathered to watch the spectacle.

On the day, Fighter Command disposed of 55 German aircraft – less than the 60 of 18 August – and damaged many more, at a cost to itself of 27 aircraft. By the time the men from Ministries had finished though, this score had soared to a peak of 185, plus 41 "probables" and 72 damaged. Even that number was a fraction of the 304 aircraft lost by the *Luftwaffe* on 10 May 1940. In actuality, the number shot down represented less than 20 per cent of that single day's loss.

Despite that, according to the post-war legend that turned this event into the day of victory, now commemorated as Battle of Britain Day, Dowding gazed at the empty skies and declared the battle won. Fighter pilots roared off to the Dog and Duck and other pubs in their bright red MG sports cars for a celebratory pint or two. Hitler cancelled *Sealion* and the invasion ports emptied. Churchill declared: "This is not the end; it is not even the beginning of the end, but it may be the end of the beginning". The music played and the credits rolled.[9]

Churchill had actually spent much of the day at No. 11 Group HQ, watching the action as it unfolded. At one point, with all the aircraft in the sky, he had asked Park, "What other reserves have we"? Park, who "looked grave", had answered, "We have none", a point Churchill had subsequently laboured in a lengthy, post-war account of the action when he had labelled 15 September as the date of the demise of *Sealion*.[10] In fact, though, Park's squadrons were often wholly committed. The theatre reserve was in fact No. 12 Group, and his anxiety on this day may well have been exacerbated by wondering just where and when reinforcements from the Group would turn up.[11]

Interestingly, from the start of the battle on 10 July, to the end of this day, the *Luftwaffe* had lost 1,155 aircraft. RAF losses totalled 1,134. By contrast, in the Polish campaign and the invasion of the Low Countries and France, the *Luftwaffe* lost nearly 2,000 aircraft.[12]

And before the German bombers had crossed the coast on this day, British radio monitoring services picked up an identical signal broadcast on every German naval frequency – an unprecedented occurrence. It presumably contained details of Hitler's order from the previous day, postponing the invasion for three days. The British could not know this but when the signal was followed by a marked decline in radio traffic, it was assumed that it was in some way associated with a postponement or even cancellation of the invasion.[13]

For the people of London, though, nothing had changed. Came the night, came the bombers. Increasingly desperate East Enders decided to act. Led by Ted Bramley, Phil Piratin and other Communist Party workers, they challenged the prohibition on using the Underground. "Various implements such as crowbars happened to be available," wrote Piratin, "and while the police stood on duty guarding the gates, they were very quickly swept aside by the crowds, the crowbars brought into action and the people went down". Variously, Liverpool Street Underground Station, Warren Street, Goodge Street and Highgate have been named as those broken into.[14]

And while the *Luftwaffe* streamed over London, the RAF was going the other way. A "maximum effort" had been mounted by Bomber Command and, despite having over 150 aircraft in hostile skies, there were no losses. However, a Hampden of No. 83 Sqn, while attacking Antwerp from low level took a direct hit from flak in its bomb bay, which set it on fire. As the aircraft started to disintegrate, first the gunner and then the navigator baled out. Eighteen-year-old Sgt John Hannah, the wireless operator, stayed to quell the flames. Badly burned in the process, he still managed to help the pilot fly the stricken aircraft back to base. He was awarded the Victoria Cross.[15]

DAY 69 – MONDAY 16 SEPTEMBER 1940

The BBC the previous day had made the most of the victory, the last main bulletin of the day parading 185 Nazis downed. This was too late for the *Daily Mail*, which offered, "Greatest day for RAF", recording: "350 came – only 175 returned". Early editions of the *Evening Standard* ran the figure of 185, calling it a "record".

The front page also carried the obligatory "puff" for the Anderson shelter, recording how a family had just completed the erection of one when a raid had started and they were forced to take refuge in it. Their house had been demolished, while the shelter "was left safely on the edge of a crater and all escaped injury". Page three offered a picture of a brick-built surface shelter in a south London street, amid the ruins of houses, with the legend, "… the surface shelters stood fast".

The *Daily Mirror* leader, however, was concerned this day with bigger things. "We reach the climax of the war", it proclaimed. The question for the week was: "Invasion or not?"

> As each hour passes now Hitler's evil star is on the wane. Unless he destroys Britain his fate and the fate of his German rats is sealed. We are ready! Every man and woman knows what to do. The fighting Services and civil defenders are all in the front line. If Hitler attempts this monstrous vanity we shall smite him a hammer blow and may win such a resounding victory that the whole Nazi system, foul and rotten to the core, may begin to topple.

Home Intelligence recorded "enthusiastic praise" for the junior service. It also noted that "most people anticipate an invasion in the next few days, and are confident that it will be a failure". The *Guardian*, though, was picking up the *Basler Nachrichten* sources which had led the *Sunday Express* to question whether the invasion would take place. Its headline was: "Invasion not necessary".

In his train, parked just outside Beauvais, Göring had called a meeting of his local commanders. He "fulminated" about the previous day's raid, complaining that "the fighters have let us down". Revised tactics were agreed for day bombing raids, using smaller bombing groups and stronger fighter escorts, "nuisance" raids were to be made by single bombers or fighter bombers in all weathers, and the main weight of the air offensive should be transferred to the night bombers.[16]

Göring was not the only one to "debrief" his commanders though. Park called a meeting of his controllers and rehearsed a number of complaints. Squadrons were failing to rendezvous before attacking the enemy, individual squadrons were being allocated to raids that were too big for them and the enemy fighters were being allowed to draw up the Group aircraft prematurely, with the German bombers approaching later while the British aircraft were on the ground refuelling.[17]

Despite the triumph of the previous day, Churchill took it upon himself personally to raise at the War Cabinet the demonstration at the Savoy two days earlier. "Episodes of this kind," he declared, "could easily lead to serious trouble." John Anderson joined in. He added that there were "some signs of organised demonstrations". Together, he and Churchill convinced the Cabinet that "strong action" should, if necessary, be taken to prevent further demonstrations. If allowed to grow, they "might easily lead to serious difficulties", said Churchill.[18] Piratin's reputation went before him. In 1936, he had brought 100,000 Londoners on to the streets in the "Battle of Cable Street", and stopped Mosley's Fascists from marching through Whitechapel.[19]

And, to illustrate how life want on, among other problems the Cabinet then had to deal with the monthly report from the Secretary for Mines on the coal situation, in which he noted "temporary shortages in the Southern counties" and that "certain high priority consumers" had recently been found "dangerously short of supplies".[20] As bombing damage and disruption intensified, this was a problem that was to get worse.

In very poor weather during the day, air activity was minimal. Fighter Command lost three aircraft, none to enemy action, and the *Luftwaffe* lost nine, several to accidents.

DAY 70 – TUESDAY 17 SEPTEMBER 1940

For all their talk of "strong action", there had been neither any record of War Cabinet concern about the state of London's shelters, nor any declared intent to improve them. The Cabinet considered that the accommodation was sufficient. But the *Daily Mirror* and many other dailies reported that the Ministry of Home Security was looking at the use of the Underground, and a fresh effort was to be made in the House of Commons to persuade Sir John Anderson of the need for building deep shelters.

Lord Horder, the King's physician, had been appointed to head a committee to look at the health aspects of using the Tube stations for sleeping. The *Guardian* thought the shelter problem in general was "becoming urgent". No means of alleviating it must be neglected. One idea was to requisition factory and office shelters where no night shifts were operating. Tens of thousands of spaces were lying unused during the nights, in shelters locked up after workers had gone home.

The *Daily Express* seemed to be indicating that the Underground was only being considered for people who had "no alternative air-raid cover". And, having so cavalierly dismissed this issue, the paper's lead editorial focused on the need to keep up levels of production when the sirens went.

> If you want Spitfires and Hurricanes to continue to throw back the assault of Goering's *Luftwaffe*, then you've got to work in the air raids … If you want the bombers over London to continue night after night, dropping death and devastation on our factories, on our hospitals, on our homes, then you may stop work.

For Churchill, his monthly report to the Commons beckoned. He avoided the shelter issue and stressed the threat of invasion. The deployment of barges and ships in preparation "continues steadily", he told MPs. We must expect that Hitler "will make an attempt at what he judges to be the best opportunity. All our preparations must therefore be maintained in a state of vigilance". The Prime Minister then referred to the air fighting of 15 September, "the most brilliant and fruitful of any fought upon a large scale up to that date by the fighters of the Royal Air Force".

As to the figures for the number of aircraft shot down, he told the House: "to the best of my belief – and I have made searching inquiries and taken several cross checks – these figures are not in any way exaggerated". Turning to the bombing, he declared:

> The German attacks upon the civil population have been concentrated mainly upon London, in the hopes of terrorising its citizens into submission or to throw them into confusion, and, of course, in the silly idea that they will put pressure upon the Government to make peace.[21]

Thus did Churchill identify a German war aim. This could not be entirely random nastiness – *schrecklichkeit*. The violence had a purpose. It was not a "silly idea". Churchill knew this. The use of aerial bombing was an idea he himself believed could be thrown back at German civilians whom he hoped would depose Hitler and force a new government to make peace – the concept of "regime change" that was to have an outing in Iraq in 1992, where the "shock and awe" was almost exactly a parallel of the Second World War thinking – and as effective.

For the 1940 version, the *Glasgow Herald* felt that the recent attacks on London must have had two main objects. These were "the exhaustion of the RAF and the creation of a spirit of defeatism in the Metropolis such as could have made a lightning success possible for an invading force". Neither of these objects had been achieved, it said. London "stands firm" and our Air Force was more formidable than ever.

German Supreme HQ would have agreed. The OKW *War Diary* recorded: "The enemy air force is still by no means defeated; on the contrary it shows increasing activity. The weather situation as a whole does not permit us to expect a period of calm". Hitler now had to make formal the decision taken long ago. It was pointless keeping the invasion fleet intact as it was not going to be used. He postponed *Sealion* "until further notice" (*Wird bis auf weiteres verschoben*).[22]

Hitler's decision was soon transmitted to operational formations, mostly via secure landlines. According to some accounts, a radio signal to Holland concerning air-loading equipment was intercepted by the British, decoded and passed to Churchill. It was supposedly discussed at the Chiefs of Staff Committee that evening and Churchill had asked the Chief of the Air Staff to explain it. Newall had told him that "this marked the end of Sealion", at least for this year". Wreathed in a "very broad smile", Churchill lit a cigar and suggested to his chiefs that they took "a little fresh air".[23]

Bomber Command, meanwhile, was mounting its largest night raids to date against invasion barges in the Channel ports and shipping in the German ports. Ripping through the Channel at this time was what Alan Brooke called a "mild hurricane". An agency correspondent in Dover telephoned an on-the-spot report: "There's a nasty cross-sea running and the channel would be bad for regular steamers in peace time, let alone for any flat-bottomed troop barges". Later, Churchill wrote that all now depended on the battle of the air, with the question to be resolved as to whether "the British people would stand up to the air bombardment, or whether they would crumple and force His Majesty's Government to capitulate". Confidently, he asserted, "About this, *Reichsmarschall* Göring had high hopes, and we had no fears".[24]

Harold Nicolson did not share this unbridled optimism, and he was not alone. "Everybody is worried about feeling in the East End," he wrote. "There's much bitterness. It is said that even the King and Queen were booed the other day when they visited the destroyed areas." That had been on 9 September, over a week earlier, but Nicolson had been right to be concerned. Chamberlain, he recalled, had told him that if only the Germans had had the sense not to bomb west of London Bridge, there might have been a revolution in this country.[25]

This was by no means an exaggeration. During June 1917, when Gotha bombers had raided London, a bomb had fallen on the Upper North Street school in Poplar, killing 18 infants. When on 7 July, in a second raid, 22 Gothas had returned, most of the bombs had fallen on the East End. Of the resulting 54 deaths and 190 injuries, many were caused by falling anti-aircraft shells – for which no compensation was offered. There had been significant unrest and some reports of rioting.[26]

On this day, George Orwell wrote:

There has of course been a big exodus from the East End, and every night what amount to mass migrations to places where there is sufficient shelter accommodation. The practice of taking a 2d ticket and spending the night in one of the deep Tube stations, e.g. Piccadilly, is growing … Everyone I have talked to agrees that the empty furnished houses in the West End should be used for the homeless; but I suppose the rich swine still have enough pull to prevent this from happening … When you see how the wealthy are still behaving, in what is manifestly developing into a revolutionary war, you think of St. Petersburg in 1916.[27]

The *Guardian* was articulating complaints "on every side" about the apparent failure of transport to adjust itself to the raids. It noted that ordinary Londoners had had to adjust, but the transport system had not. There had been "considerable hardship". One girl from the office had been forced to walk ten miles to her home. A man had had to walk 5½ hours to get to his home in the East End because the buses had not been running. Londoners were asking why the Minister of Transport did not take a firm grasp of the situation and do whatever was needed.

No such view prevailed in the House of Lords. Alongside Churchill's statement in the Commons, the Viscount Caldecote delivered a statement to their Lordships. Speaking of the consequences of the bombing, he declared: "Sleep has been disturbed, windows smashed, business interrupted, public services disorganised. But what has evidently not been broken is the public spirit, and that is as high as, if not higher than, ever".[28]

Home Intelligence seemed to inhabit the same parallel universe. "Intensified raids have not affected morale; rather the reverse: confidence is increased, opinion is stiffer and there is a feeling of growing exhilaration," it reported. "The spirit of the people in raided areas is excellent." Certainly, different people reacted in different ways. This was a Tottenham postman:

> I was on a delivery in Westbury Avenue when the warning went. I carried on until the guns started when a man offered me shelter in his dug out, as it was getting a bit hot overhead and a few tramlines and old bedsteads started whistling round, I accepted. Just as I entered the shelter he said "Look postman". I turned round and there on jerry's tail was one of our Spitfires, he put a burst into the jerry who rolled over, our boy was after him, then jerry straightened out and tried to turn, then the Spitfire flew right over and under him and gave him another burst. I think he must have killed the jerry because he roared down with his engine full out. It was a grand fight, after seeing that I don't mind paying another ½d on fags.[29]

The official line was "London can take it", but the actual response was often more like: "give some back". Where people could see this happening, morale was bound to improve. But there was also some solace in shared misery, and to the very great but unspoken relief of many senior politicians and others, the focus of the bombing had been moving westwards. More and more properties in the West End were being hit. Alan Brooke remarked in his diary that bombs had dropped overnight in Burlington Arcade, Bond Street, Berkeley Square and Park Lane. "It is hard to believe that it is London", he wrote.[30]

Adverse weather kept air activity light, although Bomber and Coastal Commands defied a howling gale to keep up their pressure on the invasion ports. The RAF lost two bombers on an unrelated operation, Fighter Command lost eight aircraft and the total losses to the *Luftwaffe* were eight.

DAY 71 – WEDNESDAY 18 SEPTEMBER 1940

The howling gale in the Channel through the night was being described as "Churchill's weather". Newspapers carried reports of the German invasion fleet having variously been driven to shelter or "scattered". And the RAF had carried out attacks on barges and shipping, which were being bombed and "harassed". Almost a hundred bombers had been deployed. Later edition newspapers and the US media played down the invasion though. The *New York Times* led on: "Gales scatter Nazi Channel fleets", with allusions to the fate of the Spanish Armada. This led Churchill to write to General Ismay, asking him to inquire "whether in view of the rough weather" the invasion alert could be downgraded.[31]

"London's West End had its worst bombing of the war in the two vicious raids during Monday night which had in them more than a hint of baffled desperation", wrote the *Daily Mirror*, allocating this news to its page eleven. Doubtless, the Germans were confident that their bombing was having the desired effect. The German-controlled Paris radio confidently broadcast that "the legend of British self-control and phlegm is being destroyed". In triumphal manner, it continued:

> All reports from London concur in stating that the population is seized by fear – hair raising. The 700,000 Londoners have completely lost their self-control. They run aimlessly about in the streets and are the victims of bombs and bursting shells".[32]

The Times and The *Daily Express* were actually reporting that the Queen had made personal donations of wardrobes, chairs, and beds from Windsor Castle to people in the East End, remarking that several items had "been in use at the Castle since the early days of Queen Victoria's reign", nearly a century earlier.

More prosaically, the *Express* reported that London Tube stations were now filled with people every night. Thousands of people, said the paper, had invaded various Tube stations. Extra staff members were being drafted to the stations to deal with the crowds. The shelterers lay with mattresses, blankets and pillows along the platforms, on the subways and on the stairs, chatted, ate sandwiches and played cards. Thousands of home-going City workers, many of whom had to change at one station, added to the crowds. People standing packed, heaved and surged on as trains came in.

The *Daily Mail* in a leading article recalled that Sir John Anderson, the Minister for Home Security, had rejected deep shelters, not least because he was opposed to gatherings of large numbers of people during raids. "But he has not stopped mass movements of the people," the paper observed. "The fact is that the people themselves have adopted a deep shelter policy turning the Underground railway stations into shelters, which is officially prohibited. Once the people are in, however, they cannot be ejected." In what was remarkably candid criticism, the paper then concluded: "Experience is proving that the policy of Sir John Anderson was mistaken. It is not too late for him to reverse his policy and provide the deep shelters that are urgently needed".

Overnight, there had been considerable bombing in Oxford Street. The world-famous John Lewis was left a smouldering, gutted shell.[33] And grumbling continued. Even Home Intelligence could not now entirely conceal the disquiet – not after eleven continuous nights of Blitz. "Civilian morale is fragile under the weight of bombing", it warned. Londoners were still outwardly calm and putting up with difficulties extremely well. But, it said, there were still numbers of people anxious to get out. The report also admitted there had been a certain amount of panic shown in individual cases, where people had had horrible experiences. But this was often due to temporary physical reaction, it said, adding that people were "beginning to wonder how long London will be able to go on taking it".[34]

Official strategy now was to talk up the success of the anti-aircraft defences – the only visible sign that the nation was able to fight back. This was reflected in the *Express* front page, but even its absurdly optimistic headline could only record four raiders downed. Offering a highly condensed version of the Prime Minister's speech, the paper attempted to stiffen resolve by declaring: "Mr Churchill urges you to carry on". Terror raids "will not force Britain to sue for peace".

Also attempting to hold the line was Archibald Sinclair. In his capacity as Air Minister, he spoke at a lunch in London hosted by the National Defence Public Interest Committee. A new secret device against bombers was being developed, he told his audience. "We are working hard on the solution of the problem of dealing with enemy night bombers, and are making progress," he said. "I am now able to look forward to the time when the pleasure of night bombing over Britain and the blowing of humble London homes to pieces will cease to be attractive to Reich Marshal Goering and his aerial minions".[35]

J. B. Priestley had continued to broadcast, and his most recent Sunday talk had been reported by the *Guardian*. He had made one of his best points so far, the paper thought. Civilians under air bombardment "should be encouraged not to think of themselves as civilians trying to lead an ordinary life but as soldiers actually engaged in a great battle". As indeed they were, the *Guardian* observed, going on to say that Priestley's usual insight made him stress this point, for strange and devastating events are much easier to accept as a normal part of battle than as an abnormal part of civilian life.

Churchill had not got the point. In his speech to the Commons the previous day, his had been an appeal to authority. "Firm confidence" was felt "by all the responsible officers of the Royal Air Force in our ability to withstand the largely increased scale of attack." Now was "the chance of the men and women in the factories to show their mettle, and for all of us to try to be worthy of our boys in the air and not make their task longer or harder by the slightest flinching". But behind the scenes, Churchill was badgering the Home Secretary for information on the area of glass destroyed by bombing and the "stimulation and standardization" of honours, and the Postmaster General on complaints about Post Office service during air raids (three times), which he had picked up from *The Times*.[36]

It was small wonder, perhaps, that the *Mirror* found itself delivering a robust condemnation of official inertia. Its particular concern was the growing homelessness crisis. It asked:

> Why allow the homeless to wait in odd holes and corners, in amateurish shelters and improvised dugouts, until Somebody or Something – some local pundit or fussy official gets on with the scheme for opening every West End or other comparatively safe basement to all comers. The work is already done – in parts. Make it complete and do it at once. A few words in the right quarters.

Strongly echoing the Priestley line, it then launched a strident attack on Anderson. There was, the paper complained, still time to get on with further evacuation schemes and with provision of deep shelters hitherto rejected "with unparalleled obstinacy by Sir John Anderson". The homeless people of London were not just nondescript, improper persons wandering "without visible means of subsistence". They were "soldiers, fighters in the front line; and as such worthy of all the first aid we can give them". They, the paper concluded, must be denied nothing that can be provided.

During the day, the Germans put up high altitude fighter sweeps early in the morning. Park scrambled fifteen squadrons to meet the first wave, but only six were able to engage. Successive waves followed, a mix of Ju 88s, heavily escorted by Me 109s, but those raids – mainly over north Kent – cost the Germans nine bombers. Post-war analysts marked these raids down as "failures", but the contemporary press noted: "longest daylight attacks of the war". *AP* recorded the views of military attachés and correspondents who had weathered the bombing of Warsaw, Barcelona and Madrid, saying that London had already taken more punishment than any of Hitler's conquests, including Rotterdam. But, they said, the *Luftwaffe* had failed to achieve its purpose – "to smash or terrorise the city and its millions into a mood of surrender".

Fighting on the day cost Fighter Command ten aircraft, with Bomber Command losing nine – nineteen aircraft lost, exactly the same as sustained by the *Luftwaffe*. *AP*, however, noted that the British claimed forty-two German aircraft downed, to nine of their own losses. The Germans claimed fifteen RAF aircraft shot down over England, for three of their own losses. "Claims on ships lost conflict", the agency remarked, by way of a headline.

DAY 72 – THURSDAY 19 SEPTEMBER 1940

On his way to Hendon where the military executive aircraft were based, Alan Brooke complained of the difficulties in getting out of town. Most roads were closed, including Piccadilly, Regent St, Bond St and Park Lane. There were big craters around Marble Arch. That evening, on his return to London, a heavy bomb shook the club building in which he was staying.[37]

The misery was being shared, the effects of which were as significant as the bombs on Buckingham Palace. A potential stress point was becoming a unifying force. And the "survivors" of Buckingham Palace were out and about, among the people. Guided by Ministry of Information officials, the King and Queen were taken to see survivors of "heroic rescues", throughout a tour of three districts of London which had sustained extensive bomb damage. A special point was made of introducing the royal couple to men and women whose houses had been wrecked by a direct hit. As he had on 9 September, the King once again talked up the Anderson shelters, this time saying: "These Anderson shelters are wonderful". The King and Queen "listened with interest" while occupants of two unharmed shelters told them of escapes when the bomb fell only a few yards away.[38]

With unconscious irony, the regional *Yorkshire Post* illustrated precisely the contradictions at the heart of media reporting. On the one hand, there was the lead story proclaiming: "Another RAF triumph". Next, there was the story declaring: "Smashing blows at invasion plans", an account of yet more attacks on invasion ports. Then, centre page, was pictured the devastation at the very heart of the West End, testimony to the RAF's failure to deny the night sky to the *Luftwaffe*. Nevertheless, the *Daily Mirror* picked up on Sinclair's speech of the previous day, headlining: "Bombing of London by night is not an insoluble problem. We are making progress".

Later that day, Nicolson noted in his diary that, "unless we can invent an antidote to night-bombing, London will suffer very severely and the spirit of our people may be broken". Already the Communists were getting people in shelters to sign a peace petition to Churchill, he wrote. One "cannot expect the population of a great city to sit up all night in shelters week after week without losing their spirit".[39]

The *AP* was almost poetic about the overnight raid. "Battered, grimy London took its 13th straight day of devastating bomb assault today, shook off the horrors of the war's worst night and dealt staunchly with the prospect of spending a winter underground," it recorded. The *Australian Associated Press* was of the same mind: "Many observers regard last night's raid on London as the most savage yet". It went on to say: "The Germans flew lower than ever previously, and took suicidal chances as they frenziedly endeavoured to pierce the hellish curtain of fire around and over London". The raiders made no effort to seek out military objectives.

Despite this, the *Guardian* led on the anti-invasion campaign – conveying the upbeat message that the RAF was on the ball, dealing expeditiously and effectively with the "most serious threat on the horizon". It retailed claims of the RAF having caused "heavy damage", but for once these were not without foundation. The OKW *War Diary* recorded eighty barges having been sunk, and an ammunition train with 500 tons of explosives blown up. It also reported a torpedo boat sunk and one damaged.[40]

The *Daily Mail* focused on the domestic situation, and it had had enough. It launched a vigorous campaign for improved air-raid shelters and better arrangements for the daily lives of the ten million residents of the Greater London area. The paper noted that the government had become aware that Underground stations were being used as shelters but declared: "something much better must be devised". It added: "no question of cost should be allowed to hold up construction". It then blamed the "reluctance to provide such quarters" on the government of the former Prime Minister Neville Chamberlain and its "cheese-paring policy". The present shelter policy had been "proven by experience to be wrong".

Joining in the criticism, the *Mirror* slammed "those unimaginative bodies or persons known as the authorities" for rejecting deep shelters and then for failing to devise a new policy. It does seem odd, the paper said, that even now, in the midst of the air war, learned persons should still be considering, inquiring, investigating and making notes.

On the other hand, Beaverbrook's *Express* had on its front page a piece recording: "Don't use tubes as shelters" – a joint appeal by the Ministries of Security and Transport, "to the good sense of the public, and particularly to able-bodied men, to refrain from using Tube stations as air raid shelters except in case of urgent necessity". It was immediately followed by another piece headed: "But they did". Thousands of Londoners again had taken three-halfpenny tickets on the Underground last night – to sleep on the station platforms. At most stations there were police in attendance to shepherd them gently to leave free passage for passengers on the trains. "The whole position is under review," said an official of the London Passenger Transport Board. "At the moment we are taking no action providing services are not interfered with and fare paying passengers are not impeded."

This was not good enough for the newspaper, which headed its editorial: "Hold fast". Addressing what it felt to be a defeatist sentiment, it spoke to the whole city:

> The *Daily Express* makes this appeal to the people of London, many of them homeless, many of them in nightly fear of being made so. On your courage and

discipline much depends. You are asked to show unparalleled fortitude in face of this great menace. Life is held cheap by our enemies and they seek to disrupt you physically and mentally. If you hold on, behaving with the bearing of soldiers, obeying the instructions you are given, then liberty will one day be yours again. But if you give way then you face the prospect of a lifetime of misery and torture under a foreign heel.

It looked as if the government was going to make a stand. The *Press Association* reported that the prime minister and government were convinced that "deep or heavily protected" shelters were impossible to construct in wartime and that the job would be "more or less impracticable" even in peacetime. Anderson complained in the House of Commons of people being misled into believing such shelters were safer and, in the evening, William Mabane, Anderson's parliamentary secretary, broadcast on the BBC. He urged the public not to leave their Anderson shelters for public shelters, saying it deprived others of shelter. "We're going to improve the amenities in existing shelters," he promised. "We're setting about providing better lighting and better accommodation for sleeping and better sanitary arrangements."

But discord could not be contained. The story even reached the *New York Times*. In a "special cable", its correspondent wrote of the Commons going into secret session to discuss the mounting housing crisis, the absence of suitable deep shelters and the failure to take care of citizens bombed out of their homes. People had been kept in rest centres "for several days" without hot food while officials tried to arrange transportation. Strain on the political consensus was showing. "Laborites" had co-operated with the government in maintaining this "people's war", said the *NYT*, but many now pointed out that the victims are not being cared for well enough. The people would put up with the hardship of this total war, but only if they were convinced the government was doing everything it could, first to guarantee their security and, second, to care for them and their families if they were bombed.

In response to the government's appeal, the paper noted that "crowds crushing into subways indicate the growing demand for security". And in what must have been a worrying development for the government, even Home Intelligence was deserting them. "People are not so cheerful today," it reported. "There is more grumbling. Elation over the barrage is not so strong: people wonder why it is not more effective in preventing night bombing." Among the many points of tension identified, "determination of the public to use underground stations as shelters" was listed.

This was becoming a trial of strength and the government was close to losing. But there was no evidence that Churchill was engaging in the issue. Colville noted:

> The PM is sufficiently undismayed by the air raids to take note of trivialities. Yesterday he sent the following note: 'The First Sea Lord. Surely you can run to a new Admiralty flag. It grieves me to see the present dingy object every morning. WSC'".[41]

But the tide seemed to be turning. The late edition of the *Evening Standard* reported that the Ministries of Transport and Home Security were examining police reports, and the reports of their own observers on the use of Tubes as dormitories. It was "understood" that these stated that there had been "no trouble of any kind" the previous night. The paper further "understood" that: "there will be no question of banning the tubes for use as dormitories. Sleepers will be allowed to continue using them unofficially, but in controlled numbers".

As to air operations on the day, these had been much reduced by frontal-driven rain. Fighter Command escaped loss, and only one Blenheim was downed, against eight aircraft lost by the *Luftwaffe*.

And in Berlin, with no fanfare, the process of dismantling *Sealion* was proceeding. Hitler had agreed that the notification time for assembling the fleet could be extended from ten to fifteen days, allowing some vessels to be put back into commercial use. With that came the release of the ships held for Operation *Herbstreise* (Autumn Journey). This was a deception operation to be mounted from Norway. Two days prior to the actual landings, three light cruisers and the gunnery training ship *Bremse* and other light naval forces were to have escorted the liners *Europa*, *Bremen*, *Gneisenau* and *Potsdam*, with ten transport steamers, towards the east coast of England between Aberdeen and Newcastle, simulating a landing in the north.[42]

Yet, in sunny Rome, Italian Foreign Minister Ciano was meeting his German counterpart, von Ribbentrop. He told Ciano that bad weather, and especially the clouds, had even more than the RAF prevented the success of the plan. The invasion would take place anyway, as soon as there were a few days of fine weather. "The landing is ready and possible. English territorial defence is non-existent. A single German division will suffice to bring about a complete collapse", he said.[43]

DAY 73 – FRIDAY 20 SEPTEMBER 1940

Rainstorms and a howling gale lashed the Channel coasts once again, making it even more evident that there could be no invasion. The weather was not sufficient to prevent two-way bomber traffic, but it clearly ruled out the idea of flat-bottomed barges crossing the Channel. RAF photo-reconnaissance brought reassuring evidence. Five destroyers and a torpedo boat had withdrawn from Cherbourg, and the assemblies of barges were already beginning to disperse.[44] Churchill told Colville that he was "doubtful whether the invasion will be tried in the near future", but said there was no doubt that every preparation had been made.[45]

The day fighting was now virtually irrelevant. The Germans were relying mainly on fighter sweeps to make nuisance raids. Nonetheless, Fighter Command lost seven aircraft, with two others lost, making nine downed against three to the *Luftwaffe*, one of which was to anti-aircraft fire. The focus had moved to the night. Everything had changed. The *New York Times* reported: "Huge bombs fall". The Germans were using mines, dropped by parachute over the city. Called "land mines" – they could flatten a whole block in a terrifying display of raw power.

The battle was now for hearts and minds. And the government, having set its face against the use of the Tubes as air-raid shelters, was now in danger of losing it. Contradicting the earlier *Evening Standard* report, the *Yorkshire Post* headlined its lead story: "A decision against deep shelters". The government, reported the London correspondent, was not going to build "deep" shelters. Nor, he wrote, "will the Government allow the continued general use as shelters of Underground railway stations. The tube's essential transport function must not be impeded". The report continued:

Ministers feel sure that the public will realise that the use of tubes to carry workers to and from work at night is vital to the war-effort, and will accordingly appreciate the attitude which the Government have felt obliged to take. If need be, Ministers are prepared to ensure that the public do not use them as shelters. The authorities will, however, continue to allow limited numbers of genuinely stranded persons to remain on the stations during raids.

The increasingly unpopular Anderson ventured out of his Whitehall office to have a look for himself, but showed little understanding of what was at stake. Reporting to the War Cabinet, his main concern seems to have been "the character of the persons who took refuge there". He came up with a scheme for requisitioning basements of commercial premises and, for areas where there was insufficient provision, setting up an elaborate transport scheme run by local authorities to move people to areas where there were shelters.[46]

Anthony Eden was far more concerned that photographs in the press of ruined houses and buildings were giving an "exaggerated idea" of the general aspect of London in the present time. It was "bad propaganda", disturbing to Londoners in the fighting services who were serving at a distance from their homes, he said. Churchill was preoccupied with the dislocation of production by air-raid warnings, reminding colleagues of the scheme to deal with single aircraft flying over. Policy was already not to give a "red" siren warning, and this "must be adhered to".[47]

Earlier in the day, the *Daily Express* had not only given its front page to the shelter crisis but had run an editorial which had bordered on the frenetic. "Listen people of London," it said, "this is the truth". In like vein, it continued:

> It is your destiny to lead Britain to victory. It is your right as citizens of the greatest city this world has ever known to show all others the way. It is not an easy way. Victory cannot be achieved by seeking safety and forgetting the rest. But the results of your endurance will be glorious. There will be a crown for your courage.

"Keep the tubes free," it implored:

> Here is the situation. It is true that there is more safety from bombs in the London tubes than anywhere else. But the tubes were built to get the worker to and from his desk and bench. That is their function, which is a hundred times more vital now that the siege is on.
>
> For the tube is the one means of transport unlikely to be seriously damaged by bombs. And it must be kept free for the workers. Your safety will count for nothing if the work of the City is allowed to slow and falter and stop.

The *Glasgow Herald* noted that Göring, having failed to get results so far, was "trying to force an early issue by trying to destroy London's morale". It argued that the Cockney, "that stout fellow", is determined that the effort will fail, then pronouncing that "patience is required from everyone for a little longer until the menace of night bombing is mastered". But patience was running out and the menace of night bombing was very far from being mastered.

Thousands of Londoners were taking matters in their own hands. They had again flocked to the Tubes for shelter. At some stations, they began to arrive as early as 4 p.m., with bedding and bags of food to sustain them for the night. By the time the evening rush hour was in progress, they had already staked their "pitches" on the platforms. This time, police did not intervene. Some station managers, on their own initiatives, provided additional toilet facilities. Transport Minister John Reith, and the chairman of London Transport, Lord Ashfield, ventured into Holborn Station to see things for themselves.

The atmosphere was unpleasant. Travellers were jostled by "Tube night boarders" carrying their bedding. The overcrowding was "disgraceful", a passenger said, and the station actually "stinks". But virtually every station between Edgware and the Strand had been occupied, turned into an overcrowded dormitory. The atmosphere had been so thick and heavy at one station that a reporter investigating conditions felt "faint". The situation was untenable.

DAY 74 – SATURDAY 21 SEPTEMBER 1940

Overnight, the *Guardian* observed, East Enders had not been taking the least bit of notice of the government's call to "refrain" from using the Tubes as shelters. Still less were they listening to the entreaties of the *Express*. The government had two options. It could try to enforce its ban, calling out the police and perhaps even troops to evict women and children at the points of bayonets. Or it could cave in and make the best of the situation. It took the sensible option. And, as what it called part of its "deep shelter extension policy", it decided to close the short section of line from Holborn to the Aldwych and turn the tunnel into an air-raid shelter.

Only now did Churchill send an "action this day" minute to his permanent secretary, Sir Edward Bridges, copy to Anderson and Reith. In it, he recalled having asked the Cabinet "the other day" whether the Tubes could be used as air-raid shelters, "even at the expense of transport facilities". This would have been on 13 September, when he had been told by Reith that their use as shelters was "inadvisable". Now, after eight days of inaction from himself, Churchill was now asking what had happened to supersede "the former decisive arguments".

"Pray let me have more information about this," he wrote. "I still remain in favour of widespread utilization of the Tubes", he added, asking for a "short report on one sheet of paper" on details of changes necessary to make the Underground system more accessible.[48] That evening, Reith wrote in his diary of a "Silly 'action this day' memo from the PM about Tubes".[49]

It was certainly "silly" in the sense that the immediate crisis was past. There can be no doubt at all that the people of London – or, at the very least, tens of thousands of Londoners – had openly defied the government in an egregious episode of mass civil disobedience, with the acquiescence of the police and transport authorities. The government had thus been confronted with the choice of enforcing its policy or backing down, and had chosen the latter.

Had it taken the "strong action" that Churchill had wanted, not only against demonstrators but against those who were openly defying the government, one can only speculate as to what might have happened. It may even be the case that the police would have refused to obey orders. Had they not done so, there could well have been bloody riots. There had been a riot in Portsmouth when the police had sought to enforce a policy of keeping air-raid shelters locked through the day, to prevent interruptions to war production. When a group had tried to force their way into a shelter, the police had drawn their truncheons and made a baton charge.[50]

London riots, in front of the world's press, would have been far worse and, in the febrile mood of the times, might not have ended there. A perverse decision could have triggered the very event that Hitler and Göring so much wanted – and expected. At this point, the people possibly came as close to rebellion as they ever did throughout the war. Never again did there seem to be the precise combination of circumstances and the degree of tension experienced in these closing days of September. If there was a true pivotal moment in the entire war, when it could have been lost, it was maybe this day, 21 September.

To what extent this was ever a threat is almost impossible to tell. Political correspondent Laurence Thompson, writing of the general period, recorded that on the nights of 7 and 8 September there had been something which an eye witness "choosing the words with care" described to him as "near panic". It had not been on a large scale, nor lasting beyond that short time, but it had been watched with anxiety because of pre-war anticipations, and the contagious quality of the panic which had so recently been seen in France and Belgium.

Such had been the sensitivity of even the suggestion of panic that Sir Harold Scott, chief administrative officer of the London Civil Defence Region was at pains to dispel any idea that it had been seen. He assured Thompson that he was "certain there was no panic of any importance". By coincidence, a long piece by Ritchie Calder was published in the *New Statesman*. Among other things, he set out the background to the South Hallsville School incident. He was caustic about those who so glibly claimed to be able to characterize the state of morale of the East Enders, as he described the inefficiency and incompetence of the officials and government institutions.

But, the crisis had now passed. That evening, in a postscript to the 6 p.m. BBC news, Clement Attlee, then Lord Privy Seal, spoke to the nation of the "Battle of Britain", telling his audience:

> Those who have been killed in air raids have died for their country no less than the soldier killed in battle, for this present air attack is not directed primarily on our factories, docks, and public services, but on the spirit of our people. It is here that Hitler is sustaining his heaviest defeat.

Stating that he was one of those charged with the duty of working at the centre, and thus was able to survey the whole field with a full knowledge of what was happening, Attlee said, "I speak with a deep sense of confidence in the success of our cause".

After paying a tribute to the work of the RAF, he continued:

> Our forces on land are in good heart I include in these forces, not only the Navy, Army, Air Force, and Home Guard but also the civil defence services, police workers in industry and, indeed, all the men, women and children of our nation. We are all in this war. I believed that the Battle of Britain was "the turning point of the war.

Defeat of this attack, he said, marks the turning of the tide. We may have to endure worse things yet. There is no room for easy optimism. But there is very cause for confidence.[51]

Churchill was at Chequers later that evening, and gave no hint of the passing of the crisis. He was joined by Lord Gort and Dowding for dinner. This was the first day that the existence of the codename *Sealion* had shown up in the top secret Enigma intercepts of German radio traffic, and conversation turned to the invasion. The Prime Minister hypothesized that the Germans could mount a surprise invasion during the autumn fogs. Ismay, his military advisor, was sceptical, but too polite to tell the Prime Minister he was talking "rot".[52] Colville, in his record of the discussion, did not mention shelters, and remarked not on the distant drone of German bombers as they pounded London once more, for the fifteenth consecutive night.

Churchill, on the other hand, sent Alan Brooke a paper from Samuel Hoare in Spain, giving details of a talk with a reliable American who had come from Germany. Speaking on 7 September, he had said he was certain that Hitler would attack within a fortnight. This day was the last day of the fortnight, and the weather forecast was for a perfect sea.[53]

Through the day, Fighter Command had only lost one aircraft, a Hurricane colliding with a machine-gun post at its home base, as it was taking off. Bomber Command despatched aircraft to attack shipping and barges at Calais, Ostend and Boulogne, without loss. It was also reported that Jersey Airport had been "heavily attacked".[54] A combination of accidents, enemy fighters and flak lost the *Luftwaffe* eleven aircraft. This had been one of those better days.

12.

Consequences

I am aware, of course, that there are many demands, including anti-invasion preparations, made upon our limited naval forces but I should be failing in my duty if I did not represent, in the strongest possible terms, the necessity for putting a stop to the present exorbitant risks to which our Merchant Shipping is being exposed.

Ronald Cross, Minister of Shipping, 30 September 1940

The day battle was about to peter out. The objective (as far as it was ever real) of gaining air superiority for the invasion had ceased to have any relevance. If the theory of Douhet "terror bombing" meant anything, then the adverse effect on morale should also have been measurable, but that moment had passed as well. Instead, a new crisis was emerging – a catastrophic and increasing loss of merchant shipping, which threatened the very survival of Britain. And convoy escorts were sitting in the ports waiting for an invasion, while the U-boats enjoyed a killing spree.

DAY 75 – SUNDAY 22 SEPTEMBER 1940

The British Government climb-down was hailed by the *New York Times* with the headline: "Public opinion wins demand for use of subways in raids -- government yields". The paper added, with neat irony, a sentiment that was to be repeated down the decades: "Slum clearance by Nazis – homeless move to West End". And, already, there was an element of organization creeping in. At Piccadilly Underground Station, a broad white line was being painted on the platform, to mark the division between shelter and throughway for passengers. People were queuing as early as 2.30 p.m. and by six, every available space on the City line platforms was occupied.[1]

Home Intelligence captured a shift in mood. Morale was "excellent". People were more cheerful, it said, adding a note which perhaps reflected the essence of J. B. Priestley's talk: "The feeling of being on the front line stimulates many people and puts them on their mettle in overcoming transport and shelter difficulties". The mood of crisis had gone. London conversation was now almost exclusively about air raids, "gossipy, not panicky, and it is centred in personal matters".

Priestley was back in the *Sunday Express*, telling his readers: Let us say what we mean. "We are fighting for liberty and democracy. You have said it, I have said it, and they have said it. And most of us have meant what we said", he wrote. But, he added, the words picked out as a pull-quote in a white-on-black box:

> To put it bluntly, millions of people do not believe yet that we are really fighting for democracy. They consider that our talk is on the same level as Hitler's talk about a new and more equitable European order. They think it is all eyewash.

A post-war world, he argued, should be a democratic one. "If our representatives seem to stand for the Right People rather than the Whole People, then there will be some excuse for outsiders imagining that our talk of democracy is a mere trick of propaganda".

In Berlin, there was talk of a different kind. Shirer recalled that the Berliners he spoke to were beginning for the first time to wonder why the invasion of Britain had not come off.[2] And, in an extraordinary illustration of the power of propaganda, and control of information, the *Sunday Express* was reporting how captured Germans, shot down over Britain, believed that half the country was already in German hands and that London was making a last stand. Victory was "inevitable in a few weeks, or even days". In almost the same league, D. R. Grenfell, the Secretary for Mines, was telling the Labour Party Conference in Glasgow, "I am convinced there will be no coal shortage".

The air war over Britain saw a few lone raiders, but there was little daytime air activity. Fighter Command flew 158 sorties, the lowest number since July. One Spitfire on the ground was lost to a hit-and-run bomber at Duxford. There were no Bomber Command losses. The Germans lost a Ju 88, shot down by a Spitfire over the Channel. Three aircraft were written off after accidents. Come the night, around 120 bombers visited London. With the continuous flashes of the guns, the sparks of bursting shells in the sky and the haloes of searchlights,

London "looked like approaching Dante's inferno", wrote General Brooke. The RAF sent up twelve night fighters – Blenheims and Defiants. They failed to make a single interception.

As for the invasion, the small article in the *Observer* noted that the Navy was "our first defence". This was a reference to Churchill's speech earlier in the week, but there was more to it. Special anti-invasion patrols had been carried out nightly by destroyers in the Channel and the southern North Sea. They had been joined by MTBs which carried out a sweep off the mouths of the Dutch rivers on the night of 22/23 September.

The Polish destroyer *Blyskaivica* sunk a French fishing vessel by ramming off the Brittany coast, having first removed the crew. E-boats had been active in the Channel and North Sea. The armed trawler *Loch Inver* had been sunk on the night of the 21st, and the armed trawler *Edwina*, which was in the vicinity, claimed to have hit an E-boat with her 12-pdr. Brooke noted the lack of invasion.[3]

Before the bombers had droned through the night sky over London, Priestley was back in the public eye, speaking once again on the BBC. In this broadcast, he chose the theme of "women". There isn't an airman, submarine commander or unnamed hero in a bomb squad who hasn't behind him at least one woman, and perhaps half a dozen women as heroic as himself, he said. And as for those women who had been bombed out of their houses, turned away by "middle class women ... with any amount of room to spare in their houses", he spoke of the need for a society "where nobody will have far too many rooms in a house and nobody have far too few".

Listening to the Broadcast was Harold Nicolson, who was in Sissinghurst, dining with Major General Laurence Drummond and his wife, where there was a "sense of mahogany and silver and peaches and port-wine and good manners ... All the virtues of aristocracy hang about these two crippled and aged people and none of the vulgarity of wealth". Priestley, he later wrote, gave a broadcast about the abolition of privilege. He speaks of the old order which is dead and of the new order which is to rise from its ashes. "These two old people listen without flinching," Nicolson wrote. "I find their dignity and distinction and patriotism deeply moving".[4]

DAY 76 – MONDAY 23 SEPTEMBER 1940

The Times on this day decided that British morale was "in excellent shape". Any tonic that it might require, it pronounced, "has been supplied by Hitler".[5] Nevertheless, all the newspapers were agreed that the most important story was the sinking by a U-boat of the liner *City of Benares*, *en route* to Canada. It had one hundred and two evacuated children on board, ninety of whom were on the government-funded scheme. Only thirteen were reported to have survived, with two of their nine adult escorts. In a "tempestuous sea" 600 miles from land, one newspaper reported, many children had been killed in the explosion or trapped below decks – the torpedo hitting at 10 p.m. The ship had foundered so quickly, developing a steep list, that many of the lifeboats had not been launched.

The ship, the name not as yet disclosed to the press, had been torpedoed on 17 September, but the government had withheld the news. The War Cabinet had been told on 19 September, four days previously. Duff Cooper had been "invited … to arrange for suitable publicity".[6] He had held a press conference the following day (Thursday 20 September).[7] Why the newspapers chose to hold over publication to the following Monday is not clear.

With the *City of Benares*, the shelter issue was being driven down the agenda, but it had not been forgotten. The King had made a broadcast the previous evening. People had feared the worst, but his main concern was to announce the new George Cross and Medal, second only in rank to the Victoria Cross, specifically for civilian bravery. The *Daily Express* also noted: "King praises people of the shelters".

He had paid tribute to the way the civil defences had faced constant danger, but then added: "No less honour is due to all those who, night after night, uncomplainingly endure discomfort, hardship and peril in their homes and shelters". This would not have been a spontaneous tribute. The message was getting through to the authorities that the home front needed bolstering.

The *Daily Mirror* had a different take. "London should be ashamed of the way it is treating some of its refugee citizens," it wrote.

> When German bombs drove them from their shattered homes, their spirit remained firm. Now, bungling officialdom is achieving more than ever Hitler could, and the people who held their heads high before the terror of the skies are becoming dispirited and discontented.

One special correspondent had visited a rest centre with a "varying population of between 150 and 250 men, women and children". Some had been there close to a fortnight, their only air-raid protection bricked-up windows in a few rooms into which everyone was crowded, sharing one indoor toilet and two roller towels. In a fortnight, one family had had only four hot meals.

A London County Council official said the conditions were almost the same at several other centres. "If my wife and children were homeless," he said, "I would do anything to keep them away from such conditions as these. It just seems as though the authorities were taken by surprise when the blitzkrieg started and only now are things beginning, slowly to improve".

Behind the scenes, the War Cabinet was pushing for unrestricted revenge attacks on Germany. These, at the moment, were not favoured by the Air Staff, who wanted to maintain at least the appearance of concentrating on military targets. Thus, as the drone of deadly *Luftwaffe* bombers filled the night skies of London once more, with others hitting Merseyside, 119 British bombers were winging their way to Berlin, ostensibly targeting gasworks, railway stations, power stations, the aero-engine factory at Spandau, and Tempelhof Airport. But only a small fraction of the bombers would get anywhere near their targets and still fewer bombs would do any damage to the city.

The lack of accuracy was brought home to Churchill somewhat forcibly when he was shown photographs of bombing results for the invasion ports. He later admitted they "had several times disappointed me". This day, having seen photographs of barges in Dunkirk, published in *The Times*, he wrote to the Secretary of State for Air, lamenting:

> What struck me about these photographs was the apparent inability of the bombers to hit these very large masses of barges. I should have thought that sticks of explosives thrown along these oblongs would have wrought havoc, and it is very disappointing to see that they all remained intact and in order, with just a few apparently damaged at the entrance.[8]

"Can nothing be done to improve matters?" the Prime Minister asked, only then, at an early evening meeting of the War Cabinet, putting to his colleagues whether the bombing effort should be concentrated on the invasion ports or Berlin. He confided that "a number of indications had been received pointing to the possibility of an attempt at invasion over the weekend". One of these,

Churchill stated, "had suggested that invasion would start at 3pm on Sunday, 22nd September".[9]

Guy Liddell, on the other hand, was advised by an Intelligence colleague that his "best sources" indicated that the invasion had been meeting with considerable difficulty. The German Naval experts considered the craft entirely inadequate. The troops and naval ratings were tired of waiting and did not view with any enthusiasm the prospect of crossing the Channel in a barge at eight knots. The Air Force was apparently quite ready to have a cut at it but they were feeling their losses rather acutely. Hitler had been told by his High Command that he must make up his mind one way or the other, as it was impossible to keep the troops up the mark indefinitely.[10]

As for that Air Force, the Germans had during the day concentrated mostly on fighter sweeps, keeping the RAF busy, so much so that the Fighter Command launched as many sorties on this day as it had on 15 September.[11] The day saw them lose ten aircraft. Bomber Command lost three aircraft, and the Fleet Air Arm lost a Swordfish, bringing total losses to fourteen, against the *Luftwaffe's* sixteen. Overnight, 261 German bombers visited Britain, with the British despatching 119 on raids to Berlin. Shirer was later to report, "The British really went to work on Berlin last night. They bombed heavily and with excellent aim for exactly four hours".[12]

DAY 77 – TUESDAY 24 SEPTEMBER 1940

Overnight, the War Cabinet was told, enemy activity had been "rather more intense" than recently.[13] The main attack had been against communications. Liverpool Street Station and the Brighton line at Wandsworth Common had been blocked. Traffic at Euston was stopped by a UXB (unexploded bomb). Also, the Northern Outfall sewer had again been damaged at Abbey Mills, and the southern outfall had been hit. Direct hits had been sustained by several shelters, and the casualties had been rather heavier than on the preceding two or three nights.

Prominently its morning edition, the *Daily Mirror* announced government plans to distribute a million sets of ear plugs to shelterers who found it difficult to sleep. The paper was distinctly unimpressed, offering a critical editorial, complaining about the lack of preparedness: "The new or newly announced plans for London's security are of course hurried improvisations to meet an emergency. Yet an emergency foreseen for years!" Its cartoonist Zec produced a distinctly unflattering picture of Sir John Anderson, his head buried in a pile of sand as bombs fell around him, a notice on his pin-striped backside declaring: "This is not a military objective – by order".

The newspaper might have been less than impressed by a memorandum produced under the names of the Chiefs of Staff, advising on the defence of Whitehall against air attack. However, after proposing an impressive array of weaponry, they were conscious of the impression it might give. It has occurred to us, the Chiefs wrote, that the provision of such defences for government offices in Whitehall "may react unfavourably on the morale of other sections of the community", and on the East End of London in particular. Therefore, they suggested that the War Cabinet should consider the wider issues before the guns were put in position.[14]

At last, though, the government was moving to improve the conditions of the people. A million bunks were to be fitted to existing shelters and extra shelters were being opened up. First-aid posts were also to be provided. The stations were being occupied by sleepers under police supervision. Sanitary arrangements were being improved, drinking water was being supplied and better heating and lighting was being arranged.

Security Minister William Mabane admitted to the *Guardian* that the shelter policy had "been been guided largely by the conduct of the people in London". He said that although the London Passenger Transport system must be carried on, the fact that people had been using the Tube stations had now been "recognised". The government was going to "relate shelter policy to the conditions of the time and the behaviour of the people". Instead of trying to dictate what the people would do, it would accept and make the best of present shelter arrangements and the popular attitude to them. The *Guardian* noted that it was "not easy to gather from Mr Mabane what the government thought about London's invasion of Tube stations, but it is clearly prepared to accept it". The government cave-in was complete.

This day had been marked by the Germans as meeting its optimum requirements for tides, moon and daylight for the invasion. One suspects that, even had the British media known this, it might not have even remarked on it. "Except in certain areas, invasion talk has receded into the background", Home Intelligence reported.

On the front pages, newspapers were covering a new subject, unrelated to the air war but one that was to rock the Churchill Government to the core – another heroic failure. At the moment, it was just "breaking news" – not that such an inelegant phrase had been invented yet – on the Prime Minister's adventure in Dakar, which went by name of Operation Menace, supporting an effort by de Gaulle to claim the West African Vichy territory in the name of "Free France". It was too early to report the outcome, but the media had picked up the arrival of Vichy French warships after they had been permitted to pass unhindered through the Straits of Gibraltar. The press sought to discover who had allowed this, and why the naval authorities had apparently stood idly by while the Vichy Government had sent reinforcements to its colonial outpost. Soon, highly critical leaders would be complaining of another Churchillian "blunder".[15]

What was not yet known, although soon perceived, was that there had been a more profound change in *Luftwaffe* tactics over Britain. Following the mauling that his air fleets had suffered, Göring had decided that his aircraft should revert to attacking the British aircraft industry. This was evident when the élite bombing unit, *Erprobungsgruppe* 210, equipped with Me 110 fighters and bomber conversions, made a direct attack on the Spitfire factory at Woolston, on the edges of Southampton. The raid lasted a mere eight minutes and little damage was done, although a works shelter was hit, killing ninety-eight skilled workmen and injuring forty others.

No Spitfires were destroyed in the raid but, in air combat, the RAF lost eleven fighters and five bombers – sixteen aircraft in all. By way of exchange, the *Luftwaffe* lost seven aircraft during the day. That included three to the anti-aircraft guns of Southampton and Portsmouth, small recompense for the people they had killed.

DAY 78 – WEDNESDAY 25 SEPTEMBER 1940

The bombing had temporarily receded in intensity as a media event, with the *Daily Express* devoting its front-page lead to the Dakar operation. Other newspapers followed suit. Nevertheless, there was no slackening of the bombardment. On the contrary, the War Cabinet was told that the previous night's raids had been heavier than usual, mainly directed against the West End. The Tottenham Court Road area had suffered severely. The new police station at Savile Row had been badly knocked about, railway communications had suffered very severely and Waterloo Station was again out of action. The East End had suffered very little.[16]

Home Intelligence reported that "responsible people" were saying emphatically that women, children and old people should be got out of the heavily raided areas. Many women were showing "great nervousness and fatigue" and there was "a lot of bitter feeling" about the government's slowness in coping with the emergency.

For once, the situation was not quite as black as painted. The *Guardian* reported that "enormous crowds" had spent the night at the Aldwych Tube Station, even though the tunnel had not been officially opened. The overflow was being accommodated in Aldwych House basement. Slow it was but, very gradually under the pressure of events, the system was responding – mostly through voluntary initiatives. However, according to Hilde Marchant in the *Daily Express*:

> One thing stands out in the East End. Voluntary work is excellent. The WVS under the drive and initiative of a good leader has a smooth and sympathetic organisation. Red tape is official. One woman told me that all her work, covering hundreds of people a day, depends on one harassed, overworked clerk who is so busy that he occasionally forgets. His lapse leads to the discomfort of many. There are too many natural officials who are too ready to cipher the people they are dealing with, and forget that each name represents a story of human misery.[17]

And now that the crisis was contained, if not yet completely over, *The Times* weighed in with another ponderous editorial. Headed, "The shelter problem", it noted that in Mabane's broadcast statement of the preceding Monday was "an admission of the insufficiency of the present provision" and of the need for "urgent and large-scale action". Nothing of that could have been deduced from earlier reports in the "paper of record", but having reviewed the options, and pronounced on the need to make good use of the deep shelters available, it observed dryly that the people had decided this question "very largely for themselves". It also added that their claims to space on Underground railway platforms had been "irresistible".

The *Guardian* joined in, to make this a chorus of criticism, with an interview of former prime minster, David Lloyd George. He called for the "provision of adequate, comfortable, and well-equipped shelters deep underground". My daughter raised the issue in the House of Commons fully eighteen months ago when she and other members urged the construction of deep shelters, he said.[18] That was before the war, and particular mention was made of the need for adequate protection for the people in the East End of London, because their houses are so fragile and so many jerry-built, and because so many are without cellars and basements. The answer given then was that everything was being done or going to be done. They ought to have been provided.

Lloyd George thus argued that there has been "an appalling lack of foresight, drive, and imagination in our plans for protecting our people and our industries against the inevitable perils of an unparalleled attack from the air".

Still the bombers came. Fifty-eight Heinkels, escorted by fifty-two Me 110s, attacked the Bristol Aircraft Company at Filton. Serious damage was caused and shelters were hit by a stick of bombs, killing 60 and injuring 150. Production was seriously affected. The *Luftwaffe*'s own magazine, *Der Adler*, proclaimed: "this factory will not produce many more aircraft". But bombers had scattered their loads over the general area as well, leaving a total of 132 dead and 315 injured. Other areas in the south-west were hit, the naval towns of Portland and Plymouth in particular. In the evening, bombers visited coastal towns from Margate to Worthing. They made a nuisance of themselves in the south-east area of Essex.

Then came the night bombers. From just past ten, the asynchronous drone was heard as far apart as east and south-east England and the Midlands. Liverpool was attacked. South Wales and the Bristol Channel areas were also targeted. In the London area, many places were hit, including the approach road to Vauxhall Bridge. The main targets were the railways again. A crater was made on the GWR line near Ruislip Garden Station. Bombs were dropped on the railway at Kensington. Lines were completely blocked by debris. The railway bridge over Thames Road, Chiswick, was hit by high explosive just after midnight.

RAF Bomber Command continued its counter-offensive. Eleven Blenheims made a night attack on five enemy minesweepers off Dover – so-called *R-boots*. They claimed two direct hits and four near misses. Had not *Sealion* already been cancelled, the significance would have been enormous, the Germans unable to protect their vital minesweeping force. And that night, no less than twenty-seven Blenheims were abroad, attacking targets as far afield as Boulogne, Calais,

Antwerp and Brussels. Fourteen Battles attacked shipping at Ostend and thirty-three Wellingtons joined in raids on Calais and Boulogne.

The day's fighting lost Fighter Command nine aircraft, the RAF thirteen in total. The *Luftwaffe* lost fifteen. Meanwhile, the RAF Whitehall warriors were focused on their more immediate enemy: Dowding. Sir John Salmond, fortified by his position on the Night Defence Committee, was writing to Trenchard, part of an organized – and ongoing – campaign to unseat the head of Fighter Command, complaining that Dowding lacked the qualifications as a commander in the field. He was without "humanity and imagination".[19]

Salmond also complained about the Chief of the Air Staff, Cyril Newall, who was:

> so impressed with the possibility of invasion that he will not even tell off a couple of day fighting squadrons to be trained for the night, even though they could be at once used for day work if invasion took place.[20]

DAY 79 – THURSDAY 26 SEPTEMBER 1940

The war looked very different in Berlin. "We had the longest air raid of the war last night", wrote Shirer in the German capital. The damage was not great but the psychological effect was tremendous.[21] Nevertheless, it was not good enough for the former Chief of the Air Staff, Lord Trenchard, who had written deploring that bombers should be taken off attacking military objectives in Germany in order to bomb the invasion ports. Churchill told the War Cabinet that "we should be assuming a great responsibility if we allowed invasion concentrations to accumulate in the Channel ports without taking action against them". When the weather in the Channel was unfavourable for invasion, he told his ministers, it might be possible to divert more aircraft to targets in Germany.[22]

The Cabinet was getting daily reports of bomb damage to the United Kingdom, and was also told of bombs being dropped at random over the country. Most had been directed against London, mainly in northern suburbs and the areas just south of the river. The casualties in the London area were around 50 killed (probably more than half of them in Hendon) and 370 injured. Thirteen parachute mines had been dropped, some of which had exploded in the air.[23]

This evening Londoners would see their twentieth consecutive night of bombing. There was now an entrenched belief that the network of surface shelters provided by the government was unsafe. This was far from unjustified. In the summer of 1940, there had been major – if localized –shortages of cement and the government had permitted the use of lime mortar. With their reinforced concrete roofs, concrete floors and weak walls, in the dark humour of the time they would come to be known as "Morrison's sandwiches", named after the then minister for home security.[24] That was unfair as Morrison was not to be appointed until early October, long after the surface shelter policy had been devised and implemented and the faulty shelters had been built. A rush remedial programme was put in hand, but public confidence was never really restored, as was evidenced in the Home Intelligence report of this day. It noted that the Tube stations were "as crowded as ever".[25]

Crucially, in just one sentence, the report also noted: "The work of voluntary organisations in stricken areas has done much to prevent the breaking down of morale". Famous for its provision of canteens, mobile and static, very much in evidence was the Salvation Army. Historically, it had had a strong presence in the East End and had been a major supplier of social services in the area. Private enterprise also played a strong part. The first canteens in the shelters were set up by Marks and Spencers, and the Co-operative Societies took a pivotal role in keeping the capital, and the nation as a whole, supplied with food. "In the most deadly hours of Britain's history, the Co-operative Movement was the unbroken ally and support of the people", wrote Bill Richardson, editor of the Co-operative Party's own newspaper, *Reynold News*.[26]

Fighter Command was not doing that well. It was even unable to protect its own supplier, the Woolston Spitfire factory. In the late afternoon, a force of nearly sixty Heinkels, covered by a heavy screen of seventy Messerschmitt 110s, roared up the Solent to deliver another precision attack. Thirty-seven workers died this time, and hundreds were injured. It was nine weeks before production was back to par. Also lost was project B12/36, the Supermarine bomber prototype. This might have given the RAF a bomber equivalent to the B-29. It was abandoned.[27]

Across the river, watchers had seen the works "burn up like a piece of brown paper". Then it was their turn. A phalanx of thirty bombers broke away from the plant and targeted Phoenix Wharf, on which they stood.

In ten seconds a hundred bombs burst on the wharf, on the gasworks alongside or in the river. Fifty-two more people were dead. The wharf, the gasworks and a grain warehouse had been destroyed. As the dust began to settle, a policeman emerged asking for a volunteer to send a message from the telephone exchange. A girl telephonist offered her services and the policeman led her to a wrecked office. She was asked to put a call through to ARP, telling them: "there is an unexploded bomb underneath the telephone exchange at Phoenix Wharf". She calmly sent the message, and was later awarded an OBE.[28]

That night, as well as London, Merseyside was hit – badly. In Birkenhead just before eight, incendiary bombs started falling between Central Station and Morpeth Docks. Fires were started at the GWR warehouse, the Customs Offices, a theatre and a shop. The tunnel between Birkenhead Park Station and Hamilton Square Station was damaged by a bomb. Liverpool got even worse. At nine, explosives and incendiaries were dropped causing very considerable damage to property and starting severe fires in the dock areas. The ships *Peterton* and *Diplomat*, and warehouses, were left burning. There was considerable loss of stocks of food, copra and palm kernels, and other goods. And this was the second night running. The previous night, among other premises, a large cotton warehouse had been hit, with major losses.

While Liverpool burned, joined once again by London, with attacks also on the north-east and even Wales, fighter pilots were safely tucked up in their beds. The officers would have batmen to wake them with morning tea and polished shoes. It was not their fault. The technology and the equipment were not up to the job. Still, the day job had cost Fighter Command five aircraft. Bomber Command lost four, and another Dutch Fokker went down. That was ten aircraft lost against nine to the *Luftwaffe*.

Back in London, Lord Halifax was reviewing recent events. He could not exclude the possibility, he confided to his diary, that Hitler was "deliberately scaring us with invasion in order to check reinforcements to Egypt where the main blow is to be delivered".

DAY 80 – FRIDAY 27 SEPTEMBER 1940

It had even reached the War Cabinet that the local pride of the Liverpool people was suffering owing to their being described in communiqués as "a North-West coastal town".

But these high officials had more important business to deal with. Three days previously, Lord Beaverbrook had submitted to the Cabinet a memorandum deploring the diversion of resources abroad. "Everything should be centred on the defence of Britain," he wrote. "All available supplies and material, all resources of every sort, including man-power, should be retained here." In his view, if the Germans failed to attack Great Britain, that was a victory. If the Germans attacked and were hurled back, that was a decisive victory. Thus, he had declared: "If we can prevail until the winter months, the Americans will come into the war and the issue will be settled in our favour".[29]

At Beaverbrook's insistence, the Cabinet had agreed to discuss the issue and, after deferring it from the previous day, finally got round to considering the matters raised. But Beaverbrook found no allies. The Chief of the Air Staff said that he naturally wanted more aircraft for the Battle of Britain. But the limited number of aircraft being sent to the Middle East "would have an effect in that area out of all proportion to the loss occasioned by their withdrawal from this country".

The First Sea Lord also favoured the despatch of the aircraft to the Middle East. Lord Halifax thought likewise. "The consequences of a bad setback in the Middle East might be very serious", he said. The Lord Privy Seal agreed, and Archie Sinclair gave figures for Hurricane availability in the country. There had been a "considerable improvement", while there was a "great numerical inferiority in fighters in the Middle East".

Grudgingly, Beaverbrook conceded that the fighter situation had improved, but was still strongly opposed to further withdrawals of either aircraft or pilots. "The Battle of Britain was the only battle that counted", he insisted. But, with otherwise unanimous support, Churchill over-ruled his Minister for Aircraft Production. The despatches to the Middle East would continue.

Beaverbrook's hopes of the Americans joining the war, however, looked closer than even he might have imagined. In the remarkably well-informed *Cassandra* column in the *Daily Mirror*, William Connor wrote of increasing reports that Japan was about to join the Axis, in what was to be called the "tripartite pact". Japan actually signed this day, declaring that it recognized and respected "the leadership of Germany and Italy in the establishment of a new order in Europe". Germany and Italy reciprocated with a declaration which recognized Japan's interest in the "Greater East Asia".

Predictably, the USA saw this as a hostile move, leading to short-lived hopes that it would drive Roosevelt to join the war with Britain. Ultimately, though, it was to bring America into the war, but not until December 1941, after the Japanese attack on Pearl Harbour. Then it was the German membership of the pact which had Hitler declare war on the USA. Unrecognized at the time, this day was a significant turning point.

Guy Liddell, meantime, had lunched with Stewart Menzies, the chief of MI6 and the man who was supervising the code-breaking efforts at Bletchley Park. Menzies told Liddell that the German invasion "had been worked out in every detail including practice in climbing cliffs". He then revealed that it had previously been postponed for some reason unknown. Appearing to be remarkably well-informed, he also disclosed that the Navy and Army had both had misgivings and "the matter had been referred to Keitel". Meanwhile, the situation as understood was that "people in Berlin and elsewhere in Germany were getting impatient and were unable to understand the delay".[30]

The day's newspapers were dealing with a different fare. Their front pages were devoted to the "miraculous" discovery of a lifeboat from the *City of Benares*, with forty-six survivors, including six children. But that did not prevent the *Mirror* ripping into the government for its performance on Dakar. In a piece headed "Major blunder" and a cartoon that had Churchill in a highly unflattering pose, no punches were pulled. "Are we still in the stage of gross miscalculation, of muddled dash and hasty withdrawal, of wishful thinking and of half measures," it stormed. "We have another setback to face, another disappointment, more evidence of shuffle and makeshift."

Meanwhile, both sides in the air war were branding each other's bombing as "indiscriminate". The British expended much effort on telling its own population how careful Bomber Command crews were to avoid civilian targets. At night though, claims of precision were pure cant. For the British, to get within five miles of a target was regarded as a "hit". But in daytime, it was a different matter, and one of the reasons why the *Luftwaffe* was persisting with this form of attack, despite its obvious dangers. So it was that, after some early morning manoeuvring over the Channel, with small-scale attacks on Dover, three German formations totalling some fifty aircraft were seen crossing the coast at Dungeness at an altitude of approximately 20,000 ft.

Apparently headed for London, they had failed to rendezvous with their fighter escorts. They were met by some 120 Hurricanes and harried all the way from the coast to the suburbs of the metropolis. After intervention by Me 109s, confused dog fighting took place but the bomber wave was turned back. Many bombs were jettisoned indiscriminately, causing widespread misery. Nineteen girls were killed in a Clapham works shelter, when it was struck by a bomb and the entrance caved in.[31] A main sewer was breached in the area and the railway line between Brixton and Loughborough junction was damaged. In Battersea there was considerable damage to the weighbridge and the Albert yard.

Late morning, another force carved its way into Bristol. But an additional squadron had been moved into the area and this raid was also turned back, with heavy losses. Two more raids were directed at London, but neither got through in force. Some found targets and the Houses of Parliament suffered their first recorded hits. The famous bronze statue of Richard the Lionheart was lifted from its pedestal by the blast, the tip of the king's sword bent forward.

The *Mirror* reported that the first London shelter had been fitted with bunks – a surface shelter in Stoke Newington, setting an example to the rest of the city. Unusually, page eleven of the newspaper also carried a report of a direct hit on an Anderson shelter in North London. The bomb had killed the five members of the Martin family – father, mother, and three children – and twelve-year-old Eileen Dickinson.

Home Intelligence, in the last of its daily reports, wrote: "the spirit of London is extremely good, even where people have suffered seriously". The fact that daily reports were no longer required itself told a story. The state of public morale was evidently no longer so volatile that daily reports were thought essential. The moment of greatest danger, it would appear, had passed. George Orwell seems to have thought so. "The *News-Chronicle* to-day is markedly defeatist," he wrote in his diary:

> But I have a feeling that the *News-Chronicle* is bound to become defeatist anyway and will be promptly to the fore when plausible peace terms come forward. These people have no definable policy and no sense of responsibility, nothing except a traditional

dislike of the British ruling class, based ultimately on the Nonconformist conscience. They are only noise-makers, like the *New Statesman*, etc. All these people can be counted on to collapse when the conditions of war become intolerable.[32]

Orwell might also have been thinking of US Ambassador Joseph Kennedy, who was in a decidedly defeatist mood. In a much leaked and damning letter sent to President Roosevelt this day, he wrote of the "substantial damage" done by the raids, and of his own feeling that the British were "in a bad way". He added:

> I cannot impress upon you strongly enough my complete lack of confidence in the entire [British] conduct of this war. I was delighted to see that the President said he was not going to enter the war because to enter this war, imagining for a minute that the English have anything to offer in the line of leadership or productive capacity in industry that could be of the slightest value to us, would be a complete misapprehension.[33]

For the RAF though, it had been a successful day. Not one of the daylight raids had broken through, and a toll of fifty-one aircraft had been extracted. But Fighter Command's losses had not been insignificant either, at thirty-one. Two British bombers were lost. And by night, the German bombers were back.

DAY 81 – SATURDAY 28 SEPTEMBER 1940

The *Daily Express* announced that the war was one year, three weeks and four days old, and the "Air Battle of Britain" began fifty-two days ago, which put the start on 8 August. The RAF, flushed with success from the previous day, could not resist over-egging it, claiming 130 kills. The "score" was given prominent coverage in the day's newspapers. Churchill was so taken with this "victory" that he sent a telegram to Archie Sinclair at the Air Ministry. He instructed:

> Pray congratulate the Fighter Command on the results of yesterday. The scale and intensity of the fighting and the heavy losses of the enemy ... make 27th September rank with 15th September and 15th August as the third great and victorious day during the course of the Battle of Britain.[34]

One of Churchill's main activities of the day, however, seems to have been addressing the disruption arising from workers stopping work when the sirens sounded. He had become obsessive about the amount of production lost. Now he personally introduced a scheme where the warning was to be regarded as an "alert", with a system of "spotters" to give local warning if aircraft appeared.

Only then were workers supposed to take cover. Another of his preoccupations was the number of UXBs. By the end of October, there were 3,000 in London alone. Their disruptive effect was huge. Churchill took a very keen interest in the minutia of deactivation techniques.

In *The Times* though, there was a bombshell of a different kind – a small article with the innocuous title of "Empire publicity". It announced that the Ministry of Information was to start a publicity campaign on 7 October, to bring home to people that "the war is not a fight between Great Britain as an island and northern Europe but something that is of interest to the Empire as a whole". The bombshell was tucked in the end, with the statement: "The Government are working out a policy of war aims and post-war plans, and part of the Empire Publicity Campaign will be to give some definition to these aims". If that was the case – especially in the context of Churchill's refusal on 20 August – this was major news. A lot of people wanted to know more.

As for the shooting war, this day saw something of a reversal in the fortunes of Fighter Command. It lost four Spitfires and nine Hurricanes, with nine pilots killed. Accidents and other losses brought the balance to eighteen, in exchange for ten *Luftwaffe* aircraft. Total RAF losses in two days of fighting, including bombers, had the two sides close to parity: 59–65. Nor did the sea war offer any comfort. The British steamer *Dalveen* was sunk by German bombing off the north-east coast of Scotland. SS *Queen City* was damaged. HMT *Recoil* was lost on patrol in the English Channel, presumed mined. Then a flotilla of German destroyers from Brest laid mines in Falmouth Bay. Five Allied ships were to fall foul of them. And this was only the tip of the iceberg.

Very substantial merchant shipping losses were being suffered, attributable in large part to the general shortage of escorts. A. V. Alexander had raised the alarm back on 29 August. But the situation had continued to deteriorate. Furthermore, it was felt that Churchill had contributed to the problem. On 1 July, as a precaution against invasion, he had instructed the Admiralty to "endeavour" to raise the flotilla in the "narrow seas" (the English Channel) to a strength of forty destroyers, with additional cruiser support. These could only come from the convoy escorts, as Churchill was very obviously aware. "The losses in the Western Approach must be accepted meanwhile", he had written in his minute. But those losses were reaching dangerous proportions.

C-in-C Home Fleet, Admiral Sir Charles Forbes, had never been at ease with his original instructions. There would be sufficient warning, he argued, to permit destroyers to be employed on convoy escort and other duties. Should an invasion seem imminent, they could be rapidly redeployed. This had become a running sore in the relations between Forbes and the Admiralty acting under the direct instructions of Churchill. This culminated in Forbes writing a letter, suggesting that "the Army, assisted by the Air Force, should carry out its immemorial role of holding up the first flight of an invading force". The Navy, he asserted, "should be freed to carry out its proper function – offensively against the enemy and in defence of our trade – and not be tied down to provide passive defence of our country, which has now become a fortress".[35]

In what must surely have been a complete coincidence, the *Mirror* made exactly the same point, headlining its lead editorial: "Too much invasion?" It asked whether the "invasion scare" was subtly serving one of the Nazi aims. That aim was to fix the attention of our government and people on the danger of direct attack and on the necessity for vast defensive preparations by ourselves. But now the mere threat of invasion had immobilized millions in the country. "A huge and a hugely expensive Army, with another auxiliary army, tramps, marches, stands, waits and gets fed up". It says something though that what was obvious to Forbes, and to the editorial writers of the *Mirror* seemed somehow to have evaded Churchill. Here though, the issue was not the diversion of escorts, but manpower. With the civilians rather than the Army in the front line, could not at least a portion of the Army be used to help clear up the bombing damage?

Come the night, in this fortress island where this huge idle army waited, air activity started at about eight. London was the main objective again, but the south and south-east of England, East Anglia as far north as Lincolnshire, Nottingham, Derby, Liverpool and South Wales all received visits. To add to the damage done by the *Luftwaffe*, eighteen Fighter Command aircraft were downed during the day, plus five "heavies" from the other Commands. Against those twenty-three, the Germans lost a mere ten aircraft. Nine British fighter pilots lay dead.

DAY 82 – SUNDAY 29 SEPTEMBER 1940

The *Sunday Express* was asking whether the raid on the Friday might have been something more than "merely an unusually vicious air attack", speculating that it might have been part of another invasion attempt, smashed once more by the RAF. The paper also recorded Churchill sending his message congratulating Fighter Command on the results of that day.

But there was no respite. The *Luftwaffe* came soon after dawn, clocking in just before seven and again at nine, the bombers visiting Berkshire, Essex, Kent and Surrey. But, in the dry words of the official log, "no incident of importance took place". Later in the morning it was the turn of east and south-east England. Just before eleven thirty, eighteen bombs were dropped near the naval base at Lowestoft. A land mine detonated and some ammunition exploded, causing damage to property, water mains and telegraph wires. There were several casualties. Then came a sweep by about a hundred Me 109s, shortly after four in the afternoon, flying at great height from the Dover–Dungeness direction. Part of this force approached central London, but most of it had remained over Kent. In the evening, Sittingbourne was heavily bombed.

The night brought a fresh wave of bombers. They started their murder at about eight in the evening, hitting London but spreading death around south and south-east England once more. South Wales and the Midlands suffered visitations. Bombs were dropped just after nine at the Royal Military College, Sandhurst. Unfortunately, as some averred, the only result was a burst water main. Many bombs were dropped on the Guildford–Sevenoaks line.

Liverpool's visits were later, but before midnight, when fires were started at Duke's and Salthouse Docks. Four warehouses, including one containing grain, caught fire. Birkenhead Docks were also attacked. Railways generally took a hit again, but not on any great scale. A number of factories were damaged and the City of London received its quota of bombs. From just after midnight, they caused several fires, the most serious being in Upper Thames Street. An unexploded bomb was also reported in the south-east corner of St Paul's Churchyard, causing major traffic disruption. Cheapside and Queen Victoria Street were already closed. Horse Shoe Wharf, Cannon Street and Carter Lane were also affected.

So went the war. The *Luftwaffe* dropped their bombs, and the people endured.

Fighter Command lost six aircraft in what was rapidly becoming its own private war. Three British bombers went down and the *Luftwaffe* lost eight machines.

DAY 83 – MONDAY 30 SEPTEMBER 1940

The *Daily Mail* gave its front-page lead to air correspondent Noel Monks, under the headline "Triumph in 'crisis month'". The RAF, Monks wrote, have weathered, with the passing of September, the "crisis month" of the war. He continued:

> On the first of the month that ends to-day a high Air Ministry official said to me: "As far as the RAF are concerned, this is the critical month of the war: I will be glad when it is past." Now it IS past. And the RAF, who have hurled back every attack made on them, the airmen who have destroyed more than 1,000 German aircraft for the loss of only 286 of their own fighters, have come out on top.

The Air Ministry "spin" failed to impress the *Daily Mirror*. Giving its page lead to the weekend raid on Berlin, it then attended to domestic matters. A Sunday lie-in for Tube shelterers had caught the eye of one of its reporters, who noted how Londoners had taken advantage of the late start to the traffic, the men going topside to collect hot tea for their womenfolk. The *Daily Express* also featured the raid on Berlin and the claims of damage to "Nazi bases". But the paper's war reporter, Sefton Delmer, warned: "Revenge bombs will not win the war". He wrote: "I spent five hours yesterday morning driving round London and its suburbs carefully observing the damage done by Hitler's bombs in last night's raids". From this he had concluded: "Random bombing, of the kind the Germans carried out over London on Saturday night, just does not pay. And it's not worth imitating. Let us stick to our careful selection of economically and militarily important targets".

One man in particular was especially concerned with economically important targets – the Minister of Shipping, a Conservative MP by the name of Ronald Cross. This day he was not the bearer of good tidings, submitting a paper to the War Cabinet which raised the alarm about the increasingly severe merchant shipping losses. "In a matter of this vital importance," he wrote, "remedial, measures should not be delayed." He urged an immediate increase in the number of escorts for the convoys.[36]

Entirely in tune with Admiral Forbes and his representation to the Admiralty only two days previously, Cross could not have been clearer. He said:

> I am aware, of coursethat there are many demands, including anti-invasion prepara-
> tions, made upon our limited naval forces but I should be failing in my duty if I did not
> represent, in the strongest possible terms, the necessity for putting a stop to the present
> exorbitant risks to which our Merchant Shipping is being exposed.[37]

The most senior of the intelligence bodies, the Combined Intelligence Committee (CIC), had information that supported a reduction in the forces held on standby. On this day, it had received a report from the RAF, indicating that the total of barges photographed in the five main ports between Flushing and Boulogne had, since 18 September, reduced from 1,005 to 691. The evidence, however, was judged to be "inconclusive", possibly only an attempt to move the barges out of the reach of RAF attacks.[38]

The *Luftwaffe*, meanwhile, sent over two attacks, totalling two hundred aircraft. The first crossed the Kent coast at around nine in the morning. It was met by eight squadrons of Hurricanes and four of Spitfires. The bombers got as far as Maidstone before they were turned back. An hour later, a formation of Me 109s and 110s tried its luck. It was met by a strong force of sixty Hurricanes and eighteen Spitfires. A second wave followed, a hundred bombers escorted by two hundred fighters. Crossing the Sussex coast, it headed towards London but only one *Gruppe* got as far as the outskirts, suffering heavily for its folly. A final raid was tried on the Westland factory at Yeovil. Forty Heinkels, escorted by Me 110s, crossed the coast near Weymouth. Once again, a welcoming committee forced them to scatter. They dumped their bombs over Sherbourne and district and fled.

The *Mail* was right about the RAF getting "on top" of the threat – but only the daylight attacks. All Fighter Command had achieved was to establish an airborne "Maginot line", which was now being circumvented. The main bombing effort had already been transferred to the night, when the slaughter continued unabated. This night, the attacks were concentrated mainly on south and west London, with the Home Counties getting attention as well. There was light bombing on Merseyside. But the traffic was not one-way. Unfavourable weather did not stop the RAF visiting northern Germany. A small number of bombers again raided Berlin. These and other operations cost nine bombers and a Fleet Air Arm

Albacore. With nineteen fighters downed, that brought RAF losses to twenty-nine, as against forty-two *Luftwaffe* losses, including twenty-eight Me 109s.

On the month, Fighter Command had lost 393 aircraft, bringing its total losses for the battle to 818. Total RAF losses for the month were 511, and for the battle as a whole, the number reached 1,324. *Luftwaffe* losses were 548 on the month, and 1,374 from the start of the battle. Despite the hyperbole and exaggerated claims, the two side's losses were very closely matched, as they were to remain throughout the battle.

That night, the 15in gun monitor HMS *Erebus* took up station four to five miles off Calais and bombarded gun emplacements. Her two guns, weighing a hundred tons each, were capable of hurling shells each weighing nearly 2,000lbs. They fired seventeen rounds before the ship retired. The Germans responded with nine 240mm rounds from the radar-guided Prinz Heinrich Battery. Curiously, no mention was made of this action in official communiqués. No details were publicized in the British or foreign press, despite reports of RAF activity over the Channel ports.

DAY 84 – TUESDAY 1 OCTOBER 1940

Now it was the turn of the *Yorkshire Post* to declare that the tide of the war was turning. As with the others, it was partially right. During the day, in that now tiny fragment of the war, the RAF was successfully fighting off the raiders. At night, it was letting them through. Nevertheless, there was clearly a concerted attempt to mark up a "turning point" and the *Guardian* joined in the fray with an article headed: "First phase of the air war". Citing "official opinion", it declared that one phase of the air war had ended and Britain was ready to face the next round "full of confidence".

Nevertheless, in the article it was "recognised that the question of stopping enemy bombers raiding London and other cities by night remains to be solved", but it was pointed out "in authoritative Air Ministry quarters" that the prospects of developments "soon" were "favourable". The attacks on London, these "quarters" said, had been part of the invasion plan "aimed at disrupting communications within and to and from the capital". If the enemy had won this fight, "it would have gone down as one of the most decisive battle of history". As he had not succeeded, it was only a phase.

As a clue to the real authors' grip on reality, however, the article went on to state that, among other types of German aircraft, the fictitious Heinkel 113 had been "tried and severely beaten". Unabashed though, the RAF continued its propaganda war, adding forty-nine aircraft to the score of the previous day, bringing the claimed total of *Luftwaffe* aircraft downed in September to 1,095, almost exactly double the true number. Thus, the "summer phase of the war" had come to an end in a resounding propaganda victory.

Adding to the sense of triumph, the *New York Times* told of RAF raiders pounding Berlin for five hours. The Germans claimed only one bomb had been dropped, but there was no independent witness. William L. Shirer had no diary entry for this day. Nevertheless, his earlier reports had referred to damage as "negligible", although he reported that the psychological effects of the RAF raids were profound. The bare statistics were unimpressive, though. Forty-two bombers had been despatched on the night of 30 September/1 October. Only seventeen reached the target and bombed it, for the loss of two aircraft.

To be fair, the *Luftwaffe* had the easier job. The distances involved were shorter and, for London, the crews had the Thames to guide them to the city. For other targets, it had radio navigation aids, far in advance of British equipment. Göbbels wrote that following "absolutely massive attacks" on London, it was "possible to see the demoralising effect from the English press". Of the British attacks on Germany, he claimed: "one can no longer discern English intentions with any certainty". He was wrong about the effects of the bombing on London. Although the physical damage was significant, the psychological effect was less so. The shock effect had worn off and Londoners were adapting.[39]

On this day, a shelter "dictator" was appointed, Admiral Sir Edward Evans, one of two London Regional Commissioners for Civil Defence, charged with bringing order to the chaos. As importantly, the authorities were learning how to deal with the extraordinary situations with which they were daily confronted. Projects which would in peacetime have taken months in the planning and weeks in execution were finished in hours or days. At Kilburn in North London, for instance, the almost complete demolition of a major viaduct was dealt with almost as a matter of routine. A heavy wooden framework was constructed to replace the missing stone and brickwork, and the train service was restored two days after the bombing.[40]

DAY 85 – WEDNESDAY 2 OCTOBER 1940

With the RAF having made daylight conditions dangerous for medium bombers, a major conversion programme was under way to equip large numbers of Me 109s as fighter bombers – or *Jabos*. Already they were being sent over in large numbers, usually at high altitude, where only the Spitfires could reach them. The tactic was not without cost. This day, the *Luftwaffe* lost sixteen aircraft, against the RAF's three Spitfires – two of those lost in a ground collision.

Churchill was finally confronting the human consequences of the shelter policy. He had been given a copy of the *New Statesman* article by Ritchie Calder, which had details about the conditions in the notorious "Tilbury shelter". This was the area beneath the massive Fenchurch–Tilbury railway goods terminal just off the Commercial Road, part of which had been organized by the local authority as a shelter for 3,000 people. Other parts were used for the storage of margarine. Communist councillors had led residents to break into this area, bringing the occupation on some nights up to as many as 14–16,000 people. There was no sanitation. Poorer families were forced to occupy the more unpleasant areas where the floors were covered by excrement and discarded margarine. One observer reported: "The place was a hell hole. It was an outrage that people had to live in these conditions".[41]

Now, at the War Cabinet, Churchill urged strong action – as a general rule, he was keen on "strong action" – to prevent large numbers of people crowding into the building until it had been made safe. He wanted the man in charge fired. Admiral Evans, the Regional Commissioner, had been given the fullest powers to deal with this matter, taking over from local authority officials.[42]

In the wider world, Drew Middleton of the *AP* was speculating about *Sealion*. The "zero hour for [the] invasion of Britain this year has passed", he wrote, citing "neutral military observers and unofficial British sources". There were "signs that the battle of Britain will be fought in Africa", where Germany would reinforce the Italians. They would also keep troops in the Channel ports, but only to tie up the British North Sea fleet.

DAY 86 – THURSDAY 3 OCTOBER 1940

Overnight had seen much reduced *Luftwaffe* activity, clearing the way for the newspapers to concentrate on Neville Chamberlain's resignation. Worn down by the stress of office and age, and now aware that he had a terminal illness, he had resigned from the government.

Headlined on the front page of the *Daily Express*, before the details had been formally released, the reshuffle brought in Labour MP Herbert Morrison as Home Secretary and Minister of Home Security. He replaced Sir John Anderson, who took Chamberlain's vacated post as Lord President of the Council, and joined the War Cabinet as a permanent member.

Morrison, a one-eyed son of a policeman – having lost an eye as a baby, due to infection – had been a Hackney councillor and Mayor, and leader of London County Council. During the First World War, he had been a conscientious objector and he was to become grandfather to Peter Mandelson. One of his first acts in his new post was to appoint Miss Ellen Wilkinson ("Red Ellen") as Parliamentary Secretary, responsible for shelter policy.[43] Formerly a member of the Communist Party, she had walked with the Jarrow Hunger Marchers of 1936 and had spoken passionately for their cause in parliament. As a people's representative, she could not have been a better choice.

Back in the war, autumnal weather prevented any concerted air attacks. The *Luftwaffe* resorted to its standard bad weather operating pattern, despatching single aircraft on raids throughout the country. One Ju 88 found the de Havilland works at Hatfield. From a height of 50ft, it machine-gunned workers as they ran for shelter and then dropped a stick of four bombs on the plant, killing twenty-one and injuring seventy. Anti-aircraft fire brought the aircraft down. Fighter Command losses for the day were limited to one Blenheim, crashing in driving rain during a patrol, killing the whole crew. The *Luftwaffe* lost nine aircraft, including two to accidents.

Alan Brooke wrote to his diary that he was "beginning to think that the Germans may after all not attempt it [the invasion]".[44] He might have been intrigued to have read the War Cabinet minutes, in which the Foreign Secretary drew attention to two telegrams. They reported that the German Government "did not now expect to succeed in invading England", but hoped "by bombing the Midlands and South to bring about the collapse of the present Government and its replacement by a more amenable one".[45]

This identified the German objective as "regime change", another phrase yet to be invented. But that was the essence of Douhet theory being played out, even if there were no indications of how serious were German expectations. However, Field Marshal von Leeb entered in his diary the comments from General Phillip Zoch, the *Luftwaffe* Commander attached to Army Group C. Over the September fighting, he claimed RAF losses at 1,100 aircraft, as against 350 *Luftwaffe*. As a result, the British were flying older types of aircraft. It was thought that their reserves were running low and the losses could no longer be replaced by new production. Zoch believed that the English could be forced to give up the fight.[46]

But of far greater immediate significance was the sustained attack on Allied shipping. To add to the already considerable losses, a merchant ship of 4,600 tons had been lost on the previous day, and belated reports had been received of three other merchant ships sunk far out in the Atlantic. Joining the First Lord of the Admiralty, the C-in-C Home Fleet and the Shipping Minister now came Minister of Food, Lord Woolton. He submitted a memorandum to the War Cabinet. During the last few weeks, he wrote, "I have been seriously disturbed by the extent of our food losses at sea". If the current rate of loss was sustained, imports would have to be increased, taking up a much larger proportion of shipping, with serious effect on other supplies.[47]

Alongside Woolton's paper was yet another memorandum from Alexander. He repeated the point so heavily emphasized by Forbes that the only short-term way of improving the situation was "the return to trade protection of the forces which were withdrawn for anti-invasion duties".[48] Invasion was no longer a threat, if it ever had been. The response to the perceived threat was now itself threatening the very survival of Britain.

DAY 87 – FRIDAY 4 OCTOBER 1940

Trailing in the wake of its competitor, the *Daily Mail* led with the reshuffle, focusing on John Reith being moved from the Ministry of Transport and given the job of planning for post-war reconstruction. Reith was also charged with organizing immediate repairs for those buildings which could not wait, and "in all probability" starting an immediate investigation into the question of providing "more and better air-raid shelters". The other big change the paper highlighted was the promotion of Ernest Bevin, Minister of Labour, into the War Cabinet in order to "represent the trade unions".

In Berlin, reported the *Daily Express* citing Nazi radio, Hitler had ordered the authorities to rush the construction of deep shelters under Berlin's big public buildings, which were to be reserved for young children and expectant mothers.

Effective confirmation of the diminishing invasion threat came from the Italian press. It, like the rest of the world's media – including the *Daily Express*, which gave the story the front-page lead – was monitoring a much advertised meeting between Hitler and Mussolini. This was at the Brenner Pass, where the two dictators spent three hours together in an armoured train, a gift from the *Führer* to the *Duce*. And what was particularly noteworthy was that Hitler was no longer talking about invading Britain.[49] In Rome, the newspaper, *Il Popolo di Roma*, spoke of a long war in prospect, with Germany unable to invade Britain this year. That may have been unwelcome to Hitler, who had wanted a short war, but it spelled grave danger for Britain, which could not sustain its current shipping losses.

The line in Berlin from Foreign Office spokesmen was that the two leaders had discussed an appeal to the British to call off the war. Shirer covered the meeting from Berlin. "The best guess here," he wrote to his diary, "is that Mussolini is sore because the Germans apparently have abandoned the idea of invading Britain this fall, leaving him holding the bag with his offensive in the Egyptian desert".[50] *AP* writer Kirke L. Simpson wrote that "[t]he battle of England seems slated to bog down into a tragic winter stalemate of attrition". Yet it also meant that England "will enjoy surcease from fears of the worst – successful Nazi invasion". On the other hand, it faced new fears – of increasing shortages and grave economic stress.

The productive Simpson also wrote of Spain that it had voted to stay out of the war. General Franco was not convinced Britain was beaten. He was apprehensive that an airtight British blockade of Spain would invite starvation-bred disorders that could unseat him as military dictator. He had no intention of stepping in to grasp at the Axis-preferred Gibraltar prize until it was far more certain that Britain had been beaten.

Mrs Churchill had been out and about in Chingford, the Prime Minister's constituency, accompanied by Jock Colville. It had not been all sweetness and light. One woman, who had been bombed out, looked at the party, and complained: "It is all very well for them, who have all they want; but we have lost everything".[51]

Meanwhile, Winston appeared to be responding to the chorus of concerns about the shipping situation when he addressed the War Cabinet. He had, he told his ministers, discussed the matter with the Defence Committee. Their view was that suitable weather for an invasion "was not likely to prevail on many occasions during the winter months", so it would be right to divert a number of destroyers and anti-submarine trawlers from anti-invasion duties, to reinforce shipping escorts. He also hoped to have ten further destroyers and six corvettes available for service in the next four weeks, including vessels received from the USA.[52] The growing crisis, though – as was shortly to become apparent – had not been resolved.

DAY 88 – SATURDAY 5 OCTOBER 1940

Admiral Evans, the newly appointed shelter "dictator" told the *Evening Standard* that he "should be quite happy to snuggle down for the winter in a properly-built Anderson shelter", although he admitted to sleeping under his own kitchen table. Herbert Morrison, in his new role of Minister of Home Security, inspected Bethnal Green Tube Station, declaring that it could be used as a shelter. The building "is considered absolutely safe by experts of London Transport who have examined it", reported the *Standard*.

The "sensational" domestic news of the day was the appointment of Air Marshal Sir Charles Portal, Chief of Bomber Command to Chief of the Air Staff. Newall had been sent to New Zealand as its governor general. The *Daily Mail* gave it front-page treatment, noting the relative youth of Portal, and his replacement, Air Marshal Sir Richard Peirse, 47 and 48 respectively. Correspondent Noel Monks emphasized the experience of the two men. Both were great believers in offensive operations. Both strongly maintained that the winning of the war would be greatly assisted by large-scale bombing offensives against the Nazis in their own territory

However, the meeting between Hitler and Mussolini continued to dominate most newspapers, with the *Daily Express* reporting an Axis "boast" of a "Suez-to-Thames blitz". The *Hamburger Frendemblatt*, in a report picked up by the English-language press, asserted that the war had changed from a

European dispute into a great final struggle of a new world. It would not only be carried out in the regions of the British Isles, but also on African soil. This was something the *Express* correspondent developed. "Hitler has not quite abandoned his dreams of a Blitzkrieg against the British Isles," he wrote, "and wants to engage Italy in an intensive campaign of divertive (sic) action".

Shirer, monitoring Italian comment, told of a *Duce* angry that the plan to invade Britain had been abandoned. It could have reduced pressure on Italian forces in Africa. Now the Italians were the only Axis partner confronting British ground forces. Shirer further wrote that the Germans were "in a great state of mind because the British won't admit they're licked". They cannot, he said, "repress their rage against Churchill for still holding out hopes of victory to his people, instead of lying down and surrendering, as have all Hitler's opponents to date". In Shirer's view, the Germans could not understand a people with "character and guts".[53]

The Times, on the other hand, had the measure of the beast. In a leading article headed, "The mood of Britain", it noted that "the Nazi tactics of indiscriminate bombing for the purpose of mass terrorisation have established beyond all possibility of doubt that this is, in the current phase, a people's war". We know now the meaning of total war, the paper said, and we know that we, as a people, can face it without flinching. "The truly remarkable thing about this determination is that it has generated and maintained itself without any appeal to the highly coloured emotions of jingoism."

For "the few", though, it had also been a busy day. Despite patchy weather, the *Luftwaffe* had returned in considerable strength, launching five major raids and a number of diversionary attacks. Fighter Command was forced to fly 1,175 sorties, losing eight aircraft. Bomber and Coastal Commands together lost seven of their aircraft, the combined loss of fifteen exactly matching the *Luftwaffe* – whose losses included three accidents, and several in overnight raids, one from flak damage. The British were still overclaiming. The Air Ministry announced twenty-three raiders downed during the day, for a loss of nine fighters.

13.

The widening war

We are seeing more and more clearly that the Battle of Britain is only a part of the world war. And within the Battle of Britain, conflict between the German Air Force and the civilian population is itself only a part. But what a vitally important part it is! How the whole fortune of war turns upon it!

Herbert Morrison, Draft Ministerial Broadcast (script), 31 October 1940.[1]

Some regard 6 October as the start of the fourth and final phase of the "official" battle, for others, the phase started a few days earlier, for others it was the fifth phase. Variously described as the *Luftwaffe* in retreat and "the anti-climax", it marked the progressive reorientation of the *Luftwaffe* effort to night bombing, with high-level daylight fighter sweeps escorting fighter bombers. Churchill called it the battle of attrition. But, for the people, there was a victory in the offing. The new Home Secretary and Security Minister, Herbert Morrison, was about to give them a deep shelter policy.

DAY 89 – SUNDAY 6 OCTOBER 1940

Overnight, London had been lit up by anti-aircraft fire. At times the barrage had seemed to be far greater in intensity than anything reported since the attack on London began. Thus reported the *Sunday Express*, telling its readers: "Viewed from a distance of twelve miles, the barrage appeared a terrific affair. It was like a great curtain of leaping flames".

The big story of the day though – apart from the US mobilization of 27,000 naval reserves – was a "retrospective" on "How the RAF smashed the invasion". Assembled from "facts given … by people who reached London last week from Hitler's battered invasion ports", it detailed how RAF bombing had smashed the fleet and its environs. Boulogne, it claimed, "has practically ceased to exist as a port, so serious is the damage. Neither is Dunkirk of much use today. Nearly all the port equipment has been put out of action".

Nevertheless, the paper was at pains to emphasize that the Germans would like to lull the British into a false sense of security, creating a slackening of the war effort and decreased vigilance. "One possibility must not be overlooked", it said. "While the Germans have suffered a most serious setback, it does not follow that the High Command have abandoned their hope of invading Britain." Playing to a different script, however, German shortwave broadcasts were stoking up the invasion threat, claiming that "maybe" the waves of German bombers flying towards England would be followed "soon" by hundreds of thousands of troops.

The *Express*, at least, however, seemed to understand the Nazi tactics. In an article headed "Watch for the peace offer", it warned that "[a]nother peace move, accompanied by the usual threat that the British Empire must accept it forthwith or be obliterated, is expected almost immediately from Hitler and Mussolini". This was believed to be one the outcomes of the Brenner talks. Hitler would make the offer, "because he is still under the delusion that the bombing of London has made the people of this country hanker for peace even on his terms". The offer, though, was likely to come in a roundabout way and be in rather non-committal form as neither Hitler nor Mussolini wanted to risk a public rebuff from Britain. And, according to the *Basler Nachrichten*, the offer was "extremely likely" to come via a Spanish intermediary.

This day being a Sunday, another double dose of J. B. Priestley was on offer, making him easily the most influential commentator of the period. In the *Sunday Express*, he wrote of decentralization, asking "Is this the end of the lure of London?" The threat of invasion and the London bombing had compelled the government to think in terms of decentralization of power and authority in many different departments of life. This, to Priestley, seemed "all to the good". The war was doing for us what we had not the sense before to do for ourselves.

Come the evening, he was delivering his evening *Postscript* on BBC radio. Recalling recent travels where he had found hotel rooms almost impossible to get because they had been taken up by long-term moneyed residents, escaping the bombing, he tartly observed:

This has, for a long time now, been a country in which there are far too many pleasant, able-bodied persons who, because of private incomes or pensions and all kinds of snobbish nonsense, are condemned to yawn away their lives, forever wondering what to do between meals; in startling contrast to the other people who wonder how to get it done between meals.

His criticism of the "private incomes or pensions" was to provoke a storm of protest from the Right, with complaints that his broadcast might have been "calculated to set rich against poor and to annoy country districts".[2] Priestley's days with the BBC were numbered.

With newspapers this day carrying for the first time pictures of people sheltering in the Underground, even sleeping between the rails on the track bed, the weather intervened to make the shelters, for one night only, almost redundant. Atrocious conditions over the Channel and northern France prevented almost all air operations. London was visited by a mere seven bombers – the lightest attack since the offensive had begun on 7 September. Come the night, when the sirens sounded, nothing happened: no aircraft, no bombs, no gunfire. Cautiously, people emerged into the night and the pubs and restaurants were soon doing a roaring trade. Many slept in their own beds for the first time in over a month.

DAY 90 – MONDAY 7 OCTOBER 1940

The *Daily Mail* announced: "RAF preparing a great new bomber offensive", with "powerful new RAF bombers now being produced in great numbers". Portal was getting down to work. "Hitler's people can look forward to more than a taste of the medicine their Luftwaffe is administering over here", the paper declared. The *Daily Express* headlined, "Strangest night for a month", thus announcing the "Blitzpause". Göbbels, on the other hand, bemoaned the fact that that air was "slowly grinding to a halt".[3]

This "Blitzpause" marked the eve of the annual congress of the Trades Union Council (TUC) in Southport, where representatives of five million union members were meeting. The *Mirror*, noting that the Westminster Parliament had disappeared for the moment, awarded it the title of "the voice of democracy". Two members of this "Workers' Parliament" were also in the War Cabinet, Labour MPs Clem Attlee and Ernest Bevin, former General Secretary of the Transport and General Workers Union (TGWU). The paper asked whether they were doing enough to make this a People's War; a war fought "for the people by the people".

Addressing the War Cabinet that day, Churchill was more interested in taking the war to the newspapers – particularly the *Mirror* and its stable-mate the *Sunday Pictorial*. With the daily having called the Dakar affair a "blunder", the Sunday newspaper had repeated the jibe. Now, the *Pictorial* had published an article by H. G. Wells, contained a slashing attack on Field Marshal Sir Edmund Ironside and General Viscount Gort, the leader of the British Expeditionary Force in France. According to H. G. Wells, until the Army was better led, we stood no chance of beating the Germans. Ironside was "a model of incompetence" and Gort our "praying general".

The same issue of the *Pictorial* had contained a leading article making a "scurrilous attack" on several members of the government, and obviously seeking to undermine confidence in it. Halifax was singled out as "the quintessence of everything that an Englishman should not be". Churchill even objected to the attack on Attlee and Bevin that morning, with the *Mirror's* complaint that they were not doing enough to make this a war fought "for the people by the people".

To Churchill, the immediate purpose of these articles seemed to be to affect the discipline of the Army, to attempt to shake the stability of the government and to make trouble between the government and organized labour. But, "in his considered judgment", he told the War Cabinet, there was far more behind them: "They stood for something most dangerous and sinister, namely, an attempt to bring about a situation in which the country would be ready for a surrender peace". Said Churchill: "It was intolerable that any newspaper should indulge in criticism and abuse, far beyond what was tolerated in times of acute Party strife, in a time of great national peril".[4]

To his evident dismay, however, the Donald Somervell, the Attorney-General and John Anderson, as Lord President of the Council, advised against criminal prosecution. It might do more harm than good. Beaverbrook offered a possible way out, through the Newspaper Proprietors' Association, which had "considerable disciplinary powers". The matter was adjourned.[5]

Trouble for Churchill was also brewing on the diplomatic front. US Ambassador Joseph Kennedy was asking Washington to send another "rescue ship" to remove Americans from "embattled Britain". Negotiations were "understood" to be in progress between Kennedy and Washington, the main question hinging on whether Germany and Britain would give safe passage to such a ship.[6]

Kennedy was not the only one contemplating getting out of London. Announced by Health Minister Malcolm McDonald was an inspired scheme for evacuating all mothers and children of school-age or under. They were offered guaranteed transport out of the capital. Billets would be found and lodging paid. Those wishing to make their own arrangements were being offered travel warrants and lodging allowances. There were to be no bureaucratic obstacles.

In the event, only around 10,000 women and children took advantage of the scheme. But the offer had been made. Those who stayed put were "volunteers" for whatever was to come. This would defuse much of the local criticism and remove those most likely to destabilize morale.[7]

Meanwhile, the air war went on. The *Luftwaffe* sent an almost continuous stream of fighter-bombers over Kent through the morning, leaving the RAF hard-pressed to deal with them. A raid on the Westland Aircraft factory in Yeovil left more than a hundred casualties as a shelter took a direct hit. Fighter Command losses on the day amounted to fifteen write-offs. Bomber Command brought the total loss to nineteen, only one short of the *Luftwaffe's* twenty aircraft downed.

DAY 91 – TUESDAY 8 OCTOBER 1940

That morning, 150 German aircraft crossed the coast and headed towards London, mostly high-flying *jabos*, with top cover flying as high as 32,000 ft. Bombs were scattered over a number of areas, including central London. Several raids developed in the afternoon, again involving substantial numbers high-flying fighter bombers. The tactic gave Park considerable problems, even if the bombing damage was relatively slight.

In the *Daily Mirror*, the first day of the TUC annual congress was reported. Demands had been heard for better air-raid shelters, the homeless dealt with and an end to profiteering. The shelter problem was "not insoluble and its remedy is overdue", and the homeless should get "immediate and comprehensive compensation", to enable them to "restore their shattered homes". On profiteers, TUC President William Holmes declared that the government "must restrain them and make it impossible for anybody to slink away at the end of the war richer than he entered it".[8]

Doubtless, delegates had been fortified by copies of a leaflet produced by the National Union of Railwaymen. Featuring the General Secretary John Marchbank, it bore the legend in large capitals, "This is the PEOPLE'S WAR". The text opened with an unequivocal declaration: "This is our war – the people's war. If there were ever any doubts about it, the tragic events of the last months have brought the truth home to working people". It is our war, the text continued, on the second of the densely printed pages:

> because the risks and responsibilities of national defence have fallen on us. The men of the Home Guard, the ARP workers, the auxiliary firemen, the ambulance units, every section of the civil defence organisation form part of our mobilised nation. We are in arms as a people, to repel any invasion of our soil and preserve our homes.

The concluding message was equally uncompromising: "It is our war, the people's war, because the people are fighting to secure a rebirth of freedom, so that government of the people, by the people, for the people shall not perish from the earth". This was Churchill's opposition, openly pronouncing the message he had to beat if he was to retain political control of the post-war nation.[9]

Of more immediate concern, Beaverbrook submitted two memoranda to the War Cabinet, equally stark and uncompromising. "The country waits on a declaration now in terms that will persuade the men to stay at their benches", the first one said. The second: "The siren is still the signal for laying down tools in most places. The issue involved is bigger than any other domestic question and requires immediate and vigorous treatment".

In his second memorandum, the two occupying less than one page, the Minister for Aircraft Production spelt out the losses for the week ending 28 September. Airspeed had lost one-third of their total working time; Bristol one-sixth; De Havilland were out more than half of their working time; Fairey, Hayes, out about half total time; Hawker, Kingston, where the Hurricane was built, also half total time. The Supermarine works, where the Spitfires were built, were out over one-third of their time. The accessories factories, equally important, showed the same unsatisfactory condition.[10]

The event of the day though was Churchill addressing the Commons for his monthly report.[11] Curiously, having ignored it at the time, he made a reference to Hitler's speech of 4 September, noting that the *Führer* had then said "he would raze our cities to the ground". Since then, the Prime Minister observed, "he has been trying to carry out his fell purpose".

In a strongly analytical speech, he observed that 400 German bombers on average had visited the UK every 24 hours. It was doubtful whether "this rate of sustained attack could be greatly exceeded". He looked at the weight of explosives dropped, some 22,000 tons by 23 September, and then at the weight the previous Thursday week, 251 tons on London in one night. That was "only a few tons less than the total dropped on the whole country throughout the last war". That night, there had been 180 killed – one ton of bombs per three quarters of a person. In the last war, one ton had killed ten people in built-up areas. Approximately, mortality was less than one-tenth of that rate.

The expectation had been up to 3,000 killed and 12,000 wounded, night after night. Hospitals had been geared up for a quarter of a million casualties "merely as a first provision". But, up to the previous Saturday, figures stood at 8,500 killed and 13,000 wounded. Furthermore, since the heavy raiding had begun, the casualty rate had declined steadily. From over 6,000 in the first week, it had dropped to just under 5,000 in the second, to about 4,000 in the third week and to under 3,000 in the last of the four weeks. The arithmetic was clear. In Greater London and its population of 8,000,000 spread over 700 square miles, it was beyond the resources of the *Luftwaffe* to inflict terminal damage.

As the speech developed, a two-stage strategy became apparent. Having talked down the bombing threat, Churchill then talked up the invasion. "Do not let us be lured into supposing that the danger is past." In a fine burst of rhetoric, he told the House:

> On the contrary, unwearying vigilance and the swift and steady strengthening of our Forces by land, sea and air which is in progress must be at all costs maintained. Now that we are in October, however, the weather becomes very uncertain, and there are not many lucid intervals of two or three days together in which river barges can cross the narrow seas and land upon our beaches. Still, those intervals may occur. Fogs may aid the foe.
>
> Our Armies, which are growing continually in numbers, equipment, mobility and training, must be maintained all through the winter, not only along the beaches but in reserve, as the majority are, like leopards crouching to spring at the invader's throat. The enemy has certainly got prepared enough shipping and barges to throw half a million men in a single night on to salt water – or into it.

Then there was the hugely embarrassing failure of the Dakar expedition to deal with. It was another to add to the list of his many failures. Churchill needed good news, a victory to counterbalance the humiliation. For that he offered "the succession of 297 brilliant victories gained by our fighter aircraft, and gained by them over the largely superior numbers which the enemy have launched against us". He added:

> The three great days of 15th August, 15th September and 27th September have proved to all the world that here at home over our own Island we have the mastery of the air. That is a tremendous fact.

The response came from the acting leader of the opposition, Labour MP Hastings Lees-Smith. A strong personal supporter of Churchill, he spoke of Dakar: "after an episode like that, the country may, for a moment, lose its sense of proportion", he declared. It may "not realise that victory in the Battle of Britain is, in its final effect, more important than anything which happens elsewhere, even at Dakar". The one trumped the other. Never mind the failure, look at the victory. But short-term political expediency was creating a long-term legend. Meanwhile, the US press was reporting that rumours of another Axis peace offensive were circulating Europe – the same, presumably, that had been picked up by the *Sunday Express* over the weekend.

And the air war continued, this day costing Fighter Command five aircraft. Eight were lost by other Commands, including two reconnaissance Spitfires. The thirteen losses compared with the twelve sustained by the *Luftwaffe*.

DAY 92 – WEDNESDAY 9 OCTOBER 1940

The RAF had despatched thirty bombers to Berlin overnight. The Germans claimed they had driven them off. By contrast, it had been a rough night for London – one of the worst since 7 September. Ninety-four locations had been bombed. An air-raid shelter harbouring 150 people, including children, had been hit. At least 8 had been killed, some poisoned after a gas mains fracture. Many more were injured. East Ham Memorial Hospital was badly damaged by a land mine. Three complete floors had been wrecked, destroying wards housing 108 elderly men and women, killing more than fifty. In the morning, as the rescuers were reaching the trapped and injured, another aircraft dropped incendiaries. Horrified rescuers scrabbled through the wreckage to put a small fire out and assist the injured.[12]

Many of the newspapers out on the streets had taken the cue from Churchill and proclaimed that the invasion threat was not over. Few seemed to have understood the point he was making about the casualties. The media analysis generally was poor. That said, lower down the front page in the *Express* was a small article, clearly seen as important enough to have such a prominent spot, but hardly given the attention it deserved. Under the heading, "It's not a blitz-krieg any more", a high German Air Force officer at a press conference in Berlin had announced the "lightning war" abandoned. The Germans had decided to go in for "hammering and destruction".

For the people at the receiving end, life was already miserable. And there were fears that it was about to get a great deal worse. Aware that coal stocks had not built up at the rate necessary to keep London supplied through the winter, and conscious of the effect of enemy bombing on transport facilities, the Cabinet Civil Defence Committee raised the alarm. This brought the War Cabinet into play, which then asked the new Lord President, John Anderson, to look at what was needed to ensure that coal supplies were maintained.[13]

A concern of the War Cabinet, however, remained the "subversive articles" in the *Mirror* and *Sunday Pictorial*. Churchill argued that the articles consti-tuted, "a serious danger to this country". These newspapers were trying to "rock the boat" and to shake the confidence of the country in Ministers. They were attempting to weaken discipline in the Army and were trying to poison relations between members of the government. "It was intolerable that those bearing the burden of supreme responsibility at this time should be subject to attacks of this kind."[14]

Churchill declared that he was determined to put a stop to these attacks and to obtain protection for the War Cabinet. "It would be quite wrong that two members of the War Cabinet should be in the position of asking favours of the Newspaper Proprietors' Association." The War Cabinet agreed that the articles in question were highly objectionable, and that, while no one objected to fair criticism, a continuance of such articles could not be tolerated.[15]

Tucked away in the War Cabinet minutes, however, was another important item, a request for a study on possible German intentions in the Middle East. Details of the Brenner Pass meeting had now reached the Cabinet, via the embassy in Madrid. This brought confirmation that the invasion of Britain had been abandoned, and of the Axis moves towards the Balkans. It was thought that this was another way of putting pressure on British Middle East possessions – with no suspicions that the intention was to clear the way for the invasion of Russia. The point, though, was that the threat to Britain was demonstrably weaker.

Oblivious to these developments, in the House of Commons, some MPs seemed at last to realize the extent of the humanitarian crisis caused by the bombing. In a long debate, notes were exchanged about the multiple and continuing failures of the authorities charged with bringing relief.

Charles Key, representing the East London constituency of Poplar, Bow and Bromley, complained of the parsimony of the Ministry of Health in equipping rest centres for the bombed-out homeless. There were no mattresses and only a very limited number of blankets. As for food, there was a store of dry biscuits and very little else – no provision for hot meals and no opportunity at all for providing hot drinks. There was no method of getting kettles boiled, and nobody had thought of providing stoves. Official indifference was rife, complained Kilmarnock MP, Kenneth Lindsay: "If it had not been for the Salvation Army, the Quakers, the WVS and the people who brought in blankets, nothing would have been done, because it is nobody's business".[16]

The *Mirror* picked up grief of a different sort, reporting on the latest Admiralty communiqué, one of the very few newspapers to do so, with a headline: "U-boats – 15 ships in a week". Ten British ships, total tonnage 55,927, four Allied ships, 12,119 tons, and one neutral ship, 4,291 tons, had been sunk during the week ended 29–30 September. The week before, said the newspaper, we lost twenty ships, totalling 134,975 tons. By contrast, total RAF aircraft losses on the day were nine, against the *Luftwaffe*'s eleven.

DAY 93 – THURSDAY 10 OCTOBER 1940

Churchill this day assumed leadership of the Conservative Party, succeeding Chamberlain. This news competed for space with reports of the TUC Conference, which had been addressed by Ernest Bevin. He had appealed for "the last ounce of energy" to build up "overwhelming forces" to defeat Hitler. He was not to get it. Strikes were to proliferate and, by the following year miners' strikes had become endemic.[17]

Appropriately, in view of Bevin's message, the War Cabinet had before them the two memoranda from Beaverbrook about the working time lost through air-raid warnings. But, as reference was made to a strike which had been in progress at Coventry for more than a fortnight, with public feeling said to be running high against the strikers, discussion was adjourned until the Minister of Labour and National Service could be present.[18] It was to be raised again on 14 October.

Meanwhile, the bombing had almost become routine, "dulled by familiarity and resignation", as London-based journalist Maggie Joy Blunt later put it.[19] The media was struggling to show any interest. The overnight raids, nevertheless, managed to maintain their quotas of horror, this particular night marked by an attack in Hackney, which wrecked the Anderson shelters in the gardens of Mapledene Road.[20] That did not prevent Herbert Morrison, in his maiden speech to the Commons as Home Security Minister, singing the praises of the shelter. He did, nevertheless, order additional Tube provision in the East End of London to be opened to the public.[21]

The Ministry of Home Security, Morrison's new home, produced its periodic summary of Civil Defence activities, this report covering the period from 1 to 29 September – the start of the Blitz. Of the attacks on 7 September, it noted that "[a]part from attempting to lower public morale, the main objectives appear to have been docks, railways and public utilities".[22] Maggie Joy Blunt, gave adequate testimony to the failure to lower public morale, but the very declaration in the report indicated that British officialdom was very well aware of the German objective.

And while the attempt was most powerfully focused on night attacks, German daylight tactics were also achieving little, other than causing a nuisance and tiring out British pilots. The word "attrition" was finding its way into more reports, although the Germans still seemed to believe a rapid decision was possible. Reich Propaganda Minister Göbbels noted that the *Luftwaffe* was attacking London "without pause day and night. And to considerable effect … Just now there are dramatic reports of this from London. If these are true, all hell must be loose over there".[23]

But Civil Defence had vastly improved, especially the fire services. In London, the first twenty-two days and nights of the Blitz had been the most testing. The fire brigades had attended nearly 10,000 fires. The nightly total exceeded 1,000 on three nights and the totals on other nights fluctuated between 40 and 950. As the last aircraft had departed on the first night of the Blitz, there had been nine conflagrations, nineteen fires that would normally have called for thirty pumps or more, forty ten-pump fires, and nearly a thousand lesser blazes, a score of which would have made front-page headlines in peace time. In October, the total still reached 7,500 with nearly 2,000 over two nights. But there had been no conflagrations and only twelve fires of more than thirty pumps.[24]

The Combined Intelligence Committee also seemed to be coming to terms with the invasion threat. Its assessment for the day was that the venture was on hold, but with the administrative structures kept in place in the event that a favourable opportunity presented itself. But the main reasons for keeping them in place were to tie up British forces, and also to avoid the adverse effect on German morale if the operation was openly abandoned. Nevertheless, it held that the threat of an invasion would remain as long as the Germans had numerical superiority in the air, although its failure to win the air battle, the shortening days and the worsening weather combined to make an invasion a "hazardous undertaking".[25]

Out at sea, but given little prominence by the media, the naval war went on, with its steady toll of casualties. HM Patrol Craft *Girl Mary* was the latest. She was sunk in the Firth of Forth by a mine. Two of the crew were lost, the skipper seriously wounded. The British steamer *Till* was also damaged by a mine.

DAY 94 – FRIDAY 11 OCTOBER 1940

The newspapers gave considerable space to Herbert Morrison's maiden speech as Minister of Home Security. The *Daily Express* noted that he had praised the Anderson shelter, called deep shelters impossible, promised new not-so-deep shelters that would be noiseproof, and taken new powers to develop basement shelters. His predecessor, Sir John Anderson (affection-ately described as "war-horse" by Churchill), heard the speech, the paper remarking that Morrison did not say a word to which Sir John would say, "Nay, nay".

And after the calm came the storm. The *Luftwaffe* had stepped up its tempo. Göbbels remarked on the "ideal weather", boasting of causing "wild devastation". It had covered a wider area than any previous raid, one in which the roof of St Paul's Cathedral had been breached and the high altar devastated. But, although many houses were wrecked, only one major fire was started.[26]

While the German bombers were circling over London, Bomber Command was again in action over Cherbourg – but with a difference. Aircraft were acting as spotters for the battleship HMS *Revenge*. Starting at half past three in the morning, for twenty minutes she fired 120 15in and 800 4.7in shells into the port complex. "Very large fires" were reported, visible from forty miles. This was operation *Medium*, which had the battleship escorted by seven destroyers and a similar number of anti-submarine boats, its flanks guarded by cruisers and more destroyers. As an assertion of sea power, it had been a huge success. All ships returned safely to their bases, without damage.[27]

Come the morning, there was less welcome news. Destroyer *Zulu*, fourth ship in a line, was damaged by an acoustic mine in the Firth of Forth. Then the patrol yacht *Aisha* was sunk, with two wounded, and HMS *Jersey* was damaged in the Thames Estuary. These too had succumbed to acoustic mines.

While this was happening, five German torpedo boats, *Falke*, *Grief*, *Kondor*, *Seeadler* and *Wolf* were headed for the convoys on the roads around the Isle of Wight. They were spotted by the anti-submarine trawler *Warwick Deeping* and the former French armed trawler *Listrac*. Although heavily outclassed, they still engaged the Nazi boats and were rapidly sunk, the *Listrac* skipper and eleven ratings dying with their ship. Past midnight, the German force sank two French submarine chasers, both captained by British officers. The encounter left twenty dead and twenty taken prisoner by the *Grief*. Their sacrifice, however, bought time. Five destroyers had raced out of Plymouth, with two more from Portsmouth. Just after three in the morning, HMS *Jackal* engaged two of the German ships. They turned and ran.

The same night, though, Royal Navy MTBs were in action off the Belgian coast, attacking a convoy. The German trawler *Nordenham* was sunk, and thirty-four prisoners were taken. As with the Isle of Wight action, no details were given to the press.[28]

Despite the high intensity of *Luftwaffe* air operations, aircraft losses overall were light, reflecting the general immunity from RAF interference that the night bombers enjoyed. Eleven losses to the RAF, including a torpedo-carrying Albacore, damaged on a mission over Boulogne, compared with a mere seven lost to the *Luftwaffe*.

DAY 95 – SATURDAY 12 OCTOBER 1940

The *Daily Mirror* was in high spirits this morning, with a leader noting that "Seldom does a minister confess that he could possibly have been wrong!" It went on to say: "We must salute the Minister of Health, Mr Malcolm MacDonald. He has astonished us all this week by bravely accepting responsibility for delays in the feeding and housing of the homeless. He admits mistakes!" And in a comment that resonates down the age, it added: "It is well to realize that one cannot be always right because, after that, one may learn by experience and humility not to be always wrong".

Many newspapers covered the raid by HMS *Revenge*, the *Daily Mirror* announcing: "Navy guns Nazi port". In the *Glasgow Herald*, however, the political correspondent had news of a very different kind. It is known in political circles, he wrote, that not many days ago "peace feelers" reached the Cabinet by a circuitous route. Their authenticity was not definitely established Mr Churchill and his colleagues did not reply directly to them. However, the whole tone of the Prime Minister's speech in the Commons on Tuesday had been, in effect, an answer – conveying "an unswerving determination to carry on the war until complete victory was won".

What made this current report different is that the "feelers" were said to come directly from the Germans, as opposed to the expected indirect route. Limited support for the idea that there had indeed been a peace offer was to come from the US media. At the beginning of November there was a news agency report which referred to *sub rosa* peace feelers being put out again and again for some time. Usually, said the report, they came from Swedish sources, sometimes conveyed by prominent Frenchmen, but always on a vague "on-an-if, but-and-when" basis. They were just persistent enough to indicate that Hitler would like to make peace if he could pretty much dictate the terms.

Then there was a syndicated report which did the rounds in mid-November. This had imminent European peace deals floating around London, Berlin and Washington just before the US presidential election, held on 5 November.

The "inside fact" was that some very tentative ideas had been discussed by Sir Samuel Hoare and a leader of the British appeasement group.

These were said to have dated from the time "Hitler's proposed invasion of England was frustrated last September". According to this narrative, Nazi diplomats had sent out feelers "to the effect that Germany now had almost the entire continent of Europe and might be satisfied to drop the war, leaving England to stick to its own islands". So powerful and persistent did these rumours become that, on 5 November an *AP* report via the *Irish Times* carried a German denial. Germany and Italy had no reason to make a peace offer, the statement said. Finally, the presidential election seems to have marked the end of peace offer speculation.

On top of this, the hostile press over the Dakar affair and the signals given off by the recent Cabinet reshuffle might have led the Germans genuinely to believe that Churchill was politically weak. On 8 October, the very day the Prime Minister addressed parliament with his monthly review of the war, the *Glasgow Herald* noted that:

> if ... Hitler really believes the reports given to him and sent all over the world that London is beaten to its knees, he may try the peace trick in the hope that ... the Government will be compelled by public opinion to listen to his offer.

Seen in this light, the Churchill statement to the House on 8 October did fit quite neatly as a rejection of a peace offer – or a pre-emptive move. It set out an unequivocal case for continuing the war, embodying in it an analysis of why the German air offensive had to fail. Similarly, the Bevin's bellicose speech to the TUC could have served the same purpose. In that context, the heavier than usual raids on London on 9 October and in the nights following could be taken as a response to Churchill's response. The Germans were saying: "Very well, the war goes on".

But this day marked the death of *Sealion*. Hitler issued a secret message to his operational services, formally cancelling any further invasion preparations, although the planning infrastructure was to remain in place, in order to exert "political and military pressure" on Britain. The barges, fishing boats and tugs were to be returned to their former duties, the soldiers to prepare for the invasion of the Soviet Union.[29] As the British reconnaissance picked up the dispersal of the shipping, it was assumed that this was a response to the Royal

Air Force and naval raids, and in particular the recent attack by the battleship *Revenge*.

But there is no evidence in German records that Hitler was in any way influenced by the materiel losses. Despite the intensity and frequency of the British counteraction, less than 10 per cent of the shipping had been sunk or damaged – a level which could be replaced from reserves. Equally compatible with events was a response to Churchill's rejection of the recent peace feelers, leading Hitler to conclude that there was little chance of an immediate peace deal. He may at this point have been reconciled to a long war and thus his transport fleet was not needed for the time being.

Alongside this, though, there was quite clearly a conviction that the strategic bombing was having the desired effect. As the *Luftwaffe* once again headed over the Channel, Göbbels noted in his diary: "Horrific reports from London. A metropolis on the slide. An international drama without parallel".[30]

DAY 96 – SUNDAY 13 OCTOBER 1940

A small but important part of the battlefield this night was Stoke Newington, an inner London suburb, then quite unfashionable and with a large Jewish (and Irish Catholic) population. It was one of those areas of North London poorly served by the Tube, relying on the surface railway. With a large number of flat dwellers, the effects of the government's refusal to develop a deep shelter policy was at its most apparent. They had to rely on surface shelters and reinforced basements. One of the latter had been constructed from the shallow basements of three terraced shops on Coronation Avenue, Stoke Newington Road. Overnight it had afforded illusory shelter to the best part of 250 people.

It took only one large bomb to convert the illusion into terror and then, for many, oblivion. Late in the night, it hit the parade of shops, causing the five-storey terrace to collapse, blocking the exits from the basements, and trapping scores of people. In total, 173 were killed, many – it was thought – poisoned by town gas from a fractured main.[31] The censors were quick to stifle comment, although a report made page five of the *Daily Express*, on the following Tuesday, with no location identified. Nevertheless, it was described as "[t]he greatest bombing tragedy in the whole of London", from which fifty-seven had survived.

The weekly *Hackney Gazette* referred to the event but was not allowed to release details. It reported: "On Friday the King and Queen … paid an informal visit to an area where there had been casualties owing to a bomb demolishing a block of tenements underneath which was a shelter". Until the end of the war, nothing further publicly emerged.[32]

Göbbels wrote once more in his diary: "Gloomy pictures of morale in London. The city is gradually experiencing the fate of Carthage. But Churchill will not have it any other way. And so on with the fight".[33] But that "fight" was not to include an invasion – as the British were becoming increasingly aware. The Secret Intelligence Service (SIS) was circulating a report from one of its trusted agents – 9 October – stating that *Sealion* had been postponed until the spring.

In the public eye this day, though, was a "million to one chance" of the Liverpool to London express being derailed as it approached London, when a porter's barrow had fallen off a platform into its path. The engine had struck it and pushed it forward until it became lodged in some points, causing the derailment. A number of people were killed and more than fifty were injured.[34] As the news leaked out, the Germans claimed credit for the disaster.

Meanwhile, Priestley was again writing in the *Sunday Express*, his column this time headed: "Tattoo this message into your mind". The theme was propaganda and civilian morale.

Being a new kind of war, "total war", Priestley wrote, it depended, as previous wars did not, on civilian morale. "There could not be a better proof of the Nazi's belief in this," he wrote, "than the recent costly indiscriminate raids upon London, which have no conventional military value at all." That the Nazis had been ready to discontinue attacks upon purely military objectives for the sake of this assault upon civilian morale, he argued, showed how much importance they attached to this aspect of their "total war". Their assault had failed, but the fact that it had been made at all was "very significant".

The core message, then, was that, if the state of the civilian mind was so important, it followed that anything that affected public morale had to be considered a real war factor, "no more to be despised than the condition of our planes and guns".

As to the daylight air war, it was of little moment on this day. In fact, "friendly fire" was the greatest hazard for the British. Fighter Command lost four aircraft

– a Hurricane shot down by anti-aircraft fire over Chatham, a Blenheim fighter shot down by Czech pilots, off Liverpool with all three crew killed, and another damaged, only to be written off on landing. Just one aircraft was lost to enemy action. The Germans lost two.

DAY 97 – MONDAY 14 OCTOBER 1940

At 8.02 p.m. a 1400kg semi armour piercing bomb penetrated 32 ft underground into Balham Tube Station in south London. It exploded just above the cross passage between the two platforms causing debris partially to fill the tunnels where about 500 people were sheltering. Water poured in from fractured water mains and sewers. Sixty-six people in the station are believed to have been killed.[35] The roadway collapsed into the void, leaving a huge crater into which a No. 88 double-decker bus plunged. Substantial damage was caused to surrounding buildings, leaving some close to collapse.

As with the other major shelter disasters, news was suppressed, the government fearing adverse public reaction. The picture of the bus in the crater later became an iconic representation of the Blitz. But it was only one small part of the violence of which visited the citizens of London on the Saturday night, continuing through into Sunday night and even into the early hours of Monday morning. So intense and savage was the bombing that some saw it as a new phase of the Blitz.

It was somewhat ironic, therefore, that the War Cabinet resumed its discussions on how to prevent workers taking cover when air-raid warnings sounded. Ernest Bevin was now present, expressing the view that the air-raid warning system was only one of a variety of causes leading to the loss of working time. Other causes, he said, were faulty management, lack of consideration in handling men and bad lay-out of factories. Beaverbrook was having none of that, and insisted the problem lay with the warning system. Eventually, after a long discussion, it was agreed that a supplemental system of localized area warnings should be examined.[36]

However, the meeting had been preceded by the circulation of a revised system, which had been prepared jointly by Morrison and Sinclair. It proposed decentralizing the warnings and formalizing an "alarms within the alert" system, to give factories more precise details of the threats.[37] This seems to have brought some improvement as, apart from a brief reference on 18 October, the matter was not brought before the Cabinet in the remainder of the year or the two following.[38]

DAY 98 – TUESDAY 15 OCTOBER 1940

The savagery of the previous day's bombing provoked a classic "damage limitation" report from the *Daily Express*, which featured a front-page banner headline claiming, "Soon we may bomb Berlin by day, too". The story was about the possible introduction of the American Boeing Flying Fortress into RAF service. It was a transparent attempt to divert attention from the carnage.

The diversion simply concealed the fact that London had had a truly dreadful night. Even the *New York Times* was moved to report: "London is rocked by heaviest raid", while the *Daily Mirror* headlined "Great London raid". A full moon had given Göring's bombers maximum opportunity to spread havoc and mayhem, which is precisely what they had done. Over nine hundred fires had been caused, roads were blocked throughout the city, and the Underground rail network was severed in five places. A reservoir, three gasworks, two power stations and three docks were hit, causing extensive damage. Then there was the human cost. Over 400 people had been killed and more than 800 badly wounded. Some incidents particularly stood out. One was the destruction of Morley College, on the Westminster Bridge Road.

As an educational institute, the college had been abandoned. It was being used as a rest centre for people who had been bombed out of their homes. Nearly 300 people were taking refuge when a high-explosive bomb fell on the main building, ripping it apart. Of the 195 people known to have been in the building, 84 came out unhurt. Of the injured, 54 were sent to hospital and 57 were killed. Ten died in hospital. More may have been buried under the debris, their bodies never recovered.[39]

This was certainly the case in an even worse incident at just after eight in the evening – almost exactly twenty-four hours after Balham Tube Station had been bombed – when the public shelters in Kennington Park were hit. It had only been a 25kg bomb, but this was a trench shelter, shored with wood, roofed with corrugated iron and covered with earth. Fatally vulnerable to blast effect, the walls collapsed, killing at least 104. Only 48 bodies were recovered, the rest lying buried in the park. In November 1940, the damaged trench was filled in, but others in the complex continued in use.[40] Prior to the war, critics of trench shelters had bitterly suggested that their provision would at least save the cost of burials. The prophesy had come tragically true.[41]

The fatal inadequacies of the shelter policy were now laid bare – or would have been but for the intervention of the censor. In three days, there had been as many shelter incidents and a rest centre bombed. The deaths – nearly 500 in total – were all linked in some way to the policy.

Unease even percolated the War Cabinet. There was considerable discussion about the effect of the bombing on civilian morale. But there was no discussion about shelters. The people of London, it was said, were beginning to wonder whether we were hitting back hard enough at Germany in our bombing operations. If this feeling was allowed to grow "it might have an unfortunate effect on our war effort". Churchill told his Cabinet that those concerned were "straining every nerve to improve means of countering night bombing", with good prospects that defensive measures would be greatly improved within the next two or three months. He would consider whether it would be desirable for him to make another broadcast speech.[42]

The War Cabinet also considered the "likelihood of invasion". The agenda item referred to Churchill's promise on 4 October, to release warships on anti-invasion duty for convoy escort. On this day Churchill said it would be premature to suppose that the danger of invasion had passed. Intelligence reports, he said, had indicated that enemy plans were still moving forward and, in these circumstances "it would not be possible for the Navy to withdraw any more of their forces from the invasion front in order to strengthen shipping escorts in the north-west approaches".[43]

With that, the Prime Minister went to the House of Commons to answer questions … on war aims. He was challenged by Samuel "Sydney" Silverman the Labour MP for Nelson and Colne, a prominent activist on Jewish causes and a pacifist who had spent time in jail in the First World War. He was a reluctant supporter of the current war, in response to Hitler's anti-semitism. Silverman asked Churchill:

> [I]n anticipation of the time when this country and its Allies are in a position to resume the military offensive,[will you state] in general terms, our aims in this war, so that this country may take its rightful place as the leader of all those, wherever they may be

found, who desire a new order in Europe, based not upon slavery to Germany but upon collective justice, prosperity, and security?[44]

Silverman, however, was given the opportunity of repeatedly questioning the Prime Minister, in a way not seen in contemporary Commons exchanges, asking him whether a "continued negative attitude in this matter" fostered "the quite false impression that we are fighting this war merely to retain the status quo". This elicited what amounted to an affirmation that this was precisely the Prime Minister's intent, with his clearest statement yet on his position:

> I do not think anyone has the opinion that we are fighting this war merely to maintain the status quo. We are, among other things, fighting it in order to survive, and when our capacity to do that is more generally recognised throughout the world, when the conviction that we have about it here becomes more general, then we shall be in a good position to take a further view of what we shall do with the victory when it is won.[45]

What had brought up the matter at this time had been the announcement by the Ministry of Information that they were working out a policy of war aims, as reported in *The Times* on 28 September. It had also been the subject of a Zec cartoon in the *Mirror* on 30 September, which had Duff Cooper as a dove reading from "the Great Peace Manifesto" – with Hitler in the bushes attempting to shoot him with a revolver.

The prospect of a statement had excited the interest of Sir Geoffrey Mander, a Liberal MP, wealthy industrialist, philanthropist and Parliamentary Private Secretary to Archibald Sinclair. He had tabled a question which had been "dead batted" on 10 October and had responded by initiating an adjournment debate, bringing Duff Cooper to the House to discuss the issue.[46] But, if Members had come expecting a firm statement, they were to be disappointed. There was no intention of making one, even if Cooper showed where his sympathies lay. He told the House: "I admit quite frankly the desirability of issuing a statement as soon as possible, but … there should be no undue haste".

Having spoken at length of the "threat of tyranny" and of taking up arms to "defend our liberty and the freedom of the world", he was sharply corrected by Richard Stokes, the Labour MP for Ipswich, Military Cross winner in the First World War and soon to become an arch critic of the area bombing policy. Cooper, said Stokes, had enunciated what we were fighting against, but not what we were fighting for. "[It] is no use fighting for a negative object. You must have a positive one, and the sooner that [is] stated the better." His interjection brought an impassioned response from Cooper:

> We are fighting for our liberty. When we walk about the streets of London we see how buildings have been destroyed. Some of them may have been beautiful houses, and some may have been ugly houses. If we had been asked a year ago whether we wanted to destroy those houses in that way, we would have said, "No, let them stand and serve their purpose as long as possible." But now naturally it is our duty to take thought of how, when the time comes, we can build them up again, better and more useful than ever. Equally this world which is now being destroyed by this terrific war, a war which we never desired and which we were prepared to do almost everything to avoid, when this war shall have destroyed a great part of the modern world, it will be our duty then, as it must be our duty now, to think how we can rebuild a more and more beautiful fabric.

But the Prime Minister had spoken. Despite his claims to the contrary, it was to be the *status quo*. There was to be no discussion of how we could rebuild "a more and more beautiful fabric", much less of what that fabric should look like.

Meanwhile, the dirty business of war continued. At noon, six large enemy motor torpedo boats were sighted nine miles off Dover proceeding westwards. They were engaged by shore batteries, but not hit. After nightfall, HMS *Erebus* was again in action, this time off Dunkirk when she fired fifty rounds from her 15in guns. The air war, however, did not yield dividends for the British. Nineteen Fighter Command losses, plus two others, brought the total to twenty-one, against twelve *Luftwaffe* losses.

DAY 99 – WEDNESDAY 16 OCTOBER 1940

Formally published this day was a propaganda film on the Blitz, called "London can take it". Narrated by American journalist Quentin Reynolds, it was intended for a US audience in a country where there was less than a month to go before the presidential election. The RAF was not mentioned. The film was about Londoners and the Blitz. Opening the narration, Reynolds said:

> The searchlights are in position, the guns are ready, the people's army of volunteers is ready – they are the ones who are really fighting this war, the firemen, the air raid wardens, the ambulance drivers – and there's the wail of the banshee (siren sounds) … the nightly siege of London has begun. The city is dressed for battle.

The People's War imagery, already having been strongly promoted by the trades unions, was wholly distinct from the élitist vision that encompassed Churchill's "few". But the message had been tailored for an egalitarian US audience, selling the war to which was an important part of the British propaganda effort.[47] Even then, many might have had difficulty seeing any similarity between their circumstances and the scenes depicted. Nevertheless, Reynolds was not a propagandist simply parroting a script. In November 1942, he was to pen a widely syndicated piece, where he stated unequivocally: "This is a people's war". He went on:

> The Battle of Britain was not won by the RAF alone. It was won by thousands of civilians who three times saved the city of London from complete destruction. It was won by the sweat and toil of men and women who bent over lathes and drill presses in Manchester, in Birmingham, in Coventry and Sheffield, turning out guns and aircraft, bombs and ships, molding (sic) the sinews of war.

Back on this day, in the House of Lords, shelters were the issue. The Earl of Listowel, a Labour Peer and member of the London County Council for East Lewisham, led a debate on Greater London's war problems. It was generally admitted, he charged, that "existing facilities for the protection of the civilian population of London from air attack have been and are still inadequate". There had been "a remarkable lack of foresight when envisaging the sort of onslaught that would be launched by the Luftwaffe on the London area". We had to remedy our unpreparedness as speedily as possible, he said.[48]

The War Cabinet, by coincidence, was discussing shelter disasters, including Stoke Newington. But its focus was on the offensive. The concern remained that morale might begin to suffer if the public felt that the reply to night bombing was ineffective. It was of the utmost importance, the Cabinet agreed, that every effort should be made to counter it. This was a fond hope, not backed by anything of substance. And John Anderson, immersed in studying the coal supply situation, was getting worried about keeping the east coast coal traffic going – sufficient to put down a marker with the War Cabinet.[49]

Once again, though, discussion was dominated by the "subversive press", the issue having come to a head after Clement Attlee and Beaverbrook had met representatives of the Newspaper Proprietors' Association. Subsequently, they had met representatives of the *Sunday Pictorial* and the *Daily Mirror*, including the executive editor, Cecil King. Attlee had told an unrepentant King that many people thought these articles were "a deliberate Fifth Column activity". What then exactly transpired was not revealed, but King was recorded as appearing "somewhat chastened", and undertaking "to exercise care in the future". Beaverbrook thought the two newspapers would amend their behaviour, "at any rate for the time being".[50]

In the air war, Birmingham had taken the hit overnight. A bomb on RAF Ternhill in Shropshire struck a hangar, destroying it and twenty training aircraft inside. Two Fighter Command losses, plus fourteen from Bomber and Coastal Command brought the total to thirty-six, against eleven *Luftwaffe* losses.

DAY 100 – THURSDAY 17 OCTOBER 1940

The specialist aviation magazine *Flight* commented on the use of Me 109s as fighter bombers, arguing that it indicated "the Germans have admitted to themselves that the attempt to overwhelm Britain from the air has failed". Curiously, the analysis was being based on developments in the day fighting and while it doffed its cap to the damage done by the night bombing, the magazine went on to declare:

> sufferings do not affect our power to carry on the war, and indignation at the tragedies makes the British people all the more grimly determined that this barbarism must be stamped out of the world. From the military point of view, the Battle of Britain is going well for the enemies of the Axis.

The magazine had conducted many discussions in past editions about total war, and Douhet's theorizing. Despite that, it was still looking at the conflict as a joust between military forces. Yet, in the week up to this day, German bombing had killed 1,567 civilians, nearly three times the number of Fighter Command aircrew killed in the entire battle period. Many had been killed in the line of duty. In Streatham, a direct hit on the fire station wrecked two heavy appliances. Twelve firemen were killed and eight injured.

On page five of the *Daily Express*, there was a detailed report of the previous day's debate in the Lords, but nothing of the Earl of Listowel's complaints. The space was given to the Duke of Devonshire, speaking for the Home Office. Government policy on air-raid shelters was "running more and more strongly in favour of dispersal, in favour of the Anderson shelter, the street brick shelter and the reinforced basement, rather than the large communal shelter which collects too many in one place".

"I do not think it indiscreet to say that Mr. Morrison (the new Home Secretary) will come down on the side of dispersal so far as possible – which was the policy of his predecessor in office (Sir John Anderson) – rather than in favour of the policy of concentration", Devonshire was reported as saying.

There was another huge "elephant in the room" – the sea war. The German destroyer flotilla based in Brest was out hunting. It was joined by six torpedo boats out of Cherbourg, intent on raiding British shipping at the western exit of the Bristol Channel. Three convoys were in grave danger, although the raiders were sighted by Coastal Command aircraft, shortly after they had left Brest and ships at risk were rerouted. Light cruisers *Newcastle* and *Emerald*, with five destroyers, rushed out of Plymouth and after five hours hard steaming they sighted the German force. At a distance, gunfire was exchanged and the Germans turned for home. They were pursued by Blenheim bombers, one of which failed to return. All three crew were killed, the only casualties of the action.

This action was barely mentioned in the newspapers. The war at sea was rarely given "star treatment". Yet, the action never ceased. As they had been virtually every day of the war, the convoys were on the move. OB.230 departed Liverpool escorted by destroyers *Antelope* and *Clare*, corvettes *Anemone*, *Clematis*, *Mallow* and two anti-submarine trawlers. FN.311 departed Southend, escorted by destroyers *Verdun* and *Watchman*, and headed north. Convoy FS.312 at the other end of the chain started its southward journey, escorted by destroyers *Wallace* and *Westminster*. Anti-aircraft cruiser *Curacoa* transferred to convoy SL.49A east of Pentland Firth and escorted it towards Buchanness, then joining convoy EN.10.

For U-boat commanders, the period July to October was "happy time". In those four months, 144 unescorted and 73 escorted ships were sunk. The Germans lost only six boats, and only two during attacks on convoys. October was shaping up to be their best month. On this day, U-38 sunk Greek steamer *Aemos*, a straggler due to bad weather from Convoy SC.7. U-48 attacked Convoy SC.7, sinking British tanker *Languedoc*, and the steamer *Scoresby*. It damaged the *Haspenden*. U-93 attacked convoy OB.228 and sunk a Norwegian and British steamer, killing twelve seamen.

E-boats also extracted a toll, sinking SS *Hauxley* in convoy FN.311 and damaging two others. Then there were the mines. The British steamer *Frankrig* was sunk in the North Sea, the fishing vessel *Albatross* off Grimsby and the *Cheerful* off the Faroes. Steamers *Ethylene* and *George Balfour* were damaged. Over twenty crewmen were killed. In the air, there had been ten RAF aircraft lost, with twelve to the *Luftwaffe*.

DAY 101 – FRIDAY 18 OCTOBER, 2010

Thirty-five merchantmen making up Convoy SC.7 had been sailing from Nova Scotia since 5 October, headed for Liverpool. Such was the shortage of escorts, only the 1,000ton sloop HMS *Scarborough* accompanied them, armed with one 4in gun and fifteen depth charges. Leading the convoy was the SS *Assyrian*, with Vice Admiral Mackinnon acting as convoy Commodore.

The largest of the ships had been the Admiralty tanker SS *Languedor* of 9,512 tons – but she had already been sunk. The majority of the remainder were also British registered, but others had their home ports in Norway, Greece, Holland and Sweden. The range of goods carried was typical of that which Britain most needed to import to sustain her: pit props from East Brunswick destined for British coal mines, lumber and grain from the Great Lakes area for the daily bread, steel and ingots from Sydney, iron ore from Newfoundland. A load of important trucks filled the holds of SS *Empire Brigand*.

Attacks had started in the early hours of 16 October, when one ship had been lost, but the convoy was joined by the sloop *Fowey* and corvette *Bluebell*. Two further escorts had then arrived, the sloop *Leith* and corvette *Heartsease*. That night, the convoy came under sustained attack from one of the first "wolfpacks". Seven submarines coordinated their attacks. The SS *Creekirk*, with a cargo of iron ore, was hit early on by torpedoes from U-101. She was gone so quickly that none of her thirty-six crew escaped.

Over Britain, the *Luftwaffe* was back, its aircrew fortified by an Order of the Day from Göring. He had told them:

German airmen, comrades! You have, above all in the last few days and nights, caused the British worldenemy disastrous losses by uninterrupted, destructive blows. Your indefatigable, courageous attacks on the heart of the British Empire, the city of London with its 8½ million inhabitants, have reduced British plutocracy to fear and terror. The losses which you have inflicted on the much vaunted Royal Air Force in determined fighter engagements are irreplaceable.

The *Luftwaffe* "celebrated" with four fighter sweeps over Kent. Some reached the Thames Estuary and London. Approximately 300 fighters were deployed. Twelve aircraft were lost by the *Luftwaffe*. Fighter Command lost six of its own, including four Hurricanes from No. 302 (Polish) Sqn, after they had run out of fuel.[51] Come the night, Birmingham took the strain. The first bomb dropped just after eight in the evening. By the "all clear" at 11.29 p.m., approximately 116 bombs had dropped, 34 of which did not explode. About 107 incidents involved incendiaries, and about 78 fires were started.

For all that, the total casualties were ten fatalities and eighteen injured. But, over term, Birmingham was the third most heavily bombed UK city of the war, behind London and Liverpool. From 2,000 tons of bombs dropped, 2,241 people were killed, and 3,010 seriously injured. Some 12,391 houses, 302 factories and 239 other buildings were destroyed, with many more damaged. Each time the Brummies dusted themselves off, buried their dead, treated their injured and repaired the damage. Life went on.

DAY 102 – SATURDAY 19 OCTOBER 1940

The agony of Convoy SC.7 continued. SS *Empire Brigand* and her load of trucks disappeared beneath the waves. Six died. Even the Commodore's SS *Assyrian* was sunk. SS *Fiscus*, loaded with five-ton ingots of steel, sunk like a stone. Only one survived from her crew of thirty-nine. Twenty ships had now been sunk, some 79,592 tons, worth millions even at 1940 prices. The German U-boat "star" was Otto Kretschmer. In U-99 that night, he took seven ships. And still the killing had not finished. U-boats with torpedoes remaining joined U-47, commanded by ace captain Gunther Prien, to attack HX.79, another Liverpool-bound convoy. This one was completely unescorted. Twelve more ships were sunk, with no lost U-boats, the worst 48-hour period in the entire war.

U-boats were not the only predator. Condors, operating from Norway and later from France, were able to fly far into the North Atlantic, well out of the reach of shore-based fighters. They found convoys for waiting submarines, collected weather data and bombed ships, accounting for over 365,000 tons between June 1940 and February 1941.

As to the fate of SC.7 and HX.79, it was too early for news to break. H. Taylor Henry, writing for *AP*, his copy to reach millions of Americans, reported on the war in London. "High explosive bombs dropped by raiders in the heaviest early-evening assault since the battle of Britain began killed many Londoners last night and caused 'severe' damage in the British capital", he wrote. "One bomb landing outside a hotel," he added, "killed an unannounced number of people in the bar; two others were killed in a cafe, and a direct hit which demolished a London club killed an undetermined number of casualties."

The report captured the flavour of events. The bloody war just got bloodier. This was corroborated by the Home Security activity report, which told of the bombing commencing at dusk, with the first four hours abnormally heavy, then continuing on a large but more usual scale. The main attacks had been against the London area, but Liverpool, Manchester and Coventry districts received considerable attention. Bombs were unloaded blindly and, as on the previous night, there were long lulls. A pub was blown into the roadway, and people were buried under the wreckage. A cafe and a shop were demolished by the same bomb. Close by, incendiaries fell on a hospital.

The main news in the dailies, however, was an account culled from US newspapers of how aircraft from Bomber Command under their former leader Charles Portal, had in mid-September pounded the assembled German invasion fleet so hard – killing 40–50,000 troops – that it had forced the cancellation of *Der Tag* – the projected invasion day. The account was almost entirely fictional but, according to the *Express*, "officially confirmed". The Air Ministry was crediting Bomber Command, rather than Dowding's fighters, with victory.

In the *Evening Standard*, though, the banner headline was given over to: "Shelter speed-up: State will pay". Morrison had undertaken that the government would take over the funding of shelter construction, and pay local authorities to build them – a measure to speed up the provision. Additionally, the first of what were to be a million bunks had been delivered to shelters, and doctors were to be stationed in the larger shelters. Canteens and even "waitresses" were to follow. By December, refreshments were available in 80 Tube stations, sheltering 100,000 people. Consumption of tea and cocoa amounted to 12,500 gallons a night, while the food eaten weighed five tons.[52]

DAY 103 – SUNDAY 20 OCTOBER 1940

The bombing was becoming routine, witness a story bearing the headline, "Many bombs in fierce night raid on London". The report was consigned to the bottom of the front page of the *Sunday Express*, with the lead story recording Mussolini's move to the "Jugo-Slav border", a move which presaged that long-expected start of a Balkans war. There could have been little better evidence that Hitler had lost the battle to smash British morale.

Across the Atlantic, and for some months, politics in the US had been gripped by the presidential election campaign, with Roosevelt standing for an unprecedented third term. It was now just over two weeks to the election. It would decide Britain's fate. If Roosevelt won, America might enter the war. His opponent, Wendell Wilkie was running on an isolationist ticket, which could auger ill for the UK, except that Roosevelt looked to have a two-to-one lead in the electoral college. This too was the beginnings of a defeat for Hitler.

In a tribute to the men of a hidden war, C. G. Grey in the *Sunday Express* wrote of the pilots and navigators of the Fleet Air Arm (FAA), flying land-based Swordfish biplanes on extended minelaying missions to the Baltic. Night after night, they had been conducting sorties to Baltic waters, taking twelve hours in open-cockpit aircraft, laden with overload tanks of petrol, each carrying a mine which if it exploded in a crash would leave nothing to pick up. These couples, wrote Grey, deserve to be recorded in history, because they have made so much history themselves.[53]

Back in the war, the *Luftwaffe* was continuing to pursue its daylight tactics of sending over high-level fighter bombers. They and their escorts amounted to 300 aircraft, in 5 separate waves, keeping RAF pilots busy and tired. Fighter Command flew 745 sorties and lost 4 aircraft, the *Luftwaffe* combat losses amounting to 8, including a reconnaissance Dornier. As always, the RAF exaggerated its score, claiming 14 aircraft downed.

That evening Priestley made his last *Postscript* for some time … "perhaps the last I shall ever do", he told the millions glued to their wireless sets, listening to every word. Insisting that the decision to stop had been his, and that his relations with the BBC were "excellent", he also rejected the idea that he had been taking advantage of his position to bring party politics into his talks. He was not, he said, a member of any political party.

As a parting shot on the airwaves, he emphasized that "we should mean what we say; be really democratic …". Alluding to the post-war period, there was a danger, he said, that "apathy will return to some sections of the community and selfishness and stupidity to some other sections". Our greatest potential ally, he added, is "the growing hope in decent folk everywhere that civilisation can be saved". Democracy was not an experiment that had been tried and had failed but "a great creative force that must now be released again".[54]

Overnight, bombers revisited London. Coventry was heavily bombed and considerable damage was done. Rescue parties were heavily tested as several people were trapped in wrecked buildings. German minelayers were active off East Anglia, and from the Humber to the Tees.

DAY 104 – MONDAY 21 OCTOBER 1940

Bomber Command had also been active. It had detailed 192 aircraft for missions, of which 135 reported successful attacks on targets ranging from the Channel ports, German marshalling yards, armament factories in Czechoslovakia and factories in Italy. Nine aircraft were lost. The exercise gave the *Mirror* its headline for the morning: "RAF's 100-a-minute bombing".

Despite the newspaper's attempt to project "good news", with over 70 people killed in London the previous night, and over 300 seriously injured, public dissatisfaction with the failure to deal with the night bombers was growing.

The War Cabinet morosely noted that promises on forthcoming antidotes had not been realized, concluding that "Londoners were at the moment a little pessimistic". Some were a little more than that. Work had been going on at the Stepney shelter, making structural improvements. But when an air-raid warning had sounded, the shelter had not been opened quickly. Fighting had broken out and a breakaway group had attempted to rush the ARP Control Office in Stepney. The police had drawn their truncheons, and a number of men had been arrested, leading to strident complaints from the *Daily Worker*.[55]

Nothing of this was reported, but the *Daily Express* noted that German fighter-bombers the previous day had flown over the country in the sub-strat-osphere, "sometimes at a height of nearly six miles". This was part of Göring's latest plan to escape the deadly attentions of the Spitfires and Hurricanes. But, for the Nazis, this was "only an improvisation after repeated failure to press home their attacks by any other daytime tactics".[56] Bizarrely, the newspaper claimed that US-built Brewster Buffalo fighters were being fielded to counter this new tactic. The type had in fact been appraised by the RAF and classed as "unfit for duty in western Europe", not least because of poor high-altitude performance.[57]

In England during the day, deteriorating weather conditions had ruled out intensive air operations. The RAF lost three aircraft to accidents and none to combat. This, once again, was regarded as a "quiet" period. Come the night, though, Coventry again suffered heavy raids, with considerable damage done to the Armstrong–Siddeley works. There were also raids over London, Birmingham and Liverpool.

Perhaps the most significant news was a report in the *Yorkshire Post* on "New drive for shelters". Measures announced over the weekend, it said:

> suggest a determined attempt by the Government to come to grips with the shelter problem. To speed up the provision of shelters, the whole cost of building and equipment in future was to be paid by the Government as long as local authorities could show reasonable economy in their schemes. Herbert Morrison had been hard at work – and more was to follow.

Behind the scenes, the Chiefs of Staff were reviewing the invasion threat. Despite the growing evidence from intelligence and diplomatic sources that the Germans had abandoned the idea of attacking Britain this year, they judged that it remained an operational possibility. They expressed their concerns, therefore, that the widespread feeling that the danger was passed was premature.

DAY 105 – TUESDAY 22 OCTOBER 1940

Overnight, twenty Wellingtons attacked the *Bismark* at Hamburg. The War Cabinet was told that the target area had been heavily bombed, "though heavy ground haze made identification difficult" went the official report.[58] However, hits would have been difficult to achieve. Hitler's latest battleship had left its berth on 15 September to conduct sea trials in the Baltic with her base in Gotenhafen (now Gdynia). On this day, she conducted high-speed trials, reaching 30.1 knots, confirming her as one of the fastest battleships in the world, faster than any battleship in the Royal Navy.[59]

Back home and too close to the convoy disasters of SC.7 and HX.79 to be a coincidence, the *Daily Mirror*, told of a "Big U-boat blitz on our ships". The paper noted that Hitler had started an intensified U-boat war in the hope of starving Britain into subjection by blockade, now that his air attack and invasion plans had been rebuffed.

Capitalizing on Churchill's reluctance to release escorts from anti-invasion duties, more U-boats had been ordered into the Atlantic than at any time since the outbreak of war. The shipping losses over the previous weekend had been "the worst ever experienced". The Admiralty were taking all steps possible to deal with the new situation, War Cabinet members had been told. Worryingly, Churchill had to admit that shipping losses of the last two or three days had been "without precedent". Some 100,000 tons of shipping had been sunk, in spite of the fact that *one* of the convoys attacked had been strongly protected.[60]

DAY 106 – WEDNESDAY 23 OCTOBER 1940

"Weather here good", wrote Göbbels in Berlin, bad over England: "Few incursions into the Reich, but neither do we drop much in England".[61] Low cloud and drizzle, with concomitant poor visibility, were preventing any significant German air operations, either by day or night. The *Luftwaffe* sent out reconnaissance flights and single bomb-carrying fighters. One Hurricane was lost to an Me 109 and the *Luftwaffe* lost three bombers, two from the night contingent. Only one of the three was a direct combat loss – the other two crashed on home territory.

Bizarrely, the OKW *War Diary* noted that the effects of the German attack on London and the British industry had not been very strong during September. During October, the effects were said to have been stronger. "The British people is said to be fatalistic," it noted. "The people, however, do not appear demoralised".[62] Separately, in relation to the dispersion of forces intended for operation *Sealion*, it recorded that "long periods of time will, in future, be required to get this operation going". It then added: "The measures to deceive the enemy are to be continued but the main effort of this deception should be directed to Norway".[63]

The diary also carried a report on *Luftwaffe* operations. "The morale of the flying units is excellent," it said. "These units are strained but not over-strained".

In general, only fighter-bomber aircraft equipped with 250kg bombs were to be committed in daylight operations against London and alternate targets. These were to fly at extremely high altitudes and, it was thought, the damage caused in London was "very considerable".[64]

In Britain, the media focus was not on the domestic front. Big events were being staged in France, only 24 hours after Churchill had made a radio appeal to the French to rise up and set Europe aflame. Predictably, Göbbels was less than impressed. "Impudent, insulting, and oozing with hypocrisy", he had called it, "A repulsive, oily obscenity". He released the speech to the [German] press for them "to give it a really rough and ready answer". Otherwise, he wrote, the English will carry on living an illusion. We shall battle on remorselessly to destroy their last hopes. As for London: "Fantastic reports ... there it is hell on earth", he wrote.[65]

The event was that Hitler arrived "secretly" in Paris for a long conference with Pierre Laval. Reports emerging from Berlin indicated that Hitler was offering final peace terms to France in exchange for the surrender of the remnants of the French fleet. With the help of the French, Hitler and Mussolini were said to be planning a "decisive blow" against the British Fleet in the Mediterranean. According to the *Express*, "Jubilant Nazi officials in Berlin boast that the three navies could either destroy the British Fleet or drive it off our great Empire lifeline".

DAY 107 – THURSDAY 24 OCTOBER 1940

A few individual raiders and reconnaissance flights were the extent of German daylight air operations. From a British perspective, this was seen to be a ritual to keep the British defence system on alert, with no strategic significance. The main effort now was through the night. *Flight* magazine thereby decided that the Battle of Britain was over. It had degenerated into unimportant but spiteful slaughter and destruction – the purpose of which it did not specify.

The Germans saw things differently. General von Bötticher, the German Military Attaché to Washington, reported that the situation in England was becoming more precarious. The objective to make life more difficult was being achieved, he said. Production had decreased and the traffic situation was difficult. There was a danger that epidemics might break out. Reports from the embassies in Lisbon and Sofia agreed. There had been an "impressive change" in the tone of the British press.[66]

In Britain, internal politics rather than the Germans were keeping Dowding busy. He had let the enmity between Keith Park at No. 11 Group and Leigh Mallory at No. 12 Group go too far. The knives were out, and Dowding's own position was under grave threat. But, while the internal politics focused on the "big wing" controversy, the national politicians were mainly dismayed at the lack of protection Fighter Command could offer against the night bombers. To prove the point, London was on the receiving end of fifty raiders that night, Birmingham was targeted and Basingstoke was also hit. The *Luftwaffe* owned the night sky.

News was emerging of a meeting the previous day between Hitler and Franco on the border of Spain. The days in the immediate aftermath of the fall of France were now looking pure and simple, with just the straightforward issue of survival against the enemy across the Channel to contend with. But now, the war was widening, and getting more complicated. For once though, Hitler was on the back foot. Reacting to rumours that Spain's dictator, Franco, had decided to stay out of the war, Hitler was trying to head off a decision. In a two-hour, head-to-head discussion, though, he failed. Famously, he later confided with Mussolini that he would "rather have three or four teeth pulled" than go through another meeting with Franco. Gibraltar was safe – a huge relief to the UK.

From the Spanish border, Hitler travelled to Montoire in France to meet Pétain. News had since come through that Pétain had rejected any deal with Hitler over the transfer of the French Navy. However, the fleet was said to be massing in Toulon. The only explanation for this "mysterious move", was said to be that the French Navy Minister, Admiral Darlan, who was a strong supporter of deputy premier Laval, gave the orders on his own initiative. While the world waited with bated breath for news of developments, the War Cabinet was treated to a sombre appraisal on the current fighting. In particular, it learned that mines were having a significant effect on the shipping in coastal waters and on the Royal Navy in particular.

In the preceding week, they had accounted for numerous ships. Minesweeper *Dundalk* was badly damaged on 16 October off Harwich and foundered early the next day while under tow. HMT *Kingston Cairngorm* was sunk off Portland on the 18th. HM Destroyer *Veneti* went down in the Thames Approaches on the 19th. There were ninety-six survivors from the latter ship, but five officers, including the captain, were missing. HMT *Velia* was also sunk in the same locality. The minesweeping trawlers *Wave Flower* and *Joseph Button* were sunk off Aldeburgh, apparently by mines, on the 21st and 22nd respectively. HMT *Hickory* sunk off Portland on the 22nd.

The picture for merchant shipping was no better. During the period, 36 ships (150,091 tons) had been reported sunk. In addition, three British ships (21,059 tons) previously reported as damaged were now known to have been sunk. Damage by aircraft, mine or submarine to twenty-one British ships (79,791 tons) had been reported and two more (10,232 tons) were known to have been damaged in the previous period.

As to civilian casualties, the approximate figures for the week ending 6 a.m. on 23 October were 1,690 killed and 3,000 injured. These figures included the estimated 1,470 killed and 1,785 injured in London, 56 killed and 261 injured in Coventry. There had been 30 killed and 203 injured in Birmingham.[67] But there was one thing few were concerned about – the invasion. Lord Halifax wrote to Hoare in Madrid that " it really does seem as if the invasion of England has been postponed for the present".[68] Yet still Churchill was preventing more escorts from being released.

And now Churchill and the War Cabinet had to address the looming coal crisis. The problems, Anderson told his colleagues – speaking to the paper he had lodged earlier – was not a shortage of coal. Compared with the same time the previous year, nine million tons more coal had been stocked in the country, including 1½ million more in the London area. This latter figure represented London's consumption for one month. The problem was distribution.

Since the beginning of September the intensification of air attack had involved considerable congestion and delay in the delivery of coal into the London area and beyond London to the south. Damage to railways had prevented coal reaching its destinations in Central London and onwards, and damage to consignees' premises had, in some cases, prevented coal from being delivered to them. This had caused congestion of coal wagons in marshalling yards, exchange sidings and stabling points. Traffic was now backed up to the pits. It was now even affecting production, as some pits had run out of storage space.

Anderson had numerous administrative and practical suggestions to make, including establishing dumps on the periphery of London, and using road transport to ship the coal from there, and more extensive use of the canal network. But never had the "Coal Scuttle Brigade" been so necessary. Anderson was now proposing to step up sea transport. More coal would go by sea to South Thames and Medway Ports, additional small craft were being put into the coal trade and the Admiralty had agreed to increase to sixteen the number of vessels in convoys.[69]

DAY 108 – FRIDAY 25 OCTOBER 1940

The newspapers had little more to add to the Pétain affair than when they first reported the meeting with Hitler. The *Yorkshire Post*, however, rather stiffly informed its readers that Germany might be about to launch a monster propaganda campaign carrying falsification to lengths far exceeding those already attempted designed to show that Britain's chances of withstanding German might were hopeless.

The *Mirror* announced a "Better night fighter plane". The paper, with others, was reporting on a BBC commentary the previous evening by Air Marshal Sir Philip Joubert. Amazingly, he was referring to the Defiant, saying that the aircraft, "originally designed as a night fighter and used experimentally for a while by day", had now been restored to its proper role and "with certain developments that we are considering, should be very effective". It wasn't. The aircraft was not suited to radar interception. That Joubert felt the need to talk up the Defiant simply reflected the growing unease at the inability of the RAF to deal with the night bomber, and its desperation to come up with a solution.

But even in the daytime, the RAF was finding it hard to keep the *Luftwaffe* at bay. Three people were killed when a German fighter-bomber scored a direct hit on trams in Blackfriars Road, London, during a daylight raid. The trams worst hit were in the middle of a group of five, drawn up near traffic lights. The dead included a driver, a conductor and a woman passenger. A number of women ripped up their clothing to provide temporary bandages for the injured, of which four had been taken to hospital. Many others were cut by flying glass. Adjoining buildings were badly damaged.

For the first time, Italian aircraft were committed to an operation over British soil. Thirteen aircraft took part in a raid against Harwich. A Joint Intelligence Committee report stated that assemblies of shipping and barges were still to be observed in Channel ports. It was thought that the intention was either to complete arrangements in case the situation was favourable or to maintain the threat of invasion or to continue preparations so as to prevent a fall in morale.[70]

DAY 109 – SATURDAY 26 OCTOBER 1940

The official German News Agency, reporting on the meeting between Hitler and Marshal Pétain, said: "Hitler did not hesitate to treat the Marshal as a great and honourable opponent deserved to be treated". Noting Pétain 's discomfort, evidenced by the protracted negotiations, the *Daily Express* could not resist the temptation to moralize. "Now you see what it is like to be beaten. Look at France. Look at Pétain creeping to the feet of the conqueror, asking what it is he wants," the paper stormed. "As we watch each step of that dreadful and pitiful pilgrimage we sing anew the praises of our invincible Navy and our unbeatable Air Force".

Several newspapers focused on yet another gun duel across the Straits of Dover. The narrative was familiar. The German guns shelled a convoy. German aircraft joined in. The British guns responded and bombers roared into action, this time launching the biggest raid yet on German-occupied France. Honour was satisfied. The warriors stood down and had their teas, while the servants cleaned their guns. Alan Brooke and others fretted about the enormous waste of manpower on Winnie's "pets".

For the rest, it was *déjà vu* all over again. Some *jabos* and their escorts flew across the Channel and headed towards London. Like the day before, and the day before that, some actually got to drop their bombs over the city. This time, the Royal Chelsea Hospital was hit. Fighter Command flew 732 sorties, losing nine fighters – three in accidents. Seven aircraft were lost by Bomber and Coastal Commands. The Fleet Air Arm lost a Swordfish. Seventeen British aircraft had been lost, against nine Germans.

About 150 miles off the north-west coast of Ireland, the troopship and former liner *Empress of Britain* had been bombed and strafed by a Condor. The bombs started large fires which soon crippled the ship. Many crewmen were trapped below deck, some forced to escape through portholes into the sea. A

Sunderland and three Blenheims answered calls for help. Under constant air cover from Hurricanes out of Aldergrove, the ship limped eastwards, latterly under tow, only to be torpedoed by U-32 on 28 October. Most of the 643 passengers and crew were saved. Only 45 were killed, all passengers in the initial attack. At 42,348 tons, she was the largest liner to be sunk through the entire war. U-32 was sunk by the destroyer *Harvester*, two days after she had despatched the *Empress*.

Back in Britain, the creatures of the night were on the prowl again. They hit London and Birmingham heavily. New Street Station in Birmingham was closed by an unexploded bomb. But for some, the war had become a spectator sport once more – it had lost its power to shock. The *Express* reported thousands of people crowding Kent seafronts to watch and hear "terrific battles between convoys, planes and long range guns which shook the coast from early yesterday evening to long after dark", as German long-range guns, with the aid of a terrific bombing by the RAF, lit up the whole French coast between Calais and Boulogne.

And buried deep in the "book" was the short squib headed: "Why I left the BBC by J. B. Priestley". Why, the question was posed, did J. B. Priestley leave the BBC? His popularity cannot have been in doubt. Far from it. His famous broadcasts have won for him a new reputation as the voice of Commonsense Britain. Why is it then that Priestley's broadcasts have suddenly come to an end? The piece concluded: "He will tell you himself in a vigorous, outspoken article in tomorrow's *Sunday Express*".

DAY 110 – SUNDAY 27 OCTOBER 1940

The long-running Pétain saga was coming to a close. Sombre news of a daylight attack killing six shoppers in London when a bomb dropped among them was confined to the back page. The front page in the *Sunday Express* offered the details of the Pétain deal, with the word "collaboration" featuring prominently. France, under *force majeure*, was to integrate politically and economically with Germany, as part of the Nazi's idea of a new world order. However, Pétain seemed to have avoided full military integration and a declaration of war against Great Britain. It was still a hostile power, but not a belligerent one. The USA threatened to seize French overseas possessions if military cooperation between Vichy and Germany became too close.

The settlement, however, triggered another bout of speculation on peace moves, another back-page headline of the *Express* reading: "Hitler may be planning another 'peace' attack". Vichy was "full of rumours" that tempting offers would be dangled in front of Britain once agreements had been reached with Italy and Spain – even to the extent that Germany would cease bombing British towns and regard herself at peace, leaving Britain the opprobrium of being responsible for further hostilities.

With the Vatican also said to be involved, the paper explained that the object of "this great ballyhoo campaign" was to keep up the flagging morale of the Axis civilian populations, especially in Italy, and trying to lower British morale. "If the rest of the world can be duped at the same time, Hitler will be more than satisfied", the paper said. But the real purpose of current German activity, it then said, "may be to 'hold' large British forces in this country against the threat of an invasion, when these troops might otherwise be used to operate against Nazis in other lands". It was now the belief of most experts that the invasion was now "off", except for cross-Channel artillery fire.

In London, there was good confirmation of this. A coded German radio message had been picked up and deciphered by the top-secret facility at Bletchley. It instructed German forces gathered at the invasion ports "to continue their training according to plan". Another intercept disclosed that the *Luftwaffe* had disbanded the administrative unit responsible for invasion planning and co-ordination. An invasion could hardly be imminent. Churchill was informed of the intercepts and the conclusion. The next day, photographic reconnaissance picked up substantial movement of shipping out of the invasion ports. It was moving eastwards, away from Great Britain.[71]

By 2 November, Colville was writing in his diary that the Prime Minister "now thinks the invasion is off". Even then a mixed picture emerged, as he added that this was "only because of our constant vigilance. If we relaxed that, the invasion would be an imminent danger". This meant "our keeping great forces immobilised at home".[72] If that was truly a reflection of the strategic appreciation, then it explains why, despite the accumulating evidence, Churchill did not act. But, for want of escorts, the convoys were to bleed to death out in the Atlantic and the Western Approaches.

Nor was the air war providing any great comfort. In the last week of the official battle, RAF Fighter Command flew a total of 1,007 sorties – more even than 974 flown on the memorable 15 August at the height of the day battle – mostly flown in the south-east, culling only a dozen German aircraft for the loss of ten British fighters. Bomber and Coastal Commands lost four aircraft, including a Hudson written off after an air-to-air battle with a FW Condor flying over the Atlantic. On the day, therefore, with fourteen losses against the *Luftwaffe's* twelve, the Germans were ahead.

As for Priestley in the *Sunday Express*, with his explanation of why he left the BBC, the flavour of his column came over in the headline: "The difficulties I had to fight". His oft repeated "new kind of war" was a war in which morale and prestige counted for a very great deal. Information and propaganda were of immense importance and it was hard to overestimate their value – yet under-valuing the effort was "what officially we keep on doing".

Having experienced continuous obstruction from officials, Priestley had concluded that the fault lay in the peacetime attitude of mind towards the public, "which is still expected to pay its taxes and then mind its own damn business, leaving the pundits to carry on their great task of fighting all over again the second Matabele War". He had been told his broadcasts were important, especially those to North America, in which context he had expected employees of the State to be eager to co-operate. "We are all, I take it, trying to fight the same war", he wrote, then continuing:

> You begin to suspect that perhaps we are not all in the same war when, doing a job of this kind, you find yourself day after day being obstructed instead of encouraged. You want to describe something and are told shortly that you cannot describe it, and are not even vouchsafed a reason. It is as if you are a naughty child. Then your text is absurdly mutilated on censorship grounds, though many of the corrections are nonsensical. You almost suspect yourself of being an enemy agent.

Although sometimes feeling like a man compelled to walk across a field of glue, his only complaint against the BBC was that it did not seem to be able to persuade government that "broadcasting is one of the most terrific weapons we possess". Officialdom did not in their heart of hearts believe in propaganda. Nor could they understand the necessity for a well-informed public. They wished to be left alone to fight some secret little war of their own. Either they could not or would not understand the importance of what the Nazis have treated as possibly the third arm of their state, after the army and air force.

Meanwhile, tensions were increasing along the Greek border, with the Italians camped in Albania, Late in the evening, the Italian ambassador in Athens, Emanuele Grazzi, relayed an ultimatum from Mussolini. It demanded that Italian troops were allowed to occupy strategic points in Greece. Ioannis Metaxas, the Greek dictator, remarked: "*Alors, c'est la guerre*".[73]

DAY 111 – MONDAY 28 OCTOBER 1940

Germany announced a "European Front" against England. This was the propaganda campaign predicted by Duff Cooper, Smuts, Priestley and even Churchill, way back in July. It was aimed at the USA, to position Britain as the "aggressor" against a united Europe, the obstacle to peace. The *Mirror* splashed the Italian moves against Greece on its front page. More details were retailed by the *New York Times*. Italy had attacked Greece by land, sea and air, "hurling" at least ten divisions of 20,000 troops across the Albanian–Greek border. Britain promised to keep her pledge, made on 13 April 1939, to help Greece resist the invasion.

The *Express* chose to feature RAF raids on Berlin, claiming that the heaviest bombs ever had been dropped on the city in a "fierce" ninety-minute raid that "showed Berlin what blitz-bombing is really like". There was a small item about the *Empress of Britain* in the *Mirror*, the paper noting that the Nazis were saying that the ship was still on fire, having claimed two days ago on the Saturday that it had been sunk. Back in Britain, observers asserted that three-engined aeroplanes had been used for attacks on London, confirming a German report that the *Regia Aeronautica* had been in action. Soon, there was the physical evidence.

DAY 112 – TUESDAY 29 OCTOBER 1940

The first day of the Italian invasion of Greece, and the heavy raids by Bomber Command on the Skoda works in Czechoslovakia, drove news of domestic air fighting from the front pages. Yet significant operations were continuing. Overnight, Birmingham had been heavily bombed again, with New Street Station badly damaged.

After early mist, raids had started mid-morning and carried on into the early evening. Four daylight raids on London and two on Portsmouth were recorded, the largest involving forty bombers escorted by Messerschmitt fighters. No. 602 City of Glasgow Sqn distinguished itself by shooting down eleven Me 109s in six minutes, for no loss. Fifteen Italian BR 20s, escorted by CR 42 biplanes, attacked Ramsgate. Five were damaged by anti-aircraft fire.

The War Cabinet was told that a number of German vessels had been reported in the Channel making eastwards. It was, however, too early to draw the deduction that the risk of invasion had receded. Some sixty good German divisions were ready at short notice, close to the invasion ports. So long as that situation continued, it would be essential for us to keep a number of divisions in readiness at home. Thus, the Minister of Information was invited to "inculcate the need for continued vigilance in our preparations against invasion".[74]

At dusk, RAF airfields in East Anglia, Lincolnshire and Yorkshire were attacked by Ju 88s and Me 109s. Heavy night bombing of Birmingham and Coventry was recorded. London was again bombed. On the day, Fighter Command lost ten aircraft, including two Hurricanes caught while taking off from North Weald Airfield during an attack. One pilot was killed there. But Bomber and Coastal Commands lost eight aircraft, including two Sunderland flying boats. The Germans lost twenty-four aircraft, including fifteen Me 109s.

DAY 113 – WEDNESDAY 30 OCTOBER 1940

"People need coal", said the *Express* in its editorial, but the front-page headlines were given entirely to Greece. The only reference to the domestic air war was a report on the appearance of the Italian Air Force. Memories of "the few" were fading. Sullen October weather hampered day flying. Only small numbers of *Luftwaffe* braved the rain and the autumnal gloom. Fighter Command had disappeared from the script. Never again would it recapture the heady days of the summer.

The people of Britain, bloodied and weary, were looking to their second winter of the conflict, dreading its onset. And well they might. Anderson's remedies had yet to bite, and to make matters worse, trains had been ordered to slow to 10 mph through the innumerable air raids. The delays slowed coal deliveries even more. The *Express* complained: "Mr Smith has no pile in his back yard. Mr Jones cannot order a ton and be sure of getting it".

And despite the Battle of Britain supposedly being in its closing phase, British operational intensity in the air was as high as it had ever been – higher than at the beginning of the battle. Aircrew were still taking losses. On this one day, seven fighters were written off and three pilots killed. Eight *Luftwaffe* aircraft were lost. One RAF and one Me 109 pilot were shot down over the Channel. The Briton died but the German was plucked from the sea by his air-sea rescue service, unwounded. An RAF fighter pilot's life was measured at 87 flying hours. To the very last, the Air Ministry seemed determined to make sure there were as few of the few as possible to survive the battle.

As for the night battle, the War Cabinet was wearily told that the previous night 200 enemy machines had been over London, Birmingham, Coventry and Liverpool. Thirty-seven RAF aircraft had been sent up but had made no interceptions.[75]

Herbert Morrison, since taking over as Home Secretary and Minister of Home Security, had been labouring long and hard. And despite his initial support for the original pre-war policy, expressed in his maiden speech as minister on 8 October, he was now ready with something which John Anderson had refused to deliver – a deep shelter policy. At the daily War Cabinet meeting, he revealed the details.[76] What had changed, he said, was that prolonged night raiding had led certain sections of the public to seek shelter, irrespective of warnings, towards nightfall and to stay there until morning. The "accessibility" arguments against deep shelters which had hitherto prevailed were no longer valid.

While it was impossible to apply any policy for deep shelters evenly over the vulnerable areas of the country, Morrison – in what amounted to a complete volte-face – felt that it would not be right, on this account, to dismiss the possibility of providing deep shelters in certain area. He accordingly suggested that work should be put in hand for providing additional shelter by tunnelling. In London this construction would be linked with the Tube system.

This was too early for the newspapers to report, but many published details of an equally important issue – shipping losses. The week ending 20–21 October had been the blackest since the evacuation from Dunkirk, with a cumulative total of British, Allied and neutral ships lost at 198,939 tons.

DAY 114 – THURSDAY 31 OCTOBER 1940

For once the night was quiet as well. The "raiders passed" siren sounded at the earliest time since September. People in shelters looked at each other "almost in disbelief". But, warned the *Daily Mirror*, in a front-page headline the next morning: "Don't think air war is over".

Morrison, having informed his colleagues of the new shelter policy, now planned to announce it in a ministerial broadcast on the BBC. He circulated the draft script to the War Cabinet.[77] The first section read:

> We are seeing more and more clearly that the Battle of Britain is only a part of the world war. And within the Battle of Britain conflict between the German Air Force and the civilian population is itself only a part. But what a vitally important part it is! How the whole fortune of war turns upon it! We all feel a glow of pride in the work of our Civil Defence army.
>
> A year ago could we have foreseen the performance they have put up? There they are – bank clerks, shopkeepers, stockbrokers, civil servants, craftsmen, labourers – peaceable, steady folk. The world is electrified to see them stand up as they have done to the rain of fire and death that has poured upon them night after night – stand up to it, and do their job, and never fail their neighbours or their duty. And our police – they have lived up to and surpassed their finest traditions.

Morrison, the Labour politician, was speaking to "the ordinary citizens of the country". A solid promise of victory lay in the fact that for months they had stood up to the attack, kept their nerve, and were ready for more. They had won the first round – won it hands down. "Well done, magnificently done, men, women and children of Britain!" he said.

For the fliers, on this one day, it had been the quietest day for four months – although it was not to last. A few bombs were dropped over East Anglia and Scotland but neither side lost any aircraft in combat. On the month, Fighter Command had lost 190 aircraft. Total RAF losses for the month stood at 318, compared with 306 lost by the *Luftwaffe*. On the last day of Dowding's battle, Fighter Command losses stood at 1,009 since 10 July. Total RAF losses came to 1,643 and *Luftwaffe* losses stood at 1,686. Different sources offer slightly different figures, but most agree that the two side's totals came within 50 of each other. In numerical terms, the two sides were effectively at parity. It was a score draw.

And the next day, the bombers came just the same. Out at sea, the torpedoes were running, the mines were primed and the Condors hauled their deadly bombs. John Anderson, meanwhile, laboured to bring coal to London. And, at a meeting of the Defence Committee, Churchill finally agreed that the danger of an invasion was "relatively remote". The dispositions and state of readiness of British forces would be adjusted to match what was judged to be a diminished threat throughout the winter.[78] Admiral Forbes was to get some of his escorts back. Like Dowding, and Park, though, he was not to keep his job. On 2 December, he was relieved of his command.[79]

14.

The battle won?

The Battle of Britain was the aerial conflict between British and German air forces in the skies over the United Kingdom in the summer and autumn of 1940. It was one of the most important moments in Britain's twentieth century history and a decisive turning point of the Second World War. Royal Air Force Fighter Command defeated the Luftwaffe's attempt to gain air supremacy over southern England and saved Britain from German invasion and conquest.

Imperial War Museum website

In June 1940, the fall of France had merited a major speech to the people of the country. Churchill told the nation: "What General Weygand called the 'Battle of France' is over. I expect that the battle of Britain is about to begin". There was no such speech on 31 October 1940, when that battle was supposed to be over. But then, the battle wasn't over. It had not even been properly defined and at this stage did not even merit a capital "B" to signify a specific event. The next day, it continued, just as before.

To come was the bombing of Coventry on 15 November and the Sheffield Blitz of 12–15 December. Then German aircraft dropped somewhere in the region of 450 high explosives bombs, land mines and incendiaries. During those nights 668 civilians and 25 servicemen were killed. A further 1,586 people were injured and over 40,000 more were made homeless. A total of 3,000 homes were demolished, another 3,000 were badly damaged. No less than 72,000 properties suffered some damage. Manchester was badly hit on the nights of 22–23 and 23–24 December 1940, killing an estimated 684 people and injuring 2,364.

There was the fire-bombing of London on 29 December 1940, which produced the epic photograph of St Paul's, wreathed in smoke and flames. There was the Clydebank Blitz of 13–14 March 1941, two devastating raids on the shipbuilding town. It suffered the worst destruction and civilian loss of life in all of Scotland. Five hundred and twenty-eight people died, 617 people were seriously injured, and hundreds more were wounded by blast debris. Out of approximately 12,000 houses, only seven remained undamaged – with 4,000 completely destroyed and 4,500 severely damaged. Over 35,000 people were made homeless.

But it did not stop there. Bristol, Liverpool, Swansea and Birmingham, all suffered, with Belfast also being savaged. The misery seemed endless, culminating in the so-called "Moonlight Blitz" on London on 10 May, when the debating chamber of the House of Commons was destroyed and Big Ben was damaged. Any one of the hundreds of thousand people, crouching in their shelters as hell erupted, would be justified in asking why, if the RAF had won the battle back in September, the Germans were still bombing. The answer, as the *Daily Mirror* so presciently warned on 1 November, was that the air war was not over.

The very fact that it was continuing supports the assertion that a three-part battle was involved – the parts we identified earlier as the blockade, the invasion and the attack on morale (the Blitz). As to who won the battle, the specific groups competing for the accolade of victor include the three RAF Commands, Fighter, Bomber and Coastal. Then there is the Royal Navy – and also the merchant marine; and the various civilian organizations such as the police, Civil Defence, the National Fire Service and of course the people, as individuals and as communities and groups, formal and informal.

It should be fairly self-evident already from an exploration of our narrative that the people played a very significant part in the battle, but it is still useful to carry out a more structured assessment of where the credit for the ultimate victory should lie. Thus, we look at each of the three main parts of the conflict in turn.

THE BLOCKADE

The essence of this battle was set out in Führer Directive No. 9. From our narrative, it is evident that many of the bombing raids in the early stages of the Battle of Britain, classed as *Kanalkampf* by the Germans, were primarily attacks on shipping, and therefore, implementing this directive. While formations were often protected from RAF interference, there is no evidence that the attacks were specifically intended to bring RAF fighters into the fray. And despite the dismissive attitude of Churchill and others to the coastal convoys, the shortage of coal in the winter of 1940–1, arising from distribution problems, attests to their damaging effect. The Germans perhaps had a better idea of the vulnerabilities of the British supply system than did Churchill.

There is a tendency, incidentally, to characterize this part of the conflict as the Battle of the Atlantic, and primarily as a U-boat war, the main developments taking place in 1941 and 1942. But the blockade was always more than a U-boat war, and by no means confined to the Atlantic. The east coast convoys, running the minefields and "E-boat alley" were part of that war. The bombing of the ports – from Dover, to Southampton, Portsmouth, Plymouth, Falmouth, through to Bristol, Swansea, Pembroke, Birkenhead, Liverpool, Belfast, Clydesbank, Glasgow, Aberdeen, Newcastle, Sunderland, Hull, Great Yarmouth and, of course, the Port of London – plus all the points in between – were also part of this war. And this war alone nearly vanquished Britain.

Here though, there is a definitional problem. When on the receiving end of a bombing raid, it is sometimes difficult to divine the intent. A raid on a convoy or port may be a genuine attempt to destroy the ships and goods, but it may also be a "come-on" to attract defensive fighters, the real objective being to engage and defeat the enemy air force. According to the Dowding dogma, if it is the former, then it is not part of the Battle of Britain.

There is nothing, by the way, to stop both objectives being pursued, simultaneously. There can be no real doubt, however, that the German air assault on our shipping, ports and infrastructure was a serious and hard-fought part of the war, separate from the attacks on the RAF. But this was never going to secure a rapid victory – blockades do not work that way. Nevertheless, success of the air effort and the wider blockade could eventually have induced the British Government to capitulate; just as in February 1942 the blockade of Singapore forced its surrender.

One can quite understand the temptation to over-simplify the battle, though. It is much easier to retain nice neat divisions, keeping – say – the Battle of Britain, the Blitz and the Battle of the Atlantic in separate, watertight compartments. The real world, however, does not recognize such divisions. For instance, as much as it was an attack on the physical survival of the nation – aimed at starving out the population and reducing their capacity to wage war – the blockade was an attack on morale. The shortage of food, the reduction in variety, the absence of luxury goods, the grinding tedium of queues, the need to make do and mend and the never-ending government nagging – which began seriously to irritate almost everyone – all had their effect.

What is so very difficult to convey is how interrelated everything was, and how so many things had knock-on effects. Thus, as the Germans swept across northern Europe and then occupied the Channel ports, we see that much of our shipping was rerouted to ports in the west. This meant that goods had to be moved internally to their final destinations – largely by rail – putting stress on the railway network. With increased passenger traffic and the movement of war materials, that made it more difficult to move coal. Together with the bad weather, this led to real shortages. The failure properly to defend the coastal convoys exacerbated this situation so that, by the end of the Dowding's day battle, Anderson had to be drafted in to deal with the crisis.

Now we are outside the time framework of Dowding's battle, but the coal crisis developed during the brutal winter of 1940–1. By then, on top of the damage to the rail network, the Blitz caused huge damage to the Port of London and required a further transfer of capacity to the west coast ports, with further stress on the railways. Coastal shipping, and even canals were pressed into service, but the system never really recovered. As coal backed up all the way to the pitheads this affected production, as there was no room to store mined coal at the pits. Further stresses led, by the early spring of 1942, to serious coal shortages. In a fraught labour situation, interference in production – which led to cutbacks and miners being laid off – was one of the factors that precipitated a wave of strikes. That required action by the government to bring the coal industry under tighter control. In turn, this added to the growing dissatisfaction with the management of the war, leading to Churchill calling for a vote of confidence in January 1942. All of these events, directly and indirectly, resulted from enemy action, initiated during Dowding's day battle.

At this point, the submarine war can be factored in – and the long-range air-strikes (as well as the activity of the surface raiders). What is remarkable was how quickly and severely losses here started to bite. The arithmetic offered by Minister of Shipping, Ronald Cross on 30 October 1940, attested to this.[1] Imports in the first year of the war had been 43½ million tons, but September 1940 imports had been "disappointingly low", at three million tons. Given the shipping losses already experienced, expected imports for the second year of the war had fallen to 42 million tons, and 34 million for the third year. But, at the then current rate of shipping loss, they were expected to drop to 32 million tons, as against the 34 million imported in the last full year of the First World War, when the population to be supplied had been 6.5 per cent less.

These figures made no allowance for increased demands for shipping for military purposes in the Middle East and elsewhere, made worse by the closure of the Mediterranean. Thus, what Ronald Cross was saying was that, had the then current loss rate continued, shipping capacity was set to fall below survival level. In the third year of the war, Britain could no longer have fed the population and supported then current military campaigns. But for the intervention of the USA, and her shipping, this was a battle the British could have lost.

Now let us overlay the strategic position. When the *Luftwaffe* departed from Britain in May 1941, some elements taking part in the invasion of the Balkans, Greece and then Crete, it was very far from being a defeated force. It was not the losses inflicted by the British which caused it to withdraw from the battle. The determining factor was the invasion in the East.[2] Progressively, as it redeployed to the Soviet border, it comprised a powerful and effective fleet which contributed significantly to the early victories against the Soviet forces.

It will be recalled that Hitler – and his generals – expected a quick and easy victory in Russia, with the fighting finished well before the winter of 1941–2. They were not alone in these expectations. In Britain, policymakers fully expected Stalin's defeat within three to six weeks, with minimal losses. But Hitler had also suggested that crushing the Soviet Union could strengthen Japan, the increased threat from which would force the USA to look to the Pacific, and keep it out of a European war. That was not wild assumption. Despite constant pressure from Churchill – who expected Roosevelt to declare war on Germany in January 1941 after his presidential inauguration – the USA did not enter the war of its own volition. Only after the Japanese attack on Pearl Harbour in December 1941 did the Germans declare war on the USA. In that sense, Churchill failed to achieve his own strategic objective.

That notwithstanding, imagine that Germany, successful in Russia, had stayed the Japanese hand. With America not yet in the war, imagine also that the *Luftwaffe* had returned to France in force, any time from autumn in 1941 through to the spring of 1942, confronting a UK seriously weakened by the U-boat blockade. Churchill's Government would by then have also been embroiled in the Far East, and would have yet to have given the country a single military victory. With no prospect of the USA entering the war, how long would Britain have held out?

On that basis, in the spring of 1941, when the German attacks finally petered out, the air assault was on hold. In theory, it could have restarted, with the same murderous intensity of 1940–1, at any time from the winter of 1941 to the spring of 1942.

But then, if Britain had not been forced to capitulate under the renewed weight of the Blitz, the blockade might have finished her. That issue was not settled until the USA joined the war, putting her shipbuilding resources into the pot, replacing the losses sustained in the battle. An arguable case can then be made that, in the first instance, Britain's saviour was not her armed forces (or even her own people) but the Soviet Union, and then the USA. However, neither of these countries could have had any effect if Britain had already been defeated before either had entered the war. To that extent, the blockade was not decisive – it could only have been had the Soviet Union been defeated and had the USA kept out of the European war.

Once again, though, this is not the complete story. There is clearly a relationship between the threat posed by Hitler's invasion, and the effect of the blockade. Essentially, as long as there was a credible invasion threat – and for some time after it had ceased to be credible – Churchill held back a large number of warships in domestic ports, ready to intercept an invasion fleet. This greatly weakened the convoy defences, evident from Churchill's own complaint of 4 August about the shipping losses on the North-Western Approaches. In this context, it has to be said that the British did not lose the "supplies war" so early in the conflict only because the Germans did not have the physical capability to win it.

It might also be said that Churchill was curiously reluctant to allow relief to be brought to the beleaguered convoys. This was evident on 29 August, when the First Lord, AV Alexander and the Naval Staff, made representations for the release of escorts. Perhaps it was premature at that point, with German invasion barges then being shipped down the Channel. As an aside, though, in accordance with AV's other request, Coastal Command could certainly have been strengthened. Instead, the most modern aircraft – with the full approval and active encouragement of Churchill – were used to bomb Germany. Shipping patrols had to make do, in the main, with semi-obsolescent and dangerously inadequate Avro Ansons and Lockheed Hudsons, both short-range aircraft based on civilian designs, with limited weapons-carrying capabilities.

This brings us to the crucial date of 28 September, when Churchill had good intelligence to suggest that the invasion had ceased to be a credible threat. At that time, Admiral Forbes had pleaded for the release of escorts, as he had been doing for months. Yet, despite Shipping Minister Cross adding his weight to the representations on 30 September, the Food Minister on 3 October and the First Lord of the Admiralty again on the same day, all making the same points, Churchill refused to act. According to War Cabinet records, he appeared to have done so on 4 October, but without then having taken any action for nearly two weeks, on 15 October he resiled from his promise to release warships, on the basis of what were said to be "intelligence reports" which said that the threat of invasion was not over. In fact, Churchill was not relying on intelligence but "operational considerations" from the Chiefs of Staff.

Interestingly, the official Royal Navy historian, Captain S. W. Roskill, writing in 1954, did not refer to these Cabinet exchanges – then still secret. But he did recall a discussion between Forbes and Churchill on the last day of October when, prior to the Defence Committee decision to scale down the invasion precautions, the Admiral had been asked for his views on the possibility of the invasion fleet being launched.

According to Roskill, only when Forbes had assured the Prime Minister that an invasion was "not a practical operation of war" did he at last relent and allow the return of warships to their normal functions. He could have done so six weeks earlier, and certainly by the end of September, before suffering the highest shipping loss rate of the war. But on 8 October, in parliament, Churchill was still ramping up the invasion threat, on grounds that lacked any credibility whatsoever, and still telling his Cabinet colleagues on 15 October that there was a credible risk.

Churchill was later to assert that he was more concerned about the shipping crisis than he ever was about the invasion threat, but in his history he was strangely silent about his reasons for refusing to give convoy protection more priority. Instead, there is a gap in his narrative of almost exactly four months from his 4 August communication to the First Sea

Lord on the threat to shipping and the next one he chose to cite, dated 3 December. He did not mention the multiple representations made by ministers to the War Cabinet about the diversion of escorts, or the build-up of the intelligence picture which suggested that the invasion threat had diminished a great deal earlier than he had acknowledged at the time. Nor, incidentally, does he explain his absence of support for more and better patrol aircraft for Coastal Command.

Throughout the period, Churchill thus concentrated military resources on countering the invasion. Whatever he might have said in private, or actually believed, this was what he presented as the greater threat. If we now step back from the neglected supplies war, and look at this threat, we see how this came to define the traditional narrative, not least with the assistance of Winston Churchill himself.

THE INVASION

The formal claim of the invasion being at the heart of the Battle of Britain is set out in an Air Ministry pamphlet called *The Battle of Britain*, published in March 1941. This, by common accord, defined the battle as we now know it, and in the following terms:

> What the Luftwaffe failed to do was to destroy the fighter squadrons of the Royal Air Force ... This failure meant defeat – defeat of the German Air Force itself, defeat of a carefully designed strategic plan, defeat of that which Hitler most longed for – the invasion of this Island. [3]

A distilled version of this appears on the Imperial War Museum website, reproduced at the beginning of this chapter. However, this, and the many variations, only stand up if Hitler cancelled (or postponed) *Sealion* as the necessary and direct consequence of the *Luftwaffe* failing to gain air superiority. Turning this round, it must be asserted that, had the *Luftwaffe* defeated RAF Fighter Command in the September of 1940, the invasion would have gone ahead, and would then have been successful.

The very obvious problem with this scenario is that in the face of interference from the Royal Navy's thousand ships, even with British aircraft cleared from the skies of southern England, there would have been the difficulties of landing troops on open beaches, unloading sufficient equipment and then – especially – keeping the troops supplied.

What has been less well explored, however, are the practicalities of beach landings, using barges rather than specially designed landing craft. Only a few, small-scale practice runs with the available equipment were carried out, but the rare photographs illustrate better than any words that these were not assault craft. As illustrated by Schenk and Ansel, the ramps were not of the hinged, drop-down type seen on modern assault craft, but heavy, cumbersome affairs needing up to fifteen minutes and a crew of twenty to slide them into position, even under optimum conditions. They were craft that could not have been unloaded except with extreme difficulty under fire, and then not at all rapidly.

Then, as the intention was to land on the ebb tide, each barge would be stranded for most of one tidal cycle. The difficulty of manoeuvring these barges into position, and then leaving them stranded for around eight hours, did not auger well for a successful landing. And that was without taking into account the weather. When the Allies invaded Normandy in 1944, they took with them over 1,000 converted Thames barges – all of them self-propelled, but none of them used for assaulting defended beaches. During the storm of 21 June, an estimated two-thirds of them were lost or damaged.[4] In practice, the German barges proved surprisingly capable of weathering rough seas, but the real problem was beaching and unloading them. That problem was unsolvable with the resources available.[5]

Separately, though, having gone through the sequence of events in the German camp, what so very clearly emerges is the conflict between the Army and the Navy about the nature of the landing. The Army required a broad front landing and the Navy could only deliver on a narrow front. Both believed that each other's plans were suicidal. Neither was prepared to compromise. When Hitler on 27 August decided that naval operations must be adapted "to fit in with the given facts", a compromise was imposed on the both Services. But, as far as the Army was concerned, *Sealion* had ceased to be a credible military operation. It could no longer be an opposed landing. At a stroke, it had become a transportation exercise, its purpose to deliver troops after the battle had already been won – the winning of which was left to Göring and his air fleets.

Here, an intriguing point arises. Had the Germans won the air battle, how would they have known? As long as there had been some RAF fighters to take to the skies, and a small number of German aircraft had been shot down each day, the clerks and statisticians could do the rest. The RAF only had to win on paper – as indeed it did on many days, when it had lost more aircraft than it had shot down – leaving the newspapers and the BBC to announce the victories. That these were paper rather than real victories made absolutely no difference – which was just as well. In strictly numerical terms – taking into account all aircraft losses including those of Bomber and Coastal Commands – the battle was inconclusive, neither won nor lost.

What also has to be restated here is that any invasion fleet's journey would have been at night. Aircraft could not then have interfered to any great effect, leaving the German vessels invulnerable to the RAF but also Royal Navy vessels immune from *Luftwaffe* activity. If one recalls the enormous damage done to the Peewit convoy on 8 August by a handful of E-boats, then it is not difficult to imagine the great slaughter that the Navy could have wrought with a much larger fleet. We are thus confronted with the unavoidable conclusion that gaining air superiority might have been a *necessary* condition for an invasion, but it was not *sufficient*. The Royal Navy had to be neutralized in order to render the night safe for the invasion fleet. The Germans did not achieve that. They did not even attempt it.

Nevertheless, in thousands of narratives, it is a given that an invasion was stymied by the RAF. A few, and only a very few, explore the practicalities. One of the first was Duncan Grinnell-Milne's 1958 book, *Silent Victory*. He concluded that with the equipment the Germans had available, it was not feasible. But Churchill got there first. When writing his history of the period, he had been through the invasion of Normandy. He knew in detail the huge scale of the enterprise, its hazards and pitfalls and thus made his own comparison between the situations in 1940 and 1944, writing:

> Apart from mastery of the air and command of the sea, we had as large (if not so well equipped) an army, fresh and ardent, as that which Germany assembled in Normandy four years later to oppose our return to the Continent. In that case, although we landed a million men in the first month, with vast apparatus, and with every other condition favourable, the battle was long and severe, and nearly three months were required to enlarge the area originally seized and break out into the open field.

He remarked that there had been some talk in parliament of the "invasion scare" after the danger had passed away. Yet this is precisely the term he himself had been using, when he noted: "Certainly those who knew most were the least scared". After the event, he did not hesitate to make the obvious inference: the Germans had not been equipped to succeed in an opposed landing. Others agreed. Military academic Murray Williamson, in his book, entitled, *Strategy for Defeat*, wrote:

> In retrospect, the task facing the Germans in the summer of 1940 was beyond their capabilities. Even disregarding the gaps in inter-service cooperation – a must in any combined operations – the force structure, training, and doctrine of the three services were not capable of solving the problem of invading the British Isles.[6]

This is effectively confirmed by Vice Admiral Kurt Assmann, formerly a member of the German Navy operations staff and subsequently a naval historian. He expressed his views in 1947, in a then confidential evaluation of the part played by the German Navy in *Sealion*, a treatise on which we rely extensively in this book. His view of the cancellation (or postponement) is particularly relevant. He noted that, when the time came for a decision, "not one of the responsible authorities was ready to speak decisively against the operation, although all recognised the inherently serious objections; but all were privately relieved when the failure of air supremacy afforded a good reason for outwardly justifying the abandonment of the operation". Given the favourable air situation, there seemed no need to embark on this "extreme measure" involving such great risks.

Thus we see the shift to a reliance on the air war, its pivotal role confirmed by Karl Klee, who produced the translation of so many of the documents on which we rely. He stated that the "basic motivating factor" for the air offensive was the effort "to bring about a decision of the war though strategic warfare alone".

Another authoritative and convincing assessment came from General Günther Blumentritt, the Operations Officer of Army Group A, under General Gerd von Rundstedt, the man who was going to lead the *Sealion* operation. Interviewed after the war by Captain Basil Liddell Hart, the well-known writer on military affairs, Blumentritt noted Hitler's "strangely dilatory attitude" over the invasion plans. "He showed little interest," Blumentritt said, "and made no effort to speed up the preparations." That was utterly different from his usual behaviour. "Before the invasion of Poland, of France, and later of Russia, he repeatedly spurred them [the planners] on. But on this occasion he sat back."[7]

In a far more detailed article, written exclusively for the Irish defence journal, *An Cosantóir*, Blumentritt then gave a damning evaluation of the operation.[8] Hitler's frequent pronouncements "that he wished and intended to reach agreement with England" led the planners – himself included – not to regard the operation very seriously. Further, no decision Hitler ever made could be considered final. In 1939, the Polish invasion had been suddenly halted after the reconnaissance forces had actually reached the frontier, while the "alert" orders for the invasion of France and the Low Countries had been rescinded no less than eleven times.

Von Rundstedt had taken the invasion no more seriously than had Blumentritt and, in either late July or August, had been in Berlin, when he had been told by Hitler that he did not intend to carry out *Sealion*. Taking the cue from his superior, Blumentritt's view was that the operation was a bluff. Orders were given and practical preparations were undertaken because "a bluff can only succeed when everything is done as if the operation were meant seriously and when all staffs and units believe implicitly in its execution".

Blumentritt was by no means alone. Heinz Guderian, the general commanding the spearhead Panzer Group in the invasion of France, spent August in Berlin, to where he had transferred his headquarters, enjoying a period of "leisure and relaxation". Of *Sealion*, he had to say:

> Even from the very beginning this operation was never taken very seriously. In my opinion the lack of a sufficiently strong air force and of adequate shipping – not to mention the escape of the British Expeditionary Force from Dunkirk – made it a completely hopeless undertaking.[9]

Against that, Macksey in 1980 argued that an invasion could have been successful, but he had the assault starting on 13 July when the British Army was weak. Yet, for the Germans to prevail, he had to give to them capabilities and equipment which simply did not exist in the July. For instance, his fictional invasion force relied on – among many other things – the Siebel ferry to transport the guns. Yet volume production of the craft did not begin until September 1940. By late September, only twenty-five had been completed.[10]

In 1974, a wargame was played at the Royal Military Academy Sandhurst. It presumed that the *Luftwaffe* had not won air supremacy and used previously unpublished Admiralty weather records for September 1940. Even without air supremacy, the Germans were able to establish a beachhead in England using a minefield screen in the English Channel to protect the initial landings from the Royal Navy. However, after a few days, the Royal Navy was able to cut off supplies from the German beachhead, isolating the invaders and forcing their surrender.[11] Joining the list of naysayers, Robinson, in 2005, then convincingly dismissed the idea of a successful landing. Two, more recent authors, Hewitt in 2008 and Cumming in 2010, on the basis of careful study of the relative strengths of the opposing forces, also conclude that the Royal Navy would have blocked any invasion attempt.

From the totality of the evidence, the inevitable conclusion must be that the Germans – and especially the Navy – realized that the enormous practical difficulties involved in mounting an invasion made it an unrealistic proposition. The only way that *Sealion* can be made to succeed is either by distorting the evidence, or by ignoring it altogether. Thus, while Campion attempts to adjudicate on the issue, he does so by considering only a fraction of the evidence before coming down on the side of the myth.[12] The facts, however, clearly support the idea that *Sealion* may have started off as a genuine exercise, but once the practical difficulties had been understood, any enthusiasm evaporated. It became an elaborate bluff, kept going first to pressurize the British Government, and then to divert attention from the impending invasion of the Soviet Union.

If, therefore, the RAF cannot claim credit for preventing an invasion, the question must be posed as to what Fighter Command actually achieved. The best answer is that it survived, although even that achievement was not quite as portrayed in the traditional narrative. Despite being under great stress, it never appears to have been under serious threat. Yet it is here that the myth is at its strongest. Less than a month after the *Luftwaffe* attack on RAF facilities had started in earnest with *Eagle Day* on 13 August, it is held that No. 11 Group was on the point of collapse.

Remarkably, though, no sign of that crisis is apparent in *contemporary* accounts of the battle. The crisis narrative does not seem to emerge until after the war – starting around 15 September 1945, on the fifth anniversary of the great battle with the *Luftwaffe*. Then, the media makes the running rather than official sources. Only then does the supposedly abrupt shift on 7 September from airfield attacks to the bombing of London become the error "which saved British Fighter Command and England".[13] Not until 1961, in Wood with Dempster, was the bombing of London presented as easing the "agonising strain" on No. 11 Group. And it took until 2009 for Max Hastings to pronounce that the Germans had made "a decisive strategic error".

The crisis then reached a peak in the same year when Patrick Bishop has Dowding beginning to consider withdrawing the remainder of his "battered forces" to northern England. The British Army is "tensing for action, in the belief that command of the air was about to be lost and invasion was imminent". No one told General Alan Brooke. At the time, on 15 September 1940, he wrote in his diary of his concerns, but added to the entry after the war.

> It should not be construed that I considered our position to be a helpless one in the case of invasion", he wrote. "We should certainly have a desperate struggle and the future might well have hung in the balance, but I certainly felt that given a fair share of the fortunes of war we should certainly succeed in finally defending these shores.

Brooke, however, was only the general charged with the defence of Britain.

As to the existential crisis in Fighter Command, many post-war authors have it that it was of the same order as the crisis of May 1940 when Churchill was proposing to send further Hurricane squadrons to the aid of a collapsing France. The interesting thing then is that Dowding sought an audience with the Prime Minister and followed up with a letter, telling him unequivocally that he could no longer defend the country. Thus, the issue was placed very firmly on the record. The Prime Minister was left in absolutely no doubt that the situation had reached a crisis level.

Strangely then, in late August and early September when this new crisis was supposed to be at its height, Dowding was silent. So was Air Vice-Marshal Park even though his Group was most at risk. He had a particularly good opportunity to raise the alarm when on 30 August Churchill visited his headquarters. Yet, when the Prime Minister reported on that visit to the War Cabinet on 1 September, he had returned bubbling with confidence. "We had every right to be satisfied. Our own Air Force was stronger than ever and there was every reason to be optimistic about the 1940 Air Battle of Britain", the Cabinet minutes recorded him saying.

As to the pilot shortage which was said to afflict Fighter Command, there were undoubtedly problems in keeping the front-line squadrons fully manned.

But neither the Prime Minster, who seems to have micro-managed every aspect of the war, nor the War Cabinet was troubled by any talk of a manning crisis. The Cabinet had been asked to consider pilot training on 30 August, the same day that Churchill had visited Park's headquarters, but this was only in relation to moving training operations overseas. Fighter pilots were not specifically mentioned.

Then, with Churchill having already conveyed optimism about the air war, on 2 September there was his message to Bomber Command, published in the *Daily Express*. If this had just been a morale booster, it could have remained confidential. It seems inconceivable that it would have been released if Fighter Command had been on the brink of collapse.

This was then followed by Churchill's statement to parliament on 5 September – delivered with the approval of the War Cabinet. On the public record, he said that "firm confidence" was felt by all the responsible officers of the RAF in our ability to withstand the increased scale of attack. The RAF was "more numerous and better equipped than it was at the outbreak of the war". This was mirrored in a parallel statement in the House of Lords, where Lord Halifax told their Lordships that "[m]any of our Air Force stations have been the subject of heavy attack, but sound organisation and skilful precautions have enabled them to continue to operate with scarcely a pause".[14]

A day later, both the King and Queen visited Dowding's headquarters at Bentley Priory. Had the situation been so very desperate, surely the visit would have been cancelled? Instead, a newsreel shows a relaxed, smiling Dowding acting as a guide to the royal couple. Looking from the top downwards, with a "hands on" Prime Minister, who combined his premiership with the role of Defence Minister, had there been an existential crisis, it really is inconceivable that he would not have been aware of it, and then written about it. Generally, crises of this magnitude, especially if they require more and urgent allocation of resources, are referred to the very top.

But nothing percolated to the rarefied heights. In terms of the written record, Churchill, on 25 August, complained about the number of "communication squadrons" being maintained at Hendon. The airfield could provide at least two good squadrons of fighter or bomber aircraft, he thought. Then he was worrying about delayed action bombs, about street lighting and the blackout, about the delays in filling craters in bombed airfields and repairing hangars, about developing gliders for troop transports and diverse other matters. Nothing was said at the time, and there is no record of any representations being made to Churchill, or the War Cabinet for that matter, that might even have hinted of serious problems. Thus, by mid–late August and early September, any idea of a Fighter Command manning crisis was invisible to the upper echelons of government, and was to remain so.

On the eve of that 7 September attack on London, therefore, the situation was that two air forces faced each other, neither of which had been defeated. In the 1941 Air Ministry pamphlet, it was suggested that the Germans may have believed that they had achieved success and it only remained for them to bomb a defenceless London until it surrendered. However, as do most military histories, this ignores the political dimension. And here, Göring was playing an independent hand. By early September, his strategic aim had already shifted. As Klee indicated, quite unrelated to *Sealion*, the *Luftwaffe* was setting out to bring about a decision through strategic air warfare alone. The same point is made persuasively and at length by Walter Ansel. Having assessed the overall contribution towards the success of the invasion made by the air effort, he concludes that "the score works out very close to zero".[15]

Both writers make it very clear that the objective had been the destruction of British morale, thereby to secure a political settlement – an objective of which the British were very well aware. The aim was not physical but moral domination, alongside which Hitler's and Göring's representatives were active in pushing for peace negotiations as part of a tried and tested strategy. The "one-two" dimension of aggressive diplomacy coordinated with the military action is one of the neglected and poorly understood aspects of the battle, but one in which Hitler and the Nazis excelled.

To that, then is added the invasion threat, which turns out to be just another dimension in Hitler's overall strategy. The key here to understanding what was going on were the events of 13–14 September 1940 – shortly before the invasion either had to be launched, postponed or cancelled. Good evidence indicated that, by the 13th, he had already decided that the operation would not go ahead in its originally intended form. But Hitler was also mindful of the total *psychological* effect of a decision. Cancellation of *Sealion* would have relieved some of the psychological pressure, for which reason he was not disposed *yet* to issue the cancellation order and disperse the invasion fleet.[16]

That he then "postponed" the invasion on 17 September had nothing to do with the limited tactical success of the RAF on 15 September – the details of which Hitler could hardly have been aware. It was simply a reflection of the realities. The invasion fleet could not be held at constant readiness, without physical deterioration. It had to be used or stood down. Since Hitler had no intention of using it, he had to choose the latter option.

Another of those points which is rarely made in this context is that Göring was indeed an independent player, and unlike the Navy and Army chiefs, not subordinated to OKW. As *Reichsmarschall*, not only was he the top-ranking officer in the military, he was also Air Minister, and responsible for the economic plan. As such, he was responsible to Hitler alone and after him the most prominent man in the Nazi regime. As his close confidant and a man who had played a central part in his rise to power, Göring could more or less do as he pleased. He would tell Hitler what he thought he needed to know.[17]

Furthermore, he had been actively involved in peace negotiations in August 1939, and had sought to avoid war – not least because it conflicted with his role as plenipotentiary for the five-year economic plan.[18] Good evidence suggests that he initiated two different strands of peace feelers in July 1940, one via Dahlerus, and the other – more clearly documented – through Albert Plesman. It was then open to Göring to adjust the tempo of the air operations, to improve the chances of pursuing negotiations. It would have been illogical to intensify air operations while he was actively seeking peace and, incidentally, trying to rescue his economic plan, for which he was responsible.

For all that Göring acquired the reputation as a dilettante, he headed a professional air force. It benefited from skilled fighters and strategists – not least its chief of staff, the "unusually intelligent and energetic" *Generaloberst* Hans Jeschonnek, and *Generalfeldmarschall* Kesselring.[19] They had persuaded Göring to shift to night bombing, principally to reduce losses from RAF fighters. This is often presented as a strategic defeat, but night bombing was also a tactic adopted by RAF Bomber Command for exactly the same reason. To those who suggest that the *Luftwaffe*'s move represented a defeat, would they also agree that Bomber Command had been defeated? Was the fact that its thousand bomber raids were carried out at night evidence of defeat?

In effect, what happened was sound military strategy. Faced with an obstruction, the military simply sought another way round. This had been precisely the strategy adopted to deal with the Maginot line, where the tanks had circumvented the fortifications by driving through the Ardennes. Faced with Dowding's well-organized and powerful day-fighter force, the *Luftwaffe* switched to night bombing, and was able to operate with impunity. The Spitfires and Hurricanes of Fighter Command had become Britain's own Maginot line.

As for targeting London, it was the one major port city that had so far escaped serious bombing and was overdue a major raid. Given the strategic importance of the capital, and the need to secure a decision, it made absolute sense to switch the weight of the attack and put the effort behind the Blitz, as well as stepping up the blockade. Bombing London served both those objectives.

The battering the *Luftwaffe* then took on 15 September arose through a combination of hubris and faulty intelligence. Its leaders, underestimating the strength of Fighter Command, had unwisely mounted a major daylight raid and expected the same treatment as its surprise raid of 7 September. But the fleets also suffered a strong headwind, which gave the defenders more time than usual to prepare.

Despite that, the RAF shot down fewer aircraft than on 18 August. The day was a success, but not a great victory, nor even a turning point. The *Luftwaffe* did not strike its tents and steal away – the scenario posited by the 1969 "Battle of Britain" film. As the "Maginot line" of the daylight fighter force had proved to be too tough a nut to crack, it simply accelerated changes in tactics that were already under way, The strategic objective of defeating Britain remained – but the *schwerpunkt* changed. It became the people of Britain, the immediate task being to crack their morale by means of the application of strategic airpower.

This explains why, in their study of the immediate events that led to the postponement of *Sealion* on 17 September, Ansel and others do not specifically mention the air fighting of the 15th. It was not a factor. Even had the Germans judged the air battle as successful on that day, the invasion still would not have gone ahead.

Unsurprisingly, two *Luftwaffe* pilots, Julius Meimberg and Gerhard Baeker, also reject the "take" of Churchill and other post-war revisionists. "It's all exaggerated", Meimberg said sixty years after the event. "Churchill succeeded in creating this myth that so few did so much for so many". Baeker had been twenty-five when he had flown his first bombing missions over England. He too regarded the British preoccupation with the Battle of Britain as disproportionate. August and September 1940 were just one incident in a long war. "For me, the battle lasted from August 1940 until July 1941. What they call the Battle of Britain in England was just August and September".[20]

The cold statistics confirm this view. In August, when the assault on the RAF was at its highest, the *Luftwaffe* flew 4,779 sorties. It dropped 4,636 tons of bombs and incendiaries. In September, the figure was 7,260 sorties and 7,044 tons of ordnance dropped – yet the assault on the airfields wound down on 6 September. In addition, 669 mines were laid in coastal waters and estuaries. In October, with the "great day" of 15 September long gone, the *Luftwaffe* flew 9,911 sorties, dropped 9,113 tons of ordnance and laid 610 mines. Most of the ordnance was dropped at night.

The main effect of Fighter Command, therefore, was to force the *Luftwaffe* to adopt the "Maginot strategy", whence the German Air Force converted from a largely day bombing force, into a strategic night bombing force, shifting the focus of attack from airfields and the aircraft industry to the people. But the objective never varied: the purpose of the air activity was to bring the UK to the negotiating table. The support for that thesis is overwhelming. Thus, after the supposed Fighter Command victory, far from diminishing, air operations actually intensified, peaking in October. Even in November, when weather conditions were extremely difficult for the primitive aircraft of the day, 6,510 tons of ordnance were dropped – 40 per cent more than in August. Minelaying doubled, with 1,215 mines laid.

As winter closed in, December saw 3,844 sorties and 4,323 tons of ordnance, and January 2,465 sorties and 2,424 tons. Even in the brutal month of February, in near-Arctic conditions, the *Luftwaffe* managed 1,401 sorties and dropped 1,127 tons of ordnance. Sortie rate increased during March and April, with 4,364 and 5,448 sorties flown respectively, during which period some of the heaviest raids of the war were mounted against London. On 16–17 April, 681 bombers flew against the city, followed by 712 on the night of 19–20 April. Even the first ten days of May saw renewed activity, with raids against Liverpool and Birkenhead, and Glasgow/Clydesbank, as well as London. By then, of course, the attacks were a feint, to conceal the gradual relocation of forces to the East.[21]

For most of this period, the *Luftwaffe* medium bombers operated at night, with "mosquito" raids of Me 109 formations raiding during the day, flying at high level and giving the RAF huge problems. Through the night, it operated with impunity, so contemptuous of the defence that formations commonly flew with navigation lights on. Any idea that the *Luftwaffe* had been defeated is fantasy. RAF Fighter Command aircrew cannot stand as "the men who saved England", as the 1941 pamphlet would have it. The idea is preposterous.

At best, RAF fighter aircrew were co-defendants, alongside the other RAF Commands, the other Services and their Arms, and they were partners with the people who were also fighting the battle. The real achievement of the RAF, as Park had urged of his Group in August 1940, was indeed that it survived. That was no mean achievement, and nothing can detract from it. But it was not the "close run thing" as has been asserted, and it was a shared achievement. The other Services, the diplomats and most of all the people were buying time, staving off defeat in order to pave the way for victory, all playing their own vital parts in a long and complex battle.

THE ATTACK ON MORALE (THE BLITZ)

With a more sanguine appraisal of the battle, we can now begin to see the Blitz in its proper and original context. It was part of the overall Battle of Britain, but the phase where the people became the main protagonists. They were no longer the passive bystanders, their role merely to applaud the heroic "few". By 7 September, breaking the morale of the people had become the primary means by which the Göring and the Nazi hierarchy sought to defeat Britain. The ultimate victory was to be gained by a political settlement brought about through a collapse in the civil order. Britain would have been rendered ungovernable, with Churchill deposed and a new government in place, ready to negotiate. The vocabulary had not yet been invented, but in effect this was the "shock and awe" adopted by the Americans in the 1991 Gulf War, with exactly the same objective – regime change.

However, the people in 1940, in contrast to the British Armed Forces, had to do more than just survive and endure. In the unequal battle between man, woman and child, and the bombers with their loads of high explosives and incendiaries, their main defences were effective air-raid shelters. The slated enemy may have been Germany but – as with the ill-equipped fighter pilots confronting survival in the sea – a barrier to survival was their own government, in failing to equip them with the means by which they could protect themselves.

Here, the people had to take on the government in order to enhance their own prospects of survival and thus succeed in defying Hitler.

This remarkable situation occurred largely as a result of deliberate policy, formulated primarily by Sir John Anderson, but stemming from experience in the First World War. The first aerial attack on London had been on 31 May 1915, when there had been no civilian shelters. People had taken to the Underground stations and eighty were soon adapted for constant use. But, when 12,000 people had gathered at Finsbury Park Station after police had displayed "take cover" signs, there had been tremendous concerns about hygiene and spread of disease in such densely occupied areas. Thus, after the war, there were "strenuous efforts made" to ensure that stations would never again be put to such use.[22]

Even in the immediate aftermath of the first major Gotha raid, however, there was reluctance to allow the Tube system to be used. On 14 June 1917, the then Home Secretary Sir George Cave had told the House of Commons:

> Supposing we gave warnings by such means as loud-sounding hooters. I am advised that sudden warnings in this way of impending air raids would have the effect of producing overcrowding in the streets and trams, and people would suddenly crowd into the Tubes and other places, and this of itself might result in a serious loss of life.[23]

As the debate progressed, a central figure became Anderson. In January 1924, he had been chairman of the Air Raid Precautions Committee of Imperial Defence. It was he that had ruled out the Tube station shelter option. The excuses had changed, but the thinking had not.

In the shadow of Munich on 21 December 1938, when challenged in parliament on the air-raid precautions, Anderson still dismissed out of hand any idea of providing these effective bombproof shelters, saying:

> Apart from the difficulties and delays involved in any extensive scheme for deep bomb-proof shelters, I do not think we are prepared to adapt our whole civilisation so as to compel a large proportion of our people to live, and maintain their productive capacity, in a troglodyte existence deep underground.[24]

In early 1939, under considerable pressure from parliament, Anderson as Home Secretary was forced to revisit his own decision. After complaining during a debate on 1 March 1939 of the "stir" about deep – i.e., bombproof – shelters, which was "creating something perilously near to a defeatist mentality", he appointed a conference of experts to look again at the issue. This was headed by

Lord Hailey, a fellow Indian governor who had ruled over the Punjab until 1928 and the United Provinces (Uttar Pradesh) until 1934.

Predictably, the former Indian Government colleague and his experts supported Anderson's original policy. They worked on the supposition that the bombing would be mostly short-lived raids in the daylight, the masses of bombers giving next to no warning of their arrival – as had been the case in the First World War. They had not for the moment considered the possibility of prolonged night raids, in a campaign lasting months, or even of the development of radar. From their narrow perspective, a network of deep shelters – the only type that would give full protection – would not be feasible. They would be too far apart to allow quick access in the event of the expected surprise raids, and large numbers of people attempting to use stairs at the same time risked a large-scale accident.[25]

The issue was raised in parliament on 5 April 1939, where we saw the intervention of Megan Lloyd George, daughter of the former prime minister. Her statement was extraordinarily prescient:

> There are certainly areas in this country where the risk of air raids is so great that shallow shelters cannot reduce it to tolerable dimensions. I think that that is a view which is very generally held. Whether it is the view of the Government we do not know, because they have not yet expressed any specific opinion on the matter, but there are certain parts of the East End of London, certain parts of the City of London, certain parts even of Greater London where the industrial concentration is very great, and where it would be of enormous advantage to an enemy if damage were done and great dislocation of the industrial life of the country were created. That is the case also in cities like Coventry, which are almost completely target areas.[26]

Nevertheless, on 14 April 1939, Anderson's policy committee recommended "the rejection for technical and general reasons of any attempt to provide deep 'bomb proof' shelters on a widespread scale for the protection of the civil population". With something close to breathtaking arrogance, the committee acknowledged that their scheme "may fall short in some respects of the anticipation entertained in some quarters as to the character of the protection which the Government should undertake to provide".[27]

This opened the way for Anderson to announce to the House on 20 April his idea of a definitive shelter policy. Not only did he exclude the use of the Underground, he also rejected the idea of building a network of deep shelters.

Referring to what was termed "deep shelter mentality", he had decided that if shelters were too safe (and comfortable) workers would retreat to them and not re-emerge. War production would suffer. Shelters would be proof only "against blast, splinter and the fall of debris".

Rather than allow people to congregate in large shelters – where they could possibly challenge authority – they were to be kept dispersed, in manageable packets. Instead of proper protection, they were given the prefabricated, corrugated steel structures which could be erected in gardens, which came to be called Anderson shelters. This was perhaps appropriate – like their progenitor, they were cold, dark, damp and lonely. They were incredibly noisy through the raids, amplifying the sounds of the bombs and guns, and therefore frightening. They were widely detested and many people chose not to use them. But with these and a ramshackle network of so-called surface shelters, and diverse other protection which included trenches built in public parks, the people were forced to go to war.[28]

Still, there were some MPs and others who were not satisfied. But, with less than three months to go before the East End was to be so heavily bombed, Anderson contemptuously brushed them aside. On 12 June 1940, he told the House: "I am devoutly thankful that we did not adopt a general policy of providing deep and strongly protected shelters". In this war, he said, "we must avoid at all costs what I may call the deep-shelter mentality".[29]

That position remained in September when the bombers headed towards London. Yet even though *The Times* had agreed there had been an "insufficiency of the present provision", the Prime Minister's only recorded contribution in resolving the shelter crisis was to urge "strong action" against demonstrators seeking better protection. After the War, Churchill said that he had sought from the Cabinet an explanation as to why the Tubes could not be used. He was "deeply anxious about the life of the people in London", he said.[30] But the War Cabinet minutes do not support his claims. It is perhaps germane to note that, at the time of his making them in 1949, Cabinet records were not routinely published. Publication was not introduced until 1958 and the 30-year rule did not come into force until 1967.

At the height of the crisis, upon which the fate of the nation quite obviously turned, the evidence suggests that Churchill concerned himself with "trivia": the need for a new flag for the Admiralty building; the problem of glass stocks to replace shattered windows; and post office queues. He had every opportunity to explain his role in resolving the shelter crisis – one which even the rigorously censored news media made clear was a vital political issue. But he chose not to record it, neither at the time nor after the war.

The people were left to find their own solutions, thereby saving the government from the consequences of its own indifference and folly. In the short period from 7 to 19 September, after which the government resolve crumbled and it decided not to enforce its own shelter policy, the war could have been lost. A significant number – many thousands – of Londoners rebelled against the government. And although it was a passive rebellion, it might not have taken much to have turned it into violent revolution. Fortunately, the government, or more particularly, the police, soldiers and the officials on the ground, had the sense to cave in. By 20 September, the moment had passed. The people settled down to a bloody war of attrition.

As to the consequences of the bombing, it was not only shelter policy that failed. Public administration in some East End local authority areas broke down, episodes which were dealt with at length and in great detail by Angus Calder.[31] He also records – as indeed did the War Cabinet and MPs at the time, the latter during several debates in the Commons – that central government had been slow to recognize the collapse, and even slower to do something about it. Sometimes, thoughtless action by central and local government had made things worse, for instance drafting in troops to help clear up the debris from the bombing and then requiring the hard-pressed local authorities to find billets for them.

Local initiatives, organized by people ranging from priests to the monstrous legion of women, individuals, groups, charities and officials acting on their own initiatives, collectively saved the day. The record shows that the input from the centre was minimal. Even at the height of the Blitz in London, it was the Salvation Army, with other agencies – even the Canadian Red Cross – which supplied refreshments to battling firemen who were collapsing through lack of sustenance – lacking even drinking water while they fought fires on twelve-hour shifts. The official mind had never thought of the need.

FADING AWAY

The air battle over Britain – or this phase of it – effectively ended on or around 10 May 1941 with the "Moonlight Blitz" on London, although there were sporadic raids in the days and weeks afterwards. Towards the end of the month, the newspapers were talking about a "lull" in the bombing, and thus did it fade away. Before that, on 13 May, news broke of the capture of Deputy *Führer* Rudolf Hess, who had parachuted into Scotland, ostensibly on a peace mission. Even to this day, aspects of his story are shrouded in mystery. But one thing is absolutely clear. Hess did bring a peace offer, which he asserted that Hitler would accept immediately, and which differed little from the earlier proposals.[32] Had Hitler actually approved the mission, it would have been entirely in character, and rather appropriate.[33] The Battle of Britain having been launched with a flurry of peace offers, ended as it started, with another peace offer.

Back in 1941, the Hess affair dominated the headlines for a short while but it was soon displaced by the German adventure in Crete – where its airborne invasion was narrowly successful, but at huge cost. In an example of what might have happened if *Sealion* had ever been launched, the Royal Navy over the night of 21–2 May 1941 decisively beat off a seaborne invasion, with a force of three cruisers and three destroyers, sinking twenty-two of twenty-five vessels. This was despite the *Luftwaffe* having complete air superiority in the daylight hours.[34]

Soon enough, another disaster for British arms was replaced, in the English media, by the drama of the sinking of the Bismark – for once a small victory and a cause for celebration after the stunning loss of HMS *Hood*. In time, all that was left of the Battle of Britain were the memories. But who was to claim the credit for a battle won?

15.

To the victor the spoils

In previous years a Civil Defence Day has been organised in the autumn. A suggestion has now been made that a "Battle of Britain Sunday" should be held in September, to celebrate the Battle of Britain in 1940.

War Cabinet minute, 19 July 1943

On the question of who should take the credit for "winning" the Battle of Britain, the blunt answer could be, as already addressed, the Russians. In their heroic and unexpectedly successful defence of the motherland, they prevented the *Luftwaffe* returning in force to northern Europe for Battle of Britain, round two.

A more sterile debate, however, rests with the narrow definition of the battle, with the focus on who can claim credit for preventing the invasion – assuming it was ever going to happen. There, the argument veers between RAF Fighter Command and the Royal Navy, with even the mighty RUSI (Royal United Services Institute) intervening in the debate.[1] But even to entertain that debate is to miss the point. The Battle of Britain – agreed by both sides, and evaluated exhaustively here – was a three component battle, fought over supplies, territory and morale – the blockade, invasion and attack on morale (the Blitz). Any one of the components could, potentially, have been decisive.

We have argued here, that Britain was never seriously at risk from an invasion, and the blockade could not have forced a decision in 1940 because the Germans did not have the means to make it happen. In the sense that the battle for morale could have been lost, the decisive battle was the Blitz – which was an integral part of the Battle of Britain. In that limited sense, the people won the battle.

Whether there is any agreement with that view or not, however, no one who has any familiarity with the events in Britain during the latter half of 1940

– and indeed the early months of 1941 – could fail to be moved by them. Nor can it reasonably be denied that the people played a heroic and central part in those events. But, of those who wish to argue that RAF fighter pilots played an important role, many seem to feel the need to do so at the expense of the people. The people must be written out of the script, awarded only places in the supporting cast, in order that the heroism of the airmen can shine through.

Much of this is the result of intellectual laziness. It is easier to present a simplistic "shoot 'em up" narrative than it is properly to describe and analyse a series of complex historical events. But there seem to be other, more profound reasons why history should have been distorted, and why that distorted account should have prevailed – reasons which suggest that our history was stolen rather than simply lost. The "airmen as victors" was a deliberate artefact, created for a number of reasons.

The first and most obvious is that the fighter battle made good propaganda. And, at the time, that was very much needed by the government's propaganda chief – Duff Cooper. He was the man, it will be recalled, whose inept and provocative "Silent Column" campaign had alienated both the public and the media, while his other attempts to tighten censorship, his information gathering exercises and then his poor judgement in sending his son to the safety of America made him the story.

Then the ineptitude of his Ministry, in its cumbersome and insensitive censorship, excluding important information and slowing down the publication of other material, eventually had more people turning to Lord Haw-Haw's German radio propaganda station for their information than tuned into the *BBC News*. Cooper's efforts in the early stages of the battle were, to put it mildly, disastrous.

Just as public and media tension over the "Silent Column" campaign was at its highest, though, the air war erupted, offering what appeared to be spectacular victories. Home Intelligence indicated that reports of RAF achievements went down well and one then saw the Ministry of Information enthusiastically publicize the air battle. Over sixty years before Jo Moore observed that the 9/11 disaster had been "a good day to bury bad news", the MoI had discovered its own ways of driving unwelcome headlines off the front pages.

Crucially though, the battle and "the few" had another strong propaganda dimension, linked as they were so intimately to the German invasion. Churchill, right from the beginning of the battle, was extremely doubtful that the invasion would be launched, and was then confident that it would be repelled if troops were ever landed. But, as he confided to his private secretary, he needed the threat to focus the minds of the people and to inject a note of urgency into the formation of a new Army, the one which he hoped would take Britain back to France.

With morale fragile, however, the perception of the threat had to be managed. Thus, Churchill had to have a winning battle, an ongoing drama to which he could point as demonstrating Britain's continued and successful resistance. Initially, according to Home Intelligence, the Royal Navy served that function, with the RAF gaining little public profile. But Navy anti-invasion routines lacked glamour and were largely invisible. Churchill first sought to employ the RAF's bombing campaign, but that too was invisible. By contrast, the fighters were wheeling and cavorting over the heads of the people, their gunfire audible, their vapour trails etched in the sky. They provided the necessary theatre, and the high-profile evidence of resistance.

There was, however, a third dimension. Focusing on the "shoot 'em up" narrative served to obscure the political and diplomatic manoeuvring. The British Government, with the approval of Churchill, entertained multiple German diplomatic approaches. These appear to be far more important than has been acknowledged. Through the early stages of the battle, there was continuous dialogue between the parties while Hitler sought to bring the UK to the negotiating table and discuss peace terms.

That reflected Hitler's dilemma. Although Britain's land defences were weak, and she had yet to organize and re-equip her Army, his own forces were unprepared for a major amphibious assault. And, while the *Wehrmacht* made its preparations, the British Army was strengthening by the day. The RAF had been perilously weakened by the campaign in France, but it was relatively well organized and was also strengthening. The Navy was already strong, highly motivated and well prepared. In all probability, by the time Germany was ready to mount an invasion, Britain would be strong enough to resist it.

Thus, far from seeking to "break us in this island" – which was Churchill's framing – Hitler's best strategy was to undermine British resolve with a series of peace offers. This was a means of destabilizing the fragile political coalition which formed the Churchill Government, and weakening the home front, with a view to achieving regime change. And he had good reason to believe that Britain might respond to a suitably couched offer, if backed by a raft of threats.

In the first stages of the battle, there seem to have been five substantive efforts by the Nazis to seek negotiations – the two via David Kelly in Berne, the contacts with Lord Lothian in Washington after Hitler's "appeal to reason", through Victor Mallet in Stockholm, and then the Hoare contacts in Madrid. There are also claims of attempts to suborn the Duke of Windsor. Then there were the Dahlerus and Plesman initiatives, conducted via Göring.

The fact that Hitler made his appeal in the first place, and the responses to the "feelers", strongly suggests that he believed Britain might have been prepared to negotiate. The issue is not whether Britain would have negotiated, but whether Hitler believed she might. And it is clear that he did. From the British perspective, in the early days, there was every advantage to be gained from playing along. And the intention expressed by Kelly was precisely that, in order to delay the German offensive.

At the time, there were many reasons why the manoeuvres could not have been revealed. Churchill, who had made his reputation on a "no appeasement" platform, could hardly be seen to be talking to the enemy. Moreover, on 4 July 1940, the day of the shelling of the French fleet at Mers-El-Kebir in Morocco, he had specifically told the House – and the nation – that there would be no negotiation. There could be no misunderstanding his message:

> The action we have already taken should be, in itself, sufficient to dispose once and for all of the lies and rumours which have been so industriously spread by German propaganda and Fifth Column activities that we have the slightest intention of entering into negotiations in any form and through any channel with the German and Italian Governments. We shall, on the contrary, prosecute the war with the utmost vigour by all the means that are open to us until the righteous purposes for which we entered upon it have been fulfilled.[2]

On 14 July, in his BBC broadcast, he had actually gone further: "we shall seek no terms, we shall tolerate no parley". He could not be seen to be going back on words so publically and openly declared. And had his reputation survived such a breach of faith, once it had been learned that negotiations were in hand, pressure on him to come to terms might have been irresistible. Thus, it was vitally important to suppress details of the ongoing contacts and present the public with the straightforward message of unyielding resistance.

What applied on a domestic level also applied to America. Had Roosevelt
– and the American public – seen negotiation with Germany as a realistic proposition, the President might have encouraged that endeavour, and withdrawn
support for the prosecution of the war. Thus, only when the rejection of peace
feelers had been immediate and unequivocal, as on 11 September, did the
British feel it safe to tell Roosevelt of an approach.

For these reasons, therefore, there was also sense in keeping attention
focused on the daylight air war, the by-product of which was to strengthen what
was to become the Battle of Britain myth.

But there was also the party political dimension, one which cast Churchill
as leader of the Conservative Party, pitted against the Left Wing which was
challenging him for power after the war. As war leader, we see him having
sought national unity and public commitment, and his bid to capture and
exploit "people power" in his speech of 14 July. Then, he eschewed the idea of
a war "of chieftains or of princes, of dynasties or national ambition". He was
prepared to concede that it was "a war of peoples and of causes".

However, endorsing the concept of the People's War not only contradicted
Churchill's own political doctrine, it conceded the game to his domestic political
opposition. It required of him to define "war aims" and thereby acknowledge
the right of the people to have a say in the management of the war, and then the
peace, the very essence of the Left's platform. This, as a Conservative politician,
soon to become leader of the Party, he was unwilling to do.

Thus, five weeks later, in his speech of 20 August, he very publicly rejected
demands for a statement on war aims. It cannot be a coincidence that, in the
same speech, he characterized the war as one of princes – of élites. What legiti-
mized the transition was the definition of "the few", the gallant young airmen
in their flying machines, dashing to the rescue of the passive many. By creating
that myth, Churchill found the means by which could justify his own political
creed.

Looking more deeply at Churchill's speeches, one can see how they were used
to support this stance. Ostensibly addressed to the nation, to allies and also
the enemy, they make most sense if treated as one side of a conversation. On
the other side was J. B. Priestley. As a political commentator, with his writings,
his column in the *Sunday Express* and his *Postscripts* on the top BBC slot on
Sundays, he could command vastly greater audiences than could Churchill.

Already his rival in political philosophy, he was to become his rival for the affection of the British people – regarded by some as the only broadcaster worth listening to.[3] Largely written out of contemporary histories, he was hugely influential.

The subjects of the conversation were, of course, "People's War" and "war aims" with their overtly Socialist agenda. Churchill presented his case in his speeches and broadcasts, Priestley through his diverse outlets. He represented the "people" who were doing the fighting and suffering. They were entitled to dictate how the war was fought and were earning the right to a "noble future".

How well Priestley had captured the public mood was identified by Michael Foot. In his biography of Labour MP Aneurin Bevin, he noted that the huge response to the *Postscripts* was evidence of the spirit of the age. Publishers were finding they could sell vast numbers of books on political and socio-logical topics. Soldiers were reading in their camp beds and airmen at their depots. Community life, so far from being disrupted by bombs and blackouts, was being richly renewed. Many an air-raid shelter became a miniature mock parliament, with class barriers broken, tongues untied and accents forgotten. And with this new spirit, wrote Foot, went a political ferment directed partly against the squalor of the past and partly in excited hope towards the future and the peace when it came.[4]

Opposing this "political ferment" was Churchill, the party politician, defending the *status quo*. Thus, the conversation between the men became a proxy war, a fight that Churchill could not afford to have with his Labour coalition partners or, openly, with the trades unions. It started when, in response to Churchill's "war of peoples and of causes" on 14 July, Priestley offered the Margate homily. "We're not fighting to restore the past; it was the past which brought us to this heavy hour; but we are fighting to ... create a noble future for all our species", he had told his audience. On 21 July, he repeated the call to go forward "and really plan and build up a nobler world ... in which ordinary, decent folk can not only find justice and security but beauty and delight". This, he said, "is our real war aim".

On 28 July, Priestley continued the theme, but this time he enlisted the aid of "our lads in the RAF". In his talk on 4 August, he then characterized the war as "between despair and hope", with his almost feline swipe at the Prime Minister's rhetoric, declaring: "We must not only summon our armed forces, wave our flags and sing our national anthems, but we must go deeper and by an almost mystical act of will, hold to our faith and hope". So it was that Churchill, in his speech of 20 August was trying to claw back lost ground and regain the political initiative. His "few" was not just rhetoric, or a reaction to the drama he had seen at Park's headquarters. It was the response to Priestley's "many", used to soften his public rejection of a statement of war aims, in what was quite a deliberate snub to the Left.

Three days afterwards, Churchill was confronted by something of an internal rebellion, when the War Cabinet approved Duff Cooper's "war aims" committee, charged with looking at a plan which had been instigated by the "socialist" Nicolson. Churchill intervened in the debate, and steered the discussion to his ideas on European reconstruction, thereby avoiding a discussion on domestic reforms, which were also part of the Cooper package.

Then, on 18 September, there was Churchill's next speech in the Commons. Delivered in the wake of the "great victory" in the air, his pitch was an overt appeal to authority, with his reference to "responsible officers of the Royal Air Force". In making it, he asked the public to keep the production lines rolling. He was no longer appealing the "tough fibre of the Londoners". It was more a Soviet-style call to maintain tractor quotas. The population had to prove itself "worthy of our boys in the air" – the élite which was so nobly saving it from the ravages of the Hun.

But Churchill did not only have the public to deal with. He had his "enemy within", his own political allies such as Cooper and Smuts who were pursuing a declaration of war aims. Trades union leaders and many others, not least the highly influential H. G. Wells, also continued to fight for this cause – with considerable support from the press, and in particular the *Daily Mirror* and the *Sunday Pictorial*. Hostile press articles had given Churchill particular problems in late September and early October, specifically over the Dakar operation. But it was significant that he had also taken exception to the comments in the *Mirror* on the People's War, and taken them so seriously. They "stood for something most dangerous and sinister, namely, an attempt to bring about a situation in which the country would be ready for a surrender peace".[5]

This brought forward yet another dimension to the Battle of Britain. The "victory" in the air was used as a bastion against criticism. From political friend and supporter Hastings Lees-Smith on 8 October came the declaration that victory in the Battle of Britain was "more important than anything which happens elsewhere, even at Dakar". This dynamic was seen again after the ignominious retreat from Greece, the defeat in Crete, the fall of Singapore in February 1942 and of Tobruk in June of the same year. Time and time again, when under attack for the failures of war policy, Churchill was to refer to the shining example of his 1940 "victory". Until El Alamein, this was the only major success he could offer. He talked it up as a victory because it was the only one he had.

By October, therefore, the die had been cast. Churchill had justified his political stance with the aid of the Battle of Britain and "the few", and used them to bolster his leadership. But he still had rebellious newspapers to deal with and, although a sort of resolution in the "subversive press" affair had been reached by 15 October, there were to be further battles. By October, of course, the Blitz was at its height, but on the 15th, Cooper's responses on war aims in the adjournment debate came perilously close to contradicting the Prime Minister in public.

Faced with this ongoing rebellion, Churchill could express sympathy with the people but he could not acknowledge their role in preventing defeat without conceding the political game. Thus, we see him in the House of Commons on 5 November, talking of the "danger of invasion … diminished by the victories of the Royal Air Force" and of the "plain fact" that the defeat of the invasion, "constitutes in itself one of the historic victories of the British Isles and is a monumental milestone on our onward march".

On 19 November, Churchill was again in the House, again refusing to commit to a declaration on war aims. But a further revolt was growing inside the War Cabinet when, the next day, "the general feeling" was for "some general statement of the essential fundamentals".

Lord Halifax attempted to put clothes on that "general feeling" on 13 December 1940, when he took it upon himself to present a statement in his own name. "The people of Great Britain and all those who stand with them in this war", he declared, "are fighting to realise the hopes of millions of men and women throughout the world who desire above all things the right for themselves and their children to live their lives in freedom, security and peace". This was circulated to the War Cabinet on 7 January 1941, and discussed on 20 November.[6]

Churchill, of course, could not accept this – but he could not reject it out of hand either. Instead, he damned it with faint praise. It was "admirable in many respects", but it would not in its present form, "impress public opinion". With that, the matter was never again raised in the War Cabinet and, in due course, Cooper's high-flown "war aims" committee got converted into the very pedestrian and practical "reconstruction committee". Cooper was packed off in early 1941 to become Resident Cabinet Minister in Singapore, as far away from Whitehall as possible.

On 9 February 1941, Churchill then made his "give us the tools and we'll finish the job" broadcast. In this, he mocked "Herr Hitler", who "did not dare attempt the invasion" – yet another allusion to the "victory" of the few. Only then did he allow that the bombing "so far from weakening the spirit of the British nation", had "only roused it to a more intense and universal flame than was ever seen before in any modern community". There was no linkage between the resistance to the bombing and that "victory".

Furthermore, to give the broadcast, he had claimed Priestley's slot, which had already been advertised in the *Radio Times*. On 16 February, Priestley – only recently back on air – delivered that talk he would have given earlier. But the following week, under considerable attack from factions within the Conservative Party, he retaliated with an attack on the "Commanders from the Carlton Club". These were, he said:

> [T]he gentlemen who tell me in public to stick to my business of writing books and plays, forgetting that they have made such a mournful hash of their business of running the world that I can no longer attend to mine, even if I wanted to.[7]

The next week the talk was again cautious, but on Sunday 16 March, Priestley threw caution to the wind and dedicated his talk to merchant seamen, declaring:

> We owe them something more than sentimental speeches, made at a time when our lives depend on their skill and courage and sense of duty. We owe these men a square deal. In the last war, when they served us so well we praised them to the skies, clapped them on the back, and stood 'em drinks. What we didn't stand them, though, were better conditions and a reasonably secure future. We've no right to be praising men one year and then ignoring them a year of two afterwards.[8]

That was a heresy too far. The people's favourite had to go. He was taken off air, the executioner Duff Cooper. It was always suspected, though, that it had been on the insistence of Churchill. Six months later, on 8 September 1941, Priestley was to publish his tract called *Out of the People*, which set out fully his "programme for social and political reform, and for a better world for the ordinary man".

By then, the counterstroke was already in place. Only ten days after Priestley had been fired, on 28 March 1941, the Air Ministry produced the official account of the Battle of Britain in its pamphlet of the same name. Deliberately partisan – "propagandist", according to George Orwell – it was a paean of praise for "the few", referring exclusively to "the part played by the Royal Air Force in the victory". Furthermore, it only covered the fighting from 8 August to 31 October 1940. Like the Hundred Years' War, the battle was being "invented" after the event.

Written by Hilary St George Saunders, the author of several published works, 50,000 copies of the pamphlet were printed. They sold out within three hours. A reprint of 300,000 was immediately arranged. By November 1941, 3,750,000 copies had been sold and, by 1 July 1942, when a "bitterly disappointed" St George Saunders resigned from the Air Ministry to become a House of Commons assistant librarian, sales of over 6,000,000 were being claimed.[9] From 31 March to 9 April 1941, the pamphlet was fully serialized in the *Daily Express*, the final part headed: "These men saved England". The people were being downgraded and offered alternative champions.

What was not properly realized was that this pamphlet was setting such an intensely political agenda. There is no evidence that its publication coming so soon after Priestley had been fired was anything other than a coincidence. But it was a very convenient one. For Churchill, the Battle of Britain had become a talisman with which to ward off criticism, and the ideal antidote to Priestley and his subversive ideas. In 1941, he was to mention it in the House of Commons 116 times, more than any other politician.

There now comes another dimension. It takes us away from the party political field into RAF internal politics. This becomes apparent in the May of 1941, just two months after the publication of the Air Ministry's pamphlet, with the publication of a book called *The Battle of Britain 1940*. It was written by James Spaight, recently retired Principal Assistant Secretary at the Air Ministry. But as well as the fighter battle, he covered in detail the Bomber Command "counter-offensive", together with Coastal Command and Fleet Air Arm activities. These, he declared, were an integral part of the battle. "All alike have the same purpose and contribute to the same end, the defeat of the attempt to subjugate Great Britain here at home".[10]

The book took on its political edge through the author of its foreword, Marshal of the RAF, Viscount Trenchard, sworn enemy of Dowding, a conspirator in his downfall, and a champion of strategic bombing. Spaight's book was self-evidently an attempt to strengthen the image of Bomber Command, an issue of special significance when all the different Commands were competing for scarce resources. And nor was this the only attempt. Another book published in 1941 was entitled *So Few*, recounting the "immortal record of the Royal Air Force". The series of short stories again gave coverage not only to the fighters but to Bomber Command, and even the exploits of the crew of a Sunderland flying boat, citing Churchill's "airmen" in his 20 August speech.[11]

The counteroffensive came from Dowding himself. Despite being the architect of the battle so vividly described by the Air Ministry, he had not been mentioned in its pamphlet. An offended Churchill suggested this was the equivalent of the Admiralty telling the tale of Trafalgar without Lord Nelson. As a result, the Air Council asked Dowding to write his own account, which was delivered in the form of an official "despatch" on 20 August 1941, exactly a year after Churchill's "the few" speech. Even though it was not published until 11 September 1946, then in the *London Gazette*, it was circulated widely and became hugely influential. This was the next step in locking in a myth that downgraded the role of the people.

Through this despatch, Dowding defined a new start date for the battle. Somewhat arbitrarily, he says, he chose 10 July 1940, arguing that heavy attacks made against Channel convoys on that day "probably constituted the beginning of the German offensive". To him, the weight and scale of the attack indicated that "the primary object was rather to bring our fighters to battle than to destroy the hulls and cargoes of the small ships engaged in the coastal trade".

Luftwaffe air ace Adolf Galland, in his autobiography, was less certain. "I should not care to say which one of the three following strategic aims was responsible for the order to gain air supremacy," he wrote, "the total blockade of the island, the invasion, or the defeat of England according to Douhet concepts". He added: "I rather doubt if the General Staff knew themselves, because during the course of the Battle of Britain the stress was put on all of them in turn".[12]

Nevertheless, Dowding's unsupported – and partisan – beliefs defined the battle as it is now known, its start date and end, the timing running from 10 July to 31 October 1940. In so doing, he strengthened the image of a duel between the *Luftwaffe* and RAF Fighter Command. But Dowding could not have known the bigger picture. He was offering an opinion, from a very narrow perspective. But it was not the opinion of a dispassionate historian. Rather, this was a man deposed by his enemies, writing of his own place in history before those enemies beat him to it.

Much has been written of Dowding's demise, of the unfairness with which he was apparently summarily dismissed and of the tedious office politics that attended it. But it has to be said that, while his planning and leadership doubtless saved the Fighter Command from destruction, he was not able to vanquish the night bomber. Towards the end of 1940, it was the night bomber menace which was exercising the War Cabinet, and it was this which was threatening morale and the war effort. The politicians were only too aware that assurances that the scourge would be defeated were wearing thin and that they were running out of ideas and options.

Unfortunately for his personal reputation, in the closing stages of his career Dowding had presided over failure. *Luftwaffe* bombers were roaming the night skies of Great Britain, virtually unchallenged. When the name of his replacement on 18 November 1940 had been announced, the *Express* had declared: "Sholto Douglas is the man of the hour. His task is to stop the German night bomber". That identified, far more than a shelf-full of biographies, what was really going on. But, in writing his account of the Battle, creating his own history, Dowding was not going to dwell on his failures. The people's battle did not feature in his account – it could not, without raising uncomfortable questions about his performance and the role of his precious Fighter Command.

The narrative was then further strengthened by the manner of Dowding's passing. It conferred on him a certain mystique of "victimhood" and polarized opinion. Acceptance of his narrative became a gesture of solidarity among those whom he called his "chicks". It also, it seems, attracted a powerful friend. On 15 September 1941, two years after the day when Fighter Command had claimed (falsely) to have destroyed 185 German aircraft, Dowding hosted an anniversary party for 12 of "the few". The *Daily Express* celebrated the occasion by giving it the front-page lead, with a photograph of the line-up. One of these "few" was

Wing Commander Max Aitken, son of Lord Beaverbrook, proprietor of the newspaper. The *Express* was to become one of the most prominent champions of the Dowding version of the battle.

The *Daily Mirror* covered the event as well, also retailing a claim by Dowding that the RAF had "stopped the invasion". But the following day, it ran a news piece headed: "They also fought". It had a photograph depicting a "typical East End group" – men, women and children from the East End. Heroes themselves, said the paper, those folk in the picture are some of "the many" who "owed so much to so few" in the Battle of Britain. They had been attending an open-air thanksgiving service organized for the RAF, in the grounds of a school in the East End wrecked by bombs on 15 September. But, despite the rearguard action, this was – according to the *Express* – "the second anniversary of the day the Battle of Britain reached its climax and the tide turned in our favour".

On 28 September 1942, Herbert Morrison tried to redress the balance and give the people their due recognition. He proposed to the War Cabinet a celebration of the Civil Defence of Great Britain against the "blitz" of 1940–1. This would be on 15 November – then only six weeks hence – with religious services and local parades. There would also be a National Parade, with token contingents of Civil Defence members from heavily blitzed areas.[13]

Over the last days of October and the first of November, however, the epic battle of El Alamein had been fought and won. On 10 November 1942, Churchill was speaking in the Egyptian Room at the Mansion House, delivering his famous "end of the beginning" speech. With a significant victory under his belt at last, he was confident enough openly to declare his values. He told his audience: "I have not become the King's First Minister in order to preside over the liquidation of the British Empire," an empire he described as "a veritable rock of salvation in this drifting world". The code was obscure, but this was widely seen as a final rejection of calls for a statement on war aims. Maintenance of the *status quo* was his only aim. He had seen off the competition. There would be no "new world order" while he was around.[14]

Only days after the victory, with church bells rung for the first time since the Battle of Britain invasion alert, Morrison's Civil Defence Day was celebrated. Dressed in a naval uniform, the King took the salute from a stand outside St Paul's. The march-past, comprising 1,600 in all, was led by troops of the Anti-Aircraft Command, followed by a small contingent of the RAF. Then came the National Fire Service, the police and contingents of the Civil Defence from all over the country. As they marched, the narrator from *Pathe News* intoned:

> Had it not been for Mr Everyman's courage and endurance in the Battle of Britain, the cause of the United Nations would have been lost beyond retrieve.

The day was the second anniversary of the bombing of Coventry. Perhaps significantly, there was no reference to the celebration in the *Daily Express*. But a long, illustrated article appeared in the *Mirror*. It was headed: "YOUR day and YOUR future …". Morrison was quoted heavily from a BBC broadcast, when he had declared: "[I]t was the self-sacrifice and bravery of ordinary folk which [had] provided the triumphs celebrated on Civil Defence day".

Parades, church services and celebrations were held all over the country, some the following Sunday, when civic dignitaries most often took the salutes. A week later, on 30 November 1942, Morrison's Ministry produced the official account of the Civil Defence of Great Britain. In the detailed, 162-page illustrated pamphlet called, *Front Line*, it made it absolutely clear that the "Blitz" was an integral part of the Battle of Britain. Said Morrison in his *Mirror* article: "It is the people's book of heroism, the story of democracy in action. In my opinion this war has produced no finer story".

The counterstroke came on 19 July 1943, when an item was submitted for discussion in the War Cabinet. "In previous years a Civil Defence Day had been organised in the autumn", it said. But a suggestion had now been made that a "Battle of Britain Sunday" should be held in September, to celebrate the Battle of Britain in 1940. The Blitz of 1940 and 1941 was not mentioned.[15] No source for this "suggestion" was given, but it is not hard to guess its origin. The Cabinet agreed that the new day should go ahead, organized jointly by the Ministry of Home Security, the Air Ministry, the Ministry of Aircraft Production and the War Office – Lord Beaverbrook's ministry.

On 26 August 1943, the *Express* announced that Battle of Britain Sunday and Civil Defence Day would be celebrated on 26 September. The date, it said, "falls within the most decisive phase of the massed attacks by the Luftwaffe". Prayers and ceremonies would commemorate the deeds of the RAF, AA gunners, Civil Defence, Observer Corps and aircraft workers. The same announcement appeared in the *Yorkshire Post*, but with some additional detail. The day was intended to commemorate "not any particular raid or raids but the defeat of the whole of the massed attacks which were aimed first at the invasion of this country and later at the destruction of the morale of the civil population". Even at this stage, the people and the RAF were equal partners.

On 14 September 1943, Dowding held another of his luncheon parties, again surrounded by pilots who took part in the battle. He told the *Express* that he was convinced that "divine intervention" had guided the RAF to victory. *Flight* magazine on 23 September, announcing the forthcoming celebration, wrote that "[h]istorians will surely acclaim that great and prolonged struggle as one of the decisive battles of the world". Then, on 27 September, the *Express* headlined a piece with: "BATTLE-OF-BRITAIN DAY. THE MANY REMEMBER THE FEW", offering a picture of marching RAF officers. The King, again taking the salute from a stand outside St Paul's, this time wore an RAF uniform. The *Mirror* had a large article spanning two pages, headlined, "In proud remembrance of the few", the strap declaring: "King leads the nation's thanks". The role of the people had begun to disappear.

What began to appear at this time was the Battle of Britain film made by the US Army Special Service Division, directed by Frank Capra, a Hollywood filmmaker of some fame. The fourth in the "Why We Fight" series, it had been made to inform and motivate American conscripts, but the 52-minute film was now being shown freely in British cinemas. In what was described as a "generous tribute" to Britain, it rather blurred the line between Dowding's battle and the Blitz. The narrative covered the December fire-bombing of London, characterizing the battle as the "people's war" yet finished with praise for the RAF and a quote from Churchill's "few" speech. But the outcome of the battle was that "not one single Nazi soldier set foot on British soil". The battle and the invasion were becoming inexorably linked.[16]

Of interest was a sequence some seventeen minutes into the film, where a British fighter was shot down in an air battle and crashed into the sea. The clip was Pilot Officer Mudie's Hurricane on 14 July 1940, and shortly afterwards the mortally wounded pilot was seen parachuting into the Dover Straits. Seconds more into the clip, however, a Walrus amphibian roared into the picture to pick up a smiling airman in a dinghy. As identified from *Flight* magazine, that particular sequence had not been shot until the late spring of 1942.[17] The time elapsed between the two sequences in the film was less than 20 seconds but in real life it was about two years. The impression presented was false. Such is the power of the imagery, though, that many people, even to this day, believe it represents the truth.

The thrust of the piece mirrored the line projected in an Air Ministry pamphlet, published in June 1942, called *Air Sea Rescue*. This extolled the virtues of a fully-fledged service, omitting to inform that it had only just come into being. With this and the Capra clip, the Air Ministry had perhaps expended more energy in 1942–3 on telling the public about its rescue services than in 1940 it did in actually providing them.

By 1944, there was no longer even a hint of a Civil Defence Day. Battle of Britain Sunday, celebrated on 17 September, saw the light blue ensign of the RAF flying over London from Westminster Abbey. Dr B. P. Simpson, the Bishop of Southwark, preached the sermon. The RAF, "that splendid child", had smashed completely the first move of the most powerful force this world has seen, saved us from invasion, given us respite and turned the enemy on to his eastern attempt which was to prove, thank God, his complete undoing.[18]

For Churchill, though, memories of the battle and even his performance as a war leader were not enough to win him continued tenure as prime minister. In the 1945 General Election, he chose to campaign with "Give us the tools, and we will finish the job", the slogan he had minted in February 1941. But, on 5 July, the people rejected the old man, his Empire and his *status quo*. They wanted a New Jerusalem and gave the tools to the Labour Party which was campaigning under the slogan "And now win the peace", with posters using Churchill's trademark V-sign. Clement Attlee was swept into power, to deliver the National Health Service, nationalization, a sterling crisis and more rationing. Within two years, he had also given away the jewel of the Empire, the Indian subcontinent, independence followed by partition and the slaughter of hundreds of thousands.

Back in 1945, the Battle of Britain anniversary celebrations revelled in post-war extravagance. September fifteen was dominated by the RAF, with a fly-past of 300 aircraft from twenty-five squadrons. It was led by a formation with 15 pilots who had flown in the battle, its leader Douglas Bader, flying a Spitfire.[19] The fly-past was followed by a service in Westminster Abbey, packed with RAF personnel. In a torrent of press copy inspired by "information bulletins" from the Ministry of Information, were references to the "thin blue line". *AP* wrote of the "little band of pilots", of whom Winston Churchill had said: "Never in the course of human history have so many owed so much to so few".[20] The transition was complete. The RAF "owned" the battle.

Then, on 25 October 1951, when the Attlee Government in a snap general election sought to increase its narrow majority after narrowly avoiding defeat in the 1950 contest, Conservatives scraped to a narrow victory. It had been gained almost entirely after a collapse of the Liberal vote, giving them a majority of seats even though Labour had the larger popular vote. Enough people, though, had had enough of the Labour version of New Jerusalem. They voted for nostalgia – the "good old days" of the war, the "Blitz spirit" and Winston Churchill.

At the age of 76, with the country again at war – this time on the Korean Peninsula – Churchill became the second oldest prime minister in history. Just over a month earlier, two days after the eleventh anniversary of the Battle of Britain when a mass formation of 280 aircraft had overflown London, he had broadcast to the nation via the BBC, to tell them:

> Had it not been for those young men whose daring and devotion cast a glittering shield between us and our foe, we should none of us be sitting at rest in our homes this Sunday evening, as members of an unconquered and, as we believe, unconquerable nation.[21]

The people may have won a victory in 1940–1, which they consummated in 1945. But now, in 1951, the old élite was back in power. The true meaning of deeds gone past had been forgotten. The "unconquered people" had been conquered by false memories. Their victory had been "corrected" in the history books, the narrative being strengthened with each passing year as a rash of action books, biographies and autobiographies appeared. Those retailing the exploits of Battle of Britain pilots all reinforced the ownership claim. Typical of the genre was Paul Brickhill's *Reach for the Sky*, on the life of Douglas Bader. It was published in 1954 and made into a film of the same name, first shown two years later.

By 1960, it was being suggested that there should be a memorial to the RAF, erected to commemorate the battle – even though there had already been a chapel in Westminster Abbey dedicated to "the few", unveiled by the King on 10 July 1947. Strangely, there is no specific memorial in the RAF's own church, St Clement Danes, in central London. Established in 1957, though, was what is now known as the Battle of Britain Memorial Flight, now comprising Spitfires, a Hurricane, a Lancaster and a Dakota in flying condition – described latterly as "a museum without walls".[22]

On 9 September 1960, George Ward, then Secretary of State for Air, observed in a report for Cabinet, that the Battle of Britain was still regarded by the general public as a major victory and deliverance, a fight against the odds in our own skies. It had averted invasion and was the first decisive reverse to German Arms. He thus asked his Cabinet colleagues to consider whether the twentieth anniversary might not be marked by a decision to erect a permanent memorial.[23] The Cabinet looked at the issue on 15 September, noting that there had been no national memorials to victories in the Second World War. Mindful of the need to avoid any controversy about the "respective achievements of the three Services in the war", the Cabinet recommended "further consideration" in relation to "the general question whether there should be memorials commemorating other victories in the Second World War".[24]

The following year, on 11 April 1961, Harold Watkinson, then Defence Secretary, reported, only to conclude that it was doubtful whether there would be much, if any, support, either for a single memorial to victory in the Second World War, or for a series of memorials to particular victories. Nevertheless, he observed in his two-page report, "It may well be that the Battle of Britain occupies a special place in the minds of people". But he told the Cabinet that, if the battle was to be commemorated, "it would be right for the memorial to be dedicated, not only to the Royal Air Force, but also to all who helped to make the victory possible".[25]

With Prime Minister Harold Macmillan in the chair, the Cabinet considered the report on 25 April. The discussion:

> showed that the Cabinet were doubtful whether there was any appreciable demand for a Battle of Britain memorial and whether it would be fitting to select that particular victory as the one most appropriate for commemoration by a national memorial.

It then agreed that "it was undesirable in general to provide national memorials to victories in the Second World War", although it was suggested that if the University of Kent, then under consideration, was established, there might be some suitable commemoration of the Battle of Britain within it.[26]

After other attempts to revitalize the issue, it was not until 1993 that an ultimately successful campaign to erect a memorial was launched, this time by the Battle of Britain Historical Society. It culminated in the unveiling by Prince Charles and the Duchess of Cornwall on the 18 September 2005 of a monument on the Embankment, at a cost of £1.65 million, paid for by public subscription.[27] The legend was now cast in bronze, a tableau of "the few" racing for their aircraft, so perpetuating the idea of the élite coming to the rescue of the masses.[28] The idea was well-intentioned and "the few" deserved their recognition – but so did the many. Yet their victory had been stolen from them.

Epilogue

Truth is something which can't be told in a few words. Those who simplify the universe only reduce the expansion of its meaning.

Anais Nin, 1903–77

We do not experience events in nice, neat categories. In real life, they come at us jumbled together, the edges blurred, the categories indistinct or non-existent, with confusion and overlaps. Therefore, we are grateful for the efforts of historians who supply a degree of coherence, and explain the significance of events that would otherwise be obscure.

However, the process goes too far if it confers clarity and certainty that does not exist. And that is the case when the Battle of Britain is presented as a straightforward, "shoot 'em up" event, with a clear outcome. The battle is far more complex, played out at multiple levels, with an outcome which is more obscure and difficult to read than is often presented. For it properly to be understood, it cannot be left as a series of unrelated parts. Those parts need to be integrated, to make a balanced whole.

To acknowledge this does not in any way diminish the bravery, dedication and courage of the "few". It does not make Churchill any worse – or better – a war leader. It does not change the outcome one iota. The complexity makes it a far more interesting battle than the one-dimensional narrative with which we are familiar. It allows for more actors, playing a wider range of roles, each with their own significant inputs. The action becomes more nuanced.

This was not simply a fighter battle, with "noises off". The diplomatic manoeuvring, for instance, lends an important dimension to the battle, when seen as part of the whole, and not something detached from the action. The home front was not quaint local colour, to provide a background for the deeds of the gallant pilots. The people were part of the battle, caught up in a total war where technology had allowed the aggressor to bypass the defending forces. The people deserve recognition for what they achieved.

The same applies to the other branches of the RAF and the other Armed Services – and the merchant marine. James Spaight, in his 1941 book, was absolutely right to highlight the role of Bomber Command aircrew, that of Coastal Command and the Fleet Air Arm. Their aircrews were just as much part of the battle as the airmen of Fighter Command. It is a travesty that the battle honours go only to fighter aircrew.

Further, it is just as much a travesty to exclude members of the Royal Navy, the merchant marine and the many ancillary services, from the Anti-Aircraft Command and Observer Corps, to the members of the Royal National Lifeboat Service, who did sterling and often very dangerous work.

But then properly to define the role of the people in general, who took part in the battle either within some organized, uniformed service, or as ordinary people who simply endured and survived, not only changes how we perceive our history, but also about how we feel about ourselves – and our governments.

At many levels, we can acknowledge that, under the leadership of Winston Churchill, our government played a poor hand much better than expected. Even if an outright victory was not delivered, what many expected to be certain defeat was averted. But, at another level, we can also accept that some people found themselves in a position where, had they completely trusted and obeyed their government, they might have died. Many of those took the more sensible course of seeking their own salvation, in this case by taking advantage of the shelter afforded by Underground stations, despite active, official opposition.

The result of this spirited episode of rebellion, when the people exerted their will, was that the government conformed to the wishes of the people. In this case, it went about providing the facilities, such as toilets, bunk beds and queuing systems, to make the choice tolerable and safer. And that is how it should be – the government as servant, not master.

It also cannot be denied that some who trusted government – or in the absence of choice, relied on its good sense and fidelity – were killed. These included some of the unfortunates who took refuge in the trench shelters, the reinforced basements and, for want of better provision, shallow Tube stations such as Balham.

But there was another group, the very airmen who are so fulsomely applauded as the "few". They were also let down. Putting their lives at risk, they had a right to expect their government and employer to take reasonable steps to safeguard them. Furthermore, it was in the national interest to do so, fighter pilots being a valuable asset, in short supply and essential to prosecuting the ongoing battle. Through the egregious failing of the RAF to provide anything like an adequate air-sea rescue service many died needlessly, at a critical stage of the battle. And while, in "Digger" Aitkin, there was evidence of how individual initiative could solve the problem, not only did government ignore the lessons, it disbanded the voluntary system – then taking an inordinate time to secure a replacement.

How ironic it was that in July 1940, the First Sea Lord, Admiral Dudley Pound, said of the Hitler regime that complete disregard of losses could be expected if this would help them gain their objectives. At that time, the "ruthless Nazis", with their dedicated air-sea rescue services, took better care of their pilots than did the British.

As to the consequences of its inadequate and lethal policies, the State used its powers of censorship and its propaganda resources to conceal them. That highlights another lesson, that censorship and government power over the flow of information are invariably used to protect the government from the consequences of its own actions, rather than for the purpose intended.

Without taking this too far, we could therefore aver that important lessons which emerge from a wider overview are that, if you rely completely and uncritically on government, its neglect may kill you. Having done so, it will seek to obscure its actions and its responsibility for them. From this, we could further state that, even in times of extreme peril – or, perhaps, especially so – salvation does not lie entirely in government. In such instances, it is necessary to take the initiative and make government conform to the wishes and needs of the people, rather than the other way around. Government is a poor master. But it can be an adequate servant, if forced to be so.

There is also that broader issue. Without doubt, the Battle of Britain was a victory of the people of Britain, those who endured a most grievous and terrifying assault, held fast and survived, without tearing down their government and crying for peace. But, as we have seen, over the years, credit for that most important victory has been stolen from them. They have been recast as supplicants and passive beneficiaries, rather than active collaborators in their own salvation.

To restore that history is to change the way we think about ourselves. We are part of a nation which, in time of great peril, rallied and by collective endeavour engineered its own salvation. With the considerable help of the British Commonwealth, the Empire and the fighting men and women of conquered and captive nations, as well as the USA, Churchill's island people prevailed. That makes us a different people from the passive, shadowy inhabitants of a myth – and all the more powerful. What we could do once, we can do again.

Notes

NOTES ON INTRODUCTION

1   BBC website: http://www.bbc.co.uk/archive/battleofbritain/11431.shtml

2   Even though the aircraft never existed, a Hurricane pilot of No. 213 Sqn claimed to have shot down one over Dunkirk in May 1940. Pilot Officer Boot reported having a dogfight with one in September 1940. Air Marshal Dowding referred to them in his report on the Battle of Britain. German reports of its introduction were part of an elaborate disinformation ploy.

3   A full analysis of Gardner's errors is on the Dover War Memorial Project website: http://www.doverwarmemorialproject.org.uk/Information/Articles/Incidents/Flames.htm

4   BBC Listener Research Report: http://www.bbc.co.uk/archive/battleof-britain/11432.shtml

5   Ship casualty details from: http://www.naval-history.net/xDKWW2-4007-20JUL01.htm

6   See: Dixon (2008) and Ray (2000). These two volumes, in particular, give some of the background to the controversies surrounding Dowding and his conduct of the battle.

7   First published in the London *Evening Standard* of that date. By arrangement, Low's cartoons were often reproduced in the *Manchester Guardian* a few days later.

8   Battle of Britain London Monument website: http://www.bbm.org.uk/partici-pants.htm. There are small variations between different sources.

9   For a lucid account of the anti-aircraft defences, see: Dobinson (2001). The defences were augmented by an ingenious network of decoy sites. Initially dummy airfields, known as K- and Q-sites (respectively for day and night use), were built. By the end of 1941, Q-sites had been attacked 359 times. The airfields from which they had been lured away suffered 358 raids. The idea was extended to create dummy industrial sites, some with decoy fires to attract raiders. Smoke generators were used to conceal real sites. See: Norman (1993).

10 This is the concluding statement in the official Air Ministry account of the battle. See: Anon (1941b).

11 Overy (2001), p. 121.

12 The role of No. 2 Group Blenheims is very poorly recognized. No single source attests to its considerable exploits. This is a significant lacuna, noted by Mike Henry, Editor of the *Blenheim Society Journal*, writing in the *Daily Telegraph* (letters) in May 2003. http://www.telegraph.co.uk/comment/3592017/Bomber-recognition.html

13 RAAF Museum: http://www.airforce.gov.au/raafmuseum/research/units/10sqn.htm

14 The Royal Navy was also multinational, in men and ships, including Empire warships. But some foreign assets were acquired while the Royal Navy destroyed the French fleet (or part of it) in Mers-El-Kebir on 3 July. In a parallel operation, French ships in British ports were seized, including two (obsolete) battleships, four light cruisers, some submarines, eight destroyers and, according to Churchill, "about two hundred smaller but valuable minesweeping and anti-submarine craft". The vessels were manned by about 3,500 Free French. Thus, more French sailors fought in the Battle of Britain than did British fighter pilots. In addition, most of the Polish Navy, comprising about thirty vessels, was already based in Britain, including motor torpedo boats and a complete motor gun boat flotilla. There was also a section of the Royal Navy, comprising escaped Belgian sailors. It manned two corvettes, a squadron of mine sweepers and three patrol boats. There were remnants of the Royal Norwegian Navy and a cadre of escaped Danes. Dutch and Norwegian seaplanes complemented Coastal Command patrols.

15 The firemen eventually included a contingent from the Corps of Canadian Firefighters, who came over to augment the service in 1942. See: Leete (2008).

NOTES ON CHAPTER 1

1 HC Deb 18 June 1940 vol. 362 cc.51–64.

2 War Cabinet: WP (40) 168. 'British strategy in a certain eventuality.' National Archives.

3 Douhet (1998). The currently available edition is a reprint of the 1942 English translation. The volume consists of five separate works: the original 1921 edition of Command of the Air, a second edition of 1927, a 1928 monograph titled "Probable aspects of future war", a polemical article of 1929 called "Recapitulation" and the 1930 study "The war of 19–". Douhet's book was translated into German in 1935, but many of his writings were translated as early as 1929. Douhet is widely quoted but, one suspects, little read in the original. And it is unlikely that all of the pundits citing effects of "terror bombing" in this period had actually read his works. He is very rarely cited in the British press, with only two references recorded in the *Daily Express* between 1934 and 1945 – both in 1939.

4   HC Deb 10 November 1932 vol. 270 cc.525–641. Baldwin was later to tell the Commons: "Since the day of the air the old frontiers have gone, and when you think of the defence of England you no longer think of the chalk cliffs of Dover. You think of the Rhine". Reported on the front page of the *Daily Mirror*, 31 July 1934.

5   After the bombing, sleeping gas then subdued the population, following which the city was invaded by parachutists. The film thereby also raised fears of airborne invasion (and a gas attack, with the ubiquitous issue of gas masks), so much so that the Home Guard, established on 14 May 1940 following a radio appeal by War Secretary Anthony Eden, were originally known as "parashots". Their formal title, Local Defence Volunteers (LDV – more unkindly as "Look, Duck and Vanish") was changed to Home Guard on 20 July 1940.

6   This was certainly the view of Tom Harrisson, founder of Mass Observation. He argued that many Conservative and Liberal leaders never trusted the masses and "in a way deeply, privately, despised them". This "continuing, deeply ingrained contempt for the civilian masses" undoubtedly had major effects on expectations. See: Harrisson (1976), pp. 21–5.

7   Michael I. Handel (1973), *Intelligence and Military Operations*. International Specialized Book Service. Cited by Earle Lund, USAF. *The Battle of Britain A German Perspective*. Joint Doctrine Air Campaign Course Campaign Analysis Study. 24 January 1996.

8   For the texts of Hitler Directives, I have relied on Trevor-Roper (1964).

9   War Cabinet: WP (40) 168, *op cit.*

10   Nuremberg Documents IMT 1776–PS. Parts were also read into the record during the cross examination of Alfred Jodl, on 6 June 1946. The authorized translation and of the document and the transcripts of the hearings are available online, the latter as part of the Nizkor Project. An excellent analysis is in Ansel (1960).

11   War Cabinet: WP (40) 169. 'British strategy in the near future.' National Archives.

12   Milward (1977), p. 275.

13   The techniques were well recognized, even at this early stage of the war. By far the most complete exposition was the book, *The Strategy of Terror* by Edmond Taylor, Paris correspondent of the *Chicago Tribune*. He writes of the "fabrication by propaganda of emotionally potent ideologies for the sole purpose of using them as political or diplomatic arms", demonstrating how fully integrated were the propaganda, diplomatic and military arms (pp. 106 *et seq.*). Published in July 1940, the book is reviewed by *Time* magazine: http://www.time.com/time/magazine/article/0,9171,764180-1,00.html

14   The German–Soviet Pact, also known as the Ribbentrop–Molotov Pact, was also an issue. The considerable number of Communist sympathizers in the Labour movement were opposed to a war which might threaten the Pact and provoke

a German invasion of the Soviet Union. Among these sympathizers, sentiment changed markedly after the German invasion.

NOTES ON CHAPTER 2

1 Details throughout the text relating to the German invasion planning, and related events, are a composite, mainly drawn from Assmann, Klee and Wheatley, augmented by Grinnell-Milne and Taylor, with occasional reference to Fleming and Robinson. See: the bibliography.

2 Taylor (1982) .

3 This is a theme to which Shirer constantly refers in his *Berlin Diary*.

4 The reference to Sweden was highly significant. In 1939, a Swedish businessman by the name of Birger Dahlerus, and friend of Hermann Göring, had been involved in an abortive attempt to broker peace with the British Government. In early July, he had met Lord Halifax in Germany. The Foreign Secretary had then met Göring. On 27 August, Dahlerus had flown to London to meet Neville Chamberlain, Halifax, Sir Horace Wilson and Sir Alexander Cadogan, in what has been called the Dahlerus Mission. He was again briefly involved in September when Göring was on stand-by to fly to London for last-ditch peace talks. See: Dahlerus (1946) . However, in oral evidence during the Nuremberg Trial (19 March 1946 – transcript online,, see: Nizkor Project), it emerged that Göring and Dahlerus had met in July 1940, when Göring had suggested that "His Majesty the King of Sweden should endeavour to bring the various Powers together for peace negotiations".

5 For details of *Luftwaffe* directives and orders, I have relied on Klee (1955). His work is available online via the US Air Force Historical Research Agency website: http://www.afhra.af.mil/studies/numberedusafhistoricalstudies151-200.asp

6 An account of this raid can be found in Mason (1990), with a more detailed treatment in Saunders (2010).

7 References to Ciano throughout are drawn from his diaries. I have used the 2002 unabridged edition by Phoenix Press.

8 Churchill (1949), *op cit*, p. 239.

9 War Cabinet: WP (40) 264. National Archives. The 10 July Minute was bundled with an exchange of correspondence, dated 18 July.

10 War Cabinet: WM (40) 199. National Archives. The War Cabinet met most days, except Sundays, and most often was chaired by Churchill. Copies of the records of conclusions and associated memorandums are held by the National Archives, in the CAB series – and are also available online in searchable format. References to "War Cabinet" throughout this text relate to the record on the day indicated, unless indicated otherwise.

11 The Duke of Windsor was in Lisbon at the time. Clandestine German overtures were made to him, in the hope that he would support a peace initiative. He did not respond, and sailed on 1 August for Nassau, and his post as Governor of the Bahamas. See: Domarus (1990), p. 2071. Irving (1987b) covers this in some detail.

12 The complete sequence of telegrams is appended to the War Cabinet conclusion WM (40) 199, of 10 July 1940.

13 Kelly (1952), pp. 272–4. See also: Thompson (1966) and Anon (1957), in which Hohenlohe's report of his meetings with Kelly, dated 18 July 1940 are published. The note on Hoare's meeting was also published there.

14 Roberts (1991), p. 244.

15 Kelly, *op cit.*

16 Details from Assmann, and *Appendix: OKW Directives* for the invasion of the UK.

17 The list was assembled by Clive Pontin in his book *1940 Myth and Reality.*

18 Unless otherwise indicated, figures for Fighter Command and *Luftwaffe* losses come from Mason's *Battle over Britain*. Bomber and Coastal Command losses are taken from Larry Donnelly's *The Other Few*. The air fighting narrative is a composite, based on these two sources, and on Wood with Dempster (1969), augmented by James (2000) and others. Naval warfare details are drawn largely from the website, naval-history.net. Individual entries in this narrative are referenced only when additional material is drawn upon.

19 Propaganda policy, *Joint Memorandum by the Minister of Information and the Minister of Economic Warfare* WP (40) 444, 15 November 1940. National Archives.

20 Additional material from an account published on 7 July 2010 in the *Falmouth Packet*: http://www.falmouthpacket.co.uk/news/fpboating/inport/8258392. Deadly_raid_remembered/?ref=rss The date of the attack, as 10 July, is stated in War Cabinet: WP (R)(40) 185. 'Civil Defence Report No. 20.' National Archives.

21 Donnelly (2004), pp. 28–9.

22 Assmann, Klee, Wheatley, *et al.* (composite), *op cit.* In addition, Ansel (1960) provides a very detailed account of this conference: pp. 126–30. See also: Taylor (1967), p. 63, who has it that Räder's main purpose in meeting Hitler was to impress upon him the difficulties and dangers of attempting an invasion, and to win him over to a strategy of economic blockade.

23 A good account of the propaganda effect of exaggerated claims is provided by Campion (2010). For instance, see: pp. 98–9. The issue is discussed at length by Mason (1990) and also in Wood with Dempster (1969).

24 National Archives. File KV 4/186. See also: West (2005) and Irving transcripts (online).

25 Nicolson (1967), *Diaries and Letters*, p. 101.

26 References throughout to "Home intelligence" or the "home front" refer to these reports, unless otherwise stated. See: Addison and Crang (eds) (2010).

27 The policy was not explained fully (to the Cabinet) until 7 October 1940, when it was admitted that "the results of this practice have not been very satisfactory". It had "mystified the public", "aggrieved the Provinces" and "removed from the Ministry of Information its proper function of controlling news". War Cabinet: WP (G)(40) 254. National Archives.

28 War Cabinet: WP (R)(40) 185. 'Civil Defence Report No. 20.' National Archives.

29 Mason and others give brief details of weather conditions in their daily accounts. A more detailed summary has been published by: http://forum.netweather.tv/topic/63129-the-battle-of-britain-weather-diary in the "Weather diary".

30 Brickhill (1954), pp. 131–2.

31 Mason, *op cit*, p. 123.

32 Ibid.

33 Pitchfork (2005), pp. 88–9. See also: *Daily Telegraph*, 16 January 2004 (Obituary): http://www.telegraph.co.uk/news/obituaries/1451743/Group-Captain-John-Peel.html

34 A 46-page analysis was published in 1997 under the title: "Deflating British radar myths of World War II" by Maj Gregory C. Clark, for the Air Command and Staff College Maxwell AFB. Available online: http://www.radarpages.co.uk/download/AUACSC0609F97-3.pdf

35 Wikipedia: http://en.wikipedia.org/wiki/RAF_Bentley_Priory

36 As with the First World War, there were civilian deaths from anti-aircraft fire. Levine (2006), p. 319, describes Theresa Bothwell recalling how a shell had fallen on a church hall in Birmingham, where there was a wedding reception, killing the groom and amputating the bride's legs. Thomas Parkinson describes how an unexploded shell penetrated a domestic kitchen in Kentish Town, killing a young girl.

37 The invaluable Donnelly, *op cit*, with his daily narrative and his account of losses, provides details here.

38 Launched in his own newspaper on 10 July, the campaign had been quietly forgotten by September, long after a scrap dealer had sent Beaverbrook a telegram stating: "Cannot understand your appeal for aluminium scrap. All scrap merchants have large supplies for which there is no demand". The story was summarized in *Private Eye*, 5 October 1962.

39 Details collated from contemporary news reports. A summary is published in *Time* magazine, 29 July 1940. http://www.time.com/time/magazine/article/0,9171,764264,00.html

40 Central to Nazi rhetoric was the concept of the war being "for the unity and freedom of Europe". In September 1939, the Reich Foreign Minister was being

presented with schemes for European unity, declaring the war aims to be the bringing about and guaranteeing of "lasting peace for the European countries. Security against economic strangulation and interference by outside powers". The initial stages involved the creation of a four-year plan, the plenipotentiary for which was Göring. See: Lipgens (1985), pp. 55–6.

41 Hitler's economic plans had been rehearsed widely in the British press, as had the role of Göring who, on the front page of the *Daily Express* of 24 January 1938, was being referred to as "economic dictator".

42 War Cabinet: WP (40) 270. National Archives. The correspondence is bundled, under the one reference, dated 19 July 1940.

43 War Cabinet: WP (G)(40) 153. 'Hitler interview.' National Archives.

44 *Dairy and Letters* (*op cit*), p. 101.

45 An extraordinarily detailed account of events in the north-east, on which this narrative is based, is available at: http://www.ne-diary.bpears.org.uk/Inc/Dindex.html

46 Film footage of the aftermath has been preserved by the National Library of Scotland, available online: http://www.ne-diary.bpears.org.uk/Inc/Dindex.html

47 The weekly editions are held in the National Archives, but are now available online. The official Battle of Britain period is covered by 19 editions, numbered 44–61.

48 Diary references to Alan Brooke, throughout, are taken from Danchev and Todman (2001).

49 References to Colville are taken from Volume 1 of his published diaries.

50 War Cabinet: WP (40) 264, *op cit*.

51 Ansel, *op cit*, refers, marking this as the formal start of the operation, born in "deep pessimism". The report opens: '*Die Landung ist schwierig*' (The landing will be hard).

NOTES ON CHAPTER 3

1 Churchill Centre website: http://www.winstonchurchill.org/learn/speeches/speeches-of-winston-churchill/126-war-of-the-unknown-warriors

2 Such was the fevered atmosphere that, on 10 July, Sir Edward Grigg, Parliamentary Under-Secretary to the War Office, rebuked the House of Commons for sitting until 11.30 p.m., telling them: "At this moment it may be that bombers are over many or our towns. Tonight thousands of our soldiers will be on the alert waiting for an attack which may come". *Daily Express* 11 July 1940.

3 Texts of non-parliamentary speeches are taken from the website of the Churchill Centre and Museum.

4 Texts taken from Hansen (2008).

5 Reported in the *Irish Times*, 16 July 1940.

6 References to Shirer, throughout, rely on his *Berlin Diary* (1984).

7 Cited in Lawlor (1994), p. 62.

8 Comment recorded by Assmann, *op cit*. Ansel cites comment suggesting that Hitler had made the lead-in time short in the hope that the services would find it impossible to meet.

9 War Cabinet: WP (40) 264, *op cit*.

10 Cumming (2010), p. 150. In total, 30,248 lost their lives during the entire war, of 185,000 who served, a death rate higher proportionately than in any of the armed forces.

11 A comprehensive analysis (179 pages) of the German ir-sea rescue services has been written by Lieutenant Colonel Carl Hess, and published by the US Air Force. It is available online: http://www.ibiblio.org/hyperwar/AAF/AAFHS/AAFHS-168.pdf

12 See: Mitchell (1945), pp. 98–9. The basic story was augmented by a series of detailed telephone discussions with staff of the Fleet Air Arm Museum, Yeovil, and the New Zealand High Commission.

13 Trevor-Roper, *op cit*.

14 By far the best technical appraisal of the maritime equipment comes in Schenk (1990). For details of barge conversions, see: pp. 65–94, illustrated by a substantial number of photographs.

15 It is extremely doubtful whether a significant airborne assault could have been mounted. During the invasion of France and the Low Countries, the Germans had lost 475 transport aircraft. On 10 May alone, they lost 157 Junkers Ju 52 transports, mainly in Holland. This was the only aircraft equipped for delivering paratroops and more than a year's production. It would be May 1941 before sufficient aircraft could be assembled for a major assault (Crete). See: Robinson (2005), pp. 115–17.

16 *Dairies and Letters*, *op cit*, pp. 102–3.

17 Wheatley, *op cit*, p. 29.

18 Assmann, *op cit*, p. 8. See also: Ansel, *op cit*, p. 160.

19 Shirer, *op cit*.

20 National Archives: FO 371/24407/92. Roberts, incidentally, had been peripherally involved in the 1939 Dahlerus Mission.

21 Churchill, *op cit*, p. 508.

22 Apart from Mason (1990), plus Wood with Dempster (1969), who give a good account of this action, some of the background to the politics of the Defiant is given in Dixon, *op cit*.

23 See: Lukacs (1990), p. 188–90.

24 The full text of the speech is in Domarus (1990), pp. 2042–63.

25 See: Roberts (1991), a useful text on the role of Halifax.

26 During a telephone conversation on 22 July, Lothian told Halifax: "We ought to find out what Hitler means before condemning the world to 1,000,000 casualties". For context and primary sources, see: David Reynolds (1983), *Lord Lothian and Anglo-American Relations, 1939–1940*. Transactions of the American Philosophical Society, New Series, vol. 73, no. 2. Possibly, far too much is made of this. Had either wished to discover their nature, the essence had been published in the *Frankfurter Zeitung* that day. It is unlikely that the published terms would have been materially different from anything Lothian would have been able to discover.

27 See also: Lukacs, *op cit*, pp. 194–5.

28 Ansel, *op cit*, pp. 161–2.

29 Assmann, *op cit*, p. 10.

NOTES ON CHAPTER 4

1 War Cabinet: WP (40) 275. 'Propaganda for the future.' National Archives.

2 His fine was later reduced to £2, on the recommendation of the Home Secretary. *Sunday Express*, 28 July 1940, p. 1.

3 *Sunday Express*, p. 6: "The Nosey Parkers are having a fine time".

4 Cited in Wheatley, *op cit*, p. 22.

5 Details of the meetings, see: Wheatley, pp. 30–1. Ansel, *op cit*, pp. 162–6 also refers. Assmann deals with it on pp. 14–19. Clearly, this was one of the pivotal meetings of the entire planning sequence.

6 Cited in *Daily Express* 22 July 1940.

7 Hanson, *op cit*, pp. 224–8.

8 Chester Wilmot (1952) notes that Hitler forbade the launching of an air offensive against British ports and cities, "so anxious was he to encourage compromise by maintaining the pretence that he had no quarrel with Britain".

9 Ciano, *op cit*, p. 372.

10 The reference to Sweden is Churchill's own. It is not known whether any initiative was linked with the Swede Birger Dahlerus, and through him Hermann Göring, although the timing is such that Göring may well have been involved (see: note XX, p. XX).

11 Cited at length in the *Yorkshire Post*, 22 July 1940, p. 3.

12 See: Lipgens, *op cit*, p. 61.

13 *Glasgow Herald*, 23 July 1940, p. 3.

14 The old term for the Soviet secret police.

15 Reported in the *Daily Express*, 22 July 1940. It was called the "Rout the rumour rally".

16 Assmann, *op cit*, p. 16.

17 The date is asserted by the website World War II Today: http://ww2today. com/25th-october-1940-u-boats-now-operate-from-france. Elsewhere, it is claimed that Lorient was first used by a U-boat on 7 July. http://www.uboat.net/ flotillas/bases/lorient.htm

18 *Berlin Diary, op cit*, p. 459.

19 Kubizek (1955).

20 *Daily Mirror*, 23 July 1940, p. 12; *Daily Express*, 23 July 1940, p. 6.

21 HC Deb 23 July 1940 vol. 363 cc.597–9.

22 Thompson (1966). See: pp. 148–53.

23 Details in Ansel (1960), who provides the fullest account of the initiative, having interviewed Plesman. There is also a reference to a Dutch peace plan being denied by President Roosevelt in a press conference on 28 July (*AP*). At the same time, London denies receiving a peace document "via Stockholm". Further details come from the KLM corporate history and the Dutch *wittebrugpark* history project website. The latter records that, in May 1941, the Gestapo found out about Plesman's initiative, and that Göring was freelancing. Heydrich was briefed and Göring was confronted with the file. To cover his tracks, he ordered the arrest and imprisonment of Plesman.

24 The front page of the *Daily Mirror* bore the headline: "How your tax will be stopped off pay". Standard rate of income tax was raised to 8s 6d in the pound.

25 HC Deb 25 July 1940 vol. 363 cc.983–4

26 The initiative came from the Vatican, via Cardinal Maglione, the Vatican Secretary of State. Communications had been sent to Rome and Berlin, and to London via the Apostolic Delegate, urging the three powers to negotiate. Maglione was still attempting to bring the parties together on 26 July and did not abandon that endeavour until 2 August. See: Chadwick (1987). There was also an earlier approach from the Papal Nuncio in Berne, which was rejected by Halifax on the direct instructions of Churchill – the minute dated 28 June 1940. See: Wilmot (1952), p. 24, and Churchill, *op cit*, p. 151.

27 Garfield (2005), p. 316.

28 *Berlin Diary, op cit*, p. 461.

29 Lipgens, *op cit*, pp. 65–71.

30 Wheatley, *op cit*, p. 31.

31 Air action, see: Mason *op cit* and Wood with Dempster, *op cit*. The naval action is described, at length, by McKee (1957), pp. 9–15 (paperback edition).

32 Although the attacks on Cooper came from across the political spectrum and from most of the newspapers, the *Daily Express* was especially persistent. Lady Diana, writing to her son the day previously (25 July) wrote of the personal animosity of the newspaper's proprietor, Lord Beaverbook, noting claims that

he had declared he "was not going to stop until he got Papa … out of office". The other target of Beaverbrook's ire was Archie Sinclair. See: Charmley (1986).

33   War Cabinet: (40) 213. 'Conclusions of meeting, Minute No. 12.' National Archives.

34   Roskill (1954), p. 235.

35   Churchill (1947), *op cit*, p. 168–9.

36   The next day (4 August 1940) the *Sunday Express* ran a report under a front-page headline "Last moments of the greatest sea tragedy of all time". It had a picture of the capsized ship, the upturned hull silhouetted with men. The sea was dotted with the heads of men near two upended lifeboats. The report detailed how "the sea at the time was covered with oil which made swimming almost impossible".

37   See: http://victoriaseymour.com/ww2/index.html – another example of websites filling in local detail left out in the grand narratives.

38   *Daily Mirror*, 27 July 1940.

39   A contemporary of Douhet and Billy Mitchell, and strong advocate of strategic bombing – he recognized that the *Luftwaffe* air fleet was not sufficient to break down British resistance.

40   Hanson, *op cit*, pp. 228–31.

NOTES ON CHAPTER 5

1   Churchill, *op cit*, pp. 218–19.

2   War Cabinet: (40) 216. National Archives.

3   Wheatley, *op cit*.

4   This was the yacht in which the Duke and Duchess of Windsor had cruised in the Mediterranean in the summer of 1938. It had been converted into an auxiliary patrol vessel after war had broken out. The loss was reported in the *Daily Mirror* on 31 July 1940, but no location was specified, thereby maintaining the fiction that the raid on Dover Harbour had been unsuccessful.

5   Kent History Forum: http://www.kenthistoryforum.co.uk/index.php?topic=6801.0

6   Supplement to the *London Gazette* 5768, 30 September 1940: http://www.london-gazette.co.uk/issues/34956/supplements/5768 Photographs of the burning ship are published in the Kent History Forum: http://www.kenthistoryforum.co.uk/index.php?topic=6801.0 None of these were published in the contemporary press. The attack on this day was officially confirmed in War Cabinet: WP (R)(40) 185. 'Civil Defence Report No. 20.' National Archives. Only there is it acknowledged that one of the ships was saved by the fire services.

7   http://www.naval-history.net/xGM-Chrono-10DD-19D-Delight.htm

8   Between April and December 1940, mines destroyed 151 ships accounting for 342,000 tons – 10 per cent of the total losses. See: naval-history.net website.

9   Wheatley, *op cit*, p. 33; Ansel, *op cit*, pp. 178–81.

10 According to *General de Flieger* Josef Kammhuber, then on the *Luftwaffe* General Staff, Göring was unenthusiastic in his response – which may have reflected the fact that he was still pursuing freelance peace initiatives. Kammhuber maintained that Hitler himself never intended the air war against England to be anything other than a gambit to force her to negotiate for peace. It was never intended as "a decisive test of strength". In Kammhuber's opinion, Göring was aware of the coming conflict with the Soviet Union and its implications for the *Luftwaffe*. See: Suchenwirth, *op cit*, pp. 64 and 134.

11 http://en.wikipedia.org/wiki/Hull_Blitz

12 Gilbert (1997), p. 595.

13 See: Ansel, *op cit*, pp. 182–6, for the background to the discussion.

14 Wheatley, *op cit*, p. 34; Assmann, *op cit*, pp. 22–5.

15 http://ajrp.awm.gov.au/ajrp/remember.nsf/pages/NT000011C2

16 Page 11. "MPs attack research nosey parkers".

17 HC Deb 31 July 1940 vol. 363 cc.1218–20. See also: Churchill, *op cit*, p. 169.

18 Page 3. "Lancastria: Mr Cooper explains".

19 Calder (1969), pp. 103–4.

20 There is no evidence to support claims that the Duke of Windsor was prepared actively to support Hitler, although he had been cautioned by Churchill about taking a view about the Germans or Hitlerism "which is different from that adopted by the British nation or Parliament". However, there is credible evidence to suggest that, at some stage, Hitler believed the Duke could be suborned, and thus provide the nucleus of a plot to oust the Churchill Government. It is not unrealistic, therefore, to suggest that the Duke's action on this day, in sailing to the Bahamas, may have influenced the timing of Directive No. 17.

21 Trevor-Roper, *op cit*, pp. 79–80.

22 Ansel, *op cit*, pp. 194–7.

23 Overy (1984) argues that Göring's peace initiatives via Dahlerus in 1939 were simply a ploy to detach Britain from France. Irving's far more detailed account (and the Nuremberg transcripts) suggests that the initiative came from Dahlerus. Interestingly, neither author mentions Göring's initiative in July 1940, when it would be hard to dismiss German peace attempts as a "ploy". The evidence suggests that Göring and Hitler genuinely wanted peace, if they could have it on their terms.

24 Taylor, *op cit*, p. 250.

25 *Diaries and Letters, op cit*, p. 104.

26 The reference is in Churchill's second volume on the history of the Second World War: *Their Finest Hour*. This, and a brief mention of the Papal Nuncio's attempt, are the only references in the entire book to peace feelers. It is perhaps

his reluctance to discuss such matters, matched by similar reticence on the part of his official biographer, Martin Gilbert, that lends weight to diverse conspiracy theories.

NOTES ON CHAPTER 6

1   Churchill (1949), p. 474.
2   See: p. 306.
3   Battle of Britain London Memorial website: http://www.bbm.org.uk/BrittonHWA. htm
4   Ansel, *op cit*, p. 199.
5   Excerpts from the broadcasts can be found on diverse websites. One useful site is: http://www.war44.com/secret-war-resistance-espionage-during-wwii/346-william-joyce-treason.html Audio files are also available: http://www.archive.org/details/LordHawHaw-WilliamJoyce-GermanyCalling17-23of23
6   Simpson's work was widely syndicated, often in the *New York Times* and *Wall Street Journal* – archives of which are protected by a paywall. However, they were also published in provincial journals, this one in the *Lewiston Daily Sun*, is freely accessible via Google: http://news.google.com/newspapers?id=NcE0AAAAIBAJ &sjid=jmgFAAAAIBAJ&pg=962,2793419&dq=barges+invasion&hl=en
7   Taylor, *op cit*, p. 226.
8   Assmann, *op cit*, p. 25. Wheatley offers a detailed account: *op cit*, pp. 44–5.
9   A remarkable online database, recording details of the convoys run can be found on Convoy Web: http://www.convoyweb.org.uk
10 Roskill (1954), p. 141; *Daily Express*, 11 October 1940, p. 4: "Let's talk about the weather".
11 Deighton (1977), p. 147.
12 There is no single source for what amounts to another untold story of the Battle of Britain. Statistics and a narrative covering wartime adjustment were issued by the British Railways' press office in 1943, now online: http://freespace.virgin.net/neil.worthington/jx/1943.htm. For obvious reasons, details of wartime transport movements and difficulties were secret, and therefore press coverage was limited. However, the transport issue was rehearsed many times in parliament, from which debates, some of the detail is drawn. As the transport crisis developed, in October and December, Sir John Anderson, then Lord President of the Council, produced two secret and highly detailed reports for the War Cabinet: WP (G) (40) 269 and WP (G)(40) 328, concerning the transport of coal . These reports make very clear the extent of the crisis, which was then discussed several times by the War Cabinet, for instance on 27 December 1940: War Cabinet: 310 (40). Documents from the National Archives.

13 For an overview, see: http://www.secondworldwar.org.uk/merchantnavy.htm

14 Most accounts have the convoy leaving in the afternoon. Saunders (2010) is adamant that it left in the morning. His book offers a detailed account of the action.

15 An account of the night battle is given in McKee (1957). Air and naval detail from Saunders, *op cit*, Mason *op cit*, and Wood with Dempster, *op cit*. There is also a detailed account, with commentary, in James (2000), pp. 49–55.

16 Kent (1971), p. 101.

17 Mason, *op cit*, p. 172 – he puts the date as 12 August and the recipient of the congratulations as Dowding. The Cabinet Record, however, is dated 9 August, with the recipients as stated. War Cabinet: (40) 223. National Archives. The message (to the Secretary of State for Air) was published on the front page of the *Daily Mirror* on 12 August.

18 Colville, *op cit*, p. 250. Two days earlier, Churchill had written to the Minister of Mines asking about coal stocks and, on 13 August, was asking about the stocks held by railways, assuming that "with the stoppage of our export trade to Europe there should be a great surplus just now". Churchill, *op cit*, pp. 515 and 517. It would thus appear that the Prime Minister had little knowledge of the distribution problems being experienced.

19 Colville, ibid.

20 Mason, *op cit*, p. 195.

21 Details from a local history website: http://www.goosemoor-lane.com/history. htm

22 See: http://1940homefrontbritain.com/#/the-liverpool-blitz/4545612278 and also Wirall News, 11 August 2010. http://www.wirralnews.co.uk/wirral-news/ local-wirral-news/2010/08/11/wirral-marks-70-years-since-prenton-maid-became-first-merseyside-blitz-casualty-80491-27032518/2

23 Colville, *op cit*, p. 250.

24 Assmann, *op cit*, p. 28; Wheatley, *op cit*, p. 45.

25 http://cylchgronaucymru.llgc.org.uk/browse/viewobject/llgc-id:1078288/ article/000016932 Morale in Swansea

26 *Daily Telegraph*, 10 August 1940.

27 There is no direct support for this assertion, but there is much evidence, such as contemporary photographs of British fighters. The camera gun port is visible externally, usually fitted on the leading edge of the port or starboard wing root. The absence in so many dated photographs tells part of the story. That there were so few films published (then and now) tells another part. The processing of the films required laboratories, staff and offices. It stands to reason that squadrons based on satellite stations would not have the facilities. Further, the clips do not always show what was expected. A montage produced by the Imperial War

Museum (http://www.youtube.com/watch?v=s9mDy8jH0jo) has a clip (1:40 into the film) showing an RAF Hurricane in the gunsight of an RAF Spitfire flown by Sgt Alan Feary of No. 609 Sqn. There is a fuller treatment of the issue at: http://www.google.co.uk/ig?brand=DSGJ&bmod=DSGJ

28 Orange (2001), p. 98, suggests this might have been in late July. There is an acknowledgement here, though, that a fully equipped air-sea rescue service was not created until August 1941.

29 Richards (1953), p. 160.

30 *Yorkshire Post*, 12 August 1940, p. 3.

31 *Daily Mirror*, 12 August 1940, p. 10, and *Yorkshire Post*, ibid.

32 *Documents Relating to New Zealand's Participation in the Second World War 1939–45: Volume III*, p. 18. Online edition: http://www.nzetc.org/tm/scholarly/tei-WH2-3Doc-c1-11.html

33 Addison and Crang, *op cit*, pp. 316–17, 319 and 321.

34 Assmann, *op cit*, supplement (OKW Directives), p. 9.

35 Jenkins (1986), pp. 40–54.

36 Mason, *op cit*, pp. 182–7. Bishop (2009), pp. 156–9 adds colour to the narrative, as does Deighton, *op cit*, 158–65.

37 See: http://ww2today.com/12th-august-1940-bomber-commands-first-victoria-cross

NOTES ON CHAPTER 7

1 Assmann, *op cit*, supplement (OKW Directives), p. 11.

2 Orwell (2009) *Diaries*, online edition: http://orwelldiaries.wordpress.com

3 Wheatley, *op cit*, p. 47.

4 A detailed account can be found online at: http://www.airmen.dk/p014aalb.htm and http://www.flensted.eu.com/194014.shtml. See also: Donnelly, *op cit*, p. 87.

5 Domarus, *op cit*, p. 2076. These statements, Domarus writes, "once more revealed that Hitler was not at all serious about a landing in England. He was searching for excuses to cancel the undertaking while still preparing for it". See also: Wheatley, *op cit*, pp. 46–7.

6 See: Liddell, *op cit*.

7 The inadequacies of the Hurricane are adequately rehearsed by Leo McKinstry (2010), pp. 220–2. Flight Lieutenant John Cunningham, No. 604 Sqn spoke of "chaps who had just learned to fly, suddenly faced with instrument flying, were not instrument pilots. An awful lot of accidents happened at night". Flying Officer William David (No. 87 and 213 Sqns) described the idea of a Hurricane fighting at night in 1940 as "an absolute waste of time". Levine, *op cit*, pp. 310 and 309.

8   *Diaries*, condensed edition, p. 191.

9   Garfield (2005), *op cit*, p. 336.

10 *Berlin Diary*, *op cit*, p. 471.

11 See: War Cabinet: (40) 222. National Archives. "The Chief of the Air Staff said that there was little to report. The usual anti-invasion reconnaissances had been flown, without yielding any definite results … "

12 Wheatley, *op cit*, p. 47, Ansel, *op cit*, pp. 224–5. See also: Domarus, *op cit*, p. 2076.

13 von Leeb, *Diaries*. Online version (Nuremberg collection) in German, pp. 251–2 at: http://www.flenstedhttp://www.trialreview.info/webgallery_leeb_diary/index.htm#252 (author's translation). See also: Irving (2001), *Hitler's War*, online version, p. 327.

14 Partial transcript published in the *Daily Mirror*, 15 August, p. 3. The broadcast was given little coverage in the British press, but widely covered throughout the Empire and the USA. The *Ottawa Citizen*, for instance, gave it considerably more space, albeit on p. 26 – from which some of the text cited is drawn.

15 Assmann, *op cit*, supplement (OKW Directives), p. 11.

16 *Berlin Diary*, *op cit*, pp. 479–80.

17 Ansel, *op cit*, p. 229. The background is covered in detail by Taylor, *op cit*. The inland waterways were also badly damaged. Army staff at the beginning of August estimated that at least a month would be required to effect repairs. See: pp. 257–8.

18 See: Assmann, *op cit*, pp. 28–31.

19 Gilbert (1991), p. 671.

20 War Cabinet: WP (40) 317. National Archives.

21 Ansel, *op cit*, p. 229.

22 Domarus, *op cit*, p. 2077.

23 Details on the Royal Engineers website: http://www.royalengineersbombdis-posal--eod.org.uk/george_cross.htm

24 Briefly reported in the *Daily Mirror* on 19 August 1940. A longer report was in the *Yorkshire Post* of the same date. The fullest report was the previous day, in the *Observer*.

25 http://www.dornier24.com/pages/stories/story1.htm

26 The events of the day are recorded in great detail by Price (1979).

27 Personal communications. Squadron records for this period have been lost. Details were pieced together by staff at Yeovil FAA Museum. A reference to Walruses being used for air-sea rescue is at: http://www.hmshood.com/crew/biography/gdonnelly_bio.htm

28 Of rather dubious performance, these and other such devices were much favoured by Churchill.

29 Dobinson, *op cit*, pp. 221–3.

30 War Cabinet: WP (40) 322. National Archives.

31 Galland (1955), pp. 47–8.

32 See: James, *op cit*, p. 339: Group Instructions to Controllers, No. 4.

33 http://cylchgronaucymru.llgc.org.uk/browse/viewobject/llgc-id:1078288/article/000016932

34 The narrative is taken from Scott (2000).

NOTES ON CHAPTER 8

1   HC Deb 20 August 1940 vol. 364 cc.1132–274.

2   HC Deb 20 August 1940 vol. 364 cc.1112–13.

3   This appeared in Dowding's despatch on the Battle, published as a supplement to the *London Gazette* on 10 September 1946.

4   There is a useful treatment of the logistics of the Battle of Britain at: http://www.aflma.hq.af.mil/shared/media/document/AFD-100120-058.pdf

5   King (1979), 21 August 1940.

6   http://www.devonheritage.org/Places/Newton%20Abbot/CasualtiesofthebombingofNewtonAbbot.htm

7   Gilbert (1997), p. 720.

8   http://www.shottshistorygroup.co.uk/William%20Morton.htm

9   *Portsmouth Times* (Ohio), 22 August 1940, p. 4.

10 Communiqué published in the *New York Times*, 23 August 1940.

11 Pitchfork, *op cit*, pp. 19–20. As far as I can ascertain, three flights of four aircraft were rotated through No. 11 Group area. Thus, at any one time, no more than four aircraft were available.

12 Wheatley, *op cit*, p. 48.

13 Thiele (2006) explores the development and use of German aerial torpedoes. Fortunately, the *Luftwaffe* did not exploit their successes and aerial torpedo attacks on British shipping in home waters remained relatively rare.

14 War Cabinet: 233 (40). National Archives.

15 http://lower-edmonton.anidea.co.uk/leisure/leisure.html

16 Richards (2006).

17 Recounted at great length in Ray (1994); Orange (2001) and Dixon (2008), among others. It is very easy to gain to impression that this controversy was the main preoccupation of senior Fighter Command personnel.

18 Jenkins, *op cit*, p. 64. This time though – unlike in the earlier raid – there were to be no reports in the press. On the contrary, the emphasis was now on escapes, miraculous or otherwise, of people sheltering in Andersons. On this day, the *Daily Mirror* (p. 12) ran an article headed: "Be wise and be safe", reporting how the shelters had "again proved their worth yesterday". The report recalled: "One received a direct hit, but the two occupants are alive, although badly injured.

Another bomb fell a few feet away from a shelter containing five people. It wrecked six houses and buried the shelter, but the occupants were unharmed. In another instance people in shelters five yards from where a bomb fell were unhurt".

19 Jenkins, ibid.; *News* (Portsmouth), The day the bombs rained down on Portsmouth, 9 July 2010. http://www.portsmouth.co.uk/news/local/east-hampshire/the_day_the_bombs_rained_down_on_portsmouth_1_1257068

20 Churchill, *op cit*, p. 271.

21 *Sunday Express*, p. 6: "A man just back from France says:".

22 *Observer*, p. 8.

23 http://www.bbm.org.uk/Sprague.htm

24 Reporting policy and official censorship, in respect of Birmingham, is explored on this website: http://www.goosemoor-lane.com/dnotice.htm. See also: War Cabinet: WP (G)(40) 254. National Archives, for an official explanation of the policy.

25 Details of the Leeds attack: http://www.yorkshireeveningpost.co.uk/news/latest-news/leeds_bomb_raids_anniversary_1_3017

26 *Berlin Diary*, *op cit*, p. 486.

27 Composite sources, including http://www.naval-history.net/xDKWW2-4008-21AUG02.htm and http://ww2db.com/battle_spec.php?battle_id=207

28 Wheatley, *op cit*, p. 49.

29 *NE Diary*, http://www.bpears.org.uk/NE-Diary/Inc/ISeq_04.html

30 Mason, *op cit*, pp. 247–9. See also: Orange, *op cit*, pp. 121–2, and Ray (2000), pp. 94–5.

31 Klee (Volume 3, p. 66 – online edition) reports the decision having been made by Hitler on 25 August, and conveyed formally in writing on 27 August. See also: Wheatley, *op cit*, p. 48 and Assmann, *op cit*, p. 31. The latter cites the directive, stating: "The Army operation must allow for the facts regarding available shipping space and security of the crossing and disembarkation".

32 Wheatley, *op cit*, p. 49. See also: Klee, *op cit*, p. 66. *OKW War Diary* entry for 30 August 1940. In view of the "small basis" of the operation now ordered, the only objective to be reached could be to strike the *coup de grace* on an enemy already battered down by the air war.

33 Even the previous day, the *Daily Mirror* (p. 7) had reported on the Folkestone raid of 26 August, noting: "A bomb which fell in the back garden of Mr. George Bailey's house made a crater twenty feet deep and thirty feet wide, and damaged houses round about. The edge of the crater was about 2ft. from an Anderson shelter, which was still intact".

34 *Diary*, *op cit*, p. 379. The reference to rejecting the Swedish mediation seems to be a Hitlerite inversion, the peace feelers having come from the Germans and been

rejected by the British. Later, Ciano is to tell Mussolini that the Germans seem resigned to war beyond the winter.

35 Mason, *op cit*, pp. 248–9 refers to this tactic. Many general narratives refer to the Germans not being aware of British radar direction but, as Mason indicates, by this stage of the battle, they were very well aware that their formations were being tracked across the Channel and were adjusting their tactics accordingly.

36 Details from the Altrincham History Society website – one excellent example of how local historians have augmented the official record, which is very sketchy on this incident. The lack of local detail very often distorts the official narrative, giving disproportionate attention to the air-to-air fighting, when the summation of the total air effort conveys a different impression.

37 War Cabinet: WP (40) 342. National Archives.

38 *Diary*, *op cit*, p. 103.

NOTES ON CHAPTER 9

1 A copy of the complete order (verbatim translation) can be found in Wheatley, *op cit*, pp. 116–22. See also: Ansel, *op cit*, p. 236.

2 Wheatley, *op cit*, p. 49.

3 War Cabinet: WP (40) 346. National Archives.

4 War Cabinet: WP (40) 238. National Archives.

5 http://www.bbc.co.uk/ww2peopleswar/stories/73/a7467573.shtml

6 War Cabinet: (40) 238, *op cit*.

7 Orwell (2009).

8 Scott, *op cit*, p. 71.

9 War Cabinet: WM (40) 239. National Archives. See also: Colville, *op cit*, p. 276.

10 Colville, *op cit*, pp. 235–6 and Roskill, *op cit*, p. 334–5. Action details at: http://www.uboat.net/allies/warships/ship/4382.html See also: War Cabinet: 239 (40). National Archives.

11 Colville, *op cit*, p. 234.

12 The bombing was reported in the city's *Telegraph & Argus* newspaper, the next day, the editorial making precisely that point. The paper, incidentally, was not permitted to name or reveal the location of the department store, even though it was one of the most prominent buildings in the city centre.

13 Buckton (2010), pp. 159–61.

14 War Cabinet: WM (40) 239, *op cit*.

15 Churchill, *op cit*, pp. 271–2.

16 Klee, *op cit*, p. 70.

17 Ansel, *op cit*, p. 248.

18 Colville, *op cit*, p. 281.

19 The fullest account of the incident can be found on a diving website, in the original Danish, at: http://www.nolimitsdiving.dk/NLD/Projekter/Pionier/ Pionier_research.htm The action was reported on the front page of the *Daily Mirror* of 21 September, when Swedish sources were cited, claiming 4,000 troops on board, with most of them drowned.

20 http://www.royalengineersbombdisposal-eod.org.uk/george_cross.html

21 A detailed account of this raid is given in J. M. Morris (1983), 'Morale under attack'. *Welsh History Review*. vol. 11, no. 3 (June). The paper is available online from the National Library of Wales. As the title of the paper indicates, it is primarily about the effect of bombing on morale. Morris notes that despite its importance, there was no formal definition of morale in existence until October 1941. Then, Director of MoI's home intelligence division suggested that it must be measured, "not by what a person thinks or says but by what he does and how he does it". Tom Harrisson (1976) observed that there was a tendency to confuse morale with "cheerfulness". The lack of clear definition led to considerable variation, by different workers, in the estimates of morale. In these pre-psephological days, he wrote, "the noise of the general public, as interpreted by the media, could sound very different from the true, private, voice of the people, which might be saying the opposite – or nothing at all".

22 Wheatley, *op cit*, p. 48.

23 Liddell, *op cit*, reported in his 6 September entry. National Archives.

24 Taylor, *op cit*, p. 157.

25 Ansel, *op cit*, p. 248.

26 *Diary*, *op cit*, online version.

27 War Cabinet; WP (40) 352. National Archives.

28 Gilbert (1997), p. 764.

29 Wheatley, *op cit*, p. 69.

30 War Cabinet: (40) 241. National Archives.

31 War Cabinet: (40) 242. National Archives. Later, a system of watchmen, dubbed "Jim Crows" was adopted. Not until they observed aircraft approaching and had given warnings was shelter taken. It was reported that some workers negotiated extra payments for working though the alert period, and the government undertook to assume complete liability for injuries received by workers who carried on during air raids. See: War Cabinet: 14 October 1940, (40) 270, National Archives; *Yorkshire Post*. 23 September 1940.

32 Domarus, *op cit*. Full text 2081–90. The cited text is on p. 2086.

33 *Berlin Diary*, *op cit*, pp. 495–7.

34 *Daily Express, Mirror, Yorkshire Post*, and others, 7 September 1940. The hospital, not named in reports, is at: http://www.dartfordhospitalhistories.org.uk/westhill_ intro.html

35   Reference is made to 160 long-range bombers having been moved from Norway. See: HC Deb 18 November 1946 vol. 430 cc.52–7W.

36   This assertion is referred to by both Klee and Wheatley, both of whom had independent access to OKW records (each of their phrasing being slightly different). It confirms that which was self-evident. Göring personally never attended any *Sealion* planning sessions. On receipt of Führer Directive No. 16, he is said to have treated it with indifference.

37   He had previously been in Finland, from where earlier approaches had been made to the British Government.

38   The full exchange of telegrams was annexed to the War Cabinet conclusion of 11 September, referenced as WP (40) 366, marked "most secret" – and presented to the Cabinet on that day. The documents are headed "Telegrams exchanged with His Majesty's Minister in Stockholm", with a covering note from the Secretary of State for Foreign Affairs (Lord Halifax), dated 10 September 1940. National Archives. See also: Roberts, *op cit*, p. 251, and Gilbert (1997), p. 799.

39   HC Deb 05 September 1940 vol. 365 cc.28–48.

40   *Diary*, *op cit*, 31 August 1940, p. 103.

41   HC Deb 05 September 1940 vol. 365 cc.48–82.

42   Klee, *op cit*, p. 73.

43   Grinnell-Milne deals with this at length in his Chapter 11, pp. 119–26.

44   Sunderland Library Service, who have provided a publicly accessible photo montage: http://www.flickr.com/photos/sunderlandpubliclibraries/3150054025/in/set-72157611894055230

45   War Cabinet: WP (40) 361. National Archives.

46   James, *op cit*, p. 359: Instructions to Controllers No. 12.

47   War Cabinet: WP (40) 366, *op cit*.

NOTES ON CHAPTER 10

1   Cited in Anon (1942c), p. 71.

2   The full text and the context of the warning was published in a written statement by the then Prime Minister, Clement Attlee, on 18 November 1946, in response to repeated questioning by MPs (of himself and his predecessor) on how close Britain had come to being invaded. See: HC Deb 18 November 1946 vol. 430 cc.52–7W.

3   *Diary*, *op cit*, p. 105.

4   Orange, *op cit*, p. 104. Terraine (1985), p. 206, was to observe that there was foreknowledge of the raid on London, which "enabled fire-engines and other appliances to be assembled and positioned ...", thus suggesting that Park had been "caught on the wrong foot". This assertion rests in part on Terraine relying

on Winterbotham (1974) claiming that Ultra intelligence was available. This is denied in Probert and Sebastian (1991) – see: Edward Thomas, "The Intelligence Aspect", p. 42 *et seq*. Hinsley (1993) affirms that neither Enigma nor any other source was giving precise information at this time.

5 See: Ray (1996), pp. 13–16 for a comprehensive narrative of the air action. James, *op cit*, pp. 233–44, also covers the raids in considerable detail.

6 Hill (1990).

7 From accounts recorded by Mass Observation workers. See: Harrisson (1976), pp. 63–6.

8 Stansky (2007), p. 28.

9 Mack and Humphries (1985), pp. 40–1.

10 See: pp. 407–8.

11 Anon (1942c), pp. 12 and 14.

12 National Archives online provides one set of figures and preliminary police reports: http://www.nationalarchives.gov.uk/pathways/firstworldwar/spotlights/ airraids.htm There is, however, a considerable variation in reports of numbers killed and injured. A contemporary news agency report (UPI, 8 July 1917 – on the occasion of the second major raid), gave figures of 157 killed and 432 injured. There is no dispute, however, that the ratio of deaths to explosive weight dropped in the First World War raids was substantially greater than in the Second World War, leading the authorities vastly to overestimate the expected casualties (while also underestimating the number of homeless survivors).

13 On 11 September, the War Cabinet was advised that the tonnage of ships totally lost was about 29,000. In addition 15,000 tons of shipping were probably capable of salvage and ships totalling 72,000 tons had suffered minor damage. However, the Cabinet members were also told, "Such an attack had been anticipated with the result that there was not so much shipping in the Thames as usual". War Cabinet: (40) 247. National Archives.

14 Evidence of this emerges in an analysis of home opinion, disclosed by the censorship of mail to the USA and Eire. See: War Cabinet: WP (40) 407. National Archives.

15 As a result of the heavy censorship at the time, the chaos arising from the bombing and the smothering effect of "Blitz spirit" recollections, much of the detail in the immediate aftermath of these first major raids has been obscured. In its daily report Home Intelligence (pp. 405–6) resorted to the use of anodyne phrasing, stating that there was "much anxiety", the paucity of "official reassurance" and "lack of guidance". Clues remain, however, to indicate that in the hours and first days after the raids there was a lack of organization and direction – not least because it was a weekend and most Council offices were closed. Survivors in West

Ham, angry at the lack of help, turned on the air-raid wardens, and threatened to "smash" their post. Levine, *op cit*, p. 282.

16 Raymond Challinor (1995), *Class War in the Blitz*. Workers' Liberty, 18 February 1995.

17 Cited in Stansky, *op cit*, p. 120.

18 See: Gardiner, *op cit*, 369–70.

19 *Daily Express*, 14 October 1940, p. 5. The service was discontinued in October, ostensibly because it had been found to be "too expensive". The travellers found homes thirty to fifty miles away from London and travelled in by season ticket night and morning.

20 Cited in Calder, *op cit*, p. 186. See also: King (1970), pp. 74–5.

21 Boothby (1978), p. 181.

22 Challinor, *op cit*. See also: Piratin (1948) and Zeigler (1995).

23 Schwarz (2003), pp. 297–8 and p. 299.

24 Irving (1987a), p. 87. See also: p. 107. The letter did not arrive in London until early November.

25 Waller (1996), pp. 177–9. These events are also widely documented online, for instance: http://www.spartacus.schoolnet.co.uk/GERhaushoferA.htm Irving, ibid., also refers. See also: Lipgens, *op cit*, pp. 376–9. He has Haushofer meeting Hess on this day, and reproduces the text of a "peace plan" sent to a former pupil of his, Legation Secretary Stahmer in Madrid, with instructions for it to be handed to Hoare. The Ambassador is said to have refused any contact.

26 Wheatley, *op cit*, p. 53.

27 Gilbert (1991), p. 675.

28 Hanson, *op cit*, pp. 259–62.

29 Brief report in War Cabinet: (40) 245. National Archives. More detail from http://www.naval-history.net/xDKWW2-4009-22SEP01.htm

30 Details of the incident, including site plans and witness statements were supplied by the Peabody Trust. Personal Communication 13 October 2010.

31 See: pp. 408–9.

32 Much of the propaganda effort was directed at the American audience, addressing the government's strategic objective of enticing the USA into the war. A good overview of the techniques employed is in Cull (1995), pp. 99–108.

33 Personal communication. GOSH. *Daily Mirror*, 18 January 1941, p. 7.

34 War Cabinet, (40) 246. National Archives.

35 Nicolson, *op cit*, pp. 114–15.

36 War Cabinet: (40) 246. National Archives.

37 Gardiner (2004), pp. 339–40. A more detailed account is in the *Daily Mail*, 28 August 2010, by Gardiner, which forms the basis of this account. Curiously, Angus Calder, son of Richie Calder, whose book covers much the same territory,

does not appear to mention the incident. The *AP* report was widely circulated – it appeared as the front-page story in the Melbourne *Argus* on 12 September under the headline "German bomb hits school – 500 persons inside". Most, the story ran, were believed killed.

38 Ansel, *op cit*, p. 288. A draft order, provisionally labelled Führer Directive No. 18, was prepared, but not signed. The draft was withheld and has gone missing.

39 Assmann, *op cit*, p. 59.

40 Cited in Anon (1942c), *op cit*, p. 25.

41 *New York Times*, 10 September 1940. Unlike the British press, US newspapers often published German war communiqués in full.

42 Waller, *op cit*, pp. 177–9, refers. See also: *Daily Telegraph*, 5 April 1999.

43 Lipgens, *op cit*, p. 73.

44 Prime Minister's Personal Minutes, September 1940, D. 51. CAB 101/240. National Archives.

45 Gardiner, *op cit*, pp. 374–5.

46 Calder, *op cit*, p. 166.

47 See: p. 412. Earlier (30 August), a report on "home opinion", from monitoring of letters sent abroad, suggested that Lord Haw-Haw's broadcasts were getting "stale". War Cabinet: WP (40) 359. National Archives.

48 War Cabinet: (40) 247. National Archives.

49 See: entry for 5 September. WP (40) 366, *op cit*, and Roberts, *op cit*, p. 251, refer.

50 Gilbert (1997), *op cit*, p. 799.

51 Online text: http://teachingamericanhistory.org/library/index.asp?document= 1911Broadcast version online (audio): http://www.archive.org/details/EveryMan ToHisPost

52 http://www.bbm.org.uk/Sprague.htm

53 Dobinson, *op cit*, p. 243.

54 For instance, the *Daily Express*, p. 1, which offered a single column, headed "Palace Bomb".

55 Anon (1942c), p. 65.

56 *Diaries*, *op cit*, online version.

57 Wheatley, *op cit*, p. 54.

58 Wheatley, ibid. See also: Ansel, *op cit*, pp. 290–1.

59 *Diary*, *op cit*, p. 107.

60 See: Ansel, *op cit*, pp. 291–6 and Wheatley, *op cit*, p. 89.

61 War Cabinet: (40) 249. National Archives.

62 Ibid. Subsequently, Lord Reith, having returned to his room, recalled having been "pressed" by Churchill on the subject of Tube stations being used by "refugees". He had said that he thought their use "inadvisable", although as Minister of Transport, "he couldn't be completely impartial". Gilbert (1997), *op cit*, p. 806.

63 Not everyone was so awed by the news. An anonymous member of the public told *Mass Observation* that it was better for the Germans to have bombed Buckingham Palace, in preference to his own home. It was alright for these people, they can go somewhere else, he said. "It's us working people can't go anywhere else". Mass Observation Archives (MOA): Topic Collection (TC) 23/5/C Air Raids 1939–45: Observations Gathered. September 1940.

NOTES ON CHAPTER 11

1 See also: *Daily Mail*, 14 September 2009. http://www.dailymail.co.uk/femail/ article-1213027/As-biography-launched-Queen-Mothers-account-day-Luftwaffe-came-town-released.html
2 War Cabinet: WP (40) 371. National Archives.
3 Summarized from Ansel, *op cit*, pp. 295–6, and Wheatley, *op cit*, pp. 56–7. See also: Grinnell-Milne, *op cit*, pp. 163–5.
4 This extremely contentious issue is summarized by Ray (1994), pp. 155–8, and rehearsed at length by Dixon, *op cit.*
5 A full account of the incident is given in Piratin's book, first published in 1948.
6 *Diary*, *op cit*, p. 107.
7 Warrington Museum: http://museum.warrington.gov.uk/Local_History/war.aspx
8 http://www.mybrightonandhove.org.uk/page_id__6962_path__0p116p 182p446p.aspx
9 Famously, in the 1969 film *Battle of Britain* – based loosely on the narrative offered by Wood with Dempster – with Dowding played by actor Lawrence Olivier, this was the high point. The Churchill misquote was in the film, which actually related to the second battle of El Alamein, and a speech given in November 1942.
10 Churchill, *op cit*, pp. 273–6.
11 Orange, *op cit*, p. 110.
12 This issue is rehearsed fully by Robinson (2005). He, in turn, relies on Bekker (1968), who argues that the reason for the German failure was the inadequate resource in the first place, and then the failure of Göring to concentrate on one point of effort. The 15 September battle, in the grander scheme of things, was a minor footnote.
13 Hinsley, *op cit*, p. 44.
14 See: Challinor, *op cit,* and Piratin (1948). Writing eight years after the event, Piratin puts this action at "two or three days" after the Savoy Hotel incident. However, on 16 September, Home Secretary John Anderson referred to "organised demonstrations" in the War Cabinet meeting – which suggests that the Underground break-ins could have been on this day. Piratin's memory is, in any event, faulty. He has the Home Secretary as being Herbert Morrison, who was not appointed

until October. Until then, it was Sir John Anderson. However, Cull (1995), p. 106, claims that Piratin broke into Goodge St Tube Station on September 17.

15 http://www.bbc.co.uk/ww2peopleswar/stories/69/a2388369.shtml

16 Irving (1973) covers this meeting briefly, citing the *Milch Diaries*. Bishop, *op cit*, has it that the change of tactics to night bombing was decided at this meeting. He does not quote a source. Bekker (1968) offers a detailed narrative, having Göring "blustering" when presented with complaints of large numbers of RAF aircraft. "If they come at us in droves, we can shoot them down in droves." Taylor, *op cit*, details an OKW report which observes that the operations had been "unusually disadvantaged", with the major losses having occurred while the bombers were homeward bound, in small groups and without fighter escort. This was undoubtedly due to the Me 109s operating at their extreme range, having to turn for home before the raid was complete.

17 Group instructions to controllers. Reproduced in James, *op cit*, p. 371.

18 War Cabinet: (40) 250. National Archives.

19 In Dixon, *op cit*, p. 139, we are reminded that, in 1917 during the German air raids, Churchill was Minister for War Munitions and Minister for Air, and had then been alarmed at the wave of violence in the East End – arson, rioting and strikes – that had followed. In those then revolutionary times, the then government had good reason to fear an uprising. Dixon suggests that Churchill in 1940 would have remembered those events, and was "thoroughly alarmed" about the morale of people in the East End.

20 War Cabinet: WP (R)(40) 192. National Archives.

21 HC Deb 17 September 1940 vol. 365 cc.121–38.

22 Ansel, *op cit*, p. 299.

23 The most often cited source for this is Terraine (1985). However, he relies on Winterbotham (1974). Edwards (in Probert and Cox (1991)) asserts that Winterbotham's claims are "utterly without foundation". Churchill does not refer to the events in *Finest Hour*, but that is not conclusive. He deliberately omitted references to Ultra material. The intelligence is mentioned in Mckay (2010), and although no source is given, he relies on Winterbotham for other claims. Churchill's biographer (Gilbert) does not mention these events, the intelligence is not mentioned in War Cabinet minutes and there is no reference to it in the official history of British Intelligence (Hinsley, 1993), who suggests that the first indication of a unit being disbanded was on 25 October – see: p. 44. In the absence of independent corroboration, the claim cannot be taken as reliable.

24 Churchill, *op cit*, p. 259.

25 *Diary*, *op cit*, pp. 114–15 Nicolson.

26 Contemporary reports, however, seem to indicate that the violence was directed

at German interests, pacifists and the like, rather than the government. See: United Press International Report, 8 July 1917.

27 *Diary, op cit*, online edition.

28 HL Deb 17 September 1940 vol. 117 cc.401–15.

29 Wartime letters from the Tottenham Home Front: http://tottenham-summer-hillroad.com/wartimeletters_tottenham_homefront.htm

30 *Diary, op cit*, p. 109.

31 Prime Minister's Personal Minutes, September 1940, *op cit*, D. 61.

32 Cited in: Anon (1942c), *op cit*, p. 60.

33 See: http://www.westendatwar.org.uk/page_id__11_path__0p2p.aspx

34 See: pp. 431–4.

35 The *Daily Telegraph* the following day noted that "it is impossible to hint at the nature of the device, but it is simple, and costs little to manufacture. It does not need a large number of men to operate it. It is neither a gun, ray, nor a balloon. When the device has been developed, London's defences will be enormously strengthened by it". The device was almost certainly airborne radar, to equip the RAF's fleet of night fighters.

36 CAB 101/240: the printed set of minutes for September – excludes the last day of the month.

37 *Diary, op cit*, p. 109.

38 Reported in the *Glasgow Herald*, 20 September 1940. Also reported in the *Daily Mirror* (p. 7): "Looking round at the destruction, in the middle of which were two unharmed Anderson shelters, the King remarked, 'These Anderson shelters are wonderful, wonderful'". The *Yorkshire Post* had: "The marvellous escapes from death of men and women whose houses had been wrecked by a direct hit led the King to say: 'These Anderson Shelters are wonderful'".

39 *Diary, op cit*, pp. 115–16.

40 Wheatley, *op cit*, p. 58.

41 Prime Minister's Personal Minutes, September 1940, *op cit*, M. 99.

42 Wheatley, *op cit*, p. 60.

43 *Diary, op cit*, p. 383.

44 Hinsley, *op cit*, p. 44.

45 *Diary, op cit*, p. 245.

46 War Cabinet: WM (40) 255. National Archives.

47 Ibid.

48 Prime Minister's Personal Minutes, September 1940, *op cit*, M. 116.

49 Gilbert, *op cit*, p. 850.

50 Challinor, *op cit.* http://www.workersliberty.org/system/files/wl18classwarblitz.pdf

51 Date from the *Daily Mirror*, 21 September. Text from the *Argus*, Melbourne, 23

September 1940. National Library of Australia. Empire newspapers at this stage of the war did not have the paper rationing affecting the British industry and were, therefore, often able to offer fuller accounts of British events than the London papers.

52 It transpired that Churchill, having learned of the radio-navigation devices used by German bombers, assumed – without even any evidence that the system could work at sea level, much less that it was fitted to naval vessels – that the invasion fleet could use the same system to navigate through the fog. He was not aware that few of the invasion barges even had radios, and relied for communication on flags and signal lamps. See: CAB 101/240 23 September 1940.

53 Brooke, *op cit*, p. 110.

54 *Sunday Express*, 22 September 1940, front page. However, there is no record of such an attack in wartime diaries of islanders. See: *The German Occupation of Jersey 1940–1945, A Complete Diary*, by Leslie P. Sinel, published by *Evening Post*, Jersey, November 1945, p. 21. Unpublished notes from K. Troy – a 14-year-old schoolboy living in Jersey during the occupation years – affirms this. Also, there is no reference to an RAF raid in September 1940 (or at any time) by Charles Cruickshank either in *The German Occupation of the Channel Islands* (1975), or in *The British Channel Islands under German Occupation 1940–1945* (2005). And finally, there is no mention of a raid in the detailed dairies of the occupation years (at date unpublished) kept by William Troy MM who at the time of the occupation was the news editor of Jersey's only wartime newspaper.

NOTES ON CHAPTER 12

1   *Sunday Express*, 22 September 1940, p. 5.

2   *Berlin Diary*, *op cit*, p. 514.

3   *Diary*, p. 110.

4   *Diary*, *op cit*, p. 117.

5   Editorial: 'Poster patriotism', p. 7.

6   War Cabinet: 254 (40). National Archives.

7   King, *op cit*, pp. 76–7.

8   Prime Minister's Personal Minutes, September 1940, *op cit*, M. 125.

9   War Cabinet: (40) 256. National Archives.

10 *Diaries*, KV4/186. National Archives.

11 James, *op cit*, p. 272.

12 *Berlin Diary*, *op cit*, p. 518.

13 War Cabinet: (40) 257. National Archives.

14 War Cabinet: WP (40) 383. National Archives.

15 For instance, the *Daily Mirror*, 27 September 1940. In a leader headed "Major

blunder", it declared, "Narvik was quite a distinguished exploit compared with Dakar. Dakar has claims to rank with the lowest depths of imbecility to which we have yet sunk".

16 War Cabinet: (40) 259. National Archives.

17 Lead story, p. 3.

18 Megan Lloyd George, then Member for Anglesey. The debate was on 5 April 1939, in which she was highly critical of the Anderson shelter, asserting that shallow shelters could not reduce the risk of air raids to "tolerable dimensions". She was supported by Sir Arthur Salter, friend and colleague of Jean Monnet, architect of the European Union. See: HC Deb 05 April 1939 vol. 345 cc.2811–78.

19 Dixon, *op cit*, p. 69.

20 Ibid.

21 *Berlin Diary*, *op cit*, p. 523.

22 War Cabinet: (40) 259. National Archives.

23 Ibid.

24 See: Gardiner, *op cit*, p. 372. The problem arose from Circular HO 197/4 "Domestic Surface Shelters" Memorandum No.14: use of certain limes in shelter construction, issued 29 April 1940. National Archives. The issue of weak shelters was first raised in parliament in an adjournment debate by Charles Ammon, MP for Camberwell North, shortly after Morrison's appointment (HC Deb 09 October 1940 vol. 365 cc.373–464). It was further raised by William Gallacher, MP for Fife Western on 20 March 1940, when Morrison asserted that the memorandum had been "unfortunately not too clearly worded and was read by some local authorities as authorising the use of mortar ungauged with cement". Any possible misapprehension, Morrison claimed, was removed by a circular issued on 17 July (HC Deb 20 March 1941 vol. 370 cc.304–5W). By then, there were major, if localized, cement shortages, and many local authorities continued using lime mortar. The issue was thus raised by several more MPs in early 1941, and also by the superbly robust Bishop of Birmingham in the House of Lords (HL Deb 17 June 1941 vol. 119 cc.417–42). Eventually, several thousand shelters had to be taken out of use and rebuilt.

25 Consulting Engineer Ove Arup described a meeting with an unnamed senior civil servant on shelter policy, and recalled being told: "What really mattered was to keep people quiet, to give them confidence in the measures taken and to prevent panic; this psychological or political aspect was more important than the safety of the shelters". A technical note which he produced, questioning the safety of brick shelters, was rejected for publication by a leading technical body on the basis that it was not "sound policy" to add to their unpopularity. See: Jones (2006).

26 See: Richardson (1977). The Co-operative Wholesale Society (CWS) and its network of independent societies, planned and executed its own response to the

bombing, setting up a system of "fall-back centres" and mutual aid to take over when distribution centres were damaged or destroyed. By this means, the largest food production and distribution enterprise in the country never failed to provide supplies to bombed areas.

27 http://www.rjmitchell-spitfire.co.uk/otheraircraft/1932to1937.asp?sectionID=4

28 The incident is described at length by McKee (1957). The girl was 16-year-old Evelyn Harmar. An account in the *Daily Mirror*, 18 January 1941, had her remaining at her switchboard for three hours, transmitting messages for the police incident post, in danger of further attack and delayed action bombs. The paper had a picture of the "pretty Evelyn", about to travel to Scotland to get married to Pilot Officer Stanley Jefferson of Coastal Command.

29 War Cabinet: WP (40) 386. National Archives.

30 *Diaries, op cit.*

31 On the day, the *Evening Standard* (p. 1) reported twenty-two killed.

32 *Diary, op cit*, online version.

33 Online text: http://ww2today.com/27th-september-1940-kennedy-the-british-are-a-lost-cause

34 *Observer*, p. 7. In the days when the front page was given over to advertisements, and the news pages were further into the "book", this was the equivalent of the front-page lead story.

35 Roskill, *op cit*, p. 257. See: pp. 247–59 for the full context.

36 War Cabinet: WP (40) 333. National Archives.

37 Ibid.

38 Hinsley, *op cit*, p. 44.

39 Taylor (1982), p. 1256.

40 London Transport Museum. A remarkable set of photographs is published on the museum website.

41 See also: Gardiner, *op cit*, pp. 372–3, and Harrisson, *op cit*, pp. 116–18.

42 War Cabinet: (40) 264. National Archives.

43 This became public knowledge around 7 October – the front page of the *Daily Express* of that date refers.

44 *Diary, op cit*, p. 113.

45 War Cabinet: (40) 265. National Archives.

46 von Leeb, *op cit*, p. 235.

47 War Cabinet: WP (40) 401. National Archives.

48 War Cabinet: WP (40) 403. National Archives.

49 See also: Ciano, *op cit*, p. 387. He wrote in his diary: "there is no longer any talk about a landing in the British Isles, and preparations made remain where they are".

50 *Berlin Diary*, p. 538.

51 Colville, *op cit*, pp. 302–3.
52 War Cabinet: (40) 266. 4 October 1940. National Archives.
53 *Diary*, *op cit*, pp. 539–40.

NOTES ON CHAPTER 13

1 War Cabinet: WP (G)(40) 280. National Archives.
2 Hanson, *op cit*, pp. 276–7.
3 Taylor (1982), *op cit*, p. 133.
4 War Cabinet: (40) 267. National Archives.
5 War Cabinet: WM (40) 267. National Archives.
6 *Daily Express*, p. 1.
7 Reported nationally, the following day. See, for instance: *Yorkshire Post*, p. 3.
8 *Daily Mirror*, p. 1.
9 Union history website: http://www.unionhistory.info/workerswar/display.php?irn
=296&QueryPage=%2Fworkerswar%2Fimagesdocs.php
10 War Cabinet: WP (40) 408. National Archives.
11 HC Deb 08 October 1940 vol. 365 cc.261–352.
12 An account is given in the *Daily Mirror*, 10 October 1940, p. 6.
13 War Cabinet: (40) 268. National Archives.
14 Ibid.
15 Ibid. See also: War Cabinet. WP (40) 402. National Archives. A lengthy report, produced under the signature of Herbert Morrison, writing as Home Secretary, argued that it would be extremely difficult to demonstrate that the newspapers were breaching Defence Regulations.
16 HC Deb 09 October 1940 vol. 365 cc.373–464.
17 In addition, the Upton Colliery in Yorkshire, which employed 2,200 men, was at a standstill, owing to a strike by haulage hands. A week later, they had rejected an appeal by branch officials of the Yorkshire Mineworkers Association to go back to work. The owners, Dorman Long and Co. Ltd, were considering closing down the pit. See: *Yorkshire Post*, 17 October 1940.
18 War Cabinet: (40) 269. National Archives.
19 Garfield (2006), p. 103.
20 http://www.hackney.gov.uk/hackney-archives-the-blitz.htm
21 HC Deb 10 October 1940 vol. 365 cc.483–568.
22 War Cabinet: WP (R)(40) 196. National Archives.
23 Taylor, *op cit*, pp. 136–7.
24 Anon (1942c).
25 Hinsley, *op cit*, p. 45.
26 Despite the general prohibition on identifying the location of bomb-damaged

buildings, the press the following day was replete with pictures of the damage. Publication of the photographs, however, had been discussed by the War Cabinet on 11 October, and specifically approved. The Chief of the Air Staff saw no objection to publication "provided this was not taken as a ruling of general application". War Cabinet: (40) 269. National Archives.

27 War Cabinet: WP (40) 423. National Archives.
28 Details of this and the preceding actions drawn from online sources: http://www. german-navy.de/kriegsmarine/ships/torpedoboats/torpedoboot1923/seeadler/ operations.html and http://www.naval-history.net/xDKWW2-4010-23OCT01. htm, plus War Cabinet: WP (40) 423 (Weekly Résumé). National Archives.
29 Ansel, *op cit*, p. 304. See also: Assmann, *op cit*, supplement p. 17. The OKW Directive read, in part: "The English must retain the impression from now on [that] we are prepared to land on a large scale. At the same time however, [the] German domestic economy will be released of a burden". Klee, *op cit*, p. 245, has the OKW diary noting that "an outline Directive for the discontinuance of *Sealion* is to be prepared". He puts the date of the order as 23 October.
30 Taylor, *op cit*, p. 140.
31 Gardiner, *op cit*, p. 347.
32 After the war, a memorial was erected in Abbey Park Cemetery. It lists 173 names. http://www.flickr.com/photos/albedo/97603317
33 Taylor, *op cit*, p. 142.
34 *Sunday Express*, 13 October 1940, p. 1.
35 Nick Cooper: http://www.nickcooper.org.uk/subterra/lu/tuawcafa.htm#balham
36 War Cabinet: (40) 270. National Archives.
37 War Cabinet: WP (40) 417. National Archives.
38 A routine was developed, however, for the submission of statistical reports for time lost by major departments.
39 http://www.raf.mod.uk/bob1940/october15.html
40 http://www.vauxhallandkennington.org.uk/forgottentragedy.pdf
41 One particularly high-profile critic had been Sir Ove Arup, Consulting Engineer, designer of the world-famous Penguin Pool in London Zoo. He was a member of the government's air-raid precautions organizing committee and advised Finsbury Council on the provision of bomb shelters, writing several lengthy monographs on the design of shelters, and shelter policy. Ironically, although many of his ideas were rejected – largely on political grounds – his construction firm had many clients for whom he built shelters. One was the Air Ministry. See: Jones (2006).
42 War Cabinet: (40) 271. National Archives.
43 Ibid.
44 HC Deb 15 October 1940 vol. 365 cc.595–7.

45 Ibid.

46 HC Deb 15 October 1940 vol. 365 cc.653–78.

47 See: Chapman (1998), pp. 98–9.

48 HL Deb 16 October 1940 vol. 117 cc.527–44.

49 War Cabinet: (40) 272. National Archives. Reference was also made to the bombing of the Carlton Club, home of the Conservative Party. The building was virtually demolished but no one was killed. A Labour MP was heard to remark that the devil looked after his own.

50 Ibid. See also: King, *op cit*, pp. 81–2. King recalls that Attlee – a man he described as of "limited intelligence and no personality" – was most concerned about "irresponsible criticism", but very "vague or silent" on what it constituted. When challenged, he could not give an example of a "subversive influence" which could endanger the nation's war effort. King did not expect the government to do anything more, and of his papers, said only: "obviously we shall pipe down for a few weeks until the course of the war alters the whole situation".

51 Mason, *op cit*, p. 368.

52 *Evening Standard*, 10 December 1940.

53 Page 9, "The bravest men I ever met". The FAA is recognized in the Battle of Britain Memorial Window in Westminster Abbey. The Roll of Honour contains the names of l,497 pilots and aircrew killed or mortally wounded during the Battle, of which it states 449 were in Fighter Command, 732 in Bomber Command, 268 in Coastal Command, 14 in other RAF commands and 34 in the Fleet Air Arm.

54 Hanson, *op cit*, pp. 279–80.

55 War Cabinet: (40) 274. National Archives.

56 Page 5: "Nazi raiders fly six miles high".

57 http://www.warbirdforum.com/saga.htm

58 War Cabinet: WP (40) 425. National Archives.

59 http://www.kbismarck.com/testi.html

60 War Cabinet: 275 (40). National Archives.

61 *Diary*, *op cit*, p. 150.

62 Klee, *op cit*, p. 237.

63 See: Assmann, *op cit* (Appendix), p.17. The diary refers to an OKW directive of 22 October "for deception of the enemy", signed on behalf of Keitel.

64 Klee, *op cit*, pp. 237–8.

65 *Diary*, *op cit,* pp. 150–1.

66 Klee, *op cit*, p. 239.

67 War Cabinet: WP (40) 425, *op cit*.

68 *Halifax Diary*, cited in Lawlor, *op cit*, p. 146.

69 War Cabinet: (40) 276. National Archives.

70 Liddell, *op cit*.

71 Gilbert (1991), *op cit*, p. 681. See also: Hinsley, *op cit*, p. 44. The CIC observed that, if the movement of shipping was maintained, it *"could* reduce the risk of invasion" (my italics).

72 Colville, *op cit*, p. 283.

73 Conveyed via the *Daily Express* the following day.

74 War Cabinet: (40) 279. National Archives.

75 War Cabinet: (40) 280. National Archives.

76 War Cabinet: WP (G)(40) 275. National Archives.

77 War Cabinet: WP (G)(40) 280. National Archives.

78 Hinsley, *op cit*, p. 45.

79 Roskill, *op cit*, p. 267.

NOTES ON CHAPTER 14

1   War Cabinet: WP (40) 393.

2   Suchenwirth (1959), p. 67.

3   (Anon 1941b).

4   Jarman (1997).

5   By far the best technical descriptions of the invasion craft comes from Schenk (1990), with an array of photographs and diagrams which make clear how difficult the landing would have been, merely from the technical aspects. These are often neglected in the grand political narratives. The sheer practicalities of delivering the fleet to the shores of England were so daunting that it is hard to see that an unopposed landing, even in ideal conditions, could have succeeded.

6   Williamson (1983), p. 72.

7   Liddell Hart (1948), p. 201.

8   Blumentritt (1949), January.

9   Guderian (1952), p. 138.

10 Schenk (1990), p. 128.

11 Cox (1982).

12 Campion (2010).

13 As in a *UP* syndicated article on 15 September 1945.

14 HL Deb 05 September 1940 vol. 117 cc.365–81.

15 *Op cit.* See: p. 235.

16 See again: Ansel, *op cit*, pp. 295–6, and Wheatley, *op cit*, pp. 56–7. See also: Grinnell-Milne, *op cit*, pp. 163–5.

17 See: Butler and Young (1952). Presented in the war-time British media as an overweight buffoon, Göring was a far more complex man. A skilled organizer, and ruthless street fighter, he was the man behind the "night of the long knives" of 1934, in which Hitler's rivals were murdered, including Ernst Röhm, leader of

the SA. When later asked why he had assented to the murder of Röhm, Göring was to say, "The man was in my way".

18 See also: Nuremberg transcript: 5 July 1946 – Dr Otto Stahmer.

19 Nielsen (1968).

20 Hitler's pilots shoot down Battle of Britain "myth". *Observer*. 16 July 2000.

21 Statistical details from Bekker (1968).

22 Jones (2006), p. 69.

23 HC Deb 14 June 1917 vol. 94 cc.1283–92.

24 HC Deb 21 December 1938 vol. 342 cc.2880–92.

25 One such happened in Bethnal Green Tube Station on the night of 1 March 1943, when 173 people were crushed to death on the stairs while descending into the Underground.

26 HC Deb 05 April 1939 vol. 345 cc.2811–78.

27 The Committee had also produced a 24-page, printed report – dated 4 April 1939, and classified "secret". It was appended to a note to the Cabinet, with a memorandum by the Lord Privy Seal, dated 12 April 1939 – also classified secret. The conclusions of the Civil Defence (Policy) Committee comprise the final document of the set. See: CP 86 (39). National Archives.

28 Consulting Engineer Ove Arup claimed that the lack of a scientific base for dispersal policy reduced it to the status of a "religious confession", accusing the government of "prophetic utterances of the future". Jones, *op cit*, p. 84.

29 HC Deb 12 June 1940 vol. 361 cc.1277–354.

30 Churchill, *op cit*, pp. 287–8. As recorded earlier, his request for more information came after the Tubes had been opened to the public, asking why the policy had been changed, rather than urging that it should be changed.

31 Calder (1969).

32 See: Nuremberg Trial, transcript 25 July 1946. Dr Seidl. There were no surprises: "Such were the terms on which Hitler was prepared to make peace with Great Britain immediately after the conclusion of the French campaign, that it was deemed that the position of Hitler had undergone no further change".

33 There has been a continuing controversy as to whether Hess undertook his journey with the approval of Hitler. With the claimed discovery of papers in a Russian archive, it now seems more likely that Hitler was aware of the mission, and had approved it. *Scotsman*, 30 May 2011. http://news.scotsman.com/scotland/Historian-claims-to-have-solved.6765528.jp.

34 See: Hewitt (2008), pp. 170–1. The implications for *Sealion* are obvious. The naval action took place at night, as would have any attack on the fleet sailing against England.

NOTES ON CHAPTER 15

1 Goulter *et al.* (2006), 'The Royal Navy did not win the "Battle of Britain"'. *RUSI Journal*. October.
2 HC Deb 04 July 1940 vol. 362 cc.1043–51.
3 WP (40) 359, *op cit.*
4 Foot (1962), p. 287.
5 War Cabinet: WM (40) 267, *op cit.*.
6 War Cabinet: WP (G)(41) 1. National Archives.
7 Hanson, *op cit*, pp. 301–6.
8 Hanson, *op cit*, pp. 317–22.
9 *Daily Express*, 1 July 1942. He refused to explain the reason for his "disappointment".
10 See: pp. 128 and 212.
11 Masters (1941).
12 Galland, *op cit*, p. 15.
13 War Cabinet: (42) 130. National Archives.
14 *Daily Express*, 11 November 1942, p. 2. Speech text: http://www.ibiblio.org/pha/policy/1942/421110b.html
15 War Cabinet: WM (43) 101. National Archives.
16 Available from the Internet Archive: http://www.archive.org/details/BattleOfBritain
17 A two-page photo-montage published on 4 June 1942 (pp. 558–9) illustrates exactly the same scene. A similar feature on air-sea rescue was published on 14 June 1941 (p. 411), but this shows only an RAF launch and a Lysander. There is no reference in the magazine to a Walrus in RAF service used in the air-sea rescue role prior to the June 1942 article.
18 Cited in the *Daily Express*, 18 September 1944, p. 3.
19 *Flight* magazine, 20 September 1945, p. 302.
20 Published in the *Spokane Daily Chronicle*, 15 September 1945.
21 Full text on http://www.rafbf.org/The-debt-we-owe
22 http://www.raf.mod.uk/bbmf
23 Cabinet: C (60) 125. National Archives.
24 Cabinet: CC (60) 50. National Archives.
25 Cabinet: C (61) 51. National Archives.
26 Cabinet: CC (61) 23. National Archives.
27 BBC website: http://news.bbc.co.uk/1/hi/uk/4257084.stm "Monument marks Battle of Britain". In part of his speech, Charles declared: "We shall never forget that if the few had failed in their mighty struggle, the consequences for this nation would have been quite unthinkable".

28 Paul Day, the sculptor, said: "The pilots' achievements are central. But the whole structure of Fighter Command is there. It is a giant collage that resurrects the spirit of the time, a spirit that has never left us". *The Times*, 25 February 2003.

Bibliography

Addison, Paul and Crang, Jeremy A. (eds) (2010), *Listening to Britain. Home Intelligence Reports on Britain's Finest Hour – May to September 1940*. The Bodley Head.

Anon (1941a), *Bomber Command. The Air Ministry Account of Bomber Command's Offensive against the Axis, September 1939–July 1941*. HMSO.

—(1941b), *The Battle of Britain August–October 1940*. HMSO.

—(1942a), *Air Sea Rescue*. HMSO.

—(1942b), *Bomber Command Continues*. HMSO.

—(1942c), *Front Line 1940–41: The Official Story of the Civil Defence of Britain*. HMSO.

—(1944), *Merchantmen at War: The Official Story of the Merchant Navy: 1939–1944*. HMSO.

—(1957), *Documents on German Foreign Policy 1918–1945 Series D (1937–1945), Volume X: The War Years (June 23–August 31, 1940)*. United States Government Printing Office.

Ansel, Walter (1960), *Hitler Confronts England*. Duke University Press.

Arthur, Max (2010), *Last of The Few: The Battle of Britain in the Words of the Pilots Who Won It*. Virgin Books.

Assmann, Kurt (1947), *German Plans for the Invasion of England*. Naval Intelligence Division, The Admiralty.

Bader, Douglas (1973), *Fight for the Sky: The Story of the Spitfire and Hurricane*. Sidgwick and Jackson.

Bekker, Cajus (1968) *The Luftwaffe War Diaries, The German Air Force in World War II* (English Translation). Doubleday.

Bishop, Patrick (2010), *Battle of Britain*. Quercus.

Boothby, Robert (1978), *Boothby, Recollections of a Rebel*. Hutchinson.

Brickhill, Paul (1955), *Reach for the Sky – The Story of Douglas Bader DSO, DFC*. Collins.

Buckton, Henry (2010), *Voices from the Battle of Britain – Surviving Veterans Tell Their Story*. David & Charles Ltd.

Bungay, Stephen (2000), *The Most Dangerous Enemy: A History of the Battle of Britain*. Aurum Press Ltd.

Butler, Ewan and Young, Gordon (1952), *Marshal without Glory*. Hodder & Stoughton.

Cadogan, Alexander and Dilks, David (ed.) (1971), *The Diaries of Sir Alexander Cadogan*, 1938–1945. Cassell.

Calder, Angus (1969), *The People's War. Britain 1939–1945*. Jonathan Cape Ltd.

Campion, Garry (2010), *The Good Fight. Battle of Britain Propaganda and the Few*. Palgrave Macmillan.

Chadwick, Owen (1987), *Britain and the Vatican during the Second World War*. Cambridge University Press.

Chapman, James (1998), *The British at War: Cinema, State and Propaganda, 1939–45 (Cinema and Society)*. IB Tauris.

Charmley, John (1986), *Duff Cooper: The Authorized Biography*. Faber and Faber.

Churchill, W. S. (1949), *The Second World War, Volume Two: Their Finest Hour*. Cassell & Co.

Colville, John (1985), *The Fringes of Power. Downing Street Diaries, Volume One: 1939–October 1941*. Hodder and Stoughton.

Cox, Richard (1982), *Operation Sealion*. Arrow Books.

Cruckahank, Charles (1975), *The German Occupation of the Channel Islands*. Oxford University Press.

—(2005), *The British Channel Islands under German Occupation 1940–194, Société Jersiaise*.

Cull, Nicholas J. (1995), *Selling War: The British Propaganda Campaign against American 'Neutrality' in World War II*. Oxford University Press.

Cumming, Anthony J (2010), *The Royal Navy and the Battle of Britain*. Naval Institute Press.

Danchev, Alex and Todman, Daniel (eds) (2001), *War Diaries 1939–1945, Field Marshal Lord Alan Brooke*. Weidenfeld & Nicolson.

De Gaulle, Charles (1964), *The Complete War Memoirs*. Simon & Schuster.

Deighton, Len (1977), *Fighter: The True Story of the Battle of Britain*. Jonathan Cape.

D'Este, Carlo (2009), *Warlord, The Fighting Life of Winston Churchill, from Soldier to Statesman*. Allen Lane.

Dixon, Jack (2008), *Dowding and Churchill: The Dark Side of the Battle of Britain*. Pen and Sword Military.

Dobinson, Colin (2001), *AA Command – Britain's Anti-aircraft Defences of World War II*. Methuen.

Domarus, Max (1990), *The Complete Hitler, Speeches and Proclamations*. Bolchazy-Carducci Publishers.

Donnelly, Larry (2004), *The Other Few*. Red Kite.

Douhet, Giulio (1998), *Command of the Air* (trans. Dino Ferrari). Air Force History and Museums Program.

Fleming, Peter (1975), *Operation Sealion*. Pan Books.

Foot, Michael (1962), *Aneurin Bevan: 1897–1945, Volume 1*. MacGibbon and Kee.

Foreman, John (1988), *Battle of Britain. The Forgotten Months: November and December 1940*. Air Research Publications.

Galland, Adolph (1954), *The First and the Last: The Rise and Fall of the German Fighter Forces*. Henry Holt and Company.

Gardiner, Juliet (2005), *Wartime Britain 1939–1945*. Headline Book Publishing.

Garfield, Simon (2005). *We are at War*. Ebury Press.

—(2006), *Private Battles – How the War almost Defeated Us*. Ebury Press.

Gilbert, Martin (1991), *Churchill, A Life*. William Heinemann.

—(1997), *Churchill War Papers, Volume 2: Norton Edit: Never Surrender May 1940– December 1940*. Sinclair-Stevenson.

Grinnell-Milne, Duncan (1958), *Silent Victory – Invasion of Britain 1940*. The Bodley Head.

Gross, Chris (2010), *The Luftwaffe Fighters' Battle of Britain: The Inside story: July– October 1940*. Crécy Publishing Ltd.

Guderian, General Heinz (1952), *Panzer Leader*. Michael Joseph Ltd.

Hanson, Neil (2008), *Priestley's Wars*. Great Northern Books.

Harrison, Roy (1990), *Blitz over Westminster*. City of Westminster Libraries.

Harrisson, Tom (1976), *Living through the Blitz*. Collins.

Hastings, Max (2009), *Finest Years, Churchill as Warlord 1940–45*. Harper Press.

Hewitt, Geoff (2008), *Hitler's Armada. The Royal Navy & the Defence of Great Britain April–October 1940*. Pen & Sword Books.

Hill, Maureen (1990), *The London Blitz*. Chapmans.

Hinsley, F. H. (1993), *British Intelligence in the Second World War*. HMSO.

Irving, David (1973), *The Rise and Fall of the Luftwaffe*. Weidenfeld and Nicolson.

—(1987a), *Churchill's War*, Veritas Pub, Australia.

—(1987b), *Hess, the missing years – 1941–1945*. Macmillan.

James, T. G. C. (2000), *The Battle of Britain*. Cass.

Jarman, W. D. "Jim" (1997), *Those Wallowing Beauties: The Story of Landing Barges in World War II*. Book Guild.

Jenkins, Paul (1986), *Battle over Portsmouth – A City at War in 1940*. Middleton Press.

Jenkins, Roy (2001), *Churchill*. Macmillan.

Jones, Peter (2006), *Ove Arup: Master Builder of the Twentieth Century*. Yale University Press.

Keegan, John (1989), *The Second World War*. Century Hutchinson.

Kelly, David (1952), *The Ruling Few, or, the Human Background to Diplomacy*. Hollis & Carter.

Kenny, Mary (2003), *Germany Calling – A Personal Biography of William Joyce "Lord Haw-Haw"*. New Island.

Kent, J. A. (1971), *One of the Few*. William Kimber & Co Ltd.

Kieser, Egbert (1997), *Hitler on the Doorstep: Operation Sea Lion, the German Plan to Invade Britain, 1940*. Naval Institute Press.

King, Cecil (1970), *With Malice toward None, a War Diary*. Sidgwick & Jackson.

Klee, Karl (1955), *Operation Sea Lion and the Role of the Luftwaffe in the Planned Invasion of England*. US Air Force Historical Study No. 157. US Air Force Historical Research Agency. Air University.

Korda, Michael (2009), *With Wings like Eagles: The Untold Story of the Battle of Britain*. JR Books.

Kubizek, Augustus (1955), *The Young Hitler I Knew*. Online Edition: Internet Archive.

Lawlor, Shiela (1994), *Churchill and the Politics of War, 1940–1941*. Cambridge University Press.

Leete, John (2008), *Under Fire: Britain's Fire Service at War*. Sutton Publishing.

Lenton H. T. and Colledge, J. J, (1964), *Warships of World War II*. Ian Allen.

Levine, Joshua (2006), *Forgotten Voices of the Blitz and the Battle for Britain*. Ebury Press.

Liddell Hart, B. H. (1948), *The Other Side of the Hill:. Germany's Generals: Their Rise and Fall, with their Own Account of Military Events 1939–1945*. Cassell.

Lipgens, Walter (ed.) (1985), *Documents on the History of European Integration, Volume 1: Continental Plans for European Union 1939–1945*. Walter de Gruyter.

Lukacs, John (1990), *The Duel. Hitler vs Churchill 10 May–31 July 1940*. The Bodley Head Ltd.

Mack, Joanna and Humphries, Steve (1985), *London at War: The Making of Modern London, 1939–1945*. Sidgwick & Jackson Ltd.

Macksey, Kenneth (1980), *Invasion – the German Invasion of England, July 1940*. Arms and Armour Press.

Mason, Francis K. (1990), *Battle over Britain*. Aston Publications Ltd.

Masters, David (1941), *"So Few" The Immortal Record of the Royal Air Force*. Eyre & Spottiswood.

Mckay, Sinclair (2010), *The Secret Life of Bletchley Park: The History of the Wartime Codebreaking Centre by the Men and Women Who Were There*. Aurum Press Ltd.

McKee, Alexander (1957), *The Coal-Scuttle Brigade*. Souvenir Press.

McKinstry, Leo (2010), *Hurricane – Victor of the Battle of Britain*. John Murray (Publishers).

Milward, Alan S. (1977), *War, Economy and Society 1939–1945*. Allen Lane.

Mitchell, Allen W. (1945), *New Zealanders in the Air War*. George G Harrap.

Nicolson, Nigel (ed.) (1967), *Harold Nicolson, Diaries and Letters 1939–45*. Collins.

Nielsen, Andreas L. (1968), *German Air Force General Staff*. Ayer Publishing.

Norman, Bill (1989), *Wartime Teeside*. Dalesman Books.

—(1993), *Luftwaffe over the North. Episodes in an Air War 1939-1943*. Leo Cooper.

Orange, Vincent (2001), *Park. The Biography of Air Chief Marshall Sir Keith Park*. Grub Street.

Orwell, George (2009), *Diaries*. Harvill Secker.

Overy, Richard (1984), *Goering: The Iron Man*. Law Book Co. of Australasia.

—(2001), *The Battle of Britain: The Myth and the Reality*. W. W. Norton & Co.

Piratin, Phil (1948), *Our Flag Stays Red*. Thames Publications.

Pitchfork, Graham (2005), *Shot Down and in the Drink*. National Archives.

Pontin, Clive (1991), *1940 Myth and Reality*. Ivan R. Dee Inc.

Price, Alfred (1979), *The Hardest Day – Battle of Britain 18 August 1940*. Jane's Publishing Co.

Priestley, J. B. (1941), *Out of the People*. Collins with William Heinemann.

Probert, Henry and Cox, Sebastian (eds) (1991), *The Battle Re-thought*. Airlife Publishing Ltd.

Ransom, Frank E. (1954), *Air-Sea Rescue 1941-1952*. US Air Force Historical Study No. 95. Research Studies Institute. Air University.

—(1994), *The Battle of Britain: Dowding and the First Victory, 1940*. Cassell Military Paperbacks.

Ray, John (1996), *The Night Blitz* 1940-1941. Arms and Armour Press.

Reynolds, David (2004), 'Churchill and the British "decision" to fight on in 1940: right policy, wrong reason'. In Richard Langhorne (ed.), *Diplomacy and Intelligence During the Second World War*, Cambridge University Press.

Richards, Denis (1953), *Royal Air Force 1939-1945, Volume 1: The Fight at Odds 1939-1941*. HMSO.

Richards, D. T. (2006), *Ramsgate August 1940*. Michaels Bookshop.

Richardson, William (1977), *The CWS in War and Peace, 1838-1976*. Co-operative Wholesale Society.

Roberts, Andrew (1991), *The Holy Fox: Biography of Lord Halifax*. Weidenfeld & Nicolson.

Robinson, Derek (2005), *Invasion 1940*. Constable and Robinson Ltd.

Roskill, S. W. (1954), *The War at Sea 1939-1945, Volume 1: The Defensive*. HMSO.

Saunders, Andy (2010), *Convoy Peewit. August 8, 1940: The First Day of the Battle of Britain?* Grub Street.

Schenk, Peter (1990), *Invasion of England 1940: The Planning of Operation Sealion*. Conway Maritime Press Ltd.

Schwarz, Ted (2003), *The Mogul, the Mob, the Statesman and the Making of an American Myth*. John Wiley & Sons.

Scott, Vernon (2000), *In Harm's Way – Pembrokeshire and the Summer of 1940*. Paterchurch Publications.

Shirer, William L (1984), *Berlin Diary: The Journal of a Foreign Correspondent 1934–1941*. Bonanza Books.

Spaight, J. M. (1941), *The Battle of Britain 1940*, Geoffrey Bles.

Stansky, Peter (2007), *The First Day of the Blitz*. Yale University Press.

Stokes, Doug (1983), *Paddy Finucane: Fighter Ace*. William Kimber.

Suchenwirth, Richard (1959), *Historical Turning Points in the German Air Force War Effort*. USAF Historical Studies 189. Research Studies Institute. Air University.

Taylor, Edmond (1940), *The Strategy of Terror*. Houghton Mifflin Company.

Taylor, Fred (1982), *The Goebbels Diaries 1939–1941*. Hamish Hamilton.

Taylor, Telford (1967), *The Breaking Wave: The German Defeat in the Summer of 1940*. Weidenfeld & Nicholson.

Terraine, J. (1985), *Right of the Line: The Royal Air Force in the European War 1939–1945*. Hodder and Stoughton.

Thiele, Harold (2006), *Luftwaffe Aerial Torpedo Aircraft and Operations: In World War Two*. Hikoki Publications.

Thompson, Laurence (1966), *1940. Year of Legend – Year of History*. Collins.

Trevor-Roper, H. R. (1964), *Hitler's War Directives 1939–1945*. Sidgwick & Jackson.

von Leeb, Wilhelm Ritter (1976), *Tagebuchaufzeichnungen und Lagebeurteilungen aus zwei Weltkriegen*. Deutsche Verlag-Anstalt.

Waller, John H. (1996), *The Unseen War in Europe: Espionage and Conspiracy in the Second World War*. IB Tauris.

Weight, Richard (2002), *Patriots: National Identity in Britain 1940–2000*. Macmillan.

West, Nigel (2005), *The Guy Liddell Diaries: 1939–1942, Volume 1*. Routledge.

Wheatley, Ronald (1958), *Operation Sea Lion. German Plans for the Invasion of England 1939–1942*. Clarendon Press.

Williamson, Murray (1983), *Strategy for Defeat: The Luftwaffe 1933–1945*. Air University Press.

Wilmot, Chester (1952), *The Struggle for Europe*. Collins.

Winterbotham, F. W. (1974) *The Ultra Secret*. Harper & Row Publishers

Wood, Derek with Dempster, Derek (1969), *The Narrow Margin*. ArrowBooks.

Zeigler, Philip (1995), *London at War, 1939–1945*, Sinclair-Stevenson Ltd

Websites and Archives

http://www.1940chronicle.com 1940 Chronicle

http://wwar2homefront.blogspot.com A Civilian in the Second World War

http://www.spiked-online.com/index.php/site/article/9622 A Country for Old Men?

http://www.aircrewremembrancesociety.com Aircrew Remembrance Society

http://airminded.org Airminded

http://homepage.ntlworld.com/andrew.etherington/1940/07/10.htm Andrew
   Etherington

http://www.the-battle-of-britain.co.uk Battle of Britain

http://www.battleofbritain1940.net/0021.html Battle of Britain 1940

http://battleofbritainblog.com Battle of Britain Blog

http://www.bbm.org.uk Battle of Britain Monument

http://www.ibiblio.org/hyperwar/UN/UK/UK-RAF-I/UK-RAF-I-6.html Battle of
   Britain: Official History

http://wscdn.bbc.co.uk/archive/battleofbritain BBC Battle of Britain Archive

http://www.bbc.co.uk/ww2peopleswar BBC People's War

http://www.bills-bunker.privat.t-online.de/index2.html Bill's Bunker

http://fishponds.org.uk Bristol Past

http://freespace.virgin.net/neil.worthington/jx/1943.htm British Railways

http://hansard.millbanksystems.com/people/mr-winston-churchill/1940 Churchill:
   speeches in the Commons, 1940

http://www.convoyweb.org.uk Convoy Web

http://www.doversociety.org/WWII.html Dover Society

http://www.englandspastforeveryone.org.uk/resources/assets/R/Resorts_in_
   WW2___Seaside_Towns_at_War_5933.pdf Essex Seaside Towns

http://www.flightglobal.com/pdfarchive/view/1940/1940%20-%202015.
   html?tracked=1 Flight International Archive

http://www.freerepublic.com/tag/by:homerjsimpson/index?tab=articles Free
   Republic (NYT Archives)

http://www.da.mod.uk/colleges/jscsc/jscsc-library/archives/fuehrer-conferences/
   Fuehrer%20Conferences.pdf Führer Conferences on Naval Affairs

http://www.guardian.co.uk/world/interactive/2010/sep/07/blitz-timeline-second-
   world-war *Guardian*: Blitz Interactive Timeline

http://www.harry--tates.org.uk/history2.htm Harry Tate's Navy

http://www.hullwebs.co.uk/content/l--20c/conflict/ww2/bombs/bombs-1940.htm
   Hull Air Raids
http://digitalarchive.wm.edu/bitstream/10288/1945/1/LimoncelliAmy2010.pdf
   Impact of the British Monarchy on Civilian Morale
http://www.liverpoolmuseums.org.uk/nof/blitz/1200.html Liverpool Blitz
http://www.bluestarline.org/liverpool_war/law_front.htm Liverpool: Port at War
http://www.ibiblio.org/hyperwar/UN/UK/LondonGazette/37719.pdf *London Gazette*
   11 September 1946
http://www.ltmcollection.org/photos/themes/theme_top.html?_IXSR_=w4MF0EA
   uOcD&IXtoptheme=Wartime&_IXFIRST_=1&IXpage=1 London
   Transport Museum
http://www.lostbombers.co.uk/bomber.php?id=3797 Lost Bombers
http://www.ww2.dk *Luftwaffe* 1933–45
http://news.bbc.co.uk/local/manchester/hi/people_and_places/history/
   newsid_8234000/8234329.stm Manchester Blitz
http://www.secondworldwar.org.uk/merchantnavy.html Merchant Navy – Atlantic
   War
http://www.battleships-cruisers.co.uk/merchant_navy_losses.htm Merchant Navy
   Losses
http://cylchgronaucymru.llgc.org.uk/browse/viewobject/llgc-id:1078288/
   article/000016932 Morale in Swansea
http://www.naval-history.net Naval History
http://www.ne-diary.bpears.org.uk/Inc/Dindex.html NE Diary
https://www.winstonchurchill.org/images/pdfs/for_educators/Harmon__Are%20
   We%20Beasts___np1[1].pdf Newport Papers: Area Bombing
http://www.devonheritage.org/Places/Newton%20Abbot/
   CasualtiesofthebombingofNewtonAbbot.htm Newton Abbot Bombing
http://www.georgeplunkett.co.uk/Website/raids.htm Norwich Air-raids
http://www.da.mod.uk/colleges/jscsc/jscsc-library/archives/operation-sealion
   Operation Sealion: Papers
http://orwelldiaries.wordpress.com Orwell Diaries
http://www.battleofbritainbeacon.org/pilots-blog Pilot's Blog
http://www.raf.mod.uk/history/campaign_diaries.cfm RAF Diary
http://www.royalengineersbombdisposal-eod.org.uk/george_cross.html Royal
   Engineers Bomb Disposal
http://spitfiresite.com Spitfire Site
http://www.explore-gower.co.uk/Content/pid=63/page=2.html Swansea Air Raids
http://www.royal--naval--reserve.co.uk/lost.htm Trawler Losses
http://www.ukpressonline.co.uk/ukpressonline/open/index.jsp UK Press Online
   (Archive – *Daily Express/Daily Mirror/Yorkshire Post*)

http://forum.netweather.tv/topic/63129-the-battle-of-britain-weather-diary Weather
   Diary
http://www.islandfarm.fsnet.co.uk/Luftwaffe%20Attacks%20On%20South%20Wales.
   htm Welsh Air Raids
http://www.wrecksite.eu/wrecked-on-this-day.aspxhttp://www.westendatwar.org.uk/
   category_idtxt__place.aspx West End at War
http://worldwar2daybyday.blogspot.com World War II Day-By-Day
http://ww2today.com World War II Today
http://www.wrecksite.eu/wrecked-on-this-day.aspx Wrecked on This Day

Index